Battling Marketing Myths

Foxhole Lessons from a
Corporate Warrior

Battling Marketing Myths

Foxhole Lessons from a Corporate Warrior

Chris Schoenleb

RIVERCROSS PUBLISHING, INC.
Orlando

ISBN: 1-58141-066-2

Library of Congress Control Number: 2001118765

First Printing

Dedication

This book is dedicated to my lifetime partner, my wife Joanne. She shared all the foxholes. She knows all the stories told here and the ones I chose to leave out.

Without her steadfast love, without her firm guiding hand to raise our four children, without her willingness to relocate to ten different cities, I could not have survived nor succeeded in corporate America.

Table of Contents

Acknowledgements

To all who read this book: I would have never completed this book without an enormous amount of help and encouragement from friends and family. I want to particularly thank:

Jane Pierotti, an outstanding consultant, seminar speaker, and author for her inspiration and work on this book. She suggested the book's title, wrote a suggested Introduction and provided many of the chapter titles. Her wit and insights are part of almost every chapter.

Perry Pascarella, my Kenyon College classmate, former Vice President for Editorial of Penton Publications and author of seven perceptive books on the business world, for his crisp insights, perceptive criticism and unflagging encouragement.

And

Peter Clark, my new friend, a retired advertising executive and co-author of two books on business writing, for his comprehensive grammatical edit and his thoughtful criticism of my writing style. I am sure this book is far more readable because of Peter's long hours of work.

I offer my profuse gratitude to:

Mary Weyenberg Willard, my long time friend and coworker. She shared two days of interviews and her extensive files on our days together at Swensen's and Bojangles'. Chapters 11 and 12 could not have been written without her help.

And

Larry Krueger, my longtime friend and co-worker, currently VP of Marketing for Popeye's fast-food chicken chain. Larry refreshed and improved my memory as he offered his comments on the Burger King and Arby's foxhole tales (Chapters 6 through 10).

Special thanks are also gratefully given to my good friends, Charlie and Doris Lee Aldag for their insights that led me to totally refocus the lessons of this book and my perspective on Ernest Gallo.

Beyond this, I owe a deep debt of gratitude to friends who read and commented on chapters about themselves and their experiences in this book. I especially thank Rogers Brackmann, Bob Swanson, Phil Currier, Quinn Williams, Eric Newman, Professor Dick Reizenstein, and a good friend from Midas who prefers to be anonymous.

In addition, you should know that this book incorporates the helpful comments of my wife Joanne, my sons Chris and Bill, and my daughters Barbara and Pat.

Last but never least, I owe special thanks to Ralph and Lettie Ann McDonald. Ralph encouraged me every step of the way in writing this book. And Lettie Ann made this book possible, because she struggled through my dictation tapes and typed them into the initial draft manuscript.

Chris Schoenleb

Introduction

Let's cut to the chase. This is a book about *how* real-life marketing decisions are made in corporate America.

Sometimes reality isn't pretty. It's almost never the way you learn it in school. So, if you think this book will tell you that American business develops marketing and advertising like it's described in textbooks, you're either naïve or living in total denial.

If you think a corporation selects the best marketing plan available, then you just haven't been there. Not in the real world. In fact, it's my experience that when any plan requires real corporate change in terms of product offerings or customer-handling systems—change that you believe can result in a marketing home run—it's usually shot down in a civil war among you, the boss, and your co-workers!

If you are a corporate marketer and use the classic marketing disciplines to build your marketing battle plan—great. But if you don't understand how your battle plan fits into your company's internal culture, your plan will never be selected. You will lose the war before you ever fight it in the marketplace.

I know. I've been there and have the scars to prove it. Now I want to share what I've learned with you.

So What, and Who's the Author?

Who am I? I'm a marketer who sought fame and fortune in corporate marketing, but was never selected for the Marketing Hall of Fame or the Advertising Hall of Fame.

Oh, I came close. I fathered the still-famous Burger King ad campaign, "Have It Your Way," that launched the Burger Wars. I was recognized for over twenty-five years as one of the top U.S. marketing executives. I was CEO of two companies and a marketing executive in four of the biggest ad industry business categories (package goods, automotive, liquor/wine, and fast food resturants)

I've qualified myself as a corporate marketing warrior by working for eleven companies, headquartered in nine different cities. Three of my employers were in Chicago, the city I still call my cultural home.

My eleven tours of duty included working for corporate giants of the marketing world like Procter & Gamble, Gallo Winery, Burger King, and

Midas. And I worked in smaller, less successful companies (Pet Inc., American Motors), three restaurant chains (Arby's, Swensen's, and Bojangles'), and two advertising agencies (Needham–Harper–Steers [now DDB] and as partner of my own agency).

I just wish I had known up-front what I'm going to tell you in this book.

What You'll Learn

This isn't a book of lists or marketing case studies. It goes beyond the usual "laws" or "commandments" so popular today. Let's face it, most of those lists can only help arm you for war, not instruct you on how to use these weapons when the going gets tough.

Although you'll see elements of such laws, this book takes you much deeper into reality. I will show you that the key to success is more than a marketing principle. It's understanding and coping with company cultures that often created the marketing problems in the first place.

In doing this I'll give you key intelligence every marketing warrior needs to know—intelligence that comes only from real-life experience. For instance, you'll be able to crack the code on

- the way to win wars even if you lose battles in the corporate world
- the joys and headaches of working with franchisees,
- how to attract and work with motivated talented people,
- how to manage the advertising agency relationship and avoid career-threatening dangers from a relationship failure, and
- the best role for a client in the client–agency relationship. (I truly believe that brilliant, strategically relevant advertising can happen only when these two parties are working on the same page. Or as my friend Burt Manning, the former chairman of J. Walter Thompson, said, "We can have great advertising only when we have a great client.")

Still, none of this is the core lesson from all the Foxhole Lessons found in this book.

That lesson is this. *To be an effective marketer, you must have more than the ability to develop solid consumer-research-based marketing plans; you must be able to sell your plans to management and your co-workers.* This is an extremely difficult task because you must address and overcome the two greatest impediments in any corporation to its marketing program's success—the company's marketing myths and its corporate culture.

What do I mean by "marketing myths" and "corporate culture"? Here's a thumbnail sketch of each.

Marketing Myths

In most organizations, its managers, employees, and advertising agencies fail because of marketing myths.

So what is a marketing myth? It's a belief in a critical "fact" that's really not a fact. A marketing myth is a false premise that can lead an organization's marketing strategy down the wrong path, usually straight to failure.

Perhaps one of the most famous myths in recent history was the "fact" that consumers wanted a new and different Coke—that they preferred New Coke to the original formula. We all know how wrong this "fact" was. Consumers were outraged and demanded the return of Classic Coke.

How does such a major miscalculation occur? My answer is that it stems from managers believing a corporate marketing myth. Almost every company has them and nurtures them.

Why do these myths develop? Usually for one of three reasons:

1. *The boss.* He (or she) believes some fact to be true either about his brand, his customer, the marketplace, or his company. This "fact" is not valid. It may have been true at some point in time, but because the boss still believes it, even though it is no longer valid, it influences all major decisions. It's tough to challenge the boss. His intimidation usually wins out.

2. *Poorly conceived/executed marketing research or poor analysis of good research.* Over the years I've seen some unbelievable statements masquerading as valid research conclusions. Sometimes it's just faulty reasoning but, more often, poor research comes from questionnaires that are worded to lead responders to answers that confirm the beliefs of management.

   The most blatant examples of questionable research in my experience were the consumer blind-taste-preference tests of cake mixes done by three reputable companies. At P&G I found many tests that showed significant consumer preference for its Duncan Hines cake mix brand over Betty Crocker and Pillsbury. Yet when I worked at Needham on the Betty Crocker account, I saw many tests at General Mills indicating consumers preferred Betty Crocker to Duncan Hines and Pillsbury. And, as if that wasn't contradictory enough, when I later worked at Burger King (owned by Pillsbury), I encountered blind tests showing consumer preference for Pillsbury over Duncan Hines and Betty Crocker.

   Okay, let's give all three companies the benefit of the doubt and admit that the tests weren't all conducted at the same time, so some product changes could have occurred. But I've seen too much. I'd be willing to bet that each company had a winner in the clubhouse because the market research was conducted with a built-in bias favoring the sponsoring company's product.

3. *Sheer laziness.* Far too few marketers and advertising agencies take the time to thoroughly investigate and analyze all the facts available to them about their products.

Corporate Culture

Culture can mean anything from tradition to values. It's a favorite (though meaningless) topic for many talking heads when discussing "old economy" versus "new economy." In this book I use the term *culture* narrowly to describe the way decisions are made and who makes them.

In each chapter, I show that corporate culture is the key to understanding the decisions made inside the company. It explains why working effectively within a company's unwritten, but real, rules of conduct will make or break your effectiveness.

In each chapter I also present a hard truth you must understand about corporate culture. *Never underestimate the influence of your boss's personality and management style on your success.* In my career I've worked for all kinds of bosses, from autocrats to consensus builders. Some delegated authority and others were complete dictators. Several, especially Bob Swanson (Chapter 3) and Ernest Gallo (Chapter 5), taught me a lot.

Speaking of bosses, in this book I describe the power of effective interpersonal relationships and the fallout when they are ineffective in almost every chapter. Along with this, I chronicle what happens when top management is changed. *I believe that changes at the top are the single most destructive act in American business.* Continuity is destroyed internally and new management can totally change a person's fit within the organization. (See Chapters 9, 11, and 15.)

What This Book is Not

Don't misunderstand.

This book does not refute the importance of your knowing marketing fundamentals. You'll never succeed without thorough knowledge of basic marketing principles—basics like how your brand compares to your competitors in distribution. And yes, you must know basics like the four "Ps" (product, package, price, and promotion) and basics like a thorough knowledge of your customers. *These fundamentals are the tickets to join the battle; they do not guarantee success.*

This book isn't written to challenge the case for marketing creativity either. A brilliantly conceived ad campaign based on good consumer data clearly beats mediocre advertising and promotion using the same strategy. *But creativity alone doesn't guarantee a successful marketing program or your marketing career.*

This book will show that success comes only if you understand the company culture in which you operate and the real marketing issues (not marketing myths) that must be addressed, and you have translated these needs into a battle plan that will work with the corporate resources available. *A marketing plan needing a bigger budget than what is available is no plan at all.*

And last, this book will emphasize that you must be able to sell your battle plan to management. Most times this isn't easy. As we tell the tale in Chapter 6, even the brilliant "Have It Your Way" campaign was almost killed by management four times before it won approval.

Foxhole Tales Lessons Guide

This book has been written to accomplish two things simultaneously: (1) tell the story of my marketing career, and (2) describe the lessons I learned at each company stop along the way so that you might apply them to your life or career.

Therefore, each chapter leads you through one or more years of my career and the lessons I learned during this period. You'll see the real world, the successes achieved, the mistakes made, and the resulting insights. Lessons learned are in *italics* and the more important **Lifetime Lessons** are in ***bold italics***. Beyond this, important lessons not identified in the chapter text are summed up at the end of each chapter along with a "Final Comment."

In the process of telling my foxhole tales I outline eight never-before-told marketing case studies: Sego Diet Food (Chapter 2), New Bisquick (Chapter 3), American Motors (Chapter 4), Burger King (Chapters 6 through 9), Arby's (Chapter 10), Swensen's (Chapter 11), Bojangles' (Chapter 12) and Midas (chapters 14 and 15). Unlike typical studies in marketing texts, these focus on how a company's culture determined the marketing decision that was made.

Mea Culpa

This is a personal remembrance. It is based on what I remember about events, the people I worked with, and the companies for which I toiled.

My memory is not perfect, no one's is. My descriptions of people and events may, therefore, not match up exactly with others' memories. I may even have a few dates or minor facts wrong, but I believe I tell the essential truth about every situation and every person mentioned in this chronicle. Certainly this has been my intent. More important, the situations are clear enough to show you how decisions get made.

Having said all of this—it's time to tell you the "Foxhole Tales" and share the lessons that emerged from them. Enjoy.

PART I
BASIC TRAINING
AN ON-THE-JOB MBA
1956–1972

CHAPTER 1
The Procter & Gamble Curriculum

(The Education of a Marketing Man)

Anyone under thirty-five, were he or she able to time travel back to 1956 to visit Procter & Gamble, would be hard pressed to believe that such a corporate world ever existed.

When I joined Procter & Gamble that year, its Brand Management department was "Mecca" for anyone seeking a career in big-time marketing.

P&G had pioneered the concept of having individual brands managed on a day-to-day basis by a brand group (usually three to five persons, age twenty-seven or younger, aspiring, ambitious men, normally MBAs). The brand group was the guardian of a brand's sales and profits. Its specific job was to develop and execute the annual advertising and promotion plan for the brand, including the brand's packaging design, consumer research, etc.

The brand group boss was the brand manager. As a rule, the brand manager was a "veteran" with three to five years' experience who had been promoted from within at least once. He was the advertising agency's primary "client" for his brand.

Other members of a brand group with titles of assistant brand manager and staff assistant had the responsibility of providing "arms and legs" support for the brand manager. In reality, these were on-the-job training positions to learn how to be a brand manager within three to five years. In general, if you did not reach brand manager within five years, you were moved out of brand management, usually to less glamorous staff positions within the company such as public relations, promotion development, etc.

Brand management was P&G's "line" management, the career path that led to the company presidency. Equally important, it was a finishing school—a place where those reporting to the brand manager, regardless of their prior training or schooling, learned the P&G marketing methodology through the tasks assigned them.

P&G hired me for brand management in the newly formed Food Products Division. I began my career in June 1956 as a Staff Assistant on Big

Top Peanut Butter. Unlike most new marketing employees at P&G, I did not have an MBA. Also, because I did not have a business education and had no business background (my parents were journalists), I was not prepared for the regimented lifestyle at P&G.

I immediately learned that *Not only did I have to learn marketing skills, I had to learn a way of life—the Procter "Way."*

You see, in 1956, at P&G, there were dress codes and office conduct codes, and there were social obligations. They were the written and unwritten rules I had to follow, if I wanted to succeed.

P&G probably rescinded all these unofficial "rules" long ago, but let me share with you the key ones—all of which seem almost unbelievable today:

Rule #1. *Men were to dress only in a white shirt, tie, and dark suit.* No sport coats. Women were to wear very conservative dresses. No bra straps were to be visible, even under a top.

Rule #2. *Working hours were 8:30 A.M. to 5:00 P.M.* To stay after work, or to use the office on the weekend, you had to have a building pass signed by your supervisor.

Rule #3. *You were to carry your work to and from home in a briefcase provided by the company.* It was expected that you would work at home. (You were also issued a slide rule. There were no electronic calculators in those days.)

Rule #4. *You and your wife were expected to attend social functions held by company managers.* Regularly scheduled invitations came from various managers in the Food Division for a social function at least once a quarter—usually dinner at the host's home. In addition, although less frequently, parties were thrown for the entire department. Conduct at all these functions was part of the ongoing personnel evaluation process. It was also a "good manners finishing school" that helped groom you for promotion.

Equally important for your future promotion possibilities were the male activity groups in which P&G senior management assumed you would participate. For example, I was a member of the Ohio River Bridge Society. This group, composed of members of the marketing staffs of the company's three divisions, (Soap, Food, Toilet Goods) played bridge once a month at various locations outside the office.

Rule #5. *You were expected to come to work in a carpool.* Human Resources, then called the Personnel Department, made sure that wherever you lived you could be part of a carpool. This was really a necessity. No one at P&G, except perhaps a few key executives had more than one car.

The carpool also enabled us to meet other employees and helped our wives to meet one another to develop an ongoing social life. I was in a carpool for my entire career at P&G. One of my favorite carpool members was Gus Priemer, who later became a legendary media guru for the Johnson Wax Company.

Rule #6. *You were expected to eat lunch in the company cafeteria unless you had a special occasion.* The cafeteria was divided by gender until 1957.

Rule #7. *You were expected to live in one of the better areas of the city near your fellow employees.* And most did! In the late 1950's in Cincinnati, most of the single marketing employees lived in a "gentleman's residence club" called the L. B. Harrison Club, and many of the married couples lived in a sprawling apartment complex called Glen Meadows.

From these rules, it is easy to see that when you joined P&G you joined a way of life—a way of life that totally surrounded you seven days a week, except for your family's choice of a church.

Please note, too, that this was basically a male society. Few professional women were part of it and their role was limited. Kathy Ashmore, with whom I shared the duties of assistant brand manager on Fluffo, told me that any woman hired in a professional brand position was advised she would not be promoted above assistant brand manager.

And wives were not expected to be working wives. In fact, in those days, babies had a way of appearing very regularly for most of us.

Of course, all these rules had a purpose. They created one of Procter & Gamble's greatest strengths—a unique, isolated, internal community in which everyone knew everyone else. And perhaps most important, they insured everyone spoke a common business language (more on that later). Last, they helped reinforce and implement P&G's dedication to the basic principle that all promotion to management positions would come from within the organization. All of the men who became president of P&G in the '60s, '70s, '80s, were there in the '50s.

One other major working fact of life built staff interaction, namely the way the office was set up for work. In those days only brand managers had offices. A staff assistant and/or an assistant brand manager did not. They sat in an open bullpen with their desk abutted to a secretary's desk or to a fellow brand group member's desk, thus forming a very close "brand group area."

I worked in such an area next to a typewriter, with a mechanical adding machine and a telephone on my desk for my first three-and-one-half years on the job. It was, to say the least, cozy and noisy. It quickly taught me how to concentrate amid chaos to get something done. It also made it very easy to ask a coworker a question about a task, or to discuss any of the latest rumors in the department.

This unique working environment, coupled with my total lack of experience, and my total naïveté about marketing, advertising agencies, etc., led to a number of unique and sometimes painful learning experiences. In retrospect, it's clear these experiences truly helped mold my adult personality, helped shape my future career and, indeed, enabled me to succeed in that career.

An Unforgettable Lesson

One of the key business lessons I ever learned was taught just six months into my career.

Chick Weaver, brand manager of Big Top Peanut Butter, was the first brand manager to whom I reported. Chick, who had an enormously successful career that culminated with the presidency of Clorox, always seemed to be rather amused at my approach to work. For the first few months after I joined the brand group, he would give me a sardonic grin and remind me almost daily, "Schoenleb, this isn't college any more."

I never quite understood what he meant until I had my first personnel review after six months at the company. These six-month reviews were mandatory for all new employees. For most, it was a formality to reassure them that they were doing well and reinforce this with a salary increase of five percent to ten percent. In my case it wasn't quite so simple.

Chick called me into his office, shut the door, and invited me to sit down. He squared his shoulders, leaned his six foot four inch frame over the table and while staring intently at me said, "Schoenleb, I'm either going to have to fire you or give you a raise. And frankly, I'm more inclined to fire you."

This was the last thing I ever expected to hear. I thought I was doing good work. In fact, it never occurred to me that I would not succeed at P&G. I had been an all-star student throughout my life. I had never failed at any mental task.

I gave Chick a startled look and shivered a little from fear. I was a new father, deeply in debt, and did not have a clue as to why I had been told I might be fired. I stuttered something like, "What do you mean? I thought I was doing well."

He replied, "Schoenleb, let's get something straight. You may have been a Phi Beta Kappa in college, but, here, you still haven't learned how to read or write English. Further, you've never shown me that you get "it." You seem to ignore how very important it is that you learn how to write the P&G way. You treat memo writing like a contest—your words versus what we want."

By this, he was referring to a major element of the on-the-job training, the legendary but true methodology employed at P&G to teach rookies like me the proper way to write a business memo (See "All That Glitters Is Not Gold" later in this chapter).

Puzzled, I looked at Chick and said, "Well, I care very much about my memo writing. I work very hard to make sure I don't have to rewrite memos."

He stared back at me, "Schoenleb, I don't believe you. You're still the cocky college kid that walked in here like he owned the place. I'm sure you'd argue with me over the meaning of the word "the," if I tolerated it."

I almost broke down and cried. I couldn't believe that Chick Weaver could not see that I was trying to conform to the P&G system. A long discussion followed in which I desparately attempted to convince Chick that I was doing everything I could to succeed.

Finally, Chick glared at me over his glasses and leaned far over the table, causing me to shrink even further back in my seat. He said, "Schoenleb, let me tell you exactly what your problem really is. You obviously don't understand that in the business world perception is reality."

He continued,

> *What people see you do, and read from your appearance, is what counts, because that directly impacts how they read what you write and whether they should respect what you write.* You have got to learn that *perception is everything—that perception is reality.* For instance, if you really want to succeed here, you should have your shoes shined every day. You have the worst looking shoes at P&G."

These statements really "did it" for me. Here I was trying to succeed in the business world, and being told I might be fired, not because I wasn't doing good work, but because of my style and my shoes! I wasn't being seen as the kind of person that fit P&G because I didn't pay enough attention to my physical appearance, especially my lack of spit-polished shoes. My appearance was sending the wrong message. I had to fix it or fail.

Yet he spoke a real corporate truth that I believe is still true today, even in the era of casual dress and office informality. *Dress and demeanor still say "volumes" about you and how you are perceived.*

Lifetime Lesson: How others perceive you will greatly determine whether you will succeed or fail in the business or marketing/advertising world.

In my case, Chick gave me a real "wake-up call." I wasn't being judged solely by my work—my personal appearance really counted, from the shined shoes to wearing proper ties, etc.

I've never forgotten that lesson, although sometimes I failed to heed it. And I've always been thankful Chick gave me the raise and didn't fire me.

The P&G MBA

In the six years that I was at P&G, first as a staff assistant, then as an assistant brand manager and, finally, as a brand manager in the Food Division, I gained a thorough understanding of the essentials of marketing. I was equipped with the "tools" essential for the rest of my marketing career. (I don't know, but I would guess P&G still gives its marketers these same tools today.)

Four key tools were truly pounded into my very being:

1. *The importance of analysis of facts.* At P&G, as at no other place I ever worked, being able to skillfully develop a concise and complete analysis of sales, consumer research, and any other relevant fact was the first requirement of any person in brand management.

   Use of such analyses was all inclusive. You were expected to be able to impart to management reasons for brand plan failures, as well as successes. While I was at P&G, no promotion was ever run, no advertising campaign was ever started, no management decision was ever made on brands on which I worked, without a thorough review of all facts pertaining to the decision

   At P&G we also had to know the "basics" about our product and track changes every month. What are the "basics"? They are knowing the *marketing ABC's* of a product. We had to know who uses the product, how many times per month the consumer uses it, the demographics and psychographics of the user and non user, the size and growth pattern of the market in which the product is competing, as well as the competitors' strengths and weaknesses.

   The result of this focus on facts was an absence of corporate marketing myths—a real rarity in corporate marketing, especially in today's world. Today there is such a premium on quick fixes and quick turnarounds that basic homework is not done often enough or thoroughly enough. There is no doubt that this fosters corporate marketing myths, which, in turn, can lead to big-time marketing mistakes.

2. *The second tool P&G provided was an approach to solving a marketing problem that can best be characterized as playing the role of a "Doubting Thomas" at all times.* The first question you were taught to ask any time you read a recommendation, or saw new advertising proposed by your advertising agencies was, "Why does this make sense?" Even if you totally agreed with a recommendation in front of you, the first statement you were to make either verbally or in writing was "I don't understand. Why should we do this?"

   As a manager later in my career, I was amazed how many times I could ask this same question and watch my own staff or even presidents of advertising agencies become pale and reply, "Well, because we like it," as opposed to giving a thorough well-thought-out answer.

3. *The third tool P&G provided was a disciplined approach to analyzing advertising recommendations.* You were to start any review of a creative recommendation with a review of whether the proposed advertising addressed the objectives set for the advertising.

P&G taught that effective advertising comes only from solving or addressing problems identified jointly by the client and the agency through proper analysis and research. I am not saying that how TV advertising is executed isn't important—probably eighty percent or more of any good commercial's effectiveness is in its execution. But, **Lifetime Lesson: You should never approve advertising that does not address the right strategic issue no matter how cleverly it's executed.**

This disciplined approach was the tool that most often chagrined the various advertising agencies I worked with over the years. It was my experience that too often advertising agencies paid lip service to advertising objectives and strategies when they developed their creative product.

In at least two-thirds of the new advertising presentations I attended as a client, I was unable to approve the advertising or even properly address it, because the agency's creative folks presenting the proposed new advertising did not understand the advertising assignment. They had not taken into account, or in many cases deliberately ignored, the basic objectives and strategy that had been agreed upon by the agency before the advertising was developed.

4. *The fourth tool that P&G forever provided me was practical strategic-planning capability.* Each year each brand produced a concise annual marketing plan with a recommended spending budget for management approval. This plan was a summary of a very detailed plan developed by the Brand Group working with its agency. It was an action plan with strategy and tactics for the following year. It did not employ the mind-numbing numbers of the financially oriented plans I later helped develop at other companies like Midas, or even Burger King.

The P&G MBA had many other on-the-job "courses" in addition to these four key lessons.

Over six years I was privileged to work with true media experts and learned the basics of television, radio, magazines, and newspaper media planning. Also, the P&G system allowed me to learn the process for developing effective ad copy as well as the ins and outs of developing point-of-purchase and other promotion materials.

Last, I was thoroughly indoctrinated on the uses of market research and advertising research as well as their importance to making any consumer marketing program successful. Anyone who left P&G marketing would affirm that they became strong believers in consumer research.

The Value of Long-term Strategy

P&G also stressed long-term strategic thinking in addition to the annual planning ritual, but again it was more strategic than a grand collection of mostly theoretical numbers that I found most companies used during my career.

The need for this long-term strategic focus and its benefits were demonstrated to me in a rather extraordinary meeting, a management meeting in which P&G made a far-reaching decision that still affects the supermarket today—the national introduction of Crisco Oil.

In P&G's structured environment, the Brand Group working on Crisco shortening was totally separate from the Brand Group assigned to develop a marketing plan for a new product, a cooking oil to compete with Wesson Oil. We were not involved at all, other than knowing the product was under development through the inevitable discussions in the company lunchroom. We knew, however, that, when the cooking oil was introduced, it would compete directly against Crisco.

It was permissible, however, for any brand group to "protect its turf." Therefore, when we learned that the cooking oil product Brand Group was going to name their brand Crisco Oil, we cried "foul."

Perhaps, because of our objection, it was agreed to test market two different oil products, Puritan Oil and Crisco Oil. The same product and package would be used by both brands. The only difference would be the brand name. This would determine whether the Crisco name on a cooking oil would be as "magic" for sales of cooking oil as it was for shortening. It would also determine the influence the use of each name would have on Crisco shortening sales.

Within eighteen months the test markets of these products were launched, measurements were taken, and research was completed.

It was determined that Crisco Oil was clearly a preferred name over Puritan Oil and that, although Crisco shortening would lose some consumers, P&G would gain market share in the overall cooking oil/shortening business. It was also concluded that Crisco Oil would expand the cooking oil market, a key criteria that P&G had for any new product category.

Now it was time for the decision—should P&G introduce Crisco Oil nationally? It was, as I remember it, in June 1959 that I was invited to my only meeting in CEO Howard Morgan's office. The meeting's stated purpose was to make this Crisco Oil decision.

At that meeting, I saw one of the real strengths of P&G emerge, namely a corporate willingness to make a long-term commitment to a brand, and put the money muscle behind it to ensure it every chance of success in the marketplace. It was agreed in that meeting that Crisco Oil would be introduced nationwide with the most powerful and expensive method available, namely in-home sampling. It was also agreed there would be a three-year "payout" before P&G would make one dime of profit.

I never participated in any meetings in any other company in which this kind of long-range decision was made. The short-term outlook has almost always been the rule at other companies.

"All That Glitters Is Not Gold"

Until now, this chapter has been almost a paean of praise for Procter & Gamble. But all was certainly not perfect. Indeed, P&G provided many experiences I wanted to avoid later in life, particularly when I became the chief marketing officer or president of a company.

Perhaps the biggest weakness at P&G was also one of its great strengths, its very structured environment. In the '50s, there were three levels of management in the Food Division above the brand manager. Furthermore, virtually all decisions were made using written communication—memos. If meetings were held, they were to discuss a written recommendation using all the carefully crafted phrases in the required P&G format.

Memos require more precise language than a typical overhead presentation; hence they create decision delays. This was abetted by the P&G memo-writing process itself. Seldom, if ever, was any recommendation written just once.

P&G had its own memo "style" and "language." It was specified, for example, that all memos to management be confined to one page and that all memos begin with a proper first sentence describing what the memo was about, etc. Invariably the first three words of every memo started with the phrase "This is to . . . . "

The avowed objective of this special language was to make sure that each word used was the exact word P&G management employed for the action being recommended or described. (In truth this was a goal never attained because every senior manager had his own favorite lexicon.)

What resulted from this search for wording perfection was at times a system that seemed more intent on fixing a memo's language than getting an idea considered or a decision made.

It was "grammar school" for a new employee because the only way he could learn the language was through trial and error. Until he learned it, his memos were subjected to rigid rewriting and rewriting and more rewriting. It was not unusual to write a memo and have it criticized and edited three or more times in a week. (Even after three years at P&G I once rewrote a memo seven times.)

As a result, everyone in P&G Brand Management understood, in those days at least, that they made very few key decisions for their brand. They were very well trained memo writers. (Indeed, the real role of the brand manager was to shepherd his brand, so that top management could be assured that the brand's fundamentals had been tended to, i.e., brand positioning, pricing, packaging, promotion and advertising, as well as sales analysis and market research.)

The top management of P&G made all key decisions on any brand. In truth, they had to do this, to ensure that the company's broader strategies were followed.

All this structure made decisionmaking a long tedious process. In fact, in my experience, six months was the minimum time for minor recommendations to be approved. Sometimes it took longer, especially on a major brand like Tide or Crisco—witness my experience described next.

Selling Top Management

After a period of sales training in the snows of Iowa, and a stint as assistant brand manager on Fluffo shortening, I got lucky; I was assigned to Crisco as an assistant brand manager. Crisco at that time was the Food Division's biggest brand, dominant in its market and a major profit maker.

In reviewing all the market research, it was clear that consumers saw Crisco as a bit old-fashioned. In partnership with our agency, Compton Advertising, we agreed an effort should be made to "update" Crisco. Now this was not to make a major overhaul of the brand, just a tune-up. New advertising would be developed, a new cookbook would be written, and a new label for the one-pound and three-pound Crisco cans would be developed.

I was put in charge of the new-label project. It was, from the first, a perfect example of how laboriously many decisions were made at P&G at that time.

Within P&G, there was an Art Department. This department did some internal packaging design, especially promotion labels. It also assigned projects, like the new Crisco label, to outside design firms.

For the first two months of this project, the outside firm (I do not remember its name) submitted a series of preliminary designs. These were rejected by Mike Barna, the Art Department supervisor for the project. Finally, in the third month Barna showed us four different possible new labels. After two or three meetings over several weeks, we (the Brand Group in toto) chose the two designs we felt best achieved the objectives we were seeking.

We then put these designs into customer research. We received the results of the research two months later, confirming that one of the two designs was indeed a winner. It was seen clearly as more modern and preferred over the label in use.

This part of the project took approximately six months. Then the real work began—selling P&G management on the change.

Any label change had to be approved by the CEO. Therefore, I drafted the inevitable memo recommending the new label design to Bob Kelly, the Crisco brand manager. After Kelly edited it, I reissued it and it was sent to his boss, an associate advertising manager. He edited it, sent it back; I reissued it again. The memo was then sent to the head of the Food

Division, Bob Shetterly, (who later left to become the first president of Clorox.) He read the memo, made comments, had it rewritten and sent back through the chain of command again. This time, he initialed his agreement and, at long last, the recommendation was submitted to top management.

All this took, as I recall, about ten days. In each case, for each of these memo approvals, we held a showing of the new label versus the old label; each on an actual Crisco can on a mock supermarket shelf in the Art Department.

Finally, the top management showing was held. I don't remember exactly who attended the meeting, but I do remember that after a great deal of discussion, it was agreed that although a label change was needed, the change proposed wasn't quite right.

We redid the work; an additional test was made with consumers, and the process of gaining approval was repeated. When approval was finally granted the Brand Group received a memo from management declaring this change approved. At last, we could go to the P&G departments that ordered labels and direct them to have the label manufacturer execute the change.

These steps took, as I recall, about four months. It then took several more months to get the label changeover to supermarket shelves.

The fascinating point to this story is how much ado there was for so little change. The difference between the old label and the new label was simply taking out a silver line over the logo, making it a dark blue line approximately half an inch wide!

Leadership: The P&G Way

The P&G brand culture gave great training, but it did not stress rewarding marketing achievement. *At P&G,* **how** *you performed your job seemed to be more important than the results you achieved.* You could be highly creative and be responsible for a most successful marketing program for a brand, but not be promoted if you were perceived as not having a P&G leadership style.

I know this statement sounds exaggerated, but it's probably an understatement. There's no doubt that the most important quality sought in P&G brand managers was the appropriate kind or style of "leadership."

What was the leadership style sought? It was once summed up for Brand Group personnel in a clumsily phrased memo on "Leadership" written by one of the senior managers of the Toilet Goods Division Brand Management in the early '60s. I quote it verbatim (including typos).

ON LEADERSHIP
1. Be positive. It is necessary to support what one is proposing in completely positive terms. This is almost always true

even if the actual decision on what is being done has been arrived at as "the lesser of evils." The benefits of what one is recommending are generally as long term ones of principle, rather than short term ones of expediency

Management people tend to belittle those who bend to every prevailing wind. Build the reputation of one who does what is right, regardless of any difficulty therein.

2. Be partisan. The brand system has been set up so that each product manager is the selfish and guardian of his brand's prerogatives. Try not to approach problems as a completely intellectual challenge; doing so tends to expose too many of the negatives which underly almost any question. Rather, after deciding what is right, edit out—from both written correspondence and verbal presentations—what is not necessary to achieve approval.

Presenting too many sides to a question not only can provide the seeds for management to adopt a different point of view, but can, in fact, imply that the actual recommendation itself represents a rather marginal choice, or that the product man hasn't really made up his mind. (Be careful of giving this impression of having trouble making up your mind, or of adopting firm points of view.)

3. Wax enthusiastically over what you recommend, both verbally and on paper. Plan your presentations so that it looks as if you really believe in what you are doing.

Management's degree of confidence in what a man is recommending is often times predicated upon the degree of confidence it is estimated the brand man himself has in the course of action he is proposing.

4. Don't get talked out of what is it is you are proposing. When doubts are raised, you will most often be smart to answer them within the context of your own original argument (which was carefully thought out), rather from jump to a different basis (which is often developed on the spur of the moment). Make sure that if you disagree with what it is suggested the brand do, such disagreement is clearly and irrevocably stated. Do not be afraid to re-recommend several times a move which has been turned down, or ask for an audience from higher authority.

5. Get there first. Most management people are quick, decisive, and impetuous. If you delay in making up your mind or in proposing a decision, you can be assured that this void will be quickly filled. Staying current may mean extra overtime man hours, but that is often necessary to stay on top of the business.

6. Deliver what you promise. Once one promise is broken others may too come doubted. If it is humanly possible to keep to what one has promised—no matter what difficulty, hours, or discomfort are involved—keep the promise. (It goes without saying that promises–whether verbal or in writing—should be reasonable ones, although it is also true that good objectives should require a "stretching" rather than being too easy to attain.)

7. Be Machiavellian as far as motivating people is concerned. Some require paying court to, others simply wish to be told what to do. Figure out what motivates people, and act accordingly. Remember "people" are the raw material of the marketing equation.

8. Look the part of a leader. Most of the people who get ahead in business are quite careful about their person and clothing. They watch their weight and diet, receive a physicians review periodically, make sure they get enough of the right kind of physical exercise and mental stimulation, etc. Most take particular pains to see that their clothing is clean and well fitted, shoes shined, ties and collars not frayed, hair neatly cut and beard closely shaven.

While many of these eight points listed make sense, note there is not one word on achieving positive sales results—the essence of what marketing leadership must achieve.

Egg Timers Etc.

Sometimes, a company will go to ridiculous extremes to enforce discipline. Perhaps the most absurd example I can remember in any company occurred at P&G.

One fine day, the Brand Groups were introduced to three-minute hourglasses (egg timers!) Everyone was issued his own personal timer. With each egg timer came a memo that stated that all employees were talking entirely too long on long-distance calls. It stated that with proper discipline, three minutes should be sufficient for any business call, and therefore, effective at once, we were to use these timers to assure our calls lasted no longer than three minutes.

This was, of course, utterly ludicrous. How could there be, for example, any kind of detailed conversation with an advertising agency about an idea in three minutes?

At any rate, this new procedure went into effect. Each time a phone call was made, a timer was turned over. The discipline of the organization held. We would simply say at the end of two-and-one-half minutes in any conversation that we had to hang up; but would the person we were talking to please call us back?

The howls of protests that emerged from our advertising agencies and suppliers over this phone charade were legion. This particular policy quickly disappeared.

Another silly attempt to "manage" how we worked occurred when I was assistant brand manager on Fluffo shortening. Someone questioned whether Brand personnel were utilizing their time efficiently.

Accordingly, a consultant, who was an industrial engineer, was assigned to work with the Brand Group. Of all the brands in the Food Division, they chose Fluffo to study first. Herb Liss, the brand manager at the time, looked at this as an opportunity to show everyone how efficient we were. At the same time, Herb recognized that standard efficiency measurements, as used in industrial manufacturing, could never apply to a marketing group. So he quickly set out to lay this whole project to rest. He scheduled a trip to New York to visit our advertising agency, Benton & Bowles, and invited the efficiency expert to come along.

Note: A trip to visit a New York advertising agency at P&G in those days was a real "treat." We left the home-office structure and went to New York to become part of all the glitter and all the glamour of Madison Avenue. We stayed at first-class hotels and lived the "good life" on the expense account.

We began our trip after normal working hours, taking the American Electra to LaGuardia. We had dinner and several cocktails on the plane. When we landed, it was about 9:30 P.M. Herb suggested after we checked into the hotel that we go out, have a late night cocktail and discuss the next day's meeting, and then go to bed. We invited the efficiency expert to join us. One thing led to another and we retired to our beds at 4:00 A.M. after consuming more drink and food than we really needed.

At 7:00 A.M. we were up for breakfast, and at exactly 9:00 A.M. we marched into the agency ready for a long day of meetings. The efficiency expert was still a little bit hung over from the night before. He clearly had a hard time following the morning meeting.

Then we went out for a long lunch. (In those days, alcohol was very much "in" for lunch.) We returned for another three hours; then went out to a long dinner with the agency again staying out late. The next morning we caught an airplane home and spent the rest of the day in the office.

We never saw the efficiency expert again. I am not sure whether he became convinced that he couldn't infuse efficiency into the operation, or whether he became convinced that when the Brand Group "worked" twenty-one hours a day on the road, he simply couldn't chart the lifestyle.

Alumni

No chapter about P&G would be complete without commenting on the turnover of high-quality people that occurs at P&G.

P&G has always served as a training ground for both advertising agency executives and other companies' executives. After getting promoted to brand manager, you became a prime target for "headhunters" to solicit you for opportunities in other companies. Because P&G did not pay well nor promote rapidly versus these other companies, many of us were willing to leave. In fact, almost all of us who were hired in the so-called Class of 1956 left for greener pastures sometime within ten years.

I can name no one who left P&G that did not have good success wherever they went. Some were very successful on the "client" or corporate side, like my good friend, Phil Currier. Phil and I had been fraternity brothers at Kenyon College and joined P&G at the same time. Phil attained brand manager status and stayed eleven years. He finished his career as CEO of Hanes Underwear and Active Wear.

Others went to the advertising agency side. My first direct supervisor, Bill Phillips, left P&G to join Ogilvy & Mather, where he eventually became CEO.

I left Procter & Gamble in 1962 to join Pet Milk as brand manager of Sego a brand of liquid diet food (See Chapter 2). My reasons for leaving were money and, quite frankly, boredom. I was working as brand manager of New Products and Big Top Peanut Butter. But I was using little of the marketing skills taught me. I was spending seventy-five percent to eighty percent of my time training those reporting to me and coping with a boss, C. Arden Smith, who would not make decisions.

Lessons Learned

1. It is possible, even at marketing's Mecca, P&G, to succeed without an MBA. Whether one could become a CEO without such a degree is problematical.
2. Even a company as successful as P&G has major weaknesses. Their marketing muscle is awesome, but their rigidity can stultify moving opportunistically in the marketplace.
3. The greatest strength in P&G's marketing arsenal is its relentless search for facts—not accepting marketing myths. And the key to this search is consumer research and sales analyses.
4. In a highly structured corporate culture, and a large company, perception of one's skills is at least as important as actually proving you have them. "Fitting in" is more important than in-market results, especially for middle managers. ***Style truly counts—perhaps more than substance.***

Final Comments

1. The education I received over six years at P&G was invaluable. It was the critical foundation of my career. It not only opened doors to new

job opportunities, but more important, it gave me the basic skills I needed for every marketing position I occupied for my entire career.

2. I never totally accepted the tenet that management style was more important than actual accomplishments to achieve corporate success—-that perception of a man and his work will in the end determine his success, not the results of his work.

Perhaps I should have. This book will show that building a successful marketing program is important but it's not a guarantee that you will achieve personal success. You also need acceptance of your management style. ***Lifetime Lesson: To have long-term success in a company you must be liked by your superiors as well as respected.***

I know. I lost several key positions in my career despite glittering job results.

For example, at the peak of my career at Burger King when I became executive VP of Marketing, I was sent to Tuck School at Dartmouth on the recommendation of Bill Spoor, the chairman of the Board of Pillsbury. There I was given four weeks of graduate business education primarily designed for persons designated as possible CEO's of their company.

I was sure this meant I could be the next president of Burger King. However, I did not become president of Burger King. To this day, I believe the reason had largely to do with my management style, not my internal record of achievement, nor my talent. The Burger King story is told in Chapters 6 through 9.

CHAPTER 2
The Politics of the Status Quo

(Continuing the Education of a Marketing Man)

I experienced a personal culture shock when I joined Pet Milk Inc. (later Pet Inc.) in February 1962. It was the "outside business world" never exposed to me at P&G. Naïvely, I had not anticipated an "outside world" so different.

Pet was a culture much more dependent on individual initiative and individual expertise than on a disciplined system. It was a world that had a management that was much more likely to be making decisions based on one or more "corporate myths" and short-term corporate bottom-line concerns than the basic marketing principles taught at MBA schools and "lived" at P&G.

Pet's systems were almost totally different from P&G's. I was initially baffled on how to do anything, and there was no one assigned to show me the ropes. I was from "Mecca" (P&G) and the Pet organization expected me to understand its fundamentals.

Further, Pet had a different attitude toward the marketplace. Pet had no brands that were market leaders—and, completely foreign to me, the company accepted such market positions. The company was used to being a second-place or "also-ran" marketer. Pet sought profitable niches, not leadership, a fact that dumbfounded my P&G inculcated mind that had been taught to focus on leadership.

In addition, Pet had a different kind of marketing talent. When I joined Pet, I had assumed that the same quality of people found at P&G were there. The few people I had met in the interviewing process had reinforced this expectation. It was never to be. Few, if any were MBA's. Most were older (in their mid-thirties) and had prior experience in sales. They were not the aggressive "tigers"—the high-IQ achievers I was accustomed to.

They were not even friendly to a newcomer! Everyone seemed to live in his or her own isolated world. This was aided and abetted by the internal office arrangement in the headquarters building in downtown St Louis. Instead of the bullpen arrangement at P&G, everyone, even secretaries, had a rather spacious office that opened to a long corridor. Instead of passing fifteen to twenty people to get to your desk, you would see per-haps one or two scurrying down the hall.

My boss was also very different kind of person. I reported to a product manager, Bob Buck. Like everything else, he was a shock to my cultural expectation. Bob was very bright, but truly undisciplined. Unlike my for-mer supervisors, Bob operated more on intuition or "feel" than waiting to review and discuss well-documented facts. Bob also loved alcohol, but did not seem to be an alcoholic. My first lunch with him was a four-martini affair that put me out of commission for the rest of the day, but did not seem to affect him.

Perhaps my biggest surprise was the actual job I was expected to do, and how I was expected to do it.

My title was brand manager. My job description read like a P&G brand manager's, but the job, in reality, was very different. I was to be a one-man band with no staff reporting to me. I was the Brand Group. In the role I was expected to be a decisionmaker and a verbal communicator, not a memo writer.

This difference in the job description and the real job was one I learned would be the "rule" in accepting a new position throughout my career. *Lifetime Lesson: The written job description for your position will not be accurate. View it as a "starting point" for delineating your position's real responsibilities. Your company's culture, your boss's per-sonality and your co-workers' business practices will determine how a job is truly positioned and how it is expected to function.*

Finally, I found a very different corporate organization structure. Compared to P&G, Pet was much smaller and less professional than I had expected when interviewing for the job. I knew that like the P&G Food Division, Pet had four Product Groups; but had fewer layers of manage-ment (Hallelujah). A product manager headed each group; he (it was an all-male department) reported to Al Hodor, VP of Marketing, who reported to the president, Ted Gamble.

The smaller size at Pet came from a lack of staff departments. Unlike P&G, which had departments for six important disciplines. Staffed by experts in these disciplines (promotion, packaging design, public rela-tions, advertising copy, media, and market research), Pet had five people for staff support. There was a three-man market research department, a Director of Advertising, and Director of New Products.

I had to adjust to what I would learn later was a quite normal type of marketing environment outside of P&G. The only "constants" from P&G were the job title and riding to work in a carpool. This cultural change was too big for me. No doubt about it, I was a "duck out of water." I never "fit" at Pet. And, initially, I yearned to return to P&G.

Getting Started

Despite my instant concern about the working environment, I dug in to my new assignment with great gusto. The reason I had joined Pet was the opportunity to market Sego Diet Food. Sego was a glamorous product in a new product category, and I wanted this job.

To me, Sego's multimillion dollar budget offered a rare opportunity to "show off" my marketing prowess and jump start my career. I saw it as a challenge, a way for me to make an impact in the marketplace, and a way to prove to myself and to the world that I had the talent to be Marketing VP in any company.

Sego

Sego Diet Food was one of the "hot" new products in supermarkets in 1961.

Pet had introduced it to be a competitor to Metrecal, the brand leader in a new business category called "complete diet foods." If you will recall, these diet foods were basically complex soy proteins mixed with water and packaged in 8- or 10-ounce cans in various flavors, chocolate being the favorite. Each can contained 225 calories. The concept was simple. Drink four cans a day as your only food intake and quickly and safely lose weight.

Why did this concept work?

Four cans of this product contained only 900 calories yet provided "complete nutrition," that is the minimum daily nutrition requirements of vitamins, protein, etc. Virtually any adult, then and now, can lose weight by consuming only 900 calories a day.

Mead Johnson, a relatively small proprietary drug company, developed the liquid diet food concept in the late '50s and brought it to market under the brand name Metrecal. They packaged Metrecal in beerlike six-packs of 8-ounce cans, and sold the brand in three different flavors, chocolate, vanilla and orange. By the early '60s, Metrecal was a major marketing success.

On TV, Metrecal was advertised with a health positioning, "Diet or Die." Its most famous TV ad showed a very fat man slowly trying to climb steps, while voice-over copy extolled the need to lose weight and stated Metrecal would enable you to do that safely and quickly.

Sego was introduced as a direct competitor and offered in the same flavors. There were only two basic differences apparent to consumers between Metrecal and Sego. Sego was sold in single cans, not six-packs, and the Sego cans contained 10 ounces versus Metrecal's 8 ounces.

When I joined the company, Sego had about a ten percent market share, a distant second place to Metrecal. My assignment was to develop the strategy and programs to achieve a twenty percent share. I was expected to immediately address the task. I had ninety days to produce a new program or reaffirm or adapt the existing one.

First Ninety Days

I started with a one-day background briefing, a so-called brand review, from the advertising agency, Gardner Advertising. In this meeting, the Account Group and Bob Buck verbally briefed me on the status of all issues concerning the brand and showed me all existing advertising materials.

The brand review really energized me. Pet's culture was disappointing, but the opportunity to build a great marketing success was still there. Equally encouraging was the agency account group, Bill Lahrmann and Bob Lundin. They were aggressive and smart. I quickly concluded they would have to be the substitute for my nonexistent internal staff.

And, other "outsiders" would also have to be relied on—for example, the sales "reps" of the media, particularly print (magazines/newspapers). In an attempt to sell ad space, representatives from each of the major consumer magazines would call on me regularly and offer promotions, or try and work with me to develop ideas for future programs tied in to their magazine. This is still an industry practice today, and a good one, especially if the inside staff is small, or nonexistent.

Despite the time deadline, I made no quick changes in the brand program. Instead, I spent the first sixty days learning all I could about Sego and its market. This investigation turned up several startling facts that gave me great hope that the brand could be the huge marketing success I sought.

We had a product advantage. I was furnished blind-product taste-test results between Metrecal and Sego. Surprisingly, Sego won the blind taste tests by a whopping margin. Preference was, as I recall, over sixty percent in favor of Sego.

Sego also had a "satiety" advantage. The research showed that not only was Sego's taste preferred, but also that people felt they did not get as hungry on a daily diet of four cans of Sego as they did on four cans of Metrecal.

Sego had two extra ounces of water in every can. Therefore, it was more filling. These extra ounces also explained Sego's taste preference. Sego had more water and this provided a superior masking of the abominable taste of soy protein.

Yet Sego only had a 10 percent market share. Why? I asked myself. Why hadn't these advantages—huge advantages in my eyes—translated into a higher market share? Was the marketing strategy or the advertising to blame?

There were no direct answers to this in the company's consumer research, but the reasons soon became apparent from other data.

First, I learned that the average Sego consumer would purchase only three to four cans of liquid at a time, whereas, the Metrecal consumer had to buy the cans in six-packs. Therefore, Metrecal had a much higher average purchase rate than Sego.

Even more important, six-pack packaging gave Metrecal a vehicle to dominate shelf space in every supermarket. Because of this, I inquired why we could not do six-packs of Sego to compete with Metrecal's six-pack.

It was then that I learned the very interesting story of why Sego existed. Sego was a product that had been developed not only to tap in to a "hot" new product category, but also to use unused capacity of an evaporated milk plant. All product and packaging decisions stemmed from this fact. For example, the plant could not handle 8-ounce cans, it could only handle 10-ounce cans.

Thus, an "accident" of manufacturing necessity gave Sego its major taste and satiety advantages.

I also learned that there was no real place to put a six-pack package machine on the packaging line of this evaporated milk plant. Therefore, we could not make a six-pack to compete directly with Metrecal.

Last, I found that Sego was positioned in the marketplace almost exactly the same as Metrecal. However, Sego seemed to have better TV advertising. Sego ads had a nice play on words, "See the pounds go with Sego" with a musical jingle to underscore it.

Gardner was proud of their creative work. They felt the ads were "right on," but were not building market share because they were being overwhelmed by Metrecal's reported five to one media-spending advantage. They had urged that the ad budget be at least doubled.

I questioned this thesis. Even though the creative was "good," I opined that the advertising message could be based on the wrong strategy. As I saw it, we would never outspend our competitor so we had to have a "cutting-edge message" to be heard over Metrecal's "noise."

I saw "See the pounds go with Sego" as essentially a more upbeat execution of Metrecal's "Diet or Die" strategy. Further, it wasn't a competitive message. It offered no reasons for consumers to try Sego instead of Metrecal, even though research showed strong consumer preference for Sego.

Still, when I joined Pet, the "Diet or Die" positioning was accepted as gospel. Gardner had been asked to develop a new advertising campaign along the same strategy and to retain the line "See the pounds go with Sego."

Challenging the Status Quo

I met with Bob Buck and explained my concerns. "Bob, we need a new strategy based on the fact that consumers prefer Sego over Metrecal in taste and in satisfying hunger. We will never be Number One with a me-too strategy. Metrecal's media and promotion dollars will kill us."

Bob, who talked with a mouth that seemed to have extra-wide hinges, did not disagree with my thinking, but he did think my timing very bad.

He said, "You may be right, but hold off trying to make any changes now. Wait till you have been here longer. If you push this now, you'll have us all out on a limb and you'll make a host of enemies, particularly at Gardner."

He went on, "Al Hodor likes the current strategy and ads. He's told me to stay the course. Why risk change nobody wants. Don't rock the boat. Try to win the support of the agency first. They don't trust you, and they, my friend, have top management's ear. Besides, number one is not the goal. We can be a solid number two with what we are doing now. We've already proven that."

I looked at Bob in amazement. Had I heard him right? "Don't do the right thing, because even if it's right, it would be political suicide?" What kind of place was I in?

After a long pause, I made the first of my many career decisions to attack the status quo and champion a major shift in strategy. (Ron Moore, president of Midas, later called me a "kamikaze pilot" for this politically incorrect streak in my character.) ***Lifetime Lesson: To be a success in marketing you must be prepared to challenge the status quo. Marketers must be willing to foment change.***

In this case I said, "Bob, I can't sit here and not fight for what I am absolutely convinced is the right thing to do. The basic marketing strategy for Sego is wrong. You know it. I know it. I'll bet that even the agency knows it. If Sego is ever going to build market share, we have to show consumers how we're different and how we're better than Metrecal. Clearly we can't do this with a me-too Diet or Die health positioning."

He shook his head and grimaced. "OK, I'll support you; but mark my words. Even if you win the battle, you will lose your future here. This is not a place that will tolerate your kind of "shit kicking" very long."

Bob turned out to be a prophet. I did gain agreement, albeit a luke-warm endorsement, to explore a positioning of being a superior product to Metrecal because Sego tasted better and had more liquid to better stave off hunger. Al Hodor agreed to this, when Leon Ullensvang, director of Market Research supported my position.

Fixing the Media Plan

One other major concern had to be addressed when I looked at the overall advertising strategy—to whom should we address the Sego ad message?

Until that time, diet foods had been positioned to a dual audience: men and women. In fact, Metrecal was advertised primarily on dual audience TV programs like news programs. Sego followed suit.

I wanted a more targeted creative and a media plan that would more effectively and efficiently use our ad funds. At a series of meetings I challenged the agency to come up with a whole new advertising plan based on a new target audience, women. I argued that we should position Sego directly against women because they were the heavy users.

I ordered this change and in doing so incurred the wrath of the agency. They clearly did not appreciate their strategy being challenged. Later in my career, I learned that *to maintain a good working relationship with the agency, you should appeal to the agency's expertise and request their recommendation before simply ordering change.*

The "Magic" Of New Flavors

Ignoring all these politics which I naïvely thought would disappear over time if the new plan worked, I went to work inside the company to create more needed changes. There were two other items that I knew needed to be addressed to make Sego more successful.

First, we had to improve the number of shelf facings the product had in the grocery store. In packaged goods marketing there is a sales-building axiom, *More Shelf Facings = Higher Retail Sales.* Second, we needed a better in-store promotion plan.

I met with the Pet Sales Manager and his staff. Not surprisingly, they took the position that Sego had to have a six-pack "or something" as an excuse for them to get greater shelf space. I already knew this couldn't happen. So lots of words led to no action. (A common occurrence in business even today.)

However, in these conversations an idea emerged that did solve both problems. Someone suggested that we have more flavors. This would give Sales an excuse to go out and push Metrecal back to less shelf facings and get more shelf facings for Sego.

More flavors rang a bell with me. My limited experience in the cake mix business (I sold Duncan Hines during my sales training at P&G) was that new flavors were the lifeblood of the product. For Duncan Hines, the marketing plan was to offer two or three new flavors each year. This not only gave the sales department additional leverage to get shelf space at the expense of competitors, it was also a built-in promotion that did not require discounting or special allowances to the trade.

Why not, I thought, apply this same new flavor strategy to liquid diet food?

I contacted the Pet product technicians at the Sego manufacturing plant. They were cautious, but interested. "Sure," they said, "We can make almost any flavor of diet food you want. It's just a matter of adding flavoring to the basic mix. In fact, we have even tried formulating hot flavors, like tomato soup, or chicken soup, or chicken bouillon flavor."

However, there was a problem. More flavors created complications at the manufacturing plant where each "run" of a flavor required separate "set-up time" which, in turn, slowed the total production efficiency of the line.

I asked for some samples of the various flavors that could be made. Then Bob Buck and I met the technicians at the plant in Greenville, Illinois, to taste them. If you've ever spent an afternoon tasting soybean liquid-flavored product, you know what a difficult task it is. Soybean-based liquid diet food simply doesn't taste good, no matter what the flavor. However, my taste buds said the hot flavors, tomato and chicken, certainly had great merit. Also several other flavors such as chocolate malt and strawberry seemed to hold promise. Bob concurred.

True to my P&G background I requested the market research department to do consumer taste tests with these products versus our existing product and Metrecal.

The research was very revealing. The new products were well liked. In fact, Chocolate Malt was the clear winner over all other products. More important, this research showed us another key insight: diet food drinkers liked variety. They hated to drink the same flavor four times a day every day for a week. Even the chocoholics sought variety.

A lot of this development work took place in a very short period of time, about one-eighth of the time it would have taken P&G. This excited me. We were able to make things happen in a hurry.

Winning the Battle but Losing the War

While this new flavor work was occurring, the agency came back with several new advertising campaign ideas.

Bob and I selected a campaign based on some added insight Gardner had obtained from consumer group interviews. This research had shown that the biggest single problem for women on a liquid diet food diet was to keep from snacking between meals. From this insight, the campaign line emerged, "Try Sego, it gets you through the Temptation Hours."

A series of print ads and TV commercials were developed. All featured women and showed the reward of dieting, looking more attractive. There was no allusion to the previous "Diet or Die" positioning. The agency, with my support, "sold" the whole campaign to Al Hodor without further consumer research.

Along with this, we gained agreement to introduce one new flavor, Chocolate Malt, immediately and follow this six months later with the two soup flavors. These would be the tools to get additional shelf space and to satisfy the consumer's need for variety.

Last, the entire media schedule was dramatically changed from primarily a network TV schedule to a national print campaign aimed at women, plus spot television to heavy-up ad weight in key markets where Sego had its best distribution.

An exciting new strategy was now in place! The campaign was launched with a two-page ad in *Life* Magazine. (Remember when *Life* was the leading weekly magazine?)

Did this stratigic shift in brand positioning plus the new flavor strategy work?

Yes. Sego became a huge success. Within a year, despite manufacturing problems and ongoing distribution problems, Sego had more than doubled its market share and was climbing. It would become the market leader.

But Bob Buck had been correct in his assessment of how Sego's success would affect me. I did not achieve internal, personal success from my work on Sego. I was never given a raise in salary. In my fifteenth month, I resigned to join an advertising agency, Needham Louis & Brorby.

Lessons Learned

1. Having an exploitable or demonstrable product advantage is the surest road to a marketing success, if that advantage is important to consumers.

2. Being a "change artist" in a corporate world has major pitfalls for your career. To accomplish change it has to be done in a way that involves everybody—management, the internal staff and the agency. Do it wrong, and even if you succeed, you could lose your job. *Lifetime Lesson: All organizational people hate change, even if it succeeds, unless its their idea or they become sold into taking ownership of it.*

Final Comment

Pet was my second lesson in the absolute importance of adapting your management style to fit the culture in which you work. This time I did not try to adapt, and my tenure lasted barely a year. *Lifetime Lesson: The most important facet of any job change is learning how to adapt successfully to the new employer's culture.*

CHAPTER 3
Never "Pitch" on a Cloudy Day
(The Education of an Advertising Man)

Leaving Pet was like waking up from a bad dream.

I went from a dead-end job in a second-tier marketing company to a challenging career opportunity at one of the biggest and best advertising agencies in the world, Needham, Louis & Brorby (Soon to be renamed Needham, Harper, & Steers—now called DDB).

Ironically, it was my P&G experience that rescued me from Pet. Dale Anderson, who had been the Crisco account supervisor at Compton Advertising, called me one day. He asked me how things were going. After I told him that I wasn't very happy and that things weren't going very well despite the success of Sego, he responded with a very pleased sound in his voice, "Well then, we should talk."

"What should we talk about?" I asked, suddenly alerted that there was more to this conversation than the casual "networking" call that occurs frequently in the close-knit advertising/marketing world.

Dale replied, "Well, I resigned my position at Compton and I am now in Chicago at Needham." I'm now the management director for General Mills account, supervising all the business we currently have from General Mills. It's a big account. Bills over $15 million. We have all of their Betty Crocker mixes, except potatoes."

"Sounds like a great job, Dale," I replied, still wondering where this conversation was going.

"It is. It's especially good because I've started a whole new life. I've remarried; and my new wife, Rosemary and I left Compton and came here to Chicago. Did you ever meet Rosemary?"

"Yes I did, and congratulations!" I replied. Then becoming a little impatient with Dale's roundabout approach, I rushed on, "But, how does that affect this phone conversation?"

He answered, "Well, we need an account executive to handle the Betty Crocker Frosting Mix business and eventually the cake mix business. You came to mind. Would you be interested?"

I almost fell through the phone with joy. Here could be my exit from purgatory in St. Louis and it was an opportunity to work on a big-time brand with a friend.

I gushed, "Dale, I am flattered you'd think of me. I'm very interested. Tell me more. I've never worked on the agency side of the business and this would give me an opportunity to do just that. After my experience here at Pet, it seems like agency work might be a better alternative for someone with my background. I know Bill Phillips is doing real well at Ogilvy."

With these words, I set a career change in motion. I was invited to come to Chicago for an interview.

When I reached Chicago, I visited with Dale and Rosemary, then went through a series of pro-forma interviews at Needham. Dale had made it clear the job was mine, if I wanted it.

It didn't take me long to decide that I wanted it. Needham was truly "love at first sight."

The Agency had an impressive client list. Its major clients at that time were true "blue chippers," Johnson Wax, Kraft, State Farm, HFC, Campbell's, and General Mills. I especially liked the fact that most of them were major packaged-goods companies. More important, I instantly felt at home with the Needham people. They seemed to be real professionals. They reminded me of P&G people and P&G agency people—exactly what I had so sorely missed at Pet.

I went back to St Louis to tell my wife that I had accepted Dale's job offer "on the spot." I would be the account executive (AE) on Betty Crocker Frosting Mixes, with a twenty-five percent pay raise.

Getting Started

Two weeks later I returned to Chicago to begin a four-and-one-half-year stint in the advertising agency business.

I was confident I could do the job, even though I had never worked for an agency. I knew that the AE had a role similar to a brand manager inside an agency. He worked with the client's marketing staff and co-ordinated completion of all the work that the client requested inside the Agency. And, an AE was also expected to have enough marketing "smarts" to provide strategy recommendations.

My bigger worry was the new working culture I faced. I knew when I joined Needham that I had joined a culture very different than P&G or Pet. The agency was, in many ways, a "Gentleman's Club." Every account group was composed primarily of WASPs, seemingly well-heeled men (no women!) from Chicago's stylish North Shore. I really did not "fit" that mold. So, for me, Needham would be a challenge to fit in.

Then too, I would have to learn how to live and work in a big city. For the first time in my life, I wouldn't be in a car pool. I would commute by train. My social life would not come from work and my family would no longer be nearby. They would live in Arlington Heights about thirty miles from the city rather than the shorter distances in St Louis and Cincinnati.

These both proved to be phantom worries. The other AE's welcomed me and I quickly became a "Needhamite." Also, my family adapted easily to the big-city suburban life-style.

"Clients are from Mars; Agencies are from Venus"

While the people culture issues proved easy to adjust to, I did have trouble adjusting to the agency mindset. I found a mind-boggling cultural divide between the agency and the client-side of the advertising/marketing business that pervaded every decision made inside the agency.

Let me explain this difference—a profound difference that still exists today.:

First there is the nature of an agency's business versus a client. The key concern at P&G and Pet was the ability to make a profit on a *tangible product*—a product that usually required capital investment in processing machinery, packaging and warehousing, a product that had inventory costs because it was a hard physical asset.

In contrast, the key product of an advertising agency is an *advertising idea,* an *intangible* product that requires *no* capital investment other than furniture and electronic devices. Its only "sales" come from services, e.g. creating advertising materials and buying media schedules. And an advertising agency's only inventory is people. Until its client company, then, an agency management's *key* concern is not its product, but attracting and retaining the personnel that make its product, particularly the creative people who develop ads and sell them to clients.

Second, there is the difference in the agency's role in marketing versus the client's. Simply put, the agency is really an advisor and "recommender." The agency has no final responsibility for a brand's success or failure. The client is the decisionmaker and has to decide whether to accept the agency's point of view or reject it.

I knew this; but I did not expect this difference to be as profound as it was. For example, I believe it explains the great difference in how each view a brand's sales performance. **Lifetime lesson: An agency is concerned about its client's product sales primarily as a measure of advertising effectiveness; a client worries about its product's sales because it affects its profit objectives.**

Third, there is a very different work ethic in agencies. Both clients and agency people work hard, but oh so differently. A client tends to be on a fairly rigid work-hours schedule. Meetings are usually during regular working hours. An agency never has nine-to-five jobs. Agencies have long crazy hours with meetings at any hour from 7:00 A.M. to midnight.

Along with these different working hours, I found that life in an agency was a series of highs and lows. Unlike my client jobs, there was rarely an "even keel" day. The account group was "up" if the client agreed to what the agency had recommended. It was "down" if things had not gone well in the last meeting or phone call with the client.

Because of this, I found all kinds of special efforts to figure out "our client." What made the client tick? Was it sports, the arts, or the daily horoscope? Were there days to avoid presenting to the client? Did the client have favorite colors? Did the client like wine? etc, etc.

I found this study of the client a special focus of most of the creative people. Many were very superstitious about any client presentation. Some carried good luck charms to client presentations. Others donned the same clothes they wore in a successful meeting to every successive presentation until they lost, much as some of our more eccentric basketball coaches do today.

All of this angst about the client was, of course, just speculative "fodder" for people who had fragile egos and an enormous amount of themselves in any idea presented to the client.

Amid this "fodder" there was one theory that I still believe today. *Weather is important.* Weather definitely affects a person's mental state. In general, all of us are happier on a sunny day than on a cloudy day. This, in turn, has to affect a person's receptivity to new ideas.

Because of this, I offer one finite piece of advice to all marketing and agency professionals, **Lifetime Lesson: Never pitch a major new idea on a cloudy day.** In my career, I never sold a major marketing program or an ad campaign to anyone on a cloudy day.

Obviously these three key client–agency cultural differences resulted in my having a job with very different responsibilities. *I did not approve the agency's work as the client; I presented it to the client.* I was no longer directly responsible for the key marketing variables I had spent my entire career learning—pricing, product, and distribution. I was now a consultant to the client for these responsibilities.

My primary job was to make sure the client had effective advertising. To accomplish this, my key responsibility was not my own work output, but getting quality work on time from others, primarily the Creative Group and Media Department.

Clearly, I had to take a very different personal approach. I could not be a one-man band, as I had been at Pet. *My first task had to be to sell myself to my fellow workers. Then I had to sell myself to the client.* I had to create a favorable perception of Chris Schoenleb before I could ever hope to sell a TV ad or marketing strategy.

Bob Swanson

When I joined Needham, I reported to an account supervisor, Bob Swanson, who in turn reported to Dale Anderson.

Bob was one of three account supervisors on the General Mills business. I was one of five account executives working on the business. All of us except Dale were very young—between twenty-seven and thirty-two years of age.

Bob had been hired from Marathon Oil only a few months before I arrived. He had responsibility for the Betty Crocker Cake Mix and Frosting Mix businesses as well new products. At first, I was Bob's only direct report. He handled cake mixes himself.

I immediately liked and respected Bob, and still do. (We have maintained contact over the years as he followed his own gypsylike career that culminated with his position as CEO of Del Webb, before he retired due to poor health.)

A former Fulbright scholar, Bob was one of the smartest men I ever worked for—perhaps topped only by Ernest Gallo (See Chapter 5). Like Ernest, he had a very practical, not theoretical, brilliance. He was a strong market analyst and strong strategist, but his greatest strength was the ability to analyze a situation and determine what would sell, and what would work in a given situation.

He taught me that the most important action to take in looking at any proposed program was to filter it through a "reality check." I labeled this "filter" the Art of the Possible. It was a filter that asked two simple but profound questions: (1) Will a program "fit" the company's "modus operandi" and (2) will it require company personnel to change their on-the-job methodologies? ***Lifetime Lesson: Before adopting a consumer marketing program that requires any change in corporate behavior, you must realistically determine how likely it is that the change will be adopted. If it requires major change, odds are the program will fail.***

In addition to his talent, Bob brought a major personal advantage to his job—his familiarity with the client. Prior to Marathon, he had worked for General Mills as a brand manager on cereals. He knew all of the General Mills management team.

This made Bob especially valuable to Needham. He could have personal, private conversations with the client and find out what was really going on. He parlayed this "in" with the client to gain overall control of all the General Mills account at Needham within two years. (Dale Anderson was simply outmaneuvered; he lost out to Bob's people advantage.)

When I met Bob, I learned he was suffering from throat cancer. He took weekly radiation treatments that virtually destroyed his vocal chords. He was able to speak only in a raspy whisper. It was touch and go for a while as to whether he was facing an early death.

Over time, he won his battle with the disease, but never recovered his speaking voice. Despite his cancer, he never sought sympathy. He stayed very focused on his work and earned the respect of everyone in the agency.

Working for Bob was not easy. Bob was the most intense workaholic I ever encountered. He was also a total perfectionist and demanded the same from his direct reports.

I always dreaded going to work on Monday morning. I knew that sitting on my desk would be a stack of papers. Each had been personally placed there by Bob. Each would have Bob's hand-written note asking me about the status of a project, or giving me information for a new project assignment. There were also notes on Tuesday, Wednesday, Thursday, and Friday morning, but Monday was by far the worst day of the week.

Agency Job = High Risk

I had been working for Needham about six months. I was just getting comfortable in my new role as an AE. I had learned to accomplish the basic job functions and had gotten to know the agency's creative and media specialists assigned to General Mills.

I had learned the basic agency accounting system—how to charge my hours and monitor the hours being charged to my account. Agencies keep P&Ls by account. For example, Betty Crocker Frosting Mix would be one account, Betty Crocker Cake Mix another. Much like consulting firms, the direct costs (cost of people's time, out-of-pocket expenses) and indirect costs (agency "overhead") are subtracted from billing income to determine account profitability.

I had learned how to be an agency person in a client meeting, namely to proffer a recommendation and await the client's decision. This had been harder than I thought it would be, because of my innate desire to be a decisionmaker.

I had established a good relationship with the Frosting Mix brand manager, John Hartwell (who was, and is, a good friend of Bob Swanson). and I had sold a couple of recommendations to him. In general, everyone seemed to be pleased with the agency's work and me.

I was also comfortable dealing with General Mills for another reason, it reminded me a lot of P&G.

I had even begun to play bridge in the Chicago Ad Agency Bridge League.

Result: I was happy. I liked the work, my boss, and my co-workers, especially the creative group—Mary Hardin, Lynn Hauldren and Dixie Buyan (one of my future agency partners who later married Jerry Fortis and was named Chicago Ad Woman of the Year).

This almost idyllic life quickly came to an end with one five-minute meeting.

Saving the Business

I was called into Bob Swanson's office. I could feel the tension as I walked through the door. Bob was exuding the most negative intensity imaginable. "Grim" would have been an understatement to describe his facial expression. I instantly wondered if he had been given bad news about his cancer.

He stared at me across his desk, " Chris, I want you to take over from me as cake mix AE."

"Bob, what's happened?" Are you getting sicker?"

He looked startled. "No, No, nothing like that" Then he told me his news. "We're in real trouble. Betty Crocker Cake Mixes have been put up for review."

He explained that General Mills had invited Doyle–Dane–Bernbach (DDB), a hot creative New York agency, to develop an advertising campaign for Betty Crocker Cake Mixes in competition with Needham. In other words, the client had initiated a "creative shootout" for the biggest billing Betty Crocker brand we had. The client would award our cake mix business to DDB unless our creative campaign was selected over DDB's.

He continued, "You've got to take over as AE on Cake Mix. Your job, from this moment forward, is to convince Art Schultze (our client, the Cake Mix brand manager) that we are smarter and more attuned to his needs than anyone at a creative shop like Doyle–Dane. You are perfect for this, since Schultze also started his career at P&G."

Then he really got my attention: " Chris, I don't expect you to get much sleep until this shootout is over. For the next four months, expect to eat, sleep and breathe Betty Crocker Cake Mix. Tell your family it is sort of life or death. If we don't keep the business, you might not have a job."

That was my first taste of one of the realities of the agency business. *No matter what kind of job you are doing personally; you can lose your job almost without warning if a big account is lost.*

I was shaken to the core. This was my third job in three years. I needed stability in my life at work and especially at home. I had just learned that my wife was expecting our fourth child.

"Bob, What will you be doing?" I wondered if I was being made a "fall guy" for the business.

For the first time, sensing my unease, he smiled. "I'll be right with you, trying to save the business. You have to do the day-to-day on Cake Mixes so I can be freed up to undo the damage your friend Dale has done with the Mills management." (I never learned what this "damage" was.)

I approached my new job as if I were the new brand manager on Cake Mix. I reviewed all the research, I reviewed all the Nielsen data, etc. I wanted to be at least as knowledgeable as the brand manager so that he would accept me as his "equal." This would not be easy. Art Schultze, like most of us from P&G, had a very good opinion of himself.

I asked our General Mills media planner, Phil Morrow, to teach me more about media, particularly network buying, as it was practiced for General Mills. My goal was to know more about media planning and buying than Art Schultze. I did not want to replace the media department but I needed to make Art more appreciative of the skills and services I could bring him. He had to see me as more than just another ex-P&Ger.

And I sat down with Dick Daub of the research department to learn all about advertising research techniques. I asked him to help me sell the creative department to use more research in the development of the new cake mix TV advertising. I knew that Art would be more inclined to accept our recommendation if it had been thoroughly researched. I also suspected that DDB would not be using much research. (The now legendary Mary Wells headed the DDB creative group assigned to the business.)

In addition, I spent a lot of time with Art Schultze. My goal was to become a good business friend. I knew that because Art was from P&G we could never be friends like Bob was with his old compatriots at General Mills. P&G had taught us to be professional, not personal, in our relationships with agency people. And both Art and I were too young to appreciate that agency executives and clients could become good personal friends.

Art and I spent several long evenings together doing what people in Minneapolis do better than almost anyone in the country, drinking cocktails and eating. We had a common background that I tried to exploit. We told each other P&G war stories by the hour.

As time passed, we began to operate more as equals than as client–subordinate. We did become business friends.

In the course of doing this, I learned one of the major truths of the ad agency business. *Agency account groups invariably believe that they are smarter than their clients.* At first, I thought this was just because of my own ego and my appraisal of Art Schultze's ability versus mine. But, it wasn't just me. It was true of every account executive versus their counterpart at General Mills. Indeed it was true of every AE and account supervisor that I knew at the agency. Universally, although many respected their client, they were sure they were smarter. In fact, most believed that part of their job was to make sure the client didn't make bad decisions.

I know in my heart of hearts that this attitude continues today. My agency friends usually reluctantly fess up to this.

In truth, this attitude can be the personal ego salvation of an account group. It enables them to cope with the inevitable "ups and downs" they experience dealing with a client. They can rationalize away their failure to sell a program or ad campaign by sharing agreement to this thought, "It wasn't our recommendation that was wrong, it was just that the client didn't know what was good for him."

With all of this activity, four months went by very quickly. I became a workaholic who rivaled or beat Bob Swanson. I was an absentee husband and father. I worked fourteen to sixteen hours a day. I worked every day, including Christmas and New Years, at the office. Bob was my companion in this; he was at the office almost all the time I was there.

Together we drove ourselves and our co-workers to put together a program that would keep the business. We knew we had to get a memorable creative campaign that would capture the imagination of the client. But we went beyond this. We strove to provide new marketing insights on the brand. We demanded a revised and freshened media plan that would push a lot of the "right buttons" with the staff members of General Mills.

In effect, we hoped our other work would create a "slam dunk" tiebreaker should the "creative shootout" need one.

The creative was, of course, the hardest part to put in place. Bob made sure that all the creative teams in Chicago, Los Angeles, and New York worked on the problem. In all, we must have seen twelve or more different campaigns before we settled on one. The amount of midnight oil burned by the creative people was astonishing to me until I understood agency politics. There was great internal prestige at stake. Every group wanted their work to carry the day. Their goal was to be able to brag that they were now "king of the agency's creative work."

"So Tender You Can Cut It With a Feather"

The day finally came for the "shootout" presentation. The General Mills conference room was full. Nerves were frayed. I noted that it was a cold, but sunny day in Minneapolis.

In addition to Art Schultze and his boss, Bruce Atwater (a future president of General Mills), the key Mills participants were three friends of Bob Swanson's—Don Swanson, who was best man at Bob's wedding; Lawry Crites, and Jim McFarland, both of whom Bob had worked for when he had been at the Mills. Also, the Mills's media maven, Dale Haworth, was in the audience. So was Jim Fish, the Mills's legendary VP of Advertising.

Bob had always had good personal relationships with all of them. In truth, we hoped that all these relationships would be another tiebreaker for Needham if our pitch were at least equal to DDB's.

For our part, we brought out all our big guns. Paul Harper, our chairman, and Jim Isham, our president, headed the delegation. Also present were the overall creative director, Irv Sohn, who would present the creative and Blair Vedder, our media guru, who would present the media plan. Bob made no presentation. His voice was almost nonexistent because of cancer treatments. I had a minor role, although I had written most of the marketing and strategic portions of the presentation.

Just prior to the start of the meeting, I observed something that I would remember later with fondness. Art Schultze was very nervous about this review. Apparently, he had sold General Mills management on having this "creative shootout" in the first place. Now, he seemed concerned that if things did not go well, it would reflect badly on him.

The pitch began and the critical moment of the meeting soon arrived. Jim Isham, a tall steel-gray-haired man who always seemed perfectly groomed, stood in front of this rather large group. He smiled. He slowly and dramatically reached inside his Brooks Brothers' suit coat. He pulled out a large white eagle feather from his pocket. All eyes were on him.

Then as smoothly and dramatically as he was able, Jim said "Gentlemen, our creative solution for Betty Crocker Cake Mix is a simple, but very dramatic promise: Betty Crocker Cake Mix is so tender you can cut it with a feather." With that, Jim stepped up to a table on which we had placed a two-layer Betty Crocker white cake that had no frosting. He took the large eagle feather and cleanly sliced the cake. A feather did indeed cut a cake.

Then, in as dramatic a fashion as possible, Irv Sohn presented several TV commercial storyboards that used this visual advertising promise. Following a brief recess, we showed the proposed media and promotion plans. The presentation was over. Questions were asked; then the agency was asked to leave.

I had presented the promotion section of the pitch, but most of the time I had studied our clients' facial reaction to our presentation. I could see shock on some of their faces; on others I was sure I read a clear acceptance. I was sure we had won.

And, indeed we had. After the announcement, Art Shultze and I went out to celebrate. Art celebrated because he had been a hero in getting new creative. I celebrated because I still had a job.

Ironically the advertising campaign was not a big success. It was visually dramatic, but an empty promise. Moistness and flavor were far more important than "tender" to cake mix users. We knew this; so did General Mills.

But in our joint search for dramatic TV we ignored reality. A new campaign to replace the "feather" campaign was developed within eighteen months. By then Art and I were both off the business.

Schultze's Legacy

Art Schultze went on to a long and successful career at General Mills. He was my client for three years, but we never kept up with each other after we stopped working together.

Art did, however, leave a lasting legacy with me. He showed me how *a totally self-centered approach to the client–agency relationship can be counterproductive.* At this point in his career, Art was prone to critical harangues in meetings, especially creative meetings. These generally illustrated how smart he was and how inept the agency recommendations were. In doing this, he showed me that self-centered bluntness could be devastating to the creative morale of the agency. Many times his harangues slowed the creative development process until creative egos could be repaired, or a new creative team could be assigned.

Lifetime Lesson: To get the best effort from your agency, you have to create a non-threatening, collaborative atmosphere that will inspire the best agency creative people to continue to work on your problem. This means that you must always give much more than a "yes" or "no" response to their work. Even if you rejected their recommendation, you have to show you appreciate them as people, and state that you are confident that they will do superior work next time.

The "Fruits" of Success and Bisquick

All was going very well.

Partly because of our success in keeping the Cake Mix business, Bob Swanson replaced Dale Anderson and was named to the Needham Board of Directors. I was promoted to account supervisor reporting to Bob, as was a Peter Nelson. (Pete had a long and fruitful career at Needham before finishing his career as VP of Advertising for McDonald's.) Within a year, at age twenty-nine, I was named a VP of the agency.

Ironically, all this led to my moving off Betty Crocker Cake Mixes and being given responsibility for some new General Mills business we had been awarded—Bisquick and new products.

This led to my hiring Phil Lincoln on Bisquick. Phil was a major "player" in my working life and became a dear friend. I worked closer with him over the next thirty years than any other person.

Phil had been at two agencies prior to Needham and was an experienced AE. He had a very different perspective on business than mine. He was not a strong strategic marketing thinker, but he had enormous "street smarts." His focus was on understanding who had the decisionmaking power and how they were going to use it.

I used to scoff at Phil and point out that knowing who could do what would never replace the need for good advertising based on solid marketing strategies. But, at the same time, we made a good team. I was always looking at the marketing problems while he analyzed the people problems.

In addition to complementing my skills, Phil also provided me with the most outrageous excuse I have ever heard for being late to a meeting.

One day we had a critical meeting with our Bisquick client. It was set for 9:00 A.M. at the agency. I arrived early, made sure the meeting room was set up and waited for Phil. He did not appear; 9:00 A.M. came and went. The client arrived and after spending the usual twenty minutes to exchange pleasantries and sip coffee, we were ready to start the meeting.

The media folks were in place; so were the other agency staffers, but, Phil had not appeared.

I called Phil's home. He wasn't there. I became more and more upset. I stumbled all over myself trying to figure out what to do about this meeting before it became a total disaster. I had no good options. Phil had the critical role and he had taken the pitch home with him the night before.

Finally, at 11:00 A.M. Phil appeared. He was totally calm, cool and collected. He began to unload his briefcase to get the meeting underway, as though everything were routine.

By this time, I was apoplectic. In front of everyone, I demanded an immediate explanation. How could he possibly be late for such an important meeting? Where had he been?

He looked me square in the eye, while glancing over the others in the room, and said in his most serious demeanor, "Well, you know Chris I would have been here on time but I ran into a real problem."

"Problem?" I demanded, "What kind of problem?"

> He said, "Well, you see, there was this dragon, this huge fire-breathing dragon. He wouldn't let me get on the train platform to catch my train. Chris, he was huge—biggest one I ever saw. I couldn't risk getting burned by his breath or bashed by his enormous tail. So-o-o, the only thing I could do was go back home and wait until the dragon left. When I learned he had finally stopped waiting for me, I got on the next train and came as quickly as I could.

I stood there stunned at this outrageous, off-the-wall explanation. Then Phil grinned and, for some reason, I began to laugh almost uncontrollably. The client, Bob Hatch, joined in the laughter. Phil had broken the ice with our client in a way I had never expected.

New Bisquick

Bisquick proved to be a far more challenging assignment than either of the Betty Crocker brands.

Bisquick had been General Mills's first big baking mix success. It was originally formulated for making biscuits, but had over the years become far more than a specialty biscuit mix. It had been used for a host of flour-based products including muffins, dumplings, and pancakes.

In the late '60s, however, for most of these nonbiscuit uses, Bisquick was being challenged by new specialty mixes, most especially pancake mixes. This, coupled with fact that the high volume "scratch" biscuit makers in the Deep South did not use Bisquick, made it a brand that seemed destined to slowly sink into oblivion.

To try to "fix" Bisquick, General Mills took two strategic steps. First, it developed a new Bisquick formula designed to specifically address this

Southern scratch-baking consumer. A mix containing buttermilk, it made lighter and fluffier biscuits than the previous product. Second, they hired Needham to revitalize the Bisquick advertising/ad promotion program.

Our assignment, when we were awarded the business, was to find a way to introduce this new Bisquick to the Southern scratch biscuit baker.

Our solution was to gain agreement to treat the buttermilk product as New Bisquick. We wanted to introduce it as a second Bisquick, a "flanker product," not as a replacement brand. We knew that the scratch bakers would be a tough sell. We were convinced that for this target market we had to totally restage the brand by focussing on "New" and the end result attained from the new mix—lighter, flakier biscuits.

We also gained client agreement to do a full-blown test market, that is selling the product with a new positioning, new creative, extra ad spending and heavy sales promotion in one TV market, before any major rollout of the New Bisquick in the south.

The key to success, as always, would be the strategic positioning for the Brand; and how this positioning was translated into advertising, particularly television. It was clear from consumer research that the only positioning that had any real chance to attract the scratch baker was a superiority claim. New Bisquick needed to be positioned as "Better Than Scratch."

This was a very tall order. We needed an advertising claim that was legally provable and demonstrable to consumers.

In research, the scratch biscuit eaters identified "lightness" as the key descriptor for a really good biscuit. (They were defining taste and texture, not the weight of a biscuit.) The ideal ad, then, would be one that promised "Biscuits made from New Bisquick are lighter than scratch."

However, we could find no research support for this claim or any other superiority claim. Consumer taste tests showed that, at best, biscuits made from New Bisquick were seen as equal to scratch, not better. Furthermore, New Bisquick was not preferred for its lightness versus a scratch-recipe biscuit.

Yet, amazingly, our Needham creative group, now headed by Jack Friedman, came up with exactly what we sought. They proposed print and TV ads that clamed in a very bold way, "New Bisquick Biscuits are lighter than scratch."

And, amazingly, despite the consumer research, this was an ad claim that was legally provable.

Jack had used truth. However, his proof of lightness superiority was not better texture or taste, but weight. It was a fact that scratch biscuits were heavier in weight than Bisquick biscuits because of the large amount of lard or butter used in them. In effect, these proposed ads tried to change the consumer definition of lightness from texture to weight and, in doing so, imply that lighter weight biscuits were superior.

Jack also developed a truly unique and dramatic *cinema verite* demonstration of lightness for TV commercials. It was very dramatic television even for this time period, the era in television of the memorable demonstration (remember the "White Tornado" for Ajax Cleanser?).

In the proposed television, real Southern housewives would be invited to bring their scratch biscuits and place them on a scale—a small brass replica of the "scale of justice." The scratch biscuit would be placed on one tray; the New Bisquick biscuit would be put on the other tray. When the scratch biscuit went down, it seesawed the lighter-weight Bisquick biscuit up, thus dramatically showing the difference in weight.

I was skeptical that this "flip" in the meaning of biscuit lightness would be effective in the long term. Even though the ads were legally correct, I was convinced that these ads were an overpromise that could create high initial consumer trial, but little repeat purchase. Why? Because in my mind this campaign "fit" my favorite quote (paraphrased) about advertising from DDB's founder, Bill Bernbach, *"Nothing kills a bad product quicker than good advertising."*

I suppressed these concerns, however, after I expressed them to Phil and Bob Swanson. Both liked the campaign. They felt I was too concerned about what might happen. New Bisquick was not a bad product. Besides, they were sure the client would buy the ads. So we presented the New Bisquick lightness campaign and, indeed, the client gave us quick approval.

The commercials were shot in the Town Square in old Savannah, Georgia. Proud Southern ladies responded to the Bisquick "challenge" to their biscuit-baking prowess. To their chagrin, their biscuits "lost" on the scales. We had a unique campaign to air.

The introductory test was launched successfully. Sales did increase, and new distribution was attained.

New Bisquick was, as I recall, eventually expanded nationally. But, most scratch biscuit bakers never switched to the new mix. The increased sales came primarily from new young Southern housewives to whom scratch baking was a mystery that they would solve with New Bisquick, rather than learning how to bake the old family biscuit recipe from scratch.

Dr Saul Ben-Zev

My career as an agency account manager for General Mills ended with work on new products.

General Mills had developed a processed soy protein and wanted to find commercial uses for it. They had developed one potential product, a high-energy nutritional candylike bar for a complete breakfast "on the run." The assignment for the agency was to determine the marketing potential for this concept, and/or find other potential product concepts, then put together a proposed marketing strategy to tap this potential

To begin, we needed more consumer research. We hired a Dr. Saul Ben-Zev to do it.

Saul was not an ordinary researcher. He had a Ph.D. in psychology from the University of Chicago. A native-born Israeli, standing about five-feet-five, he wore thick horned-rim glasses and spoke with a thick Israeli accent. He looked and talked like the prototypical rumpled college professor. In his early 30's, he had just gone into business as president of his own market research company, Creative Research Associates.

For this product study, we agreed to use a series of consumer group interviews. In this form of research, the research discussion leader recruits groups of six to ten target consumers to participate in a free-flowing discussion of questions put to them. The normal group lasts about two hours and is usually conducted in a conference room that has a two-way mirror that allows client or agency people to watch and listen unseen by the group participants.

In this case, Saul conducted the group interviews personally. Then he made a presentation of his findings to the account group. I had sat through all the consumer research groups. I had heard every word. But when Saul presented his report, he did not play back what I had heard. He gave his interpretation of what the people had really said.

This was Saul's genius. He had the unique capability of listening to people in a group session and understand not only what they said, but also what they really meant. In effect he could almost psychoanalyze a group's thoughts.

In his final report he provided more information than we ever expected. Not only did he interpret the consumer input, he developed a complete "gap analysis" of the breakfast market. In doing this, he also confirmed that there was a potential market for a soy breakfast energy bar.

From this we developed several product concepts, including a product name and positioning statement, and presented our findings to the client.

I have no idea what happened to these concepts. After this presentation I left the General Mills Account to supervise work on two new clients, Armour-Dial and Mead Johnson. Both were clients that I had worked with Swanson to bring to the agency.

[For me the most important result of this project was becoming acquainted with Saul BenZev. The General Mills study began a working relationship that we maintained for over thirty-three years. As I will detail later in this book, he played a major role in most of my biggest marketing successes.]

TONE Soap

When I left the General Mills account, one of the happiest times of my life ended.

I was now working on two newly acquired accounts with little billing—Mead Johnson for its Nutrament brand, and Armour-Dial for new products and its dishwashing liquid, Chiffon. Total billing was barely over $1.0 million.

Needham expected to lose money on both these new accounts. However, the agency eagerly added them to their client roster for two reasons, prestige and potential future billings.

In effect, the business gave us a "foot in the door" to improve our long-term chances to acquire more of these companies' business, particularly each company's major brand, Metrecal and Dial Soap.

I hired Dave Gorden to be the AE. Dave did an excellent job. He was a good marketing strategist who had more enthusiasm for a $500,000 brand ad budget than I could ever understand. Dave eventually left Needham and worked for Alberto Culver in brand management. Later, he left Alberto Culver to be a "headhunter" at his own small executive search firm. It was Dave who recruited me for Burger King.

Our job was to push Needham's long-term goal by "overservicing" these clients. Bob Swanson described my assignment very succinctly "Wow them, Chris, every chance you get."

Armour-Dial soon gave us the first "wow" opportunity. They asked for Needham's new product ideas for possible future development.

The account group brainstormed this request. We came up with a total of seven ideas for products we felt "fit" our client's current businesses. For each, we developed the concept as completely as we could. We provided a product formula description, a product name, an overall marketing positioning for the product, and samples of possible advertising in print or TV storyboard. It was true "overkill."

I don't remember any of the concepts, except one—mine. I came up with an idea for a new kind of bar soap because of a major traumatic event in my family. My daughter Barbara had recently suffered severe burns over much of her body. From this terrible accident I had learned the healing qualities of cocoa butter on the skin. It could truly soften skin as it cleansed. No major bar soap had this ingredient.

We proposed that Armour-Dial formulate a new complexion soap with cocoa butter as its key ingredient. The creative team came up with a great name for the product and we boldly recommended that it be positioned directly against P&G's Camay brand. The product we proposed Tone Soap.

The rest is marketing history. Armour-Dial adopted the idea, the name, and developed the formula as we had proposed. Two years or so later, Tone Soap was successfully test marketed in Denver and later put into national distribution. I have been told it was Armour-Dial's biggest new product success in years.

There was an ironic ending to the Tone Soap saga. William "Woody" Wood Prince Jr. left Needham to become the brand manager on Tone

Soap. As a "thank you" for my contribution to the product, he sent me a case of the new soap brand when it was introduced into test market. When I received it, I tried it out. It seemed like a great product for others, but not for me. It made my skin break out in a rash.

Leaving Needham

Despite the excitement of Tone Soap, I spent the final year of my agency career in growing frustration. My clients at Mead Johnson and Armour-Dial were very nice people on a personal basis, but professionally they were the same second-tier marketers I had fled when I left Pet.

Both clients had three qualities that drove me "nuts." They were not as smart or aggressive as General Mills. They did not seem to recognize or appreciate top-quality work. And most unforgivably, they were indecisive. Sometimes we would wait weeks for a decision on an agency proposal that the client had demanded on a very short time frame. The fact that many times late nights were required to meet the due date added "insult to injury."

In all this, another insight on life at an ad agency was reinforced forever. *Lifetime Lesson: The client's personality, both personal and corporate, directly determines the "quality of life" for the agency account group servicing the account.*

It was this insight that led me to conclude I did not want a lifetime agency career. The work took too much effort to be frustrated by mediocrity.

I discussed my frustrations with Swanson. He told me he too was considering leaving. He wanted broader management responsibilities. Now I was faced with a double whammy, a new boss and clients I did not like. It was time to move on!

Lessons Learned

1. The ideal advertising agency account person is someone with a multi-faceted personality that combines advertising knowledge, strategic-thinking capability, street smarts, personal-selling skills and the ability to motivate and direct creative people. *It is far more difficult to do this job well than a comparable corporate job, because this individual has two bosses, the client and the agency management.*
2. Developing and maintaining friendships in business will enable you to be more effective in your work. *It will also enhance your ability to find or be offered a new job.* (Most of the positions I gained in my career were through networking with friends.)

Final Comments

There is no doubt in my mind that every senior client would be better equipped for marketing success if that client has spent time at an advertising agency. Understanding an agency's perspective should at the very least, enable any client to be a more effective communicator. It should also make any client a better listener and give the client an internal standard of what is reasonable to expect from an agency.

There is also no doubt that today most advertising agencies have lost their role as a client's marketing partner that Needham and all major agencies played in the '60s and '70s. Today, agencies are usually seen as the "supplier" for advertising materials, not a partner. Most AEs are "bag carriers" for the creative group, and/or "hand-holders" of the client, not partners in planning. This role change has, in turn, hurt the ability of agencies to attract top-notch marketers for account work. This has also resulted in most agency presidents now coming from the creative side of the agency, not the account management side.

Finally, there can be no doubt that my experience at Needham forever changed my perspective on the client–agency world in three fundamental ways:

1. I learned to value talented advertising agency people. I saw firsthand how a client can get better work if the client creates the right environment for the "creatives."
2. I learned that advertising agency talent can be a reliable partner in bringing about change in a company's marketing program. *Lifetime Lesson: Agencies thrive on ideas and change; most companies (clients) do not.*
3. I became a "true believer" in the power of advertising and the importance of the agency in capturing it. At P&G I had gained the view that how advertising communicated was very secondary to content—making sure that proper positioning and product claims were communicated. I left Needham convinced that P&G had only half the formula for capturing the most impact from advertising.

Lifetime lesson: Great marketing strategy needs great advertising execution. Therefore the importance of the advertising agency to any consumer marketing success cannot be minimized.

CHAPTER 4
Outside-in Marketing

(Tactical Lessons from American Motors)

Someone once advised me, "You have to do Detroit. Only then will you begin to understand why the American automotive business operates the way it does. There's no place on earth like it."

I did Detroit for three-and-one-half years in a senior marketing position with American Motors. My experience confirmed that there is indeed no place like Detroit in the business world.

I also learned firsthand that the American automobile business had a very serious corporate disease in the late '60s, a disease Brock Yates, editor of *Car and Driver* magazine, described as "marketing myopia."

However, when I was being recruited for American Motors, I knew none of this. Instead, I saw a real marketing challenge—the challenge of trying to change a major company's consumer image to achieve a turnaround of its sales and profits. And I was convinced that at AMC, unlike at Pet, I would be part of the management team, not an outsider.

Bill McNealy, VP of Marketing of American Motors, hired me. (Bill is probably more famous today as the father of Scott McNealy, founder of Sun Microsystems.) Bill recruited me for a job that had nothing to do with advertising. I was to be Director of Merchandising. In this position I had management responsibility for consumer promotions and a lot of things with which I had absolutely no experience, including auto shows, dealer incentive programs, dealer sales meetings, dealer salesmen's training materials, and auto racing.

I was truly excited about my new job. For the first time I would be working in a high visibility product category, autos, the biggest industry in America. Furthermore, I would be a department head for a company that McNealy had convinced me could be a storybook business turnaround. I could hardly wait to apply my package goods expertise to the task.

Best of all, this new job had a very special "fringe benefit" in the form of a new car every four months for me, and a new low-cost lease car for my wife every year. I was sure that, at long last, the Schoenleb's had "arrived" economically.

Of course, the reality of the job proved to be much more difficult than I had ever imagined. *I quickly learned that I had looked too much at the challenge of the job and not nearly enough at cultural realities.*

Even more complex than P&G, at American Motors I had to adapt to both an external city-wide culture and an internal corporate culture. You see Detroit was a one-industry town—a giant culture focussed only on the auto industry.

As such Detroit was also the epitome of a capitalist culture gone amok. I experienced it as a culture almost totally based on money and power.

It was a powerful culture. It dictated that our social life outside of work be built around who I was at the workplace, not who my wife and I were as parents, neighbors, or church members. It was a culture that infected our kids at an early age. I overheard my grade-school children talking to their friends about such topics as whose Daddy had the most important job and what color car their parents would be getting in a few months, or even the merits of one car model versus another.

It was a culture that included lots of entertainment by suppliers to your company—often in lavish fashion. I will never forget a party we attended to honor Lee Iacocca's birthday. Staged by S&H Travel, the party included about 500 of Lee's "closest friends" (I have never met Lee Iacocca.) Vic Damone came on a chartered jet just to sing "Happy Birthday."

AMC "Reality"

Internally, the AMC culture was a microcosm of Detroit with far greater differences from the packaged-goods world than I had expected. It was a company culture that almost defies description today.

First and foremost, it was a world of Harvard MBAs newly hired as senior VPs. These men were brought in by the new president and COO, Bill Luneberg, to make over a failing, old-line, traditional car company (AMC had lost $73,000,000 the year I joined them). They were charged with one mission—change the company's historical culture—a corporate culture inhabited by employees who were used to being the smallest car company and trying to "stay alive" in a world dominated by the Big Three. It was a culture accustomed to mediocrity.

To begin their task, the new VPs made a simultaneous "assault" on all internal processes—bookkeeping, purchasing, manufacturing, etc. This resulted in massive personnel changes, with "outsiders" hired in all departments. Confusion reigned in almost every department for several years.

In many instances the new VPs had no prior experience for their positions. Bill McNealy, for example, had no car company experience and had no prior marketing experience. He had been a Purchasing VP at Cummins. In fact, of all the senior officers, I believe only one, the CEO and Chairman of the Board, Roy Chapin, had spent his career in the auto industry.

In retrospect I believe that these MBAs were trying to follow the model of what Ford had done ten years earlier with Bob McNamara and the "whiz kids." They were trying to bring some of the fabled MBA disciplines to AMC through the "chaos of change" they were fomenting. In the end they did not succeed. While I was at AMC, I never saw these disciplines penetrate deeply in the AMC culture, except, perhaps in the Finance department.

Perhaps one of the reasons for this was where we worked. AMC's offices were in an old Kelvinator plant, not an office building. I believe this unchanged office environment communicated subliminally to its employees that AMC was still not a world-class company like its Big Three competitors.

The Role of Marketing

In this world, I found little resemblance to my packaged-goods experience in the basic role of the Marketing Department and the corporate decisionmaking process.

First, the Marketing Department was limited to developing the advertising and promotion tactics. Marketing had little say on the key strategic decisions for the product to be sold—the size, the styling, and the specifications of the vehicles to be built.

Marketing had virtually no authority on the prices set for these vehicles. Furthermore, the use of consumer research for input and guidance for such key strategic decisions was minimal. Most decisions made at AMC were based on personal opinion, not consumer input.

I remember attending a meeting in which the Styling department reviewed several different front-end looks for the new Gremlin. We offered our input; then Gene Amoroso, Director of Market Research, suggested that we bring some consumers in to test their reactions to the proposed Gremlin styling. Instead, Styling invited CEO Roy Chapin and other top AMC executives to a second meeting. Roy said, "I like that one." He made multimillion dollar decision, and life limped on at AMC.

When I was at AMC, the CEO and the Finance Department were the product marketing decision makers. The CEO made all final styling and engineering decisions: Pricing was Finance's domain. *It was a real personal adjustment for me to know that accountants had far more "say" over what would be built and the price for which it would be sold than marketing personnel.*

Another huge difference at AMC versus packaged goods was working with a captive distribution system, the AMC dealers. No longer was capturing shelf space or gaining distribution in a grocery chain in the job description. Instead, it was marketing's role to persuade and/or cajole the dealers to adopt the corporation's programs.

Indeed, internally, AMC management defined marketing's role as "building sales" to consumers and dealers.

Marketing was responsible for attracting dealer showroom traffic and for developing the tools to sell vehicles in-dealership, including all the point-of-purchase materials and selling aids such as the sales catalog.

Most important, it was marketing's role to help "sell" dealers on buying more vehicles to build their dealership inventory. Marketing did this by developing dealer sales incentive programs to make it more attractive for dealers to grow their retail sales.

Why was this done? Because, to increase consumer retail sales, dealers tradionally had to cut their margins and make better "deals" for their customers. Hence, marketing programs started with dealer incentives usually "spiffs" (dealer discounts), and/or a special reward for volume sale increases (usually an exotic trip for the dealer and a companion).

Perhaps the most profound insight I gained about the car business had to do with this phenomenon of trying to build dealer interest in buying and selling more vehicles. *Lifetime Lesson: The auto companies and their dealers approach the marketplace with basically conflicting goals. The companies seek sales volume growth; the dealers seek maximum profit per vehicle.* You see, auto companies make their profits grow from improving retail sales volume. Selling more vehicles makes the assembly lines more efficient and gives the company more profit per car.

On the other hand, dealers are primarily concerned with how much money they can make on each vehicle they sell. They have very little interest in pushing a lot of cars out of the dealership at little or no profit to them. In general, they would rather sell ten cars for a $1000 gross profit, than fifteen for a $500 gross.

All of these differences resulted in a very different orientation to marketing planning. At AMC, marketing was focussed on short-term tactical programs, not long-term strategies. Although there was an annual budget and planning calendar, Bill McNealy viewed six months as a long-term planning horizon.

This kind of planning horizon proved to be great training for my future experience in the fast-food restaurant business. At the time, however, it was part of the overall culture shock.

Besides the difference in corporate culture, there were two major changes in the nature of my job.

First, I had to become accustomed to being a decision maker, instead of playing my former lower middle-management role of preparing recommendations for higher-ups to review. As Director of Merchandising, I was empowered to approve programs. This was a limited power. Technically, I still had to get Bill McNealy's agreement on major expenditures but he was so busy with his other areas of responsibility that I was rarely overruled. With a department of fifteen and a budget in excess of $15 million, this was "heady stuff" for a 33 year-old executive.

Second, for the first time in my career I was not involved with advertising on a day-to-day basis. I truly missed participating in the TV creative process—far more than I had anticipated. This frustrated me no end because I found myself cut off from working on advertising with a truly outstanding agency at the peak of its prowess.

The agency? A freshly hired "hot New York creative shop," the newly formed Wells–Rich–Greene (WRG), led, of course by Mary Wells. Mary tackled AMC as one of her first major clients.

There is no doubt even today that she, with the creative talents of Charlie Moss and Stan Dragoti, had one of her finest hours writing and producing advertising for the AMC product line. WRG made some of the great, funny, memorable TV car commercials of all time.

Of course, my frustration with my non-involvement with advertising must have been partially shared by Bill McNealy. Mary Wells always pitched new advertising directly to Roy Chapin, CEO.

Note: I did work with WRG on promotion projects. This, in turn, did facilitate my getting well acquainted with Mary and Charlie, a fact that was pivotal later at Burger King and Midas.

The AMC Challenge

When I went to AMC, I dug in to my new responsibilities with all the intensity I could muster. Sixteen-hour days were the norm to try to both learn a business and make an impact on it quickly.

The task was to fashion nonadvertised programs to help change American Motor's image from being the stodgy maker of Ramblers to being seen as a maker of jazzy new cars like the Javelin. To do this, the overall strategy was to make AMC acceptable to the car-purchase "opinion makers" of the late '60s—teenage males. These opinion makers made it a consumer market that valued performance and racy looks above all other things.

This basic strategy aped the Big Three. Everyone in Detroit seemed to myopically follow each other. Or, as David Halbersham put it in his book, *The Reckoning*, "Detroit was Detroit and more than most business centers it was a city that listened only to its own voice."

In short, *my task was to execute a me-too strategy, not to apply package-good strategies to cars*. I was to change the various "tools" under my leadership (auto shows, etc.) to support this new image.

For some reason—probably the glamour and excitement I felt going to AMC—this basic description of the real task did not sink in for almost two years. I was too busy "doing" and learning a new industry and a new company.

When I joined the company, my office was big but empty. There was no fact base for me to assimilate to begin applying my package-goods expertise. There was no consumer research to read, nor a detailed sales analysis to review. Indeed, there was no written past history to review.

Instead, there was an internal staff who carried the history and the background of all my responsibilities in their heads. The first task, then, was to become acquainted with this staff.

I started with the man I had replaced as department head, Guy Hadsell. Guy had been with American Motors during the halcyon Rambler years and before. He was a pleasant man, but not a marketer. He was strictly a doer of projects in the time-tested way they had always been done. He knew how to make in-store merchandising materials, how to set up auto shows, and how to develop dealer incentive programs "the American Motor's way." He had long since stopped asking why things were done the way they were done. He rarely looked to change anything.

Because he was no longer in charge, Hadsell was, at best, a reluctant lieutenant. He was not the agent for change I needed to accomplish my mandate. Others in the department seemed equally wary of new thinking.

It was clear that I had to hire new people to have any hope of success, and over the next eighteen months I did exactly that. My first hire was my street-wise comrade from Needham, Phil Lincoln, who quickly became my trusted chief lieutenant.

Trans-Am Racing

From an initial review of the "weapons" available to accomplish my assignment, I quickly concluded the most potent one to address changing AMC's image was auto racing. Racing could provide the "proof" to the new target audience that AMC was not for folks with rocking chairs but for the "in" crowd that wanted performance cars from a performance company.

This would not be easy, but clearly auto racing would get the attention of our target audience. Fortunately, the company not only had a reason to go racing it had a car that seemed ideal for it, the Javelin. (The Javelin was AMC's entry into the new "pony car" segment of the market dominated by Mustang and challenged by GM's Camaro and Chrysler's Challenger.)

Because racing was new to the company, there was no existing auto racing department or program. I would have to build it from scratch.

Ironically, I knew nothing about auto racing. I had never attended an auto race. Fortunately AMC did have a real racing enthusiast: on its engineering staff, Carl Chakmakian. Carl had been named Manager of Racing and reported to me. Initially I relied totally on Carl's expertise and knowledge of the racing industry.

So, with a $3 million budget and a one-man staff, I plunged forward to try to build a successful racing program.

One program had been dictated: we would race the new Javelin in the Trans-Am Racing Series against the Mustang, Challenger, and Camaro. To do this, we hired the Ronnie Kaplan racing team to develop the engine, modify the car for racing, hire the drivers, and run two Javelins in every Trans-Am race.

But that was just the beginning.

We instituted a drag racing program. Within six months, we had an AMC sponsored "funny car" driven by Doug Thorley. Later we hired Shirley Shahan to race a Super-Stock AMX. And in 1970, we hired Bobby Allison to race our mid-sized car, the Rebel, in NASCAR.

We also developed a highly visible design for the racing cars. Ronnie Kaplan introduced me to Brooks Stevens, an auto designer and maker of "kit" cars, who came up with an ingenious design for all of the racing programs. We were *American* Motors. Therefore all racing vehicles and support trucks would be painted in red, white, and blue; the front of the car red, the middle of the car white, the back blue, or the reverse. We also used this design scheme to develop unique and very attractive racing "gear" (jackets, hats, etc.).

Overall, I had a very steep learning curve. But, I did learn and, in doing so, fashioned a program that succeeded beyond anyone's wildest dreams.

Success was not instantaneous. It came in part because *I refused to think like the smallest car company. I developed the racing program on only one basis—spend enough money to win.* Winning was the key to changing AMC's image. We had to compete with the big boys and win.

The key "war" to be won was the Trans-Am circuit. The Trans-Am circuit was a summer-long series of pony-car races at the premier road racing tracks in North America (Watkins Glen, etc.). It was unique in that it was the only racing series in which each of the Big Three auto companies had a factory-sponsored team. The operable thesis was that if the Javelin won races over its rivals in this venue, AMC would sell more cars. This was, of course, just an opinion, perhaps a corporate myth, because there was no research to truly support this thesis.

In the first eighteen months of the Trans-Am racing program, I attended every race. I met the key factory–team competitors, Parnelli Jones and the Ford racing team, Roger Penske and the Camaro racing team, Dan Gurney of the Chrysler Challenger team (all big-name racers in those days).

The AMC team was not in this big-name league. Ronnie Kaplan was a journeyman, a solid racing team manager who had yet to make it big. Our driver, George Fulmer, fit the same description. With the resources we provided them we had a very competitive team. It would finish in the top five week after week. However, the team never won a race!

After eighteen months, I concluded that Kaplan would never win. To win, I was convinced we had to hire one of our competitors' teams that was winning. Bill McNealy agreed. So, I set out to pull a real coup in the automotive world—hiring a truly big-name racing team for the underdog American Motors Company.

Roger Penske

I approached Roger Penske. In those days, he was just beginning to build the Penske racing teams that have been consistent winners on every circuit in which they have competed over the past thirty years.

Our first meeting was by chance, at a bar near the San Jovite Racetrack outside Montreal, in the middle of the Trans-Am season. We had several drinks before I broached the issue of whether he would be willing to leave Chevrolet and Camaro to run Javelins in the Trans-Am series. He expressed mild interest and said, "Talk to me at the end of the season."

The end of season was a race at Riverside, California, in late fall. Prior to that race, I had kept in contact with Roger at every race and reminded him of "talking" at the end of the season.

At last he agreed to meet. He wanted to meet secretly, prior to the Riverside race, and "talk turkey." Accordingly, Bill McNealy and I met with him in Beverly Hills at the Century Plaza Hotel, in a suite reserved for that purpose, between 2:00 A.M. and 4:00 A.M. the Friday night before the weekend of racing began at Riverside.

It was obvious from the beginning that Roger was interested in making a deal if he could significantly improve his financial return. He had no doubt he could win. We also had no doubt that with Mark Donahue and Peter Revson as drivers he could win with any car that he and his organization set up.

It was, in short, a deal that we had to make. We paid the price Roger asked without blinking. We signed an agreement around 4:00 A.M. and agreed that we would announce our working relationship on the Monday after the Riverside race. As happened in almost every race, Mark Donahue won the final race in his dark blue Sunoco Camaro. Our red, white, and blue Javelin came in second or third.

On Monday, the bombshell was announced. I stayed on the West Coast to take over the racing materials from the Kaplan organization and hand them over to Roger and his people. The very first thing that he did was take the Javelin used in the Riverside race and have Mark Donohue drive it. Donohue cut almost three seconds off the best lap time Kaplan's team had ever run at Riverside and equaled the time he had run in the Camaro. It confirmed we were going to have a winner.

And indeed we did. The Javelin team, with Donohue and Revson driving, dominated the Trans-Am series the next year. The red, white, and blue Javelins were pictured in racing programs and racing magazines throughout the United States. It was a great triumph for the smallest U.S. auto company.

Did this racing success sell more cars? Did it begin to change AMC's consumer image? To this day, I don't know. The best answer is "probably."

"Selling" Auto Dealers

After about six months at AMC, I became convinced that the biggest obstacle to changing the AMC image was the local AMC dealer. From their signage that still featured "Rambler" to the their sales personnel, the AMC dealerships did not communicate any image change to a performance company.

Nor did most dealers understand it. They still preferred selling the older car lines, the Rambler and the Ambassador—two models neither sleek nor exciting.

Clearly this had to change. At first we tried to use the Trans-Am racing program for this task. We invited the dealers to see the red, white, and blue Javelins as special guests at the track. We set up tents and served food and drink for all of the dealers, their wives, and their employees and provided free racing jackets and hats.

This worked with our younger dealers who were more performance oriented. They and their employees quickly wanted to be part of the scene and, they traveled hundreds of miles to attend races.

However, the older dealers—most of whom had been Nash dealers in the '50's—had very little interest in racing. They had basically made their fortunes, or at least a very good living, selling Nashs and then Ramblers. They didn't show up at the races.

AMX Introduction

Obviously racing was not going to reach enough of the dealers to change the fabric of the AMC dealer culture. We needed a bigger idea, and we formed one almost immediately in the planned introduction of a new AMC sports car, the AMX.

There were three key elements to the AMX introduction.

The first element was to "personalize" the car for the target buyer. The AMX was a two-seat sports car. It was the kind of car that could appeal to the car buyer who was looking to personalize his or her wheels. This person would clearly be a new customer for an AMC dealer.

To attract this buyer, we came up with the idea of giving the AMX an elitist "personal touch." We would give each AMX its own owner number in addition to the usual serial number. This number would be put on a metal plate installed on the dashboard right by the glove compartment. The plates would be numbered consecutively as the AMXs were made. Therefore, if you bought one of the earliest AMXs, you might get a model with the number 135, etc.

The second element of the AMX introduction was to create exciting news about the car for its consumer introduction at the Chicago Auto Show. We wanted this excitement to center on a "performance story" for the AMX that would reinforce the new corporate image we sought.

We knew we could position this car as one of the fastest cars on the road if we put a 390 cubic engine into the AMX as an option. (It could propel the AMX to 135 mph off the showroom floor.) This was agreed to, but it wasn't enough. We needed a merchandising "hook"—a way to demonstrate the AMX's power and speed. We solved this in a brainstorming session when some one said, "Why not position the AMX as a speed or performance record holder?"

After some research, we learned that the twenty-four-hour land speed record for an automobile was less than 110 miles per hour. We were sure that, with proper preparation, the AMX could beat that record. Thus we could introduce the AMX as the world's twenty-four-hour land speed record holder.

The trick would be to find someone who could "set up" an AMX for this kind of record-breaking attempt. And of course, we had to find a place to set the record and get a sanctioning organization to certify that the record had indeed been broken.

All of these tasks were thrown in my lap.

Fortunately, at about that time, Craig Breedlove, then the world land speed record holder in terms of top speed attained, had been soliciting American Motors for financial support to set an even higher world land speed record with a jet-propelled machine he was building.

I invited Craig to meet with us to determine if he would be willing to work with the AMX. In the parlance of basketball, this was a "slam dunk." Craig Breedlove was willing to do almost anything in the way of land speed record holding, if the money was right.

He quickly agreed that he would prepare an AMX that could certified as "stock" by the record-measuring body. He would drive the car, along with his very attractive wife, and a third driver.

I put incentives in Craig's contract. He could make almost twice as much money over the base contract for his services, if he broke all of the land speed records between one and twenty-four hours for stock cars.

We sent Craig an AMX to modify to the extent legally possible (take off the muffler, beef up the carburation system, etc). As he was doing this, he found a site for the record run—Goodyear's five-mile oval test track in San Angelo, Texas. The certification team was contacted and a date was set for the record attempt.

At the same time, we decided to film the record attempt. Our plan was to use a brief documentary style film showing the AMX setting the record as part of the Chicago Auto Show. We hired the Tommy Thomas organization to do this for us.

The weekend finally arrived for the record attempt. It was early January 1968, about thirty days prior to the Chicago Auto Show. Time was very tight. If he did not break the record on the first try, it was very unlikely we would be able to merchandise the AMX the way we had planned. In other words, we had "rolled the dice" in an attempt to have a spectacular launch for what was a rather mundane sports car.

I arrived at the Goodyear track two days before the record attempt. Craig took me for a "spin" around the track at speed. As we sped around the track, I asked him, "How fast are we going?" Craig, a handsome straight-arrow appearing man, looked at me out of the corner of his eye and grinned, "I think we are going about 210 mph." I almost jumped out of my shoes.

Then the car hit a slight bump in the track. The car seemed to shimmy and slide toward the top of the oval track. I almost lost it. Craig brought the car under control and grimaced. "There are a couple of bumps in the track," he said. "We have to drive the car a few more times to make sure we know exactly where they are. You know, Chris, at night it could be quite a problem if we don't know the track really well."

The next day the film crew arrived, the official land speed record-measuring team arrived, and the caterers came. Final tests were made. Everything was set up.

The next morning the record run began. I noted hopefully that it was a sunny day. Craig climbed into the car about 7:00 A.M., gave a hearty wave to the film crew and took off. All went well. The red, white, and blue AMX easily broke each hour's land speed record for the first ten hours.

Then as it began to get dark, about 5:30 P.M., we noticed that the car was beginning to slow down. Craig was driving. As he reached the eleventh hour, 6:00 P.M., it was pitch black outside.

Craig came in for a refueling stop and told us that car was losing power. He thought the battery was somehow being drained by the lights. He was very concerned that he might not break the twelve-hour record and thus lose a sizable piece of his bonus incentive. As I recall, the record was over 140 mph.

He climbed back in the car and took off. About five minutes later, he turned off the car's lights. And for the next fifty minutes, he drove around that five-mile oval track in almost total darkness at speeds above 150 mph. He broke the twelve-hour land speed record and pulled in for repairs. We all let out a giant sigh of relief.

This daredevil act made very dramatic film footage. When we saw the lights go out, everybody who had a car pulled it up to the edge of the test track and turned their car lights on. Imagine the fear of driving over

150 mph with no illumination except a few lights from our cars pointing at the track. To this day I marvel at Craig's foolhardy feat.

After a forty-five-minute break to repair the car, the driving team went back and drove the remaining twelve hours without incident, easily breaking the land speed record for twenty-four hours.

We had our film and we had the record. We were ready for the Chicago Auto Show and the consumer introduction of the car.

The third part of the AMX introduction was the introductory program for the dealers. We had to get the attention of the prototypical Rambler dealer, a man over age sixty in a small town in the Midwest. We had to get these dealers interested in "getting with" the new program. Phil Lincoln came up with the solution to this issue. "Why not," he said, "introduce the AMX to our dealers at Playboy Clubs around the country? I'll bet there's a Club in every city where we plan to hold an introductory show."

He was right. I contacted the Playboy Clubs. They jumped at the idea to participate. Each had enough space to show the AMX within the club and enough seating for the inevitable luncheon with Bunny waitresses. Moreover, they suggested that because we were so interested in working with them, they might be interested in working with us. They asked if AMC would give the Playmate of the Year a new pink AMX. If so, they would name the AMX as *Playboy's* "Car of the Year." We liked that idea a lot. A deal was made.

We then developed the AMX introductory sales meeting. We wanted all the pizazz we could possibly put into one meeting. We hired a former Playmate of the Year, and Craig Breedlove and his wife to be the featured speakers to introduce the car to the dealers.

All of this glamour made the meeting irresistible to our Rambler dealers. It was February—a very slow time in the car business anyway. We were able to attract virtually every dealer in the American Motors system to one of the meetings. They loved every minute of it.

Did this unique introduction make a difference? In retrospect, "No." We had gotten the dealers' attention, but it was only on the AMX, not on the importance of "getting with" the program to push performance in their showrooms.

Introducing New Cars Differently

The most spectacular single corporate event with which I was ever associated occurred during my time at American Motors.

After introducing the Javelin in 1967 and the AMX in early 1968, American Motors had no new cars, or even minor facelifts to introduce for 1969. This meant that somehow we had to create dealer excitement for purchasing the 1969 cars without having any new product.

This may be a common occurrence in the '90s but it was unheard of in the '60s. Every year each company developed new vehicles or facelifts on existing ones. They then held introductory sales meetings to get the dealers excited and to get them to purchase quantities of cars to launch the new model season.

Clearly we had a problem. How could we create dealer enthusiasm for the year with no new vehicles?

We posed this question to Tommy Thomas and Company, our agency for dealer meetings. Tommy came back to us with a big, bold, but expensive idea. It was about $1,000,000 over budget. Backed by Bill McNealy's and my enthusiasm, Tommy sold his idea to Roy Chapin.

What was the idea? The strategy was to make the meeting itself the focus of all attention. It was to make the meeting *so spectacular that it would mask the fact that there was no new product.*

To do this, Tommy proposed we hold a spectacular *one-day national sales meeting for all dealers.* This was an almost unheard of proposition. Normally, as with the AMX, the company would go to the dealers by holding a one-day sales meeting in fifteen or more cities over a month.

The meeting was held in early September, and it came off without a hitch. It was, as promised, "spectacular."

Let me explain why it was so spectacular, by asking you, the reader to pretend that you, are an American Motors dealer in Bangor, Maine.

In mid-July, you received an invitation to attend the new car introductory show being held at the "New World of American Motors" on September 5. This invitation also advised you that there would be a special free airplane flight from Boston to fly you and your fellow dealers to this "New World of American Motors."

In mid-August you and every other dealer received a second invitation. This invitation included an airplane ticket that you were to use. Departure time was 8:00 A.M. You were told the flight would return to Boston at about 11:00 P.M.

If you were like most dealers, you immediately called your fellow dealers and asked, "What's this all about? Where are we going? Why the mystery?" No one could tell you anything. (Only five people inside AMC knew the plans for the meeting.)

Finally, you received one final reminder mailing about five days prior to the flight, specifying that it was a casual dress affair and to dress for warm weather at the "New World of American Motors."

By this time, you and your fellow dealers were in a frenzy over what was going on. Nothing like this had ever occurred at American Motors. You called your sales manager or any other contact you had in the company. You were amazed to find that no one knew anything about where the meeting was being held or what was going to happen at the meeting.

Of course, with all of this hoopla ahead of time, you wouldn't miss the meeting. Therefore, you left very early on the morning of September 5 to drive to Logan Airport to make your plane.

At the airport you went to the gate specified for American Motors. There you found a special waiting area decorated with signs for the "New

World of American Motors." Milling around were fellow dealers from all over New England and several company officials. Promptly at 7:50 A.M. you were boarded an American Airlines Boeing 707 jet. Every seat was taken by one of your fellow dealers or an American Motors employee.

The plane took off and, as soon as the plane had leveled off in flight, the American Airline stewardesses served you breakfast. It was a special menu. The food items were given American Motors names: Ambassador Pancakes, Javelin Cocktails, etc. The bar was also open and being a typical auto dealer in the '60s you quickly ordered your first cocktail of the day.

As breakfast was served everyone speculated about where you were going. There was cloud cover so you couldn't determine whether you were going north, south, or west. You were pretty sure you weren't going east. About then the pilot announced over the intercom that Fargo, North Dakota, was on the right and Miami, Florida, was on the left. Everybody laughed.

It was about this time that the betting began. A pool was organized and you put in $20 with your guess on where you were going.

After breakfast, a film came on the in-flight movie screens. You are shown a film that gushed praises for the exciting new American Motors Company and vaguely referred to the cars available for 1969.

Finally, the plane landed. You had been on the plane almost six hours and, if you had been on a typical American Motors flight that day, you and your fellow dealers had consumed all the alcohol on the plane—about 900 of those small liquor bottles. You were feeling good.

When you deplaned, a marching band greeted you. Uniformed guides at the gate then led you down some steps to buses on the runway tarmac. It was at this point you finally learned that you were at Los Angeles International Airport.

The buses took you to a massive airplane hangar at the end of the airport. This hangar was totally decorated with big signs calling it the "New World of American Motors." It had several very unique features that immediately caught your eye. There was a large above-ground swimming pool with Hollywood models sitting around the edge in bikinis. There was also an eighteen-hole miniature golf course complete with golf clubs for you to try your luck.

In front, the Trans-Am Javelins were on a schedule of performance demonstrations. So were the red, white, and blue drag racers. Oh yes, inside there was also one model of each car for 1969 on auto show turntables for you to admire and see.

Within about forty minutes, twenty-three planes loaded with AMC dealers landed at Los Angeles from all over the country (including a plane that had taken off from Los Angeles and flown around in circles for about four hours). In all, ninety percent of the American Motors dealer body and all of the officials of American Motors were gathered in a hangar at the Los Angeles Airport between noon and 1:30 P.M.

After all the dealers had arrived, you heard Roy Chapin and Bill Luneberg very briefly welcome everyone to the "New World of American Motors." These speeches were made from the top step of a motorized boarding ramp.

If you were a typical dealer, you barely noticed. You were part of a happening that you had never expected to experience. You had to talk with all your fellow dealers. You may have been one of the lucky ones who rented a swimming suit and joined the models in the pool.

More refreshments were served including a food buffet. About 1:30 P.M., the buses returned. You and your fellow dealers were taken back to your airplanes to be flown back to where you came from. On the plane, underneath your seat, you found a duffle bag full of souvenirs of the meeting, including such things as model racing cars, racing hats, decals, etc. At some point you were shown a thirty-minute film featuring Mary Wells, Charlie Moss, and the new television advertising for 1969.

Finally, a brief announcement of the new incentive programs was given. The meeting was over. Of course, you were fed another dinner and additional cocktails and, if you were like most of your fellow dealers, you slept the last hours on your way home.

In all of this, not once did you discover nor did any of your fellow dealers discover there was nothing new for American Motors for 1969. *Our strategy was 100 percent successful!*

As one might imagine, the logistics for this entire meeting were unbelievably complex. We rented, for the day, every American Airline 707 with movie-showing capability in service. We totally "dressed" the airplane hangar, held the meeting, then restored it to its original function in one twenty-four-hour period.

Those were just the "tips of the iceberg" for a staff of about ten full-time people who developed the meeting details over six months.

Perhaps the millions spent on the meeting were worth it. Like most of my AMC programs there was really no way to measure its effect.

Dealer Showrooms

In addition to trying to create a cultural change in the dealer organization, it was also my assignment to try and change the way American Motors dealerships looked. To this end, we had one short-term and one long-term tactic.

For the short term, we tried to make a "silk purse out of sow's ear" inside of the old dealerships with new red, white, and blue point-of-purchase materials. At best, we improved appearances marginally.

For the long term, we advocated that the company hire a corporate design firm to develop a new American Motors sign and dealership design. Walter Margulies of Lippincott and Margulies came to Detroit and worked his magic on Roy Chapin to be hired for the job.

Not surprisingly, when Margulies had finished his work, the new red, white, and blue sign and an upgraded dealership building was approved. A prototype new dealership was built. It was a big hit with all the dealers who saw it. Unfortunately, not many of them built one because of its cost.

Because this program was not completed until after I left American Motors, I do not know how successful it really was. I do know that it was the right thing to do, and that the company made every effort to get the dealers to invest in their dealerships.

The Bottom Line

I could tell many other stories about the "wild and woolly days" at American Motors.

I particularly remember the auto shows. We developed a special performance game in which you could use a car's gear shift and go through the gears to compete with your fellow auto show visitors to see who could reach 100 mph the quickest.

There is also the story of a consumer sweepstakes used as part of the AMX introduction that was too successful. (This may have been the most successful sweepstakes ever run.) The average return for such promotions is under three percent. Ours actually generated an almost ten percent return. One person in ten actually went to his AMC dealer after receiving the mailing piece. But it did not generate increased sales. Instead, it created a lot of unhappy people. You see, the crowds were so large, that at many dealerships, customers had to wait in line just to get in. When they did get in, they found they had not won a new AMX, but a poster.

There are also stories I could tell about very effective sales incentive programs and about international trips that we took with dealers.

It went on and on and on. I don't think I ever had a better time running programs than I did at American Motors. There was simply one event after another. Each one was full of challenges for new ideas that would revitalize a sick company.

In the end, however, all of these efforts were futile. They were efforts designed to build a me-too image that made product comparison versus the Big Three critical. And the AMC products could not measure up to the Big Three's. *The company did not change its basic product enough to win over consumers to come to an inferior dealer network.*

In this book, I have talked about the Javelin and AMX; but over seventy percent of American Motors sales were still in cars like the Rebel and the Ambassador, boxy cars designed in the earlier Rambler era.

The next new car after the AMX was no better. The Gremlin, the first subcompact car made in Detroit had unattractive styling. More important, like the other AMC cars, it had quality manufacturing problems. Door handles kept falling off. Bumpers rusted in the showrooms. Interiors were not as lush, nor as sleek, as competitors.

As in packaged goods, the best product will win out—even in Detroit.

Final Year

After two years as Director of Merchandising, I took stock of my career. *I was not a marketer at American Motors.* I was a tactical, make-something-happen merchandiser. This was not what I wanted for a long term career. It was clear I would have to leave.

Before doing that, however, I made one attempt to stay put and use my marketing knowledge. I accepted an offer to transfer to an AMC task force run by another Harvard MBA, Jack Maxwell. His small group was seeking corporate acquisitions. While in this group I looked into the purchase of airplane manufacturers, lawnmower companies, etc.

I worked alone and was miserable. I realized, for the first time, that I needed to routinely work with people to enjoy my work. Result: I set about looking for another job back in packaged goods and accepted a job offer from Gallo Wine (see Chapter 5). Life in Detroit was over.

Lessons Learned

1. *Changing a corporation's consumer image cannot be done through marketing programs alone.* The corporation must reflect newness in its product, its packaging (the AMC dealership), and in its culture. This takes an enormous amount of time and money. AMC had neither.
2. *The key to the success of any franchised retail chain is the quality of the dealer (franchisee).* Even with a poor product versus competition, the good AMC dealer could prosper. A good dealer could sell as many as ten times the number of vehicles as a weak dealer.
3. ***Lifetime Lesson: To achieve success in any franchised system, you must first sell the company's own dealers (or franchisees) on the merits of a program.*** The usefulness of well-conceived dealer meetings to do this cannot be exaggerated.

Final Comment

In retrospect, the ultimate learning from my time at AMC was from my experience in working with the dealers to develop retail promotions. I soon learned a ***Lifetime Lesson: The strength of a promotion idea in a franchised retail chain is not as important as its execution.*** If you have two ideas—no matter what consumer research says are their relative strength—choose the one the dealers like. Only with their support will any promotion be effective.

CHAPTER 5
Ernest Gallo's Way

(Lessons from the Master of Wine Marketing)

From American Motors, I went back to brand management. I accepted a Group Product Manager position at Gallo Wine.

It was another career mistake. I should have been forewarned from the job interview process that Gallo was not for me. Naïvely, I was sure that after P&G, Pet, Needham, and AMC, I had "seen it all"—that I was ready for any corporate culture.

Let me tell you about the Gallo interview process. From the first, it was an extraordinary experience.

First, the management recruiter, Bill Billington, had to convince me to take the interview. Gallo had a terrible reputation among all marketing folks. The turnover at the Winery Brand Management was very high. The average marketer usually stayed less than two years. In addition, it was well known that ad agencies found it very difficult to deal with Gallo.

Bill convinced me to talk to Gallo with a perfect sales pitch. "Sure it's a tough place to work," he said. "It's not for the faint-hearted. But, Chris, so what? You're plenty tough. You, of all people, should be able to deal with the boss, Ernest Gallo. Your personality is, I think, tailor made for the winery. There's no doubt in my mind that they will appreciate your abrasive, hard-edged personality." "Besides," he added, "what's the harm in talking to them? After all, Modesto, California, is a wonderful place to raise a family. And it's only ninety miles from San Francisco."

He sold me and that led to the second part of the process getting to the interview.

Gallo flew me first class to San Francisco where I rented a car and drove to Modesto. There was a reservation at the Sun Dial Inn for the evening. I was to show up for the interview at 8:30 the following morning.

This sounds rather routine, doesn't it? It didn't prove to be. The next morning I was twenty minutes late for my interview. I couldn't find the winery—the world's largest. I finally found it after stopping twice for directions. The problem was that Gallo had no sign in front of its head-quarters. The building, which somewhat resembled a modern-day reincarnation of the Parthenon, was partially hidden by several large refinery-like tanks holding up to 90,000 gallons of unprocessed grape juice.

Finally, the job interview began. It was in three distinct sections and was like no interview I have ever had before or since.

The first section was routine. I met individually with the Vice President of Advertising, Skip McLaughlin, and the Executive Vice President of Advertising and Marketing, Albion Fenderson, to learn more about Gallo and the Marketing department.

The only thing unique about this part of the process was Albion's office. It resembled a trophy room from an African safari. (Indeed, the decorations were from an African safari that he and Ernest Gallo had taken some years before my visit.) There was an animal skin rug on the floor. There were wooden masks and spears on the walls. There was lots of vegetation in the office, and there was a unique, huge desk.

Albion and Skip seemed to be very personable and most gracious. This part of the interview process assured me that I would like the people I would be reporting to. Despite all the stories I had heard about Gallo, they seemed perfectly rational and normal. Later I would learn that they were perfectly rational and normal except when they "performed" in meetings with Ernest Gallo.

Next came lunch. We went back to the Sun Dial. I rode with Albion, Ernest Gallo, and Howard Williams, an elderly curmudgeon who served as a personal advisor on advertising to Ernest, but who had no other apparent function at the winery.

As Albion drove, Ernest Gallo and I became acquainted. I was very curious about this very famous entrepreneur. He was a small unimposing man—hardly in keeping with the legendary ogre I had heard about. Standing perhaps five feet seven inches with a stocky build and wearing thick glasses, he looked more like a bookkeeper than the co-owner of America's largest winery.

He had a shy smile on his face as we were introduced. After an awkward silence, I asked him what his goal was for his company.

He answered very straightforwardly, "To sell more wine than anyone else in this country."

I countered his answer with another question. "Well as I understand it, you already do. Albion told me Gallo has forty-two percent of the wine business. How much more of the business do you want?"

He looked at me with a stare, as only Ernest could stare, and said without emotion, "All of it."

I found myself liking this man. He had a straightforward no-nonsense manner, with no pretense, no regal air about him. It was very refreshing after Detroit.

About this time, we arrived at the Sun Dial and I met the other members of the luncheon party who had come in a second car. First I shook hands with Ken Bertsch and Dick Witter, both of whom had the title of VP/sales manager for the Company; then David Gallo and Joe Gallo, Ernest's two sons.

I was very flattered. I was having lunch with what seemed to be all of top management on the sales marketing side of the company—Ernest's responsibility. (Julio Gallo, Ernest's brother, ran the manufacturing and distribution side). I later learned all of my lunchmates would be at any meeting in which I tried to gain agreement to do anything at the Gallo Winery.

Lunch turned out to be a "test" that started with the drink orders. Apparently, this was done quite often because the waitress never hesitated. She started at the end of the table and the first two people ordered Gallo wine. Now it was my turn. Would I have a drink for lunch; and would it be Gallo wine or what? This sounds like a minor dilemma, but Ernest Gallo was staring at me from across the table, and I wondered if I would insult him if I didn't order his wine

Finally I made up my mind that I was not going to be a "wimp" and order Gallo wine. I ordered a Coors Beer. Ernest immediately ordered Coors. Everyone laughed. And I guessed I had passed a test.

It turned out to be a very congenial luncheon. I liked Ernest and he seemed to like me. However, I did notice that everyone else agreed with whatever Ernest said, adding their comment to reinforce his statements.

The afternoon "interview" was an absolute nightmare.

Ernest invited me to sit in on a marketing presentation that would be attended by all of the lunch participants. The presentation was by one of the advertising agencies and the Brand Group that worked on a line of Gallo table wines. I sat in a chair near the end of the table and watched the show, wondering why I was invited.

The agency made its presentation. There was reinforcement from the Brand Manager that he felt this was a great idea to promote wine for the holiday season. Then no one spoke. There was dead silence for what seemed like an eternity.

Finally, Ernest looked over and said, "Well, Chris, what do you think?"

I stared at Earnest in shock. I had never anticipated this. I felt like crawling under the table. How could I answer such a question? As a professional marketer, I only knew what had been presented in the room. I did not even know whether this was accurate.

Obviously this was another test. In fact, I was told later, this was Ernest's crucial test. His question: "Would I have an intelligent opinion" or was I "an empty suit?"—the term he used for most of the candidates sent to Gallo from the various executive search firms.

Fatefully, I passed Ernest's test with flying colors. Summoning up my bravado I answered, "Ernest, it's very difficult for someone who just walked into a room and has only the knowledge presented here to give you a meaningful answer; but based upon what I heard, I don't think the idea will be very successful." I gave several reasons for that opinion, the substance of which I don't recall.

I could see by the look on the presenters' faces, especially the agency's, that I had probably made some instant enemies. However, Skip smiled; Dick Witter smiled; Howard Williams grinned; and Albion immediately came to my rescue, saying, "You know, Ernest, Chris makes some good points. I find this recommendation needs some work, so why don't we call it a day?" That was the end of the meeting and the end of my interview.

I was sent home without further ado.

Why Gallo?

As I analyzed the interviews on the long flight back to Detroit, I was confused. Gallo seemed like a very unlikely match for me; yet I was exhilarated. Gallo was truly different—truly entrepreneurial—truly something I had never experienced before.

The longer I thought about it the more interested I became. I felt intuitively (and wrongly) that at Gallo I could be happy and successful. *How we sometimes fool ourselves in order to justify our decisions to ourselves.*

In truth, from the beginning, the siren call of Gallo was almost irresistible to me after almost four years of AMC. On paper at least, Gallo represented everything I sought in a job.

Gallo was in a high-profile growth industry. Wine was "in" to the emerging yuppie consumer of the early '70s. Table wines were replacing cocktails in bars and homes. Beverage wines, the apple and fruit wines, were all the rage. In fact, Gallo's Boone's Farm Apple was undoubtedly the best-selling wine brand in the world at that time.

For me, Gallo represented a return to marketing a packaged product for the market leader. Gallo was the top-selling wine company in America. It was a true giant in its industry. The company had approximately four or five times greater market share in the United States than the next largest winery.

Gallo also had impressive advantages on which to build future marketing success. The company had the lowest overall manufacturing and distribution cost structure in the industry. It was light years ahead of any other winery in terms of processing and bottling techniques.

And Gallo was a vertically integrated company. The company owned many vineyards (managed by a third Gallo brother, Joe). It manufactured its wine bottles. It owned the largest wine-bottling plant in the world. It shipped the wine via its own trucking company, and it owned the wine distribution companies that sold wine to the retail trade in the two largest wine-consuming markets in the United States: Los Angeles and San Francisco.

Last, Gallo meant leaving dreary myopic Detroit for sunny California and earning a salary greater than what I earned at American Motors.

The rest is history. Gallo made a job offer and I accepted: sending my family to a third city in five years.

Then the fun began. The Foxhole Tales I tell you here about about Gallo may seem exaggerated, but they 're not. If anything, they tell just the tip of the iceberg.

Getting Started

When I joined Gallo, my first task was to learn the wine business. I learned about it the Gallo way.

Gallo had a unique way to introduce new marketing "hires" to the business. Like P&G, which sent all of its brand people out to the field and required them to sell products to local retail stores and wholesalers as part of their training process, Gallo required wine-selling sales experience of all its marketing people. Therefore, before moving to Modesto I was assigned to a four-week training program in Los Angeles, where I became a route salesman calling on retail stores during the day and attended training classes every evening.

In those four weeks, I learned the Gallo "basics" including:

1. An understanding of the wine business, including how to judge wines for taste and value.
2. A thorough understanding of why Gallo sold forty-two percent of all the wines in the country at that time. No one in the industry had anything like the strength and depth of its training and sales force. They could not match the manpower and depth of service provided by Gallo to its customers.
3. An understanding of the Gallo sales department culture—how a professional veneer incorporating all of the latest sales techniques and marketing techniques had been applied to the winery. I call it a "veneer" because even though the company had policies and procedures and very strong talented people to carry them out, Gallo was an absolute dictatorship. Everyone took orders on even minor issues from Ernest and/or Julio.

Upon graduating from training, I went to Modesto and was assigned my new job, the details of which, up until then had been a mystery. (Sometimes I wonder how I could have actually accepted a position without knowing exactly what it would be.)

My new job title was Group Product Manager, Gallo Wines. My responsibility was to market all wines with Ernest and Julio's names on the label: table wines, dessert wines, champagne, brandy. On paper I was marketing a complete winery.

The organization chart showed me reporting to Albion Fenderson, but, of course, in reality my boss was Ernest Gallo. He made all of the final decisions.

I had a small staff that included a Brand Manager (John Selecky) and an Assistant Brand Manager (Chip Plompteau). Unlike P&G, our little group did not work in close proximity. This coupled with the reality that only Ernest could approve a plan or any real expense, made the group a loose confederation, not a close-working team.

Advertising for Gallo Champagne

My first major challenge was advertising for the Gallo Champagne product line.

Gallo Champagne and Cold Duck were sold throughout the country but sales lagged significantly behind the market leader, Andre, a brand also made by Gallo. Gallo was a low-cost champagne but Andre was cheaper. It was the lowest-price champagne and Cold Duck sales leader in the marketplace.

Inside the bottle both Gallo and Andre brands had the same sparkling wine product. The only difference was in the packaging. Gallo had a much more upscale label than Andre and a more traditional champagne bottle. It was not unusual for wineries at this time to bottle the same product in two or three different labels, but I was still appalled that my task was to market a me-too product for an additional fifty cents per bottle at retail.

Nevertheless, I set out to achieve Ernest's goal for the brand, that is make it grow faster than Andre so that some day it would be the number one champagne brand in the Gallo family of products. (Note that I already framed my task as one of trying to please Ernest Gallo—not to sell a management hierarchy.)

Clearly, to differentiate Gallo Champagne the "reason to buy" couldn't be based on a product superiority claim. Differentiation had to come out of the aura the brand's advertising and packaging could impart to it. This made the problem similar to a lot of other product categories, particularly soft drinks or beer, where there is little or no difference between products.

The agency came up with what seemed to be a brilliant solution to the problem: use a spokesman to appeal to a new target consumer, upper-income Americans. Specifically, the agency proposed hiring Arthur Fiedler of the Boston Pops, the most famous symphony conductor in America, to endorse Gallo Champagne. Fiedler, they argued, was truly a household name with the new target audience.

The TV commercial storyboards were prepared and the agency had Arthur Fiedler's assurance that he would appear on camera to endorse our product. I was particularly pleased with this strategy because champagne consumption is primarily around the holiday season, with heaviest consumption in the East. It all seemed to be a very sound marketing move for the brand.

Armed with self-confidence, I promised wholehearted support to the agency and assured the account group that I would be a different kind of Gallo brand marketer. I would stand up to Ernest, not "wimp out" at his first facial grimace.

Presenting To Ernest Gallo

The agency prepared a typical presentation to gain approval for any marketing move proposed for any Gallo brand during my career there.

This recommendation was a "first" for me. Unlike other companies, I did not have to deal with getting approvals from layers of management prior to any CEO approval meeting. Gallo Group Product managers were not required to gain the agreement of Albion Fenderson or his two cohorts, Howard Williams or Skip McLaughlin (both of whom had titles of VP of Advertising).

Every decision-making meeting was held in the infamous second-floor Gallo conference room.

It was a typical conference room in terms of size and most of its furnishings. Long and narrow, the room had a table that seated about sixteen. It was a furniture gem, fatter in the middle and thinner at each end, and always polished to perfection. There were a series of windows with venetian blinds on one of the long sides; the other side was windowless.

There was also a complete audiovisual center, through which one could project slides, TV commercials, etc. It was state-of-the-art at the time. At the other end of the room was a tasting bar. Essentially this was a refrigerator, wineglasses, etc., everything you needed to host a wine tasting.

It was not however a typical conference room in terms of how it was used. At each meeting, the management group had, in effect, assigned seats with their backs to the windows. (This meant that any presenter would be staring into the partially shaded bright California sunlight and squinting to look at the management team.) At the center of the table, at the very fattest part, was Ernest's chair. Albion sat at his right. Next to him was Howard Williams, followed by Skip McLaughlin. At Earnest's left sat Joe Gallo, David Gallo, Howard Bertsch, and Dick Witter—always in that order.

There was some rationale for this seating order since the youngest members of the management team, Witter and McLaughlin, were at the furthest ends and the Executive VP of the company sat on the immediate right of the CEO.

When presenting in this room, the Group Product Manager sat directly across from Ernest; the agency sat to his left and his staff or other members of the Gallo marketing team to his right.

Because of my interview experience, I felt somewhat prepared for my first meeting, and was excited to be there. I soon learned that every meeting was quite different and to be dreaded.

As I entered the room for the first time, Ken Bertsch, a gray-haired older man, who was always encouraging to everyone publicly, greeted me. He said, "Well, good luck, Chris. I trust you know why the color of the rug is what it is." I looked at the rug and noted that it was burgundy, a color that seemed appropriate for a wine company and I said so.

He said "No" with only half a smile. "It's to cover all the blood that is spilled in here every year."

As the other members filed in, David Gallo looked irritably at me, "Who are you?" David, who was literally my neighbor (we lived about a block from each other) obviously didn't remember me.

What a wonderful way to start I thought—"The CEO's son is irritated and the sales VP is telling me to watch out for blood."

Everyone was seated, but Ernest had not yet appeared. Ernest always seemed to arrive about five minutes after everyone else was seated. I wondered if there was some kind of button underneath the table that Albion pushed when all was in readiness.

Finally the center seat of the table was filled. The meeting began, and it seemed to go well. There were nods of approval from everyone except for Joe Gallo and David Gallo and, of course, Ernest.

(Ernest almost always maintained a totally impassive look at meetings. Every once in a while you could see a glint in his eye, when he particularly liked something, but generally, he maintained a totally expressionless pose. It was a pose that I tried to use later in my career. The pose is somewhat intimidating, but at the same time, somewhat encouraging. It keeps people presenting with hopes of making a sale, rather than discouraging them with a disparaging look prior to hearing their reasoning or seeing their materials.)

I summed up the recommendation and told Ernest that this advertising could regain momentum for a brand that was wallowing in a sales decline, if he would give it a proper budget for television. (Note: One of the unbelievable things at Gallo was that no brand had a formal budget.)

Ernest nodded formally and turned to his fellow management members. They then began an almost formula "ritual." Each provided Ernest with their opinion in order of seniority. First, Skip McLaughlin, then Dick Witter then back and forth until everyone had spoken.

All of them seemed to say, "Well, I like it Ernest, but . . . " They would never formally take a position either for or against the recommendation. Clearly, in their minds, the goal was to "survive" the meeting.

Exceptions to this were Ernest's sons, David and Joe. David was a stocky, placid man about 5′8″ with a penetrating voice. In meetings, when he spoke, he always seemed angry. Although I understand that long after I left Modesto, David grew in stature and had some unique capabilities that made him a favorite with his father, at this time in his life he was very easily distracted with little or no power of concentration. On occasion, he would seem to fall asleep during presentations, as did his brother Joe.

David also had a peculiar habit he sometimes exercised during meetings. He would take a paper clip and unwind it so that it became just a long piece of thin wire. He would then sit there and poke this straight paperclip toward his eye intermittently throughout the meeting. To say that this was distracting would be an understatement.

Joe, on the other hand, was always very quiet and usually conveyed to all that he was bored. As the older brother of the two brothers, he was clearly sitting on his father's side hoping to replace him someday.

At any rate, after about forty-five minutes of this kind of veiled conversation, Ernest looked at his watch, stopped further comments, and spoke directly to me. "Chris, you seem to believe that this campaign will be very effective. I will agree to run it, but only if you will first do some market research here in Modesto. I want you to go down to Sixth and K Street and interview the first fifty people you see. Find out how many of them have ever heard of Arthur Fiedler. If more than half of them have heard of Arthur Fiedler, then you are free to run this campaign."

I was stunned by this response. He was giving me an emphatic "no" to an idea I really believed in, in a way that left me with no room for argument.

You see, Sixth and K Street was in the heart of downtown Modesto. Modesto was a low-income town. The population consisted mostly of people who worked on farms in the nearby area or at agriculture-processing plants in town. There was no way that even 10 percent of these people would have ever heard of Arthur Fielder. Ernest knew this. He was saying in effect that he did not want his champagne to be endorsed by some effete Easterner.

Albion Fenderson confirmed this after the meeting. He said, "To Ernest, you were saying that you need someone like Arthur Fiedler to be able to sell his name to consumers. Ernest won't accept this."

I am convinced that had this idea been presented to any major package goods company, it would have been accepted enthusiastically. *Entrepreneurs like Ernest had different rules. This decision was far more personal—it was his company.*

I had been with Gallo about sixty days when this meeting took place. It convinced me that once again I had made a poor job choice. I was not in the senior marketing role that I had expected. Instead, I was a professional "front" whose role would always be to direct and work with advertising agencies in order to get the best ideas for presentation to Ernest. Ernest would make all decisions.

"My Kingdom for a Duck"

This was quickly verified by a second experience with Gallo champagne advertising. With Arthur Fiedler now a memory, we were in a bind to develop a new advertising idea to have a program ready for the holiday season. This time, at Albion Fenderson's request, the work was concentrated on a TV commercial to sell Cold Duck, the highest volume seller in the Gallo Champagne line.

Again the agency came up with what I thought was a brilliant and very funny advertising solution to our problem. They developed a parody of Shakespeare's *Richard III*, "My kingdom for a horse" soliloquy. Then they hired a Shakespearean actor to do a "down and dirty" sixty-second video to act out the soliloquy "My Kingdom for a Gallo Cold Duck."

Several weeks later, we returned to the conference room and presented this second idea to the same management group. After a similar ritual of comments by the group, Ernest cut off discussion with a simple statement, "I like it," and offered no further explanation.

The agency immediately said that it would get bids to produce a finished commercial. Ernest stopped them dead in their tracks when he said, "No, no, no. That demo commercial will do just fine." I was again stunned and again questioned my decision to join Gallo. Running demo tapes as finished commericals was not my idea of professional marketing.

Assignment: "Sell Less"

The highest volume wine for which I was responsible was Gallo Pink Chablis. At that time it was the best-selling table wine in the Gallo line and one of the best-selling table wines in America. Pink Chablis was coupled with a white wine, Chablis Blanc, and a red wine, Hearty Burgundy, and sold to the trade as the Gourmet Trio.

In addition to Pink Chablis, Hearty Burgundy was also a major success. It was, at that time, the fastest growing table wine at Gallo. It had been "discovered" by the California wine drinkers and at a $1.49 a half gallon, it was a true bargain.

Surprisingly, my first assignment for the Gourmet Trio concerned a sales problem with Hearty Burgundy. It was perhaps one of the most unique marketing challenges I ever had.

Like all major assignments at Gallo, it began when Ernest called me into his office. He said, "Chris, we have a limited number of barrels of

Hearty Burgundy to sell this year and the current sales rate would indicate that we will sell more than double the amount of wine we have available. It's imperative that we slow down the sales of the wine as quickly as possible so that we won't lose our shelf presence before we have our new crop next year."

In other words, the marketing assignment was to reduce the sales of Hearty Burgundy.

I inquired what I was free to do or recommend. Ernest smiled and said, "Well, you know almost all of this wine is sold in California. And, we can control the price here. It's set each month in Sacramento for all retailers. If I were in your position, I would raise the price of Hearty Burgundy as quick as I could."

As in every conversation I ever had at the winery, all the focus was on retail sales. No mention was ever made of improving profits. This was never to be a concern for the brand people. I had no idea what the margins were on Hearty Burgundy. Ernest never allowed any of his marketing people to know whether we were making or losing money on any given wine. The profit margin numbers were his and Julio's domain alone.

Albion Fenderson also conferred with me about the assignment. He advised me to be aggressive with the retail price. He said that if he had the assignment, he would raise the price fifty cents of a half-gallon by the next month. And, of course, that's what I did.

This pricing move had exactly the wrong impact on the business. Hearty Burgundy sales increased.

The following month I raised the price of a half-gallon another fifty cents. Sales slowed but they were still at too high a rate. I raised the price another thirty cents, and sales finally slowed to the rate that we could maintain a supply of wine for the year.

Hearty Burgundy pricing was a wonderful illustration of the law of supply and demand and the role pricing has in wine marketing.

Assignment: Revive Pink Chablis

Pink Chablis was the biggest problem I dealt with in my brief career at Gallo. This table wine tasted a lot like the White Zinfandel brands so popular today.

Sales of the wine had begun to turn down—an absolutely unacceptable proposition for Ernest Gallo. He knew the long-term future of the wine business in America would be table wines, not dessert wines or beverage wines. He would explain to any and all that America was in its wine infancy, and that as America matured in its wine tastes, table wines would become the primary battleground for wine sales. Therefore his highest priority was to build table wine sales. (Ernest was, of course, right. Today *the* wine market is table wines.)

Ernest's strategy to achieve table wine sales growth was to make good-tasting wines for everyday drinking—to sell the vin ordinaire of America.

He was convinced this would always be the highest volume market segment, and he wanted to own it.

Gallo had, in fact, two lines of table wines during this period of the winery's history, the Gourmet Trio and the so-called Decanter wines, Rhinegarten, Vin Rose, and Burgundy. Both were significantly lower priced than Mondavi and other top-end California table wines.

The Decanter wines were priced lower than the Gourmet Trio. Packaged in a decanter-like bottle, all three table wines were selling very well under the leadership of Art Ciocca, the Group Product Manager for that line. Thus, of all the Gallo table wines, only Pink Chablis was foundering.

The reason for this was never researched. The reason laid at the feet of the brand group by Albion and Ernest, however, was "bad advertising." They said, in effect, to develop a campaign that works and all will be well. This was probably a corporate myth, but there was no evidence to refute it.

I worked for three or four months with the agency to develop a new Pink Chablis advertising campaign. A presentation was finally made; but our ideas were turned down flat. In fact, Ernest expressed total disgust with the work that was done. It frightened all of us, particularly the agency who had heard rumors that they would be replaced. (I am saying agency because, frankly, I cannot remember whether the brand was originally with Erwin Wasey or Young & Rubicam).

We went back for a second try fifteen days later. It was a most unique meeting.

The meeting began with all the usual parties present. The agency finished its presentation. I had told Albion before the meeting that the agency had not come up with a very good solution but because their credibility was on the line and the time was up, I had no choice but to let them show their work. (I was learning how to be defensive in the world of the Gallo Winery.)

This time the meeting took a very different turn. Ernest did not turn to anyone sitting at his side for their comments. Instead, he stood up and said, "Thank you very much. This meeting is adjourned. Would you please leave." The agency and I got up to leave and he said, "No, no, Chris, you stay."

The agency left and Ernest left the room for a moment and came back. When he came back, an account group from a different advertising agency came in with him.

Ernest introduced me to the new agency and said, "Chris, this is your new agency to work on Pink Chablis and the other Gallo label wines. Please brief them and let me know when we can meet again on this project." With that, he abruptly left the room.

One agency had been fired and a new agency had been hired and, as a senior marketing manager at Gallo, I had had nothing to do with it. My unhappiness reached an all-time high.

Perhaps the nadir of my career at Gallo took place after this change of agency. I was ordered to go to Los Angeles and work with the agency until we had a solution. Ernest told me, "You can come home on the weekends, but I want you down there full time until the agency comes up with a solution."

So I went to Los Angeles but I was lost. I didn't know what to do with myself. *Agencies work better without clients looking over their shoulders every day.* Still, I would make an appearance at the agency each day, then go out and explore Los Angeles. Staying at the Bel Air Hotel and leading the good life, I prepared my resume to once-again look for other work.

After several weeks of this, the new agency was ready to present to Ernest Gallo. The usual cast of characters filled the room. The presentation was made with great enthusiasm. It seemed to go well. The agency concluded its presentation. Ernest asked for the usual comments.

This time the routine changed. Each individual at the table came up with a very strong opinion either pro or con for the new proposed advertising. Skip McLaughlin liked it. Howard Williams thought it was bad and ought to be redone. Dick Witter liked it. Ken Bertsch did not. David liked it but Joe mumbled that he thought it needed further work.

All had spoken but Albion Fenderson. Ernest now turned to Albion and said, "Well, Al, what do you think?"

Albion got up from his seat and walked to the end of the table. All eyes were on him. Albion was in his fifties, stood about five feet four inches or five feet five inches with flowing white hair down to his shoulders. He had very sharp facial features. This appearance had garnered him a nickname, "The Fox."

"The Fox," dressed very dapper as always, stopped at the end of the table. Then he climbed up on table and slowly walked to almost the center of the table. There he sat down crossed-legged, Indian pow-wow style. Everyone was staring at him.

"The Fox" then took off his silver-rimmed half-eye reading glasses, which he always wore on the bridge of his nose, and slowly placed them on his left ear, where they dangled precariously. Not a sound was heard in the room. He then slowly and dramatically turned to Ernest and said, "Ernest, I do not believe this work is worthy of the Gallo Winery. I believe we should start over again." Ernest nodded his head, stood up and left.

We sat in stunned amazement. The meeting was over. I shall never forget the look on the agency's face. I wish I could have seen the look on mine.

Al, "The Fox," still sitting in the middle of the table, turned to me and said, "Chris, it was a good effort for you and the agency, but we need further work."

No specific direction was given as to the direction to be explored—it hardly ever was. But, over the next three months, the agency finally did develop a Pink Chablis advertising campaign that was approved for production.

It was then that I learned the depth in which Ernest Gallo was involved for all TV advertising. He personally approved the costs, the casting for every commercial and all the props and costumes. No other CEO in my experience ever reviewed this kind of detail

Know Thy Product Or Else

Working for Ernest was a unique experience in many ways—not just in advertising meetings in the conference room.

For example, he had a rule about product. He expected his people to be able to recognize his wine versus a competitor's and to understand the differences in taste and aroma between the wines. To do this it was ordained that each Group Product Manager hold a weekly brand group taste testing of his brand versus his competitors. The product that was sampled was taken from grocery shelves around the country.

Always eager to understand my products, I held these tastings religiously every Friday. It was only later that I learned this habit probably saved my job.

Approximately three to four months after moving to Modesto, I was holding a tasting when Ernest joined us. On this particular Friday, he walked into the conference room just as the wine was being poured into several glasses. We were tasting four competitive wines to compare with Chablis Blanc.

Ernest smiled and asked if we would like to participate in a test. We, of course, could only say "Yes." He said, "I would like to see how well you know my wine." He asked us to leave the room and return in five minutes.

When we returned we found five glasses of different, but unlabeled, wines. He asked us to taste each one and to identify his Chablis Blanc. We did and, fortunately, we all found it easy to identify the Gallo wine. Ernest was most pleased, smiled, and left the room.

I was later told that had I not identified the Gallo wine, I would have been fired summarily. Rumor had it that this had happened more than once.

Ernest had other severe rules. For example: Each marketing employee received a free case of wine each month and three cases of champagne over the course of the year. You could chose any wine you wanted and receive twelve bottles each month. However, there was a rule connected with this and the drinking of wine in general in the winery. Any employee of Gallo ever arrested for drunken driving or drunken and disorderly conduct would be automatically fired, no questions asked.

Final Assignment

Perhaps Ernest's greatest strength was his insight into the market-place in terms of long-term trends and in identifying problems that these trends represented for Gallo. He was truly the only director of Marketing. All the rest of us were "gofers" or researchers assigned to find answers for him.

This modus operandi led to my biggest assignment while at Gallo. To do it, I became a consumer market researcher.

Ernest called me into his office one day and said,

> "Chris, I want to know why we're not selling more table wines in New York City. Foreign wines outsell our wines and other California wines by a wide margin. I want you to go to New York and stay there until you have answers. I want you to personally go to every store that's selling wine in Brooklyn, Queens, and Manhattan before you make any decisions. Also, I want you to conduct some consumer taste-testing research in the city. Come back when you're done and let me know what you've learned."

It took almost two months, but I became an expert on the New York wine market. I spent three weeks on Long Island. I'm not sure whether I got into every retail outlet but I saw more retail outlets for wine than any of my peers. Visiting parts of Brooklyn was a particularly frightening experience. Often, wine was sold from behind bulletproof glass with a shotgun aimed at your head the entire time you were in the store.

I also supervised a series of blind taste tests in an apartment in lower Manhattan. From this I determined the Gallo name was synonymous with "cheap" dessert wines like Thunderbird. I also confirmed a belief of the winery that New Yorkers considered California wines in general as poorer in quality than French wines. All this led to the conclusion that there was no easy "fix." It would take a long time to change New Yorkers' attitudes.

Beyond this, I did recommend a starting point to address the image problem. I proposed that we repackage all Gallo branded wines to make them appear more upscale.

This recommendation was accepted, and I was asked to oversee its development and implementation, working with the on-staff Gallo pack-aging guru. Over the next three months we labored over the assignment and finally gained agreement to a whole new look for the line. Interest-ingly, until very recently Gallo still used the labels and bottle that were developed from this project. It was the only task I completed that had some lasting effect on Gallo in my eighteen months at the winery.

"A Square Peg in a Round Hole"

By now, you have the picture of what it was like like to work in the early 70's in marketing at Gallo. And, I hope I've made it clear how very miserable I was while I was there.

The problem was simple, yet profound. Only one man had the facts to make an informed marketing decision, Earnest Gallo. Only one man had any authority to spend any marketing funds, Ernest Gallo. Result: Ernest reduced the talented men he hired to the role of advisers and implementers. It was a culture that required you to accept that you were not empowered to be a strategic thinker, or make decisions. It was, in short, a place I felt I could not use my talents in a way that I could be comfortable. I respected Ernest, immensely; I liked him personally; but I hated the culture that he created that built his company's success. At Gallo, I was "a square peg in a round hole". I had to leave the company despite my fascination with the business and Ernest Gallo.

Result: Just eighteen months after I joyfully joined Gallo, I met with Ernest in April 1972 and told him I wanted to leave his employ. He did not seem surprised. We worked out an amicable severance arrangement and I set out to complete my six-month-old search for a new marketing job. I never saw Ernest or spoke with him again.

I was thirty-eight years old and desperately needed to find a corporate culture for my personality and my talents.

Lessons Learned

1. Entrepreneurs are vastly different to work for than a professional manager. There is something about pride in building a business that gives the entrepreneur a more passionate view of the market and his company's success.
2. *The Procter & Gamble Way is not the only method of breeding marketing success. Ernest Gallo provides another success model—Ernest's Way.* Ernest had a flat, decisive management system centered around verbal interaction with one man, not on written memos through a chain of command.
3. Ernest Gallo succeeded because of his unique persona. He had a rare blend of intelligence, common sense, and self-reliance. *He never took success for granted.* He sought superiority in all the basics of marketing with a perfectionist's zeal for all his products. He ruthlessly sought to have superior products, packages, pricing, promotion and distribution tactics.

    AND, he was a man willing to make a decision relying on his personal judgment. He sought input from his senior managers, not consensus but He never trusted anyone's judgment above his own. If his "gut" told him an idea, an ad, or anything else was wrong he would not approve it.

Final Comment

Gallo solidified a basic conclusion I had drawn from my career to this point, namely that in each industry *there is one key marketing variable that is all important to the success of that company or brand.* For example, as we said in Chapter 4, the key variable that determines sales success in the automobile business is the strength of the dealer. A good dealer will sell four times as many cars as a bad dealer.

In the packaged-goods business, assuming competitive product quality and price, the key success variable is shelf space and in-store displays. Therefore, the strength of package design and the strength of the sales force are critical to the success of any advertised product.

In the wine business, with a competitive product and price, the key marketing variable is getting adequate and consistent distribution at store level. To achieve such distribution, you must have a well-financed distributor with a strong sales force.

Lifetime Lesson: To attain career success, you must identify THE key marketing variable that determines a company's or brand's success in the marketplace and focus your efforts on attaining superiority in it.

PART II
STARTING THE BURGER WARS
BURGER KING 1972–1979

CHAPTER 6
"Have It Your Way"

(Winning in the Difficult World of Burger King)

The road from Gallo to a new marketing job in a new company began at a lunch with an old friend, Rogers Brackmann, in Chicago in early spring 1972.

I was seeking advice about a possible job as Vice President of Marketing for a fast-food hamburger chain called Burger King. I had already been to Burger King's Miami headquarters once to be interviewed for this position. Now they had invited me back. I was sure this time they would offer me the job.

I had come away from my first visit interested, but not sold. In many ways the job sounded too good to be true. On the surface it was everything that I sought in a job. But after my recent failures in selecting jobs, I was very cautious. Going to Burger King would mean moving my family cross-country once again—this time 3,500 miles to Miami, Florida, from Modesto, California. I did not want to make this move unless I was very sure I had the right job.

I had three questions for Rogers.

1) What did he think of the fast-food industry and its future.
2) What did he think of Burger King. I had never even seen a Burger King restaurant until my first interview.
3) Did Rogers think Burger King made sense for me.

I was sure Rogers could give me these answers. I had worked with him at Needham where he had been in the agency's promotion group. Now Rogers had his own firm, Rogers Merchandising, Inc. (RMI), one of the largest sales promotion agencies in America. His biggest client was McDonald's. If anyone would know what the fast-food business was all about, surely he would.

Rogers also had another critical credential. He was well known in the industry and among his friends as a man of total integrity. Rogers was, and is, a practicing born-again Christian. He lives his faith. He would, I was sure, tell me the truth even if it hurt.

Neither Rogers nor I can remember where in Chicago this lunch took place. But we both remember it vividly because of its long-term impact on both our lives.

We started with our usual glass of wine. As we ordered lunch we made small talk, catching up on the status of each other's families and Rogers's business. Then Rogers, always an impatient man, could stand it no longer. He asked, "Well, are you going to go to Burger King or aren't you?"

I looked at him across the table, hesitated, shrugged my shoulders, then waved my arms nervously and replied, "Well, that somewhat depends upon what you tell me at this lunch. I haven't been offered the job yet. But I think it'll be offered tomorrow, and I don't know if I should take it. Rog, I've run my family from pillar to post. My resume is beginning to look like I can't keep a job. I have to make the right job choice this time."

"What do you want to know from me?" he asked.

"Tell me about the fast-food business. Is it the kind of business you think I could be successful in?"

Rogers stared at me then replied rather sharply, "Chris, you could be successful in any business. You are one of the brightest, smartest men I know. What's your concern about fast food?"

"Well, what kind of business is it really?"

His eyes smiled behind his steel-rimmed glasses and he replied, "The very best kind. Because, whatever you do to try to build sales on Friday, you'll know the results by Monday. You don't need a Nielsen book or consumer research."

"No, Rog, what kind of industry is it?"

He said, "Oh, you mean is it growing, what kind of competition and all that kind of stuff?"

"Yes."

"Chris, it's one of the fastest growing businesses I have ever seen. But, as I look out to the future, I think it's going to have a major shakeout. I think that after McDonald's, which is already much bigger than everybody else, there will be plenty of room for a strong number two hamburger chain. Right now it looks like that could be Burger King. Apparently, they have the money because Pillsbury owns them. You know, Chris, I think they have a better sandwich than McDonald's. The Whopper is really the best fast-food hamburger in the industry."

He smiled. He knew he had done his usual "thing." He'd covered four distinct topics—each worthy of at least a ten-minute discussion—in just six summary sentences.

I smiled back. "Go on."

And he did. For the next forty-five minutes Rogers waxed eloquent about the growth of the industry and its lack of good marketing.

He made one statement that stuck with me the entire time I was with Burger King. He said, *"No one has really brought the disciplines of packaged-goods marketing to fast food."*

Then he added, "You could do this. Chris, there is no one like you in fast food. You bring a wealth of marketing background and experience to the game. In fact, I don't think there are any truly good marketers right now in the industry, although Needham is beginning to help McDonald's get there. Their new ad campaign, "You Deserve A Break Today," is really a great success, not only for McDonald's, but for the industry."

Of course, all of this was soothing music to my ears. Rogers had emphatically confirmed and reinforced all of the good impressions of Burger King that I had gained. He truly sold me that Burger King had the potential to be, at long last, my marketing home.

When lunch was over, I flew to Miami for my second set of interviews. I was now excited about the opportunity, but still not sure it was the right job.

I had two basic concerns. The first was my overall "fit" in the corporation. I had learned the hard way that I had to fit with the culture of the company. However, I was not sure how I could determine this. I had never been able to do it in the past. I concluded it would be a gamble and that I would just have to trust my instincts. At least for this job, I had the advantage of two complete days of interviews.

The second concern was John Hollingsworth, the man to whom I would report. He had a very big job as Burger King's executive vice president for Marketing and Franchising. John seemed to be a nice guy; I liked him personally. However, he did not appear to be very strong in terms of his marketing background. I knew far more about advertising and consumer marketing than John.

Because of this, I had decided that I would take the job only if he gave me his assurance, in writing, that he would give me complete authority over the day-to-day marketing decisions and over personnel. I wanted 100% assurance I could hire and fire without any management veto.

The second set of interviews went well. I met all of the vice presidents and liked them. They seemed talented and infused with a genuine excitement over Burger King's future. They were also very open about the difficulty of working at Burger King. Several warned me that I had better know my job well, because no one had time for training or handholding. One, Ken Horstmeyer, added another piece of advice: "You'll have to hit the ground running as fast as you can just to keep up." Later I would find these warnings to be very accurate.

Finally I met with John Hollingsworth. He wasted no time, saying, "You've impressed a lot of people today. We'd like you to join us."

I hesitated, then smiled and replied, "We need to talk. Before I can consider saying yes, we have some things we need to agree upon—up front."

He nodded. "Good. Let's talk it out over dinner. I don't know about you, but I could use a drink."

Over a long congenial dinner, we came to an agreement. If I took the job, I would have, in his words, "carte blanche authority" over the day-to-day marketing decisions and personnel. John said he would be very busy with the other parts of his responsibility, real estate and franchise operations. He explained that he felt more comfortable in both areas, because he had more experience in both than in consumer marketing. (John had come from American Can where he had never really had a big-time ad budget to spend on consumer marketing.)

Finally, the job offer details were spelled out. We parted and I flew back to Modesto to talk it over with my wife Joanne.

After much agonizing over a week's time, I accepted. The agony didn't have to do with the job. It had to do with Miami and money. I was being asked to accept a ten percent cut in pay, move across the country to a more expensive place to live—a place my wife did not like.

Getting Started

I joined Burger King as VP of Marketing in May 1972. As with every new job, I faced a new culture, new people, and a new system in which to work. This time I was determined that none of this would get in the way of doing the job. I was truly a man on a mission to prove myself to the world.

After my interviews, I was not surprised to find a culture that was, in a word, "chaotic." The biggest reason for the chaos was Pillsbury. When Pillsbury had purchased Burger King four years earlier, part of the deal was that the founder and CEO, Jim MacLamore, and his management team would stay and continue to manage the company. Pillsbury knew Jim who had founded Burger King with his partner, Dave Edgerton, had been the heart and soul of the company from Day One. They also knew their packaged-goods and flour-milling management team was ill-equipped to instantly take over the management of a fast-food restaurant chain.

Jim MacLamore was one of the finest people I ever met. He was, however, never a "corporate" man. He was a true entrepreneur who was used to running the show. He was a relatively unstructured, very hands-on, get-things-done manager. Jim had built Burger King with entrepreneurial people who were used to his entrepreneurial spirit and leadership. Jim thought Pillsbury should and would keep hands off managing his company.

At the same time, however, Pillsbury had a structured corporate packaged-goods culture. Pillsbury management was used to controlling its employees' decisions and sought to do so at Burger King, even though MacLamore was on the Board of Directors. They couldn't keep their hands off. Burger King represented too big a chunk of the company. Even in these early days, Burger King was well over twenty percent of Pillsbury's revenue.

Result: The two cultures clashed constantly over how the company should be run. It was a free flowing "get things done" culture versus "structure."

Now, as I was joining Burger King, the top management of the company was changing. Pillsbury's structure had won. After sixteen years, Jim MacLamore, the only CEO Burger King had ever had, was handing over his reins to an organization man, Art Rosewall. Art did not have the hands-on restaurant operations background of the founder. He was, however, a disciplined, professional corporate manager. He had joined Burger King from Ryder Truck about four years prior to this.

Also adding to the internal chaos was Burger King's very rapid growth. When I joined the company, Burger King was a chain of only about 400 restaurants, primarily in the midwest and south, with plans to double in size about every three years. (This was almost achieved. By late 1979, the chain had over 2,400 restaurants in all fifty states, Canada and Europe.)

New jobs were being created; old jobs changed. New professional people had been hired by Rosewall to mix with the "old-timer" entrepreneurs. Many times, people did not know their fellow workers, or worse yet, were not sure which department was now in charge of what.

Together, these two factors created an absolutely incredible internal workload. Everyone seemed to be trying to simultaneously develop new policies, cope with old policies, and manage growth. This in turn resulted in each department being almost an island unto itself.

Nothing could have suited me more than this culture at this point in my career. It made Burger King a company in need of take-charge people, particularly in the unstable marketing department. (I was the third VP of Marketing in four years.)

I found myself leading the fourteen-person marketing department that occupied one-fourth of the fifth floor in the eleven-story Burger King office building in south Miami. We worked quite independently from every other department. Unless we saw someone in the elevator, or went to a meeting, we rarely saw anyone but other members of the marketing department.

As I settled into my first-ever corner office, I cannot exaggerate the lack of organization and chaos I found.

Judith Belford and David Martin had been running the marketing department in the absence of a Marketing VP. Judith was director of Market Research. David was director of Advertising and Sales Promotion. They had nominally reported to John Hollingsworth, but had had little or no direction from John in months.

However, on my first morning at Burger King I didn't start with them. I started with Advertising Accounting. I was applying a critically important **Lifetime Lesson: To control the management of any organization you must start with understanding and taking control of the budget.**

I called Lee Rowan into my office. His responsibility was to bookkeep the four percent advertising fund, the source of all funds for the marketing department's programs including advertising, sales promotion, etc. A short, unimposing figure, Lee arrived ten minutes late for our meeting with a puzzled look on his face. With no introductory chitchat, he simply said, "Hi! What can I do for you?"

As he sat down, I decided he had set the tone for my entry into the Burger King marketing department. This was not going to be a series of friendly first meetings. I needed to send a "message" to the staff that, like Mr. Rowan, I was all business and in a hurry to get something done. I was not the laid-back persona of John Hollingsworth.

I brusquely asked him, "What is the status of our advertising and promotion budget? How much money do we have left to spend this year?"

I will never forget Lee's answer. He scratched his head, wrinkled his face, and finally replied in a fake Western accent, "You know pardner, I don't rightly know. You see we don't have a budget, really. I just keep track of what's spent." I advised him this was unacceptable, that I wanted him to go back to his office and figure out answers to my questions, "pronto" and report them to me by the end of the next day.

I then called David Martin into my office and asked, "What are our marketing plans for the next six months?" David, who was a deeply tanned look-alike for Mark Spitz, the famous Olympic swimmer, grinned with his pearly white teeth and said, "Chris, we don't have a six month plan. We have nothing planned beyond June 1st. You see, we've been waiting for you, our new Vice President of Marketing."

What a start! No budget! No plans! I went to John Hollingsworth and described my findings. Finally I asked, "John, do you have any advice?"

He shook his head and smiled, "Schoenleb, we hired you to fix marketing. Go fix it." The job had begun.

I called David back to my office and told him he had five days to develop a summer program. He smiled again (already I disliked his condescending manner) and asked, "OK, but what's my budget?"

David was obviously surprised when I replied, "Whatever Lee Rowan says it is. He will know by tomorrow or he's history." For the first time I saw a little fear on David's face and was glad.

Next it was time to meet my other lieutenant and determine what kind of market research we had. I called in "Judy" Belford. When she arrived she had an air of decadence about her. She was a very thin brunette with nervous smoker mannerisms. She dressed well, but somehow you got the feeling that she had been a Vietnam War protester and liked pot. She introduced herself as "Judith." She emphasized with a real edge in her voice that she wasn't "Judy," she was "Judith."

Judith was clearly upset to be summoned to my office. Her negative "vibes" were very loud. I saw no reason to be cordial so I got right to the point. "I'd like a copy of every market research study conducted over the past four years, and a list of your current projects, today."

She gave me a steely-eyed look. Then with a negative shake of her head and a large fake sigh, she spit out her reply, "We have quite a bit of market research but, frankly, I don't know why you're asking me about it. I don't really report to you. I work for Art Rosewall and John Hollingsworth. You'll have to ask them for approval to see the studies other than those done for your area of responsibility, advertising." Then in a condescending voice, she added, "I will *try* to let you know what market research we plan to do."

My anger was ignited instantly. She was the final straw of a very bad morning of introductions to my staff for my new "dream job."

In my most intimidating manner, I told her that I wanted all research, not just advertising, and that I expected it by day's end or we would meet in Art Rosewall's office to discuss her insubordination. Judith left in a huff, but I had the studies by day's end.

Then I met one-on-one with the rest of the Marketing department. There was no animosity here.

The department was structured with three Field Marketing Managers, Jerry Townley, Bill Hinson, and Don Harvey. They were assigned to develop local marketing plans to spend the local ad funds available for their assigned markets. In addition, there was an Advertising Manager, Jeff Campbell, (he would be president of Burger King in twelve years); a Sales Promotion Manager, Dwight Shelton; and a female product manager, Jean Hall; as well as two market researchers, Jon Ritt and an assistant.

All reported to David Martin except the market researchers and Jean. Jean, a young bleached blonde whose job was to work on new products, uniforms, and packaging, had reported to Hollingsworth. Now she reported to me.

My impression from these first meetings was mixed. They were a motley crew of eager-to-please young people. I liked their attitude. However they lacked focus and seemed very laid back. And, there was no sense of camaraderie among them. Jeff and Dwight, for example, sat in offices next to each other, yet wrote memos to each other instead of talking to one another. There was talent, but no in-depth marketing education or experience. Only Don Harvey and Jeff Campbell had MBAs; no one had more than five years' experience in business. In short, they were not even close to being a group of P&G caliber that I could count on to build a strong marketing program.

Thus, by the end of Day One, I knew the bad news of my new job. I was faced with major staffing problems. The two key lieutenants who had experience were not a fit with me. David Martin would need to be watched carefully until I could find a replacement, and Judith Belford had to be fired as soon as possible. *Clearly I had to be a one-man band until I trained this staff or hired more experienced help.*

In the hope of finding some allies and experienced marketers in all of this, I started Day Two by inviting the advertising agency, BBDO, to come to Miami and present a brand review.

The agency appeared about a week later. Like my staff, the account group was a disappointment. Dick Bonnette, the AE, and Dick White, the account supervisor had packaged-goods backgrounds. They were not, however, marketers. They were well-dressed, well-spoken account managers who obviously relied on their research department for marketing thinking. They seemed to fit Ernest Gallo's definition of "corporate suits." Meeting them, it was obvious that there was both a problem and an opportunity.

The problem was that the agency people had no respect for the marketing department. It was obvious that they viewed the people in the department and the chaos at Burger King with undisguised disdain. They seemed to believe they had been hired by Pillsbury to shape up Burger King's marketing. *Worse yet they were not immediately open to my leadership.* They, like Judith, made it clear they expected to take their direction from John Hollingsworth or Art Rosewall.

The opportunity was, of course, that BBDO was a superb advertising agency. They had done great creative for many clients, including Pepsi-Cola.

In its brand review, the agency outlined the research basis for the current Burger King strategy. The agency's position was that the "bigness" of the chain's sandwiches, especially the Whopper, was a meaningful point-of-difference for Burger King versus other fast-food hamburger chains. They also liberally quoted Jim MacLamore's support of this.

The ad campaign was, therefore, "It Takes Two Hands to Handle a Whopper. The Burgers Are Better at Burger King."

In the brand review, I was very impressed by the consumer research done by BBDO and by the individual who presented it, Larry Krueger. Larry was only an Associate Director of the agency's research department, but he was the most impressive researcher I had met since I had left Needham.

Larry Krueger was (and is today) a unique individual. Standing about five-feet-seven, in his early thirties, Larry had that rare combination of great intelligence and down-to-earth personal style. He also had a very quick wit and a barbed tongue. Although he had a Ph.D. in psychology from Purdue, Larry was basically a New Yorker from the Bronx who had never forgotten that he had grown up with a cigarette pack tucked into one sleeve of his shirt while he ran hot-rod races at 4:00 A.M. on East River Drive.

I liked him instantly. He seemed like the ideal replacement for Judith. Wasting no time, I briefly discussed this possibility with him after the meeting.

After the brand review, ten days into the job, I developed a four-part plan to address the chaos.

To buy some time, I approved the agency and Dave Martin's recommendation for a summer program without consulting John Hollingsworth or anyone else. This would test whether I really had the promised authority. (I did.)

Second, ignoring BBDO's seeming hostility, I tried to build some rapport. I asked the account group for a complete recommendation of a twelve-month plan to get out of the "What are we going to do tomorrow?" syndrome. I also asked for their recommendations on consumer research and, in general, encouraged them to bring forth all their ideas that would help transform Burger King into a more disciplined packaged-goods type marketer.

Beyond this, I requested David Martin and his staff to do replicate the agency's assignment. This would help identify who had the talent to be part of my team. I also gave them an additional assignment. I requested that they develop an on-going system to determine how much money we really had for a budget.

Why did I ask for this? Didn't Burger King have a finite advertising budget?

No, it did not. Part of the marketing chaos was that the advertising budget was a "floating" number. All advertising monies came from a separate advertising fund set up by the Burger King franchise agreement. This agreement required that four percent of retail sales be spent to advertise the Burger King restaurants in the year the funds were generated. To do this we had to spend money before we collected it. Therefore, *the budget would always be an estimate, not a "hard" number.*

The fourth part of the plan was mine alone. I needed to reorganize the department to gain total control of it. To do that, I had to prune David Martin's power and rid myself of Judith. Within four months I had accomplished this. I replaced Judith with Larry Krueger, and I isolated Dave Martin by being placing him in charge of only advertising. The net result was that I had a very flat organization. In fact, I had virtually the entire department reporting directly to me. The training could begin.

Burger King "Reality"

About sixty days into the job I began to understand that it was a very different job than I thought I had contracted for. Yes, I was the Vice President of Marketing and had marketing authority within the company, but I didn't have the authority I anticipated. *There were two "masters" to deal with, the company and the franchisees.*

Franchisees owned and operated almost ninety percent of the stores in the Burger King system. They were, I discovered, far more involved than auto dealers in the development of advertising, media plans etc.

Franchisees were key participants in the marketing planning process. The ad fund was four percent of their sales. Legally, at a minimum, we had to show them that we had spent the funds each year, and we had to consult with them regularly on how we planned to spend the money in the future.

There was a formal way in which they participated, namely a franchisee marketing committee. The marketing committee was composed of twelve franchisees chosen by the company to represent the various areas of the country. They were periodically invited at company expense to a formal two- to three-day meeting outside the corporate offices to review and discuss proposed marketing programs. Technically these were advisory meetings. In fact, if the franchisees did not agree with proposed future plans or TV commercials, we did not execute them.

I first met the marketing committee at a meeting at the Lake of the Ozarks Lodge in mid-summer. Ray Steck, VP of Franchise Operations, had arranged the meeting.

The meeting was amicable. The franchisees seemed glad to have someone on board as Vice President of Marketing, and they expressed hope that I would bring them programs to get Burger King retail sales out of the doldrums. Sales were soft and some of the franchisees were concerned about the future of their businesses. Indeed, although Rogers Brackmann had spoken so highly of the opportunity at Burger King, I had learned almost immediately that we were a troubled company. In a growth industry, Burger King retail sales were relatively flat.

This meeting brought my real job into perspective. *In Burger King, the Marketing Vice President was held directly responsible for restaurant foot traffic and retail sales.* Instead of focusing primarily on fixing the chaos inside Burger King, I needed to start worrying about retail sales growth or there would be another new Vice President next year.

It was also clear after the first meeting that *to succeed at Burger King I had to gain the support of the franchisee marketing committee. I would have to "sell" them.* And to do this, I would have to work with them as though they were the client and I was the agency.

The first step was to take over scheduling the meetings. I wanted to hold them in more attractive, more upscale, facilities than Lake of the Ozarks, so that any franchisee would be somewhat flattered just to be invited to attend. I scheduled the next meeting for the Greenbriar, one of America's premier resorts.

Needed: A New Strategy

The first six months passed quickly. All seemed to be going well. John Hollingsworth seemed very pleased with my initial efforts, as did his boss, Art Rosewall.

Chaos over the budget had been basically resolved. We knew how much money we projected we had to spend. We had developed a six-month plan—a one-year's plan just didn't seem practical given the budget-estimating difficulties.

On the people front, I had firm control of the department. Larry Krueger was proving his worth, and Jeff Campbell was beginning to emerge as man with a bright future. I was a long way from my overall goal of making Burger King the Procter and Gamble of the fast-food industry, but I felt confident I had made a start.

My biggest concern was BBDO. Surprisingly, they had not performed well in media buying and had developed new TV creative that was barely okay in my book.

Even worse, BBDO had not yet become an ally. Instead, they continued to view me with unbridled suspicion and continued to view the marketing department as a group to be educated, not take direction from. In return, all of us viewed the agency account group as arrogant. It was a situation that had to be fixed.

Another major concern was retail sales. So far we had no answer from sales analysis or from consumer research as to why sales were flat. I needed more time to focus on this issue. John Hollingsworth was in full support of "more time." Art Rosewall, who showed up regularly in my office to chat, also agreed, but he said he couldn't wait very long for answers.

The final concern was that I had not developed a working relationship with the franchisees. Now that my internal house was under control, it was time to address getting the franchisees' support.

I went to the Greenbriar marketing committee meeting to do this. We had a six-month plan, plus new "It Takes Two Hands" TV creative and a host of innovative minor programs to review with them. I hoped this would buy the time we needed to thoroughly address the sales problem.

It all started badly. At a stormy meeting the first day, the franchisees had not been impressed with any of the new TV commercials, media plans or sales promotion programs that BBDO and the marketing department had put together. They would not accept "more of same." Sales were flat, and they didn't want to hear about needing more time. They wanted action now.

The next day went equally badly in the morning and early afternoon. The BBDO account group had become very frustrated, especially Dick Bonnette. He seemed to view franchisees with much disdain. As far as he was concerned, they didn't know what was good for them. He told me that we had to ignore their negative advice and proceed.

By mid-afternoon I was very discouraged. We had a minor crisis. We were at loggerheads with the franchisees. It was the franchisee's instincts versus BBDO's buttoned-up package-goods style and consumer research.

We took a short break. I went outside the meeting room and stared into space trying to figure out where to go from here. About this time, an older couple came by. They glanced at the Burger King logo outside the meeting room. She turned to him, "Bill, that sign says Burger King. What's Burger King?"

I will never forget his answer, "Sarah, Burger King is just like McDonald's. They sell hamburgers."

As I overheard this, it was as though a giant light bulb went on in my head. All of us had been accepting as fact that Burger King was seen as different from McDonald's. I thought, "Could it be that Burger King was seen as a me-too brand. And were we following a me-too strategy? Could it be that the BBDO research was supporting a "corporate myth"—that the bigness of the burgers and the Whopper were not meaningful points of difference for Burger King in the marketplace?"

I went back to the meeting and posed my questions to the franchisees. As I did this, I saw the very pained expression on Dick Bonnette's face and the disapproval on John Hollingsworth's countenance. I was challenging the status quo, which they had been vigorously supporting.

The franchisees responded for the first time with passionate, but friendly discussion. They were sure that my questions were raising the real problem. Council members gushed forth statements like, "Nobody knows what Burger King is, except that we sell a Whopper." And, "They don't know we have other sandwiches including burgers for the kids." And "I see the same people over and over again." And, "They love Whoppers but not very many new people ever come into our restaurants."

One of the franchisees, Manny Garcia of Orlando, finally summed up this torrent of opinions. He said, "You know, Chris, we tell people our burgers are better because they are bigger, not because they taste better, or not because we put better things on them. There is more to it than "bigger" and we haven't told anyone."

Listening to this passionate outpouring, I instinctively agreed with the franchisees. I was willing to bet the current positioning was wrong. We couldn't wait. We had to respond. *It was time to look for a new strategy.*

However, I was not going to do this on opinion. I wanted to do it based on consumer research. Surprisingly the franchisees readily agreed to the use of research. In fact, they seemed relieved that I was willing to use research controlled by Larry Krueger instead of the agency. Clearly, they did not trust BBDO.

Closing the meeting, we agreed to meet with the franchisees within six months with "answers." This didn't give us much time, but as I saw it, I didn't have much time. If I did not get a program that could build retail sales, my time at Burger King would be over.

The task was clear. We needed to start with a "clean sheet of paper" and rethink the basics of the business. Was there another, more powerful market positioning for Burger King than "Home of the Whopper"? Could we find exploitable differences versus McDonald's, other than "big hamburgers"?

To answer this, we developed a complete comparison of McDonald's versus Burger King. Most of the differences we identified still exist today.

I list a few of them here because it is amazing how the more things have changed over the years the more they remain the same.

ITEM	BURGER KING	MCDONALD'S
Hamburgers	Features the Whopper	Features small hamburger
Sandwich prep.	Broiled	Fried
Size of patty	2 oz, 4 oz	1.6 oz, (Big Mac has 2 patties)
Key Customer	Adults	Families w/children

The key difference was that Burger King had bigger *broiled* hamburgers, McDonald's had smaller *fried* hamburgers. This difference gave Burger King hamburgers a "win" versus McDonald's in every consumer research taste test that we ever conducted.

In this back-to-basics review we also turned up a new fact. We learned that almost half the hamburgers prepared at Burger King were prepared to order. Many of our consumers did not take a preprepared sandwich as they did at McDonald's. Rather, they would personalize what garnished the meat with orders like, "One Whopper with extra catsup and no pickles."

This difference in sandwich ordering stemmed from a fundamentally different method of sandwich prep. At Burger King, the sandwiches were garnished after the order was placed. At McDonald's all sandwiches were made ahead of time and wrapped.

Out of all of this, we developed three alternative concepts for consumer research:

1. "Burger King burgers are better because they are broiled not fried."
2. "Burger King burgers are better because you can have them fixed the way you want them."
3. "Burger King burgers are better because they are bigger."

I believe these three concepts have been the basis for every hamburger advertising campaign Burger King has ever run, until the 1998-99 campaign featuring "taste."

The results of the consumer research confirmed the wisdom of looking for a different positioning. Of the three concepts tested, both "Broiled not Fried" and Sandwiches fixed to order" were clearly identified by consumers as more compelling reasons to choose Burger King than "Bigger Burgers."

I then turned to BBDO and requested that they recommend possible campaign theme lines for either of the winners. They did more research; then requested a meeting to gain agreement on which positioning should be chosen for developing an advertising campaign.

When BBDO was ready to present its findings, I decided to try once again to build rapport with the account management. Instead of a routine meeting at the office, I set up a two-day retreat for the entire agency account team: the AEs, creative, media, and all key marketing research personnel. Virtually all of the marketing department attended as well.

This meeting was held at the Duck Key Inn—a small hotel on a very small island just north of Marathon in the Florida Keys. In this isolated place the meeting seemed to "work." For the first time, the agency and the marketing department mixed in an informal setting and enjoyed each other's company. We played cards, we played volleyball, we talked, and we truly worked hard together.

Out of this meeting came unanimous strategic agreement. We would position Burger King as better than other fast-food restaurants, because it did not "force" consumers to purchase *pre-made* sandwiches. *Burger King fixed its sandwiches to order—the way a consumer wanted them.*

Selecting a New Ad Campaign

About thirty days after Duck Key, Dave Martin, Larry Krueger, Jeff Campbell, and I went to BBDO in New York to see the agency's initial creative recommendation.

The agency presented two campaigns. First, was a campaign called "Who's the King at Burger King? You are." The emphasis in this campaign was on how Burger King works to make you feel special with little emphasis on special ordering of sandwiches. It was not totally on strategy.

The second campaign was "Have it Your Way." It was very much on strategy.

I asked the agency for its recommendation. There was some hesitation. It was obvious that Dick Mercer, the creative director who had presented both campaigns, and the account group were not in accord. Finally Dick Bonnette answered. "We believe that 'Who's the King at Burger King?' is the stronger campaign." He rationalized why it was on strategy and gave several reasons for the recommendation.

Hearing this, I asked the agency to leave the room to allow our group to privately discuss the recommendation. This was a practice I had learned many years ago at P&G but had never used. I knew the agency didn't like it, but that didn't bother me. This decision was too big to worry about relationship problems. As I viewed it, either I made this decision correctly or my days at Burger King were numbered.

From the beginning, all of us loved "Have It Your Way." It was on strategy. It focussed directly on our strength versus McDonald's—better tasting, made-to-order sandwiches. We also thought it captured the essence of the "Me Generation" of the early '70s. And, we thought "Have It Your Way" was a phrase that might be remembered by almost everyone.

The more we talked, the more we began to believe the unthinkable; that we could beat McDonald's. "Have It Your Way" could trump their brilliant campaign "You Deserve a Break Today."

We called the agency back into the room. I told them that we preferred "Have It Your Way." I offered some minor changes we thought would strengthen the proposed TV and requested that the music they promised us for the campaign be finalized.

A long silence settled over the room. Dick Bonnette had not expected to be overruled. A lengthy argument ensued. Dick White and Dick Bonnette vainly tried to change our minds. Dick Mercer sat silently in the room. It seemed obvious that he was rooting for the client's view throughout the meeting.

Finally, I cut off our discussion and said, "Dick, this is the campaign we want to run with. Get it ready for a review with our management next week."

At this point we adjourned for lunch. I was split off from the group for a special get-acquainted luncheon with the then Creative Director of BBDO, Jim Jordan. Jim had an excellent reputation on Madison Avenue. His biggest claim to fame was the Wisk "Ring around Your Collar" campaign.

I was flattered that Jim wanted to have lunch with me, until I found out why. Jim wanted to change my mind. He spent the entire lunch selling me on "Who's The King at Burger King? You Are." I never learned why, but I decided to give him a partial victory. (I did not want to turn the agency totally against me.) I agreed to allow BBDO to present both campaigns to Art Rosewall and the rest of the Burger King management. In return, Jim agreed that the agency would not proffer a recommendation, but would state that either campaign would work.

The luncheon was the start of a very difficult relationship between Jim Jordan and me. From the beginning we were like oil and water. I think it is accurate to say that over the next two years we came to dislike each other rather intensely.

The Burger King management meeting was held the following week. BBDO had done an excellent job of finishing both campaigns. In fact, the now famous "Have It Your Way" jingle was on a demonstration tape for the meeting.

The agency finished their presentation and, of course, made it very clear its preference for "Who's The King at Burger King? You Are" without overtly saying it.

Suppressing my anger, I turned to Art Rosewall and said, "I believe the agency has done outstanding work. We need a new advertising campaign. I am sure that both campaigns would do well. However, it is my strong recommendation that we proceed with "Have It Your Way." It's the best execution of our strategy. I also believe that "Have It Your Way" will be a theme line everyone will remember. The music also has a ring to it that I believe will resonate on TV."

Art did not respond. I sensed he had real doubts. I also saw disagreement and doubt among my cohorts. I asked the agency to leave the room.

A spirited discussion followed. Jerry Ruenheck, who was in charge of company restaurants, and Ray Steck both expressed doubts about "Have It Your Way." They were very concerned that encouraging consumers to order specially-made sandwiches would slow speed-of-service and would, therefore, hurt sales. Even after I pointed out that almost half the sandwiches were already being made as special orders, they were adamant that this promise was a big risk.

After some time, it was clear that members of the Burger King management were split in their opinion, and that their opinions were becoming more entrenched by the moment. To break the deadlock I suggested we do consumer research to determine which campaign to choose.

John Hollingsworth vetoed this idea. He stated that it wouldn't solve the operations issue being raised. Rather, he proposed that we take both campaigns to the franchisees at our next marketing council meeting and let them choose. If they had the same operational concerns as Ray and Jerry, then clearly we would have to go with the campaign "Who's The King at Burger King? You Are" rather than the campaign he saw as superior, "Have It Your Way."

John's approach carried the day. "Have It Your Way" would live until its presentation to the franchisees.

Selling the Franchisees

Before the marketing committee meeting, I decided to try and cash the one personal chip that I had not used to try to succeed at Burger King.

I called Rogers Brackmann and reminded him of a long-ago promise he made to me at our luncheon. "Rog," I said, "I need you to become Burger King's promotion agency."

I reminded him, "You said you would resign from McDonald's when I was ready. Rog, I'm ready! If you do this, I can guarantee you as much income the first year as you are currently earning from McDonald's. After that, it will be whatever you can make it."

Rog called me back the next day. He had prayed about it. He would, indeed, resign McDonald's to become Burger King's promotion agency.

This was a real coup. Burger King was getting the best and most experienced fast-food promotion agency in the country, and in doing this we were hurting our biggest competitor.

I rushed to the eleventh floor to tell John Hollingsworth and Art Rosewall of our good fortune. I was surprised by their response. They didn't understand the importance of this move and were rather cool toward the idea. John seemed particularly concerned.

He said, "You know, Chris, you made this move without consulting the franchisees or me. This could really backfire on all of us. I have already heard reports that you are too arrogant and that you don't listen. Rogers Brackmann had better be some kind of special person or this could hurt you personally, big-time. If he is such a good friend, perhaps he ought to stay with McDonald's. There is no guarantee that we will be able to keep him employed here."

I had already advised Rog that I could only guarantee the first year. His work would have to speak for itself. I never told him about this conversation with John Hollingsworth.

The marketing council meeting was held in Bermuda in June 1973. Larry, Jeff, and I flew off to the Sonesta Beach Hotel along with Ray Steck and John Hollingsworth. Dick Bonnette, Dick White, and Dick Mercer were sent by BBDO.

Retail sales were still flat. Clearly this meeting would go a long way toward deciding my immediate fate. If the new strategy and its advertising didn't work, I was afraid I would be out the door.

To say that I was "up tight" would be a significant understatement. At the same time, I knew we had real ammunition for a successful meeting. We had new creative based on a new and very sound strategy. And we had Rogers Brackmann. He would be my surprise introduction. He had been exposed to the "Have It Your Way" campaign and had immediately loved it. He was sure the franchisees would buy it.

Rogers's role would be to show the franchisees how we could take this campaign into each of their restaurants. I was excited about this because, as Rogers said, "Chris, this will be the first advertising campaign in fast food that is totally integrated down to the store level. Up until now, everything McDonald's has done at the store level has not been tied to its advertising or vice versa. I'm sure this will be a big plus for us and make up for the fact that McDonald's outspends Burger King."

The meeting began on a beautiful Bermuda day. My hopes rose, *The sun was shining.*

Despite the sunshine, my heart sank. When I saw the hotel's only meeting room. I was sure we had one big strike against us before we started. The room was too small. It was an ideal room for twelve people, not twenty. It would be very warm, even for the informal garb of the tropics. We would be packed like sardines around a typical U-shaped table with the presenters using an overhead projector at the open end of the U. I promised myself that if I survived this meeting, I would never again let a meeting be held without first making sure we had a room that was the right size for the committee.

But there could be no turning back. The meeting began on time with a packed house and I pulled out all the stops. Before we showed any advertising to the franchisees, I spent an hour and a half reviewing all the facts and figures about sales, about our customers and outlined objectives and strategies for the following year. In effect, I presented a miniversion of a P&G marketing plan.

We took a quick break. One of the franchisees, Jack Jones, who had been at Leo Burnett ad agency before buying his franchise, took me aside and said, "Chris, that was the most brilliant presentation we have ever seen as franchisees. I sure hope the advertising lives up to the billing you have given it."

Dick Mercer came on after the break and put on a great show. He had everyone's head nodding as he presented "Who's The King at Burger King?" Then he launched into "Have It Your Way." I watched the audience closely. The look on Jack Jones' face said it all. He seemed excited, almost ecstatic.

We had agreed that we would let the franchisees choose the campaign. But I just couldn't do it. When Dick Mercer had finished, I immediately stood up and said, "Gentlemen, initially we had not planned to give you a formal recommendation because there are some concerns about how one of these campaigns might impact your in-store operations. I must tell you, however, that with all of my heart and soul, I strongly urge you to agree with me that the 'Have It Your Way' campaign should be adopted."

From his glowering countenance, I thought Ray Steck wanted to kill me. I knew John Hollingsworth was livid. However, the franchisees almost applauded. *One by one they stood up and enthused, "We love it. Go with it. "Have It Your Way" is just what we have been looking for."*

Finally, Ray Steck said, "We are very concerned about how this might impact operations. Aren't you concerned that this will slow down your service times?" The franchisees looked at Ray like he was from a foreign land. Their consensus reaction was something like this, "Hey, we do this every day. If this campaign will bring in more people, we will figure out a way to serve them." Case closed. Campaign sold.

Then came the "coup de grace," Rogers Brackmann. He wowed them! He explained his philosophy of bringing a marketing strategy to promotion. Then he showed them the in-store point-of-purchase materials for "Have It Your Way." The franchisees enthusiastically endorsed everything.

The meeting was an unqualified success with the franchisees. They left excited for the first time in several years. Because of this, John Hollingsworth said nothing about my conduct at the meeting, but it was clear he would never trust me again. I had bet my job on "Have It Your Way."

Now it was up to the agency to deliver great creative execution, and to Rogers to execute the point-of-purchase materials and make sure they were put up in all restaurants.

At this time, I made one other critical decision. I canceled all TV advertising for July, August, and early September in all markets. The tactic was simple: we needed to save the funds to launch "Have It Your Way" to make sure that for the initial introductory period of the campaign we could outspend all competitors, even McDonald's. It was a calculated gamble that was shared with few people. I never advised the franchisees and never told top management. Neither would have agreed.

One other important but routine step was taken. In mid-July, we sought legal approval for the TV commercials. We also asked that a trademark for "Have It Your Way" be registered. Jack Eberly, the lawyer, soon sent back a letter approving the ads and advised us he would apply for a trademark.

Launching the Campaign

The new commercials were shot at a new Burger King prototype unit in San Diego.

A young woman named Ann Spangler was hired to sing the Burger King jingle and perform in most of the initial commercials. Ann couldn't stay in tune very well so it took many "takes" to get her in tune enough to make the commercials. Her flashing blue eyes and striking good looks more than made up for this, however. She looked good even in the rather ridiculous new red-and-yellow Burger King uniforms that included a strange-looking hat.

Finally, in mid-September 1973 we launched the "Have It Your Way" campaign with the strongest media weight Burger King had ever used.

Just as Rogers had described to me in Chicago, we knew the results instantaneously. By the end of the first week, franchisees were reporting sales increases as high as fifty percent. (Later we learned that we had actually achieved a twenty-nine percent sales increase the first week of the campaign throughout the system.) Customers were coming into our restaurants singing the "Have It Your Way" jingle. There was tremendous excitement among the restaurant crews. We had a grand-slam home run.

I felt personally vindicated. This was truly what I'd prayed for over many lean years.

My euphoria started on Thursday, the fourth day of the campaign launch. It lasted twenty-four hours. On the fifth day, I received a phone call from Art Roswall, inviting me to his office. When I arrived, Ray Dietrich, the chief legal counsel, and John Hollingsworth were already there. Art, a prematurely gray man with sparkling blue eyes, did not have his usual "in charge" look. I had come expecting congratulations. It was obvious that something else was very much up.

Art began without any small talk. "Chris, I am glad you could come up so quickly. I just received a phone call from the president of Burger Chef (a major regional fast-food chain owned by General Foods). He advised me that Burger Chef has the trademark rights to "Have It Your Way." He said that they are using this theme line in Burger Chef restaurants right now. I have asked Ray here, along with John, to discuss how we got into this mess and what we can do about it. I told the president of Burger Chef that I would get back to him on Monday.''

I was stunned and sat there for thirty seconds just staring into space. Could it be that all this work and this gamble I had personally taken would be totally destroyed? How could this have happened?

Finally I turned to Ray Dietrich, "Ray, we requested legal approval for the Have It Your Way campaign and a trademark registration for the line from Jack Eberly in July. He approved the ads in writing. Didn't he do the proper legal work on the trademark?"

Ray, who was a very sharp attorney but very political in his own way, looked at me and said something like, "Chris, I don't recall seeing such a request from you."

I was stunned for a second time. I faced Rosewall and said, "Art, I would never have spent a million dollars for new television creative and gambled the good name of this company unless we had legal approval. If you don't believe this, I will be happy to go and pull this information from my files."

Art gave a slight grin and said, "Why don't you have your secretary bring this information up? We'll wait." Fortunately, my secretary, Cindy, found the correspondence with the legal department, including a brief memo from Jack Eberly giving legal approval for the campaign. After Art read the memo, he turned to Ray, "Well, Ray, now what?

It was Ray Dietrich's turn to be stunned. He gathered himself together and plunged into his response. "Well," he said "I guess we made a mistake but it's water over the dam at this point. Let's see what we can do about damage control. I suggest that we go out and make sure that what you heard from the president of Burger Chef is indeed true. We need to make sure they are really using the line in their stores. In the meantime, we will go back and do our legal homework and determine just what kind of problem we have with the trademark registration of "Have It Your Way."

Art said, "Good. Let's take the weekend and meet here again on Monday morning."

The following Monday we met again in Art's office. The news was all bad. Burger Chef was using "Have It Your Way" in several stores in Ohio, and Ray confirmed that they did indeed own the trademark. He also said the registration was somewhat flawed and began to give an explanation of what that meant.

I didn't understand nor really hear much of what he said. I had already gone to the next step. What should we do now? Art was on the same page. He looked at the group and said, "Well, now what do we do? Chris, if we wanted to pull this off the air, what would we do?"

I told him the facts. We couldn't stop advertising in less than two weeks, because we had two-week cancellation clauses in all spot TV contracts. We could pull the "Have It Your Way" commercials and put on old commercials, if we could renew the contracts of the actors in those commercials. This would be difficult but it could probably be done in a week. I summed up, "No matter what we do, we'll have another week of Have It Your Way advertising on the air."

Then Art asked Ray, "What happens if we just let the advertising run?"

Ray replied, "Well, they could sue us to stop using it, with a temporary injunction, and they could sue us for damages—probably many millions of dollars worth. However, they would have a difficult time proving their case since Burger Chef would have to show that our advertising hurt their business."

We all then turned to Art Rosewall. Clearly, he had a decision to make. Art had received many phone calls from the franchisees from around the country praising the new campaign and reporting phenomenal sales increases as were the company-owned store. Art was also under great pressure as the replacement for Jim MacLamore to make something happen.

He really had but one choice. Art took a very deep breath and said, "Well, let's continue running it and see what happens. I call the president of Burger Chef and tell him that we are still reviewing our options and stall him for a few weeks. In the meantime, Chris, you'd better figure out how to tell the franchisees about this."

One thing I failed to notice in that meeting but certainly remembered later was that John Hollingsworth did not participate in the conversation. Art was now dealing directly with me. I soon learned that John would be leaving the company and that we would have a major reorganization in which I would end up reporting directly to the president.

Winning the Legal Battle

About two weeks later, Burger Chef filed for a temporary injunction to stop our advertising. The legal battle lines were drawn.

We tried to settle the matter out-of-court. Ray Dietrich and I met with the General Foods attorneys at GF's headquarters in Terrytown, New York. We offered to buy the trademark rights for $10,000. They wanted $1,000,000. Not surprisingly, the lawsuit continued.

Meanwhile, the advertising continued to run and Burger King sales continued to soar.

When we told the franchisees of our problem, they didn't want to hear about it. It was our problem to solve. All they wanted was assurance that the campaign would continue. It was clear we would have a problem with them only if we lost the legal battle.

In most lawsuits, the first step is depositions of the probable trial witnesses. I was the first one deposed by the General Foods lawyers. They prodded and poked at my story for hours. They could not believe that I didn't know that Burger Chef owned the "Have It Your Way" trademark.

Finally, in the process of the questioning, they confronted me with a statement that one of the people who worked on the Burger King account for BBDO had previously worked for Burger Chef. They were sure he knew that Burger Chef had the rights to "Have It Your Way." Had not the agency told me this? I answered negatively. No one from BBDO had ever mentioned it.

Afterward, Ray Dietrich immediately contacted Dick Bonnette and confronted him with what we had been told in the deposition. He admitted that the agency had indeed known that Burger Chef owned "Have It Your Way." BBDO had simply ignored this because the client had given legal approval.

Ray Dietrich was furious. I was again very upset with BBDO. Their arrogance seemed to have no bounds. Now they were trying to blame their client's poor legal work for their failure to advise us of a very important legal fact. I began to wonder, in fact, if the real reason the agency had preferred "Who's The King at Burger King? You are." was because they had known the legal truth.

It was early December before the initial hearing was held on the Burger Chef lawsuit. By this time, we had run twelve weeks of "Have It Your Way" advertising at the highest spending levels in the company's history.

Our consumer research showed that over fifty percent of the American public already associated the theme line with Burger King. Virtually no one associated it with Burger Chef. We "owned" the line in the minds of the American consumer before the lawsuit was ever heard.

Our lawyers filed for dismissal of the temporary injunction to stop the campaign on the basis that we already owned the line in the American public's eyes. The judge agreed with us.

Burger Chef then decided to settle out of court. After a series of negotiations, the lawyers for both sides agreed that we would buy the trademark for $100,000. At Art Rosewall's insistence, BBDO paid most of this.

Looking back now, isn't it ironic that one of the most famous advertising lines in American history occurred only because a lawyer, Jack Eberly, failed to do his legal homework? (Jack Eberly left the legal department several years after this to become a Burger King franchisee in Oregon.)

Success!

Following the legal settlement, the first half of '74 was almost idyllic for the company and the marketing department. "Have It Your Way" had truly made Burger King a household word in the areas in which it had restaurants. Burger King sales were increasing monthly.

We kept the advertising momentum going. Within six months, additional "Have It Your Way" commercials were developed that were even better than the original set.

I promoted Jeff Campbell to replace David Martin. He enthusiastically pushed BBDO to do the best work we had seen, including the most famous "Have It Your Way" commercial that starred three young black ladies singing for a customer who asked, "I know I can get my sandwiches my way. But could I get you to sing?" It won all of the awards the advertising industry gave that year. (In '98 Burger King reused parts of this commercial as part of its revival of "Have It Your Way.")

The advertising also created quite a stir within the fast-food industry. I was told that McDonald's was extremely concerned about this campaign and had formed a special task force to figure out how to respond. The Burger Wars of the '70s and '80s had begun.

The Fruits of Success

"Have It Your Way" obviously took my career to new heights. My star was on the rise everywhere within the company. My salary woes were "fixed" with the largest salary increase of my life to that point. And, as I have already alluded, I was promoted to a different reporting relationship. I was now the chief marketing officer of Burger King reporting to the president.

Bill Spoor, CEO and chairman of Pillsbury took a real interest in me. I was invited to be his special guest at a board meeting in Minneapolis. I was introduced as "the marketing guru who has literally put Burger King on the map."

I became a good business friend of Les Paszat who was the chief Financial Officer of Burger King and the heir apparent to Art Rosewall. Les assured me as early as 1974 that he would be replacing Art before the decade was over and that, if I worked closely with him, he would make sure I replaced him as the president of Burger King.

This was heady stuff. I had at long last not only found a home but a career path directly to the top. What a difference four words can make! "Have It Your Way" looked to be my ticket not only to the top of the marketing world, but to the top of the corporate world as well.

Outside Burger King other good things happened. I was invited to give speeches to many organizations, particularly ad clubs and restaurant industry conventions including a *Restaurant News'* MUFSO conference. My favorite speech was to the Chicago Advertising Club. I couldn't have been prouder of myself than at the moment I spoke there about the success of "Have It Your Way" to a packed house, including my friends at Needham as well as the McDonald's marketing staff.

In addition to speechmaking, I began to fulfill a long held desire to go back to college and teach. Because of the success of "Have It Your Way," professor Dick Reizenstein of the University of Tennessee asked me to speak to his marketing class. He expected to do the interview by telephone. Instead, I volunteered to make an in-person talk to the class.

Following my presentation to his class, Professor Reizenstein invited me to come back the following year. He also asked me if I had any friends who might be interested in coming to speak to his classes. I scribbled down the names of five or six friends, former P&Grs, on the back of an envelope. With this list, Professor Reizenstein founded an Executive-in-Residence program that continues today.

The period 1972 to 1974 was my personal coming of age. *It was my good fortune to find a job which truly fit my job experience and my personality.* Burger King needed a take-charge marketer who could survive the chaos of growth and changes in management. My background was almost tailor-made for the assignment. It enabled me to take control and create a marketing success case history for the ages.

Lessons Learned

1. Being in top management does not provide job security. Being the marketing boss at Burger King meant "produce retail sales or lose your job." If "Have It Your Way" had failed, I would probably have lost my job.
2. There's real personal loneliness at the top. You must maintain a distance from yourself and your employees to be able to objectively evaluate them, as well as to avoid the appearances of favoritism. And, it's hard to build personal friendships inside management especially if you're pushing an agenda of change.
3. The key to selling "Have It Your Way" was my total commitment to my gut reaction to the campaign. I believe that there is no substitute for having a good intuitive knowledge or "feel" for your business. Sometimes, this "gut reaction" or intuitive knowledge leads you to a decision that cannot always be rationalized by the facts at hand, but I believe you have to follow it. *After all, isn't your "gut reaction" really the sum of all your knowledge and experience reacting to a proposal?*

Final Comments

The developing, selling, and launching the "Have It Your Way" campaign was a once-in-a lifetime experience. I never approved another campaign at Burger King or anywhere else that came close to impacting sales as positively as "Have It Your Way."

In retrospect, there seem to have been three reasons for its success—two of which have disappeared forever:

First, this campaign was launched when the impact of network TV advertising was at its peak. It was before the era of cable and the splintering of the television audience. As a result, you could effectively reach everyone in the TV audience.in a relatively short period of time with far less money than any time after this.

Second, the fast-food industry was exploding in growth, changing America's eating habits forever. This campaign helped created a viable national competitor to McDonald's and added to the attractiveness of the category.

Third, there was the strength of the message with its target audience. "Have It Your Way" fit the "Me Generation" culture perfectly.

CHAPTER 7
Internal Marketing Battles

(More Turbulent Times at Burger King)

My biggest issue after the launch of "Have It Your Way" was what to do next.

As I analyzed the situation, I finally had some job security in a job that I loved. This gave me more time to achieve my professional goal of making Burger King marketing the P&G of the fast-food industry, and an opportunity to prove I was the right man, long term, to be president of Burger King.

It was clear that focussing on building the marketing program was the key to attaining both goals. We had made progress, but we had a long way to go. The advertising issues had been solved, but we did not have the total marketing program we needed, or the personnel to manage it. Also, BBDO continued to vex me with its lack of support for the marketing department.

On the plus side, in addition to "Have It Your Way," I was particularly pleased with the market research and sales analyses we were doing. I was sure that we had identified all the Burger King "corporate myths."

Another big plus was the promotion resources of RMI, Rogers Brackmann's organization. For the first time, whatever in-restaurant promotion material we needed was professionally developed and delivered to the restaurants on time.

A final plus was additional marketing personnel, two field marketing managers, two people in market research and one important newcomer, a new personal secretary, Lou Kasper. Lou, a lady in her mid-forties, was a consummate professional and soon became a valued "right arm."

On the need-to-do side, I had to address a multitude of issues that came from system growth and the success we had achieved.

Short term the biggest concern was to maintain the sales momentum. This meant addressing two areas that could have an immediate effect on sales: local TV buying and promotions. Beyond this, I wanted to explore adding new items to the menu. I reasoned that if new products were the "bread and butter" of building packaged-goods sales successes, why not fast food?

Longer term the "need-to-dos" were harder to see, but I did identify two major issues.

First, Burger King needed a public relations department. We had none, not even to answer consumer letters! We could not concede this area to McDonald's. We had to find ways to counterattack their masterful programs like their All-American Band.

Second, management responsibility for restaurant signage, building design, and interior décor needed to be shifted to marketing from operations. (*I viewed this as the equivalent of packaging for a packaged-goods product.*)

Rewards of Management Stature

As I ruminated on how to attack all these issues, one thing was crystal clear, the success of "Have It Your Way" had elevated my role in Burger King management.

I was appointed to the management committee that authored all key policy decisions. Called NDC (National Development Committee), this committee met every Monday afternoon and served two purposes. It was CEO Art Rosewall's staff meeting, and it centralized control of the company's growth by being the final approval body for every proposed new Burger King site and every new franchisee.

NDC also served a special purpose for me. It became my on-the-job training school for franchise restaurant chain management. Through it, I learned the inner workings of managing a franchised restaurant chain, especially the nuances of real estate acquisition and franchising.

At the same time, I was given an even freer hand to direct the Burger King marketing program. My new boss, Art Rosewall, was a retired military officer. He would supervise me with the question, "Well, what's planned for next month?" He wanted total communication, but gave no dictates. He considered marketing my "command." (Of course this was hardly carte blanche to do as I pleased because every plan had to be reviewed with the franchisee marketing committee.)

In all this I learned that having greater management "stature" did not reduce the ongoing pressure for results. *Burger King was a taut pressure cooker.* This pressure came from a critical fact of life in the marketing culture at Burger King—all focus was on short-term tactics. Yesterday's success was old news. Long-term strategy was of little concern. The only relevant issue was tomorrow, "What's the tactic to build sales next month?"

This cultural fact was particularly true among the Burger King franchisees. In general, whenever a franchisee had a sales decline versus the previous year, the franchisee expected immediate changes in the marketing program, not reassurances that the program was working. He was quick to blame advertising and offer his solution to the problem.

If ten franchisees had falling sales, the marketing department would usually hear ten different solutions. There was no easy way to deal with this—someone was always sure that the marketing department and/or the agency did not listen. We generally tried to use suggested solutions as input, but not react to them with major changes.

Ironically, the success of "Have it Your Way" added to this short-term mentality. In effect, "Have It Your Way" set a standard for the influence a new advertising campaign could have on Burger King restaurant sales. When the franchisees would urge that a new advertising campaign be developed, they truly expected that this new campaign could be as successful as "Have It Your Way."

This expectation for an ad campaign's success directly affected my relationship with key franchisees. No TV advertising campaign after the first eighteen months of "Have It Your Way" was ever successful enough to satisfy them. This meant almost constant pressure from them for more change.

Finally, my new management stature did not reduce my heavy day-to-day workload: it added to it. I was always preparing for, or attending, one more franchisee meeting, one more Pillsbury meeting, one more trip to the agency or one more squabble with the operations department.

In addition, there were constant internal organizational problems spawned by the rampant growth of the Burger King system.

As restaurants and franchisees were added every month, every job inside the company changed in scope and importance. As jobs changed, the talents required for them changed. New departments were formed, more outsiders recruited. All of Burger King seemed to be in a constant state of remaking organization charts with new job titles, new more specialized departments, etc.

Result: There was a constant churning of people. Some left voluntarily; some were fired. By mid-1974, for example, there was an almost entirely new marketing department. Of the original eleven people, only three remained.

All of this resulted in my routinely averaging over sixty hours a week on the job. This in turn added pressure to my personal life. With three teenagers at home, I was also needed there as much as possible.

JAPS Meeting

Early in 1974, to address the short term issues surrounding the question, "what next?" I scheduled a planning meeting on Captiva Island north of Naples, Florida, for both RMI and BBDO account groups, BBDO's research personnel, BBDO's media planners, and the entire marketing department. At this meeting, the first of what were called JAPS meetings (Joint Agency Planning Sessions), I tried to create a unique forum—one that had multiple purposes.

JAPS' primary purpose was to plan future programs and give out assignments to accomplish these plans.

Equally important, however, JAPS was to serve as a communications forum. All new market research and sales analyses were shown and discussed as were new proposed advertising and sales promotion programs. Everyone was encouraged to critique all plans. This served the dual purpose of building consensus and providing my people with on-the-job training.

JAPS also served as the only face-to-face forum for the field marketing managers to communicate their needs. Their concerns were crucial to the success of any program. As the Burger King corporate marketing representatives responsible for the specific plans for individual markets, it was their job to sell programs to the franchisees. All of us had to understand their issues, so that the marketing department could provide creditable leadership to the franchisees.

Finally, I hoped that JAPS would improve personal rapport between the agencies and between the agencies and their client. I was confident that if this forum worked, it would eliminate hundreds of memos and phone calls, and a team could be built to address all issues.

Media Buying

After a day of reviewing marketing plans and sales results, the second day at Captiva began with a discussion of spot TV buying a major issue first identified by the franchisees.

Needham had taught me that *in many ways, buying TV advertising—both network and local markets (spot TV)—is like buying a car.* The price for the time slot in which the commercial is placed, depends almost solely on the skill of the negotiator, the agency's buyer.

Applying this knowledge to review the BBDO spot TV media buying, I was surprised and concerned. Somehow, BBDO and its client had different buying standards, probably because until this time no one but the franchisees had challenged the TV-buying methodology.

I raised two issues and soon had my hopes trashed that BBDO would work with us to address either of them.

First, BBDO was using buying specs for the wrong product category. The agency viewed Burger King as a packaged-goods brand like Campbell's Soup. They did not recognize that Burger King was a local retail entity. Result: BBDO buyers did not visit local markets. They did not seek local buys that made Burger King part of the community, such as sponsorship of a local sports events.

Second, evidence from the franchisees indicated that in most instances, BBDO had not negotiated comparable advertising costs to McDonald's. This meant that we could be getting less "bang for our buck" than our main competitor—something we could ill afford because McDonald's was already outspending Burger King in virtually every market.

According to the franchisees, BBDO's buying practices had alienated the local TV station sales managers. When they were not awarded part of a Burger King buy, these salesmen would go to the franchisees in the market, and tell them that BBDO buying practices were wasting their money. They would state that BBDO had paid twenty percent or thirty percent more than McDonalds for a TV GRP (Gross Rating Point, the measure of TV audience size).

When apprised of this cost discrepancy, the franchisees would become understandably upset and demand a review of the BBDO TV buy for their market. When this review occurred, BBDO usually admitted they could have bought a more cost-efficient schedule, and then improved the buy.

Every time this happened, the franchisees became more convinced that BBDO was not doing a good job; and that the marketing department was not doing its job.

This was very frustrating to me. Media buying should have never been a problem. It should have been a major advantage for Burger King. One of the great strengths of Burger King was its centralized marketing. All the funds (four percent of retail sales) were collected centrally to be spent by one agency.

McDonald's, on the other hand, only controlled funds from two percent of sales. The rest of the money they spent (two percent to three percent of sales) was controlled by their franchisees who determined the amount to be spent, formed co-ops to collect the money, and hired as many as seventy local agencies to spend the dollars.

Under any circumstance, as a major agency, BBDO should have been able to buy at least as well as any competitor's agency. Having the built-in advantage of a professional marketing department, not franchisees, controlling all the funds should have assured it. Yet, it didn't. Apparently, the smaller McDonald's agencies, far less powerful and prestigious than BBDO, were out-buying BBDO.

At Captiva, we asked BBDO to review its buying methods, and to provide ongoing cost comparisons with our competitors' local buys. I wanted the problem to go away as quickly as possible. As professionals, they should have gotten the message.

They did not. Instead, Bill Tennebruso, the media supervisor, vigorously defended BBDO's buying practices. He claimed that all of us were misled ("agency speak" for wrong), and that if we would just "listen to reason" we would be convinced that there were no media-buying problems, just franchisee-handling problems.

Menu Innovation

Of the three short-term issues on the Captiva Island agenda, addressing the advisability and practicality of new menu items was the thorniest problem.

I began the discussion with a statement, "I believe that, of all the things we can do, a new menu item has the biggest potential to increase sales. I'm sure that the right new item would have an immediate and, perhaps, lasting sales impact. I'm also positive that any new item would be our most effective promotion—just as new flavors were for Betty Crocker Cake Mixes."

All JAPS participants initially agreed. We quickly developed a list of potential new items. Then reality appeared amid our euphoria, when Larry Krueger stated flatly, "Chris, you haven't got a snowball's chance in South Florida to sell Art Rosewall on adding any of these items. Operations doesn't want to deal with anything new right now. We're wasting our time on this."

We knew Larry was right but new menu items were too big a potential sales-building weapon to lay aside without a fight.

Art Rosewall had to approve any changes in the menu. And, in 1974, new menu items were of scant interest to him. He liked the idea of new items, long term, but wanted no changes at this time. The reason was, succinctly, operational concerns. There was, in fact, general management agreement that new items should not even be considered until the Burger King customer service system was changed.

What is a customer service system? It is the process used by a restaurant to obtain and fill a customer order. Until 1973, all Burger King restaurants had a one-cash-register service system. The customer ordered from one person; then walked to a second person, a cashier, paid the bill, and received his order.

A McDonald's restaurant, on the other hand, had three or four cash registers with one or two order takers at each register. They would take and fill orders—only one person interfaced with a customer. With this system McDonald's could process multiple orders simultaneously.

Advantage: McDonald's. Every fact we possessed supported the premise that a McDonald's restaurant had faster customer service and generated higher sales per hour than a Burger King restaurant. Further, research showed that consumers felt McDonald's gave friendlier service.

Because of this, Art Rosewall had become convinced that Burger King had to have a multiple-cash-register service system. In early 1973 he had ordered Operations to "find a way" to accomplish this.

Within a year, under the leadership of an industrial engineer, Al Bennett, a test of adapting the McDonald's multiple-cash-register system to the Burger King restaurants was conducted. (One of the great advantages I found in the chain restaurant industry versus packaged goods was the ease of setting up in-market testing. No simulations needed.)

After Bennett modified the test restaurants and worked out most of the "kinks" in service methodology, it was clear that the new system was indeed superior to the old one-register system. But, changing to the new system was a costly change—a change that required a revised kitchen layout and increased labor costs for the restaurant owner.

Despite these increased operating costs, Rosewall had plowed ahead. Result: He left a lasting mark on the company when he decreed that all existing restaurants had to be changed to the new multiple register system, and all new restaurants had to be built with this new service system.

This decision was initially met with stiff resistance by many of the franchisees, particularly the largest franchisee, Self-Service-Restaurants. (SSR later went public, bought Chart House, and changed its name to Chart House.) Many refused to change their restaurants for years. Until they did, Burger King had a dual service system—the new multiple register system and the original system. This meant all marketing programs had to be adaptable to both systems.

The service system problem was not the only practical barrier to menu innovation. Burger King also had no formal menu development department. The little work that was done on new products was by Al Bennett and one food technologist, John Barnes.

Franchisees, on the other hand, were very interested in new products. "After all," one franchisee explained, "new sandwiches or desserts are not brain surgery. Most of the time we already have the ability to cook and assemble them."

Many franchisees would add items to their restaurant's menu only to be told by the company to drop them or lose their franchise.

Menu has always been a constant "push–pull" between the company and franchisees in every fast food chain. A consistent image requires that every restaurant have essentially the same menu. If a company starts allowing franchisees to add items unique to their restaurant, soon consumers would not find a consistent menu that can be advertised.

At the same time, no chain can afford to stifle franchisee innovation altogether. Some of the greatest menu ideas in fast food have been brought about by franchisees. McDonald's, for example, credits their initial breakfast program to a franchisee in Santa Barbara. Thus at Burger King we had to allow franchisee menu experimentation, but still be able to control and monitor results.

Another menu issue was distinct regional tastes. Some lent themselves to differences in menu offerings by area of the country. Again, for consistency's sake, this was avoided whenever possible.

I remember one particularly difficult problem with the franchisees and company restaurants in Texas. They insisted that they had to have a Mustard Whopper.

I was assigned the task of visiting them to tell them to stop selling the sandwich. When I arrived I quickly learned that the Mustard Whopper accounted for thirteen percent of their total sales—or almost half of the total Whoppers they sold. I also learned that the only difference between this Whopper and the regular Whopper was that mustard replaced the usual mayonnaise.

With sales at this level, it was not hard to believe the operators' claim that lots of Texans preferred mustard to mayonnaise and that we would lose business to a local chain, "Whataburger," without the Mustard Whopper.

I was sold. Consistency of menu had to take a back seat to survival in Texas.

Menu Merchandising

At Captiva, there was no immediate solution to management's concerns over adding new menu items.

At the same time we agreed that any Burger King marketing plan that accepted the menu status quo would be a deterrent to building sales. Too many consumers perceived Burger King's menu as one dimensional—the "Home of the Whopper." If we couldn't offer new menu items to attack this issue, then we had to find a way to build the sales of Burger King's already existing other sandwiches and side dishes and thus broaden consumers' perception of the chain.

After a long discussion, we developed a partial solution to educating consumers on the breadth of the Burger King menu. We called it menu merchandising.

Menu merchandising was to be an ongoing program of featuring a major sandwich, other than the Whopper, each month inside the Burger King restaurant, by changing the point-of-sale posters and the four-color pictures of sandwiches on the menu board. And, if we had TV scheduled that month, to feature the menu item in our commercials. This would not be a discount offer, simply a "suggestive sell."

This kind of program is now routine in fast food, but menu merchandising was a new concept for Burger King in 1974. Until that year, because of the menu board's design, it had been very expensive and very difficult to change the menu board pictures. Thus, every restaurant had a picture of a Whopper there and little else.

To rectify this, RMI designed an inexpensive "fix" for the menu board. With this modification, operators could change sandwich pictures easily and inexpensively.

With this menu board "fix," the foundation for menu innovation was laid. With menu merchandising, we proved consumers would respond to featured items. Sales of items like the Whaler, Burger King's fish sandwich, would double when pictured on the menu board. More important, almost immediately we had an unexpected triumph from menu merchandising—improved profitability. All items on the menu were more profitable than the Whopper, so when a consumer switched to another sandwich, it helped build profit margins.

New Menu Items

After Captiva I kept pounding away in NDC on the importance of new menu items. By 1975, with John Barnes's help, I was able to sell some first steps in adding to the menu. Two easy additions were identified and rolled out—a new sandwich, a Double Cheeseburger (franchisees had sold this off and on for years)—and a new side dish, onion rings.

Both were successful; both remain on the menu today.

A newcomer, Jack Wile, and Al Bennett also worked on a pet project of Art Rosewall's—developing a fried chicken product line to compete with KFC. This was an abysmal failure.

With these successes and failures, the way was paved for the future. And, I was positioned to take management responsibility for a much more formal new product effort (See Chapter 9).

Sales Promotion

The most successful result from the JAPS meeting was addressing Burger King's sales promotion needs. Rogers Brackmann was again most insightful. To begin this discussion he made a profound statement that provided a *Lifetime Lesson: "There are only three ways to build sales in any business. You can improve reach—that is, add more customers to your customer base. Or you can improve frequency—that is, convince your current customers to come back more often. Or you can increase the average purchase price—that is coax your customers to buy more items or higher priced items."*

He went on to say, "When you apply this principle to building the sales of a fast-food restaurant, you see that you affect only one of these variables through marketwide advertising, namely attracting more customers for a one-time visit. *To maximize sales, every Burger King has to have ongoing programs designed to increase frequency of visit and to increase the average check."*

This really opened my eyes to the need for ongoing promotion in fast food, as opposed to the sporadic seasonally timed promotional efforts employed in packaged goods.

More important, it led to formulating the Burger King promotion tactics utilized throughout the '70s. The main focus was to develop quarterly advertised market-wide promotions designed to build frequency of visit, to try to entice a new or existing customer to come once a week, not once a month. A good example of this kind of promotion is to offer a set of special drinking glasses or plastic cups that would require a customer to make multiple visits to collect a complete set.

Local Store Marketing (LSM)

In addition to market-wide promotion needs, we also left Captiva with a plan to address local individual stores promotion needs. I was amazed to learn that every franchisee and every company restaurant spent one percent to two percent of sales to build a restaurant's sales or to build community good-will. As a group they spent millions of dollars to sponsor Little League Teams, bowling teams, put ads in high school newspapers, etc., etc., etc. In effect millions were being spent without any direction or help from the company and much of it was poorly done and ineffective.

Rogers Brachman proposed we solve this need with a new marketing tool for Burger King—a LSM manual for a local store (within Burger King we always called restaurants, "stores"). He gave this program an acronym, "RADIUS," *R*etail *A*rea *D*ominance *I*n *U*rban *S*ituations. The RADIUS manual would provide a professional planning guide and standardized materials so that any franchisee could use his local dollars more effectively.

In this manual, for example, would be model ads for local newspapers. If a franchisee wanted to run a coupon offer in his local shopper paper or newspaper, he took the model ad to the paper and designated the coupon offer. There were also special promotional ideas such as "Freaky Fridays" or free desserts on Tuesday night. All the materials for these efforts could be ordered from RMI.

Rogers also urged that as part of improving a franchisee's LSM program that a special low-cost market research study—a trading area survey (TAS)—be conducted. The TAS would be conducted so that a franchisee could understand where his business was coming from within a three-mile radius of the restaurant. This study was conducted in-store by an interviewer with a map. Customers would be asked to put a colored dot on the map showing where they had come from and where they were going.

With a market-wide promotion development plan, the LSM program and the TAS research tool, we had the blueprint for the promotion "basics" that became standard for all chains by the '80s and continues today. I was sure that if we executed it well, we could pass McDonald's in the promotion arena, as we had in advertising with "Have It Your Way." Next stop: franchisee "buy in."

When we exposed the promotion program to the franchisees at the next marketing committee meeting, there was a mixed response. Franchisees from small- and mid-sized towns embraced the LSM book, but were lukewarm toward advertised market-wide promotions. The big city franchisees, on the other hand, had little use for LSM. They wanted more market-wide promotions to build trial; they did not like the focus on frequency. "Get us the customers once," they said, "And we'll keep 'em with our quality of service and quality of food."

This split between the small town franchisees and the big city franchisees became more and more pronounced as time went on. Indeed, providing programs that enthused the total system became one of the major problems that I was rarely able to solve.

In effect, I was "damned if I did and damned if I didn't." Whatever program was run, one set of franchisees would embrace it and make it successful; another set would dislike it and fail to execute it properly, ensuring its failure. Only by producing a "home run," a great advertising campaign or superb marketwide promotion did we gain general agreement and general system success.

All of this confirmed, of course, what I first learned at AMC. *The key to successful promotion in a franchise environment is selling the franchisee. If he likes it, he will usually find a way to make it be successful in his restaurant.*

Kids Marketing

The Captiva meeting was very successful. All parties agreed that the format worked. For the rest of my tenure at Burger King, I held JAPS meetings outside the office two to three times annually.

There was other "fallout" from the meeting. RMI replaced BBDO as Burger King's dominant agency for strategic and tactical planning. BBDO did not seem to care. Their people chose to view the agency's role to be just advertising, the creative message and media. Result: the account group was never more than halfhearted in discussions of ideas outside of advertising.

Finally, as a result of the Captiva meeting, a special consumer research study was commissioned to better understand the marketplace and our competitors. We dubbed this research the "Problem Detection Study."

From this research we gained a startling finding. "Have It Your Way" had indeed built Burger King awareness and trial, but not at the expense of McDonald's family business. Burger King had made no serious penetration into families and kids, the strength of McDonald's sales.

Further, the research showed that the reason for this failure was kids. It showed that in families, the decision-making process used in choosing a fast-food restaurant made kids' preferences critical. The process went like this: First, Mom, who was in charge of the family's dining (Dad followed Mom's lead), decided whether to eat at home or eat out. If she decided to go out, Mom then selected the category of restaurant—sit-down-formal, fast food, etc.

Finally, if she selected fast food, Mom had her unwritten list of those restaurants she thought were suitable for the family. She would then let the kids select the restaurant from her list which she would offer verbally to them: "Where do you want to go tonight? Burger King, Wendy's or McDonald's?" *The kids would make the final restaurant choice.*

McDonald's was almost always the kids' choice. Our initial research showed almost eighty percent of the kids preferred McDonald's. Conclusion: to truly add sales long-term, Burger King had to go after kids with a much stronger and more competitive program. We had to have stronger advertising to kids, and we had to redirect our adult ads to Mom and Dad, not just Dad.

This was not an entirely new insight. It simply added substance and urgency to the importance of attracting kids to build sales. Burger King had always advertised to kids and had always tried to give them special attention at each restaurant. Indeed Jim MacLamore's first major TV buy in Miami had been on a local kid's show, "Skipper Chuck." And, of course, each child was given a crown to wear on his or her head when they ate at Burger King.

In 1974, however, our focus was on advertising to adults, particularly men, not Mom, and not kids. We ran only ten to fifteen percent of our advertising weight against kids. This was primarily on Saturday morning local and network television. We used thirty-second animated TV commercials starring an animated King who was a miniature version of the old Burger King on the original Burger King signs.

Despite RMI's planning prowess, the assignment for a new kids' marketing effort had to be given to BBDO. Any new program had to build off of new advertising.

BBDO responded enthusiastically. But, from the beginning, the agency focussed on finding an advertising idea, not a complete program. They hired a child psychologist to interview children. They showed several alternative advertising approaches to kids for their response.

In retrospect, the agency's research was bogus. It was the kind that spawned a "corporate myth." It focussed on kids age six and up. We learned later we needed to attract kids at ages three to four.

At any rate, based on the child psychologist's work, BBDO came back to us recommending that "Have It Your Way" be adapted to a separate kids' advertising campaign. The agency claimed that kids who had been shown prototypical "Have It Your Way" kids commercials had responded enthusiastically to the ads. They stated that kids wanted a restaurant that would give them sandwiches their way.

We all readily agreed. I liked the idea very much because it gave us one campaign for all audiences—thus leverage our ad dollars against McDonald's.

The new campaign was introduced to the franchisee community with great fanfare in the fall of 1974. The agency put together a special film in which they explained the research that confirmed that kids would love to eat at Burger King if they were told they could get the Whopper Junior or a hamburger fixed the way they wanted it.

At the same time, remembering my success with heavier TV weights for the original "Have It Your Way," I authorized extra-heavy introductory kid TV buys.

There was no immediate response to this advertising. There was no surge of business. In fact, after six months of running this campaign, there was no evidence in any consumer research that kids had remembered or had responded to it. In short, the campaign bombed.

We confronted the BBDO account group with the sales results and research findings and told them we had to have a new kids' program that worked. Not surprisingly they disagreed. They counseled for patience and assured us it would work long term.

I reflected on the initial "Have It Your Way" advertising success and rejected their point of view. Another lunch with Jim Jordan ensued. With this lunch, my relationship with Jim Jordan reached its nadir. At lunch he sketched his solution to our kids' advertising problem on the back of a napkin. I was totally "underwhelmed." Here was a head creative guru trying to sell me a revised campaign with no research, no objectives or strategies, simply his opinion.

I never wanted Jim Jordan to be involved in Burger King advertising again. I requested a private meeting with Tom Dillon, the chairman of BBDO, to express my concerns. I told him of the deadlock in opinions and reminded him rather forcefully that as his client, I needed the agency to stop fighting my requests for change. I also told him of my dislike of Jim Jordan's methodology.

This was an awkward meeting because Tom and I had no rapport. Tom clearly communicated that he did not view me as his equal, but rather someone to be placated. In the case of Jim Jordan, however, Tom seemed to listen and agree. He gave one of has famous "harrumphs" and I never saw Jim Jordan again.

Jim Jordan was replaced by Allen Rosenshine (later the chairman of BBDO). About this time, perhaps because of all the changes, Dick Mercer, the author of "Have It Your Way" left BBDO.

I met with Rosenshine and explained the problem. He seemed very receptive. He indicated he understood that his first priority was to work on a new kids' campaign.

At the same time, I requested that the agency work on a further extension of "Have It Your Way." I was convinced that "Have It Your Way" had to be extended beyond "Hold the pickle, hold the lettuce." I was convinced that "Have It Your Way" could have lifestyle meanings to the "Me" generation.

Allen did not agree. He said that the agency wanted to stay with the initial concept. With minor "tweaking" he felt it would be effective for years. However, BBDO did develop one lifestyle "Have It Your Way" commercial. It proved to be a complete dud. Tested using a Burke Recall Test, no one remembered the thirty-second version of the commercial.

I was not convinced by this failure that the idea of extending "Have It Your Way" was wrong, but rather, that the execution idea tested was wrong. BBDO did not agree. The agency made me feel that every discussion of any major changes to "Have It Your Way" advertising were akin to starting World War III. I backed off and asked for a "freshening up" of the campaign.

Obviously, Needham and McDonald's had read the same lifestyle trends that I had, because, in late 1974, Keith Reinhard wrote a new campaign for McDonald's, "You, You're the one." It was exactly on target to reach the objectives I had set for extending "Have It Your Way."

I was furious that we had been beaten to the punch. Now we really needed to have new arresting advertising—our singing counter girls had to be replaced. I demanded that the agency find a fresh way to express "Have It Your Way." Dick Bonnette took the assignment only after another heated exchange between us.

Network TV

Not everything was bleak. As the creative problems deepened, BBDO finally began to address media and, in the process, created a national promotion opportunity.

About six months after the Captiva meeting, BBDO put together a well-thought-out recommendation to shift media funds to network television for 1975. They pointed out that because Burger King was now buying more than sixty percent of the country in spot TV we could buy the same weight on network TV in these markets and cover the rest of the country.

This was exciting. By buying network, Burger King would get national advertising exposure like McDonald's and KFC. This would be a more efficient use of our media dollars and would reduce the amount of spot TV being bought at a less than competitive price.

In addition, buying network opened up opportunities to run nationally advertising promotions. It would give Burger King a real leg up on McDonald's. McDonald's used national advertising as "image advertising" and, in those days, did not try to advertise promotions on network.

When we discussed the use of network with the franchisees, they too were excited. So, starting in 1975, Burger King became a prime time network TV buyer. Today, the company is one of the largest users of network TV in the United States.

National Promotion

The second success amid the problems over creative development was launching Burger King's first nationally advertised promotion. Like "Have It Your Way," this promotion had a unique and difficult birth.

In mid-1975, BBDO recommended that Burger King buy a partial sponsorship of the '76 Olympic Games network TV broadcasts. The partial sponsorship was half of the time allocated by ABC for fast-food advertising in the Olympics. McDonald's had purchased the other half. It required the use of almost all our network TV funds, but I agreed.

As soon as the Olympics buy was made, I called Rogers. I told him that I was once again gambling on a big idea to build sales—a major tie-in with the Olympic Summer Games in Montreal. I gave him an assignment. "Rog, to pay this deal off, we have to have a dynamite national promotion to advertise."

About two months later, Rogers called me excitedly and said, "I have the greatest idea I think we've ever come up with. Even BBDO will like it."

I held my breath because Rogers sometimes came up with some off-the-wall ideas. I still remembered the idea he had proposed at Needham of using helicopters to drop coupons in the form of feathers into shopping center parking lots to promote the Betty Crocker Cake Mix promise "So Tender You Could Cut It With a Feather."

He started his pitch, "From the beginning, we have been looking for a promotion that would entice multiple visits over the four weeks and uniquely tie in to the Olympics. Well, a few weeks ago we contacted Leroy Neiman—you know, the famous painter of sports scenes and athletes. We asked him if he would do four new paintings from pictures of the '72 Olympics that we could then copy into posters. The idea is that we offer a different Leroy Neiman Olympic poster each week for the four weeks we advertise on the Olympics. And, today Leroy called back and said 'yes'."

I was dubious. "Rog, Posters? Leroy Neiman? Why is this such a big deal?"

Rog could not believe my skepticism. He gushed out all the reasons he was sure consumers would recognize Neiman. Then he added, "Chris, one thing I forgot to tell you. Leroy is going to be painting new pictures of the Olympics in the main broadcasting booth every day that ABC broadcasts the Olympics. Everybody tuning in will see them. It will be terrific reinforcement of our promotion. And, it will be free merchandising for us."

I finally got excited. "OK, Rog, this might be good, but can we afford it?"

"Yes. Leroy has offered to do four paintings for just $80,000. With this, he will also make available 300 lithographs of each painting to sell to the franchisees and to company officials as collector's items. He'll make these available at $200 apiece, which is about twenty percent of the going rate for his lithographs."

I responded, "OK, let's pursue it. Get the contract put together. I'll bounce the idea off my guys here, call BBDO and also a few of the key franchisees. Even Billy Trotter and Dave Stein (franchisees who seemed to oppose me constantly) might like this one."

Then I paused and had a sudden added worry, "There is one thing that bothers me, Rog, how do we buy these paintings? The ad fund can't really own something like that. Do you think I can sell the company on paying the $80,000?"

"Well, that's your problem. "I'm sure you'll solve it."

To make a long story short, I did solve it. The company would buy the paintings. Then we sold this idea to the franchisees who would have to purchase the Olympic posters for four cents each. They readily agreed.

We put Leroy Neiman under contract. He painted the four pictures and from those four pictures we prepared to print eight million posters, two million to be given away with a sandwich purchase at Burger King each week of the Olympics.

By late 1975, seven months before the Olympics, all plans were in place for a great promotion.

Then trouble struck, just before we printed the posters. Rogers called me. "Chris, I have some bad news. You'd better sit down."

I responded, "Okay, I'm sitting down. What's up? You sound ominous."

"Chris, we can't call our Neiman posters Olympic posters."

"We can't do what?" I literally screamed into the phone.

"You heard me. We can't call them Olympic posters. You have to buy the rights to use the word Olympic. It's protected by Congress. I just learned that McDonald's owns these rights in the fast food category. So, we can't say these are Olympic posters."

I was stunned and shouted at the phone, "Rog, this is a disaster. How could you not have known this until now? What are we going to do? We can't . . . it's too late isn't it?" I stuttered.

"No, it's not too late," he said. "We haven't printed the posters. But I don't want to give up on this promotion. I'll think of something and call you back."

Rog called back the next day. He was all smiles over the phone. "Chris, I think we found the solution to our problem."

With a huge sigh of hopeful relief, I asked, "What is it? I'm all ears".

He replied with a question, "Chris, what is the significance of the year 1976?"

"Rog, don't play games with me. It's the year of the Montreal Olympics. We all know that."

"No, it's also something else. It's the year of America's Bicentennial. There's a big Bicentennial celebration this year."

"Yes," I said, "So?"

"Well," he replied, "We've been in contact with the Bicentennial Commission and we have gotten their agreement to call the four Neiman sports posters a Salute to America's Bicentennial in Sports. You now have four America Bicentennial sports posters."

I sat there and absorbed the news. First I grinned. Then I chuckled. "You know, Rog, you just saved us."

It proved to be one of the most successful promotions Burger King ever ran.

The four original paintings may still be in a Burger King vault somewhere. I don't know what happened to them. After the company bought them, they were considered too valuable to be hung in the corporate halls for fear they would be stolen!

BBDO's Last Year

Unfortunately, in 1975 the Olympics tie-in was a year away. As the year progressed, despite the new menu items, sales were relatively flat in existing restaurants. Franchisee unrest was growing, particularly in their perception of BBDO's lack of responsiveness.

Indeed, agency problems abounded. We had a kids' campaign that wasn't working. And, McDonald's new adult campaign seemed to be eclipsing "Have It Your Way." In addition, BBDO account service remained a major headache. Their AEs and Dick Bonnette were slow to respond to our requests, and, unfortunately, they still communicated contempt for our business and us. Jeff Campbell, Larry Krueger, and I called them "arrogant" almost daily.

We were frustrated. "Why?" we asked each other, "Why is BBDO so difficult to deal with?"

By late summer, at a marketing council meeting outside of Tampa, the franchisees demanded that BBDO be fired. Much as I agreed with most of the franchisee complaints, I defended BBDO. I argued that BBDO deserved more time, that Allen Rosenshine had just been assigned to do new creative and that we had to be patient.

By late fall, the pressure to get new advertising on the air was acute. Still BBDO was not responding. There was no sign that the agency shared the urgency we felt. We had seen no progress in finding a successor "Have It Your Way" campaign that did not bury the line, but resuscitated it. (Oh how I wish they had found the solution shown on TV in 1998. This revival of "Have It Your Way" was brilliant.) Also there was still no new kids' TV.

Worse yet, the franchisees were beginning to accuse me of being in "BBDO's back pocket." Jack Jones called and warned me to stop making excuses for the agency or I would lose all support from the franchisees on the marketing council.

Very concerned for my own credibility, I again went to Tom Dillon to try and solve BBDO's lack of responsiveness. Clearly it started with account management and this had to change. I told Tom that Dick Bonnette was not "cutting it." The franchisees had always disliked his style and manner as much as I had. He was too Ivy League, too packaged-goods oriented. He was simply not "in tune" with the rough and tumble retail orientation of fast-food marketing.

Tom reminded me that he had already replaced the creative group and that we had his best man, Allen Rosenshine.

I told him that this change was no longer enough and that unless there was more visible proof that BBDO was responding to our needs, I would be unable to support keeping BBDO as our agency. Tom finally got the message. He agreed to review the situation and make some changes.

Tom responded about sixty days later. He changed the account group senior management. He brought in Bruce Crawford (future CEO of BBDO and Omnicom) as new management overseer. Bruce hired Bob Rees, who had been in charge of the Volkswagen business for Doyle–Dane–Bernbach, to replace Bonnette.

I met with these two gentlemen following Tom's announcement and was instantly impressed. Both seemed far more willing to work with us and showed none of the disdain we had felt so often in the past. They seemed genuinely concerned that BBDO might lose the business. Most of all they seemed to share a sense of urgency. They promised a Herculean effort would be made to "get the account back on track."

While all of this was going on, rumors that BBDO would lose the Burger King business were rampant on Madison Avenue. This led to my receiving numerous phone calls from other major agencies in New York.

One agency in particular went all out to convince me that we should fire BBDO—Wells–Rich–Greene. Several times in early 1976 Mary Wells flew to Miami to take me to dinner. I also met with Charlie Fredericks, then president of WRG, and with Charlie Moss, WRG's creative guru.

Ed Meyer, CEO of Grey Advertising, also called to state his interest in working for Burger King. He reminded me of our long ago relationship when he was the account executive on Big Top Peanut Butter.

I was exhilarated by all of this. However, I remained committed to BBDO and seeing the work through with them.

Nails for the Coffin

In April 1976 two things happened that doomed the relationship with BBDO.

First, Allen Rosenshine admitted in a creative meeting that the agency had done no major work in the previous nine months on a new kids-only advertising campaign. This was a shocking revelation. A major New York agency, with some of the greatest talent in the advertising industry, had failed for nine months to work on a request made by their client. Worse yet, it had openly lied about it.

This revelation was followed by a request from Bob Rees that BBDO be given an additional sixty days to solve the kids' problem and come up with new adult advertising. He pleaded that the new organization simply had not had enough time.

I was skeptical. These were talented people, but virtually nothing had gone right in a year. In truth, I had begun to doubt that BBDO would ever solve the kids' creative problem. Still, I agreed to the sixty days to try to solve our needs. However, I told Bob, "I can only support the agency so long without some solutions."

The second event was the promotion of Art Rosewall. Art was moved to Minneapolis to head up the newly created Pillsbury Restaurant Division. Pillsbury had purchased Steak N Ale. Bill Spoor wanted someone reporting directly to him in the home office to oversee Pillsbury's fastest growing business segment. Art, in turn, promoted Les Paszat to the presidency of Burger King.

This was good news for me. Les had already promised that I would be his successor. Les Paszat was, however, an impulsive emotional man. As such, he was anxious to make his mark with the franchisees and prove that he was in control of the company.

Soon after he took over, Les met with me to understand the problems with BBDO. At the end of my recitation, he asked, "Well, why don't you fire them?"

I told him that we owed the agency more time. I also expressed concern that, from a political standpoint, we ought to talk to Pillsbury and get their agreement before we did anything. I pointed out that BBDO seemed very sure they had friends there to protect them, including CEO Bill Spoor.

Les snorted, "Chris, I am running Burger King. You are running marketing for Burger King. We don't have to get the approval of anyone." But he agreed to wait.

Finally, the sixty days promised the agency were up. We met in New York in mid June. *It was cloudy day.* There was gloom and doom in the room. Allen Rosenshine did his best to sell mediocre creative. We did not agree with any of his recommendations for adult or kid advertising.

Afterward, I met with Bob Rees. He asked for more time. I told him I did not think he would get it—that the status of BBDO would be reviewed at a management meeting the next day and results from that meeting would determine next steps.

In Miami the next day, we met in the Burger King boardroom. In attendance in addition to Les Paszat and myself, were Jeff Campbell, Larry Krueger, Ray Dietrich, and Ken Horstmeyer, a former marketing executive who was now executive VP of Operations. (Ken had seemed very disappointed when Les, not he, had been named president.)

I reviewed the status of where we were with the advertising campaign development, then expressed the opinion that I did not believe BBDO would find solutions to our needs. Furthermore, I stated that it was clear that the franchisees shared my belief.

I summarized, "No matter what the agency recommends—even if all of us liked it—the franchisees will reject it. BBDO has no friends in the franchisee community. Not one. It's time to say good-by." Larry and Jeff added their support to my recommendation.

Ken Horstmeyer, a very bright man, questioned this recommendation at length. In the middle of one of his questions, Les interrupted him. "Gentlemen," he said, "I have made up my mind. We are going to fire BBDO."

Ken rolled his eyes, smiled and said, "Well, it's your funeral. I don't know of very many agencies who could give anybody a campaign like 'Have It Your Way'. I think you're making a terrible mistake to throw them out. I'm not sure that Tom Dillon, an old friend of mine, really understands the seriousness of the situation. Why don't you meet with him and give the agency another chance to perform. What's another sixty days?"

Les was not persuaded; he was adamant. He obviously felt he needed to be decisive, particularly with his old rival, Ken. He said, "We need to show the franchisees we are listening to them and get on with it." Another translation of Les's point of view was that he wanted to show everybody who was in charge.

The die was cast. The agency which had developed the brilliant "Have It Your Way" campaign was to be fired less than three years after the campaign began.

"Taking Stock"

As we prepared to fire BBDO, Burger King was a much different company than the one BBDO had been hired to shape up six years before. Burger King was a strong number two in the fast-food hamburger arena, not one of several would-be challengers to McDonald's.

Further, my goal to make Burger King the fast-food industry marketing leader was within reach. We were the innovator in promotions. We had perfected menu management. Our market research was the best in the industry. And, we had made a major investment in people. By 1976, the internal staff had quadrupled; we had experienced experts in all facets of fast food marketing, except public relations.

Still, we had only started the Burger Wars. We had not won. Our sales per restaurant still lagged far behind McDonald's. I was sure that to "win" the Burger Wars we had to finish the task of becoming the industry leader in all aspects of marketing a chain restaurant system.

To do this, I knew we had to address four major areas in which we lagged McDonald's. The biggest battle was to win over kids. In addition, we had to find more new items to broaden the menu; we had to improve the in-restaurant décor, and, somehow, we had to match McDonald's marketing public relations efforts.

But first, we had to find the right advertising agency partner.

Lessons Learned

1. Periodic planning meetings outside the office with the agency and all key personnel are invaluable. If structured properly, they can be the

best vehicle available to build consensus for marketing strategies and tactics. Further, they are invaluable as on-the-job-training for your staff.
2. To achieve marketing success, the importance of understanding two fundamentals cannot be overstated.

- The customer decision-making process—Every market has such a decision process; few marketers delve into it deep enough. Until we understood the crucial role of Mom with the kids in the choice of fast-food restaurants, we had a flawed plan.

- A promotion plan to build sales from existing customers—Too often, ninety percent of a marketer's focus is on attracting new customers and advertising to get them. At Burger King we learned that building added frequency of purchase, and gaining higher dollar sales from every existing customer was an easier and less expensive method to build sales.

Final Comment

Chapters 6 and 7 are really a case study from the client's point of view of how BBDO lost the Burger King account. Sadly, the relationship was doomed by the agency's own actions.

BBDO destroyed client trust by simply not telling the truth about working on kids' advertising. Why they did this is an open question to this day.

BBDO never sought to build a mutual respect relationship with the Burger King marketing people. Instead, the agency people were openly disdainful of their client until Bob Rees was hired. (To this day I believe that Bob could have solved this had he been put on the account sooner.)

BBDO people never understood or accepted that Burger King was a retail entity, not a packaged-goods brand. *The agency always tried to adapt Burger King to packaged-goods tactics, rather than to try to adapt packaged-goods tactics to Burger King.*

And, finally, BBDO people never understood how to interact with the franchisees. They were never effective salesmen to an audience that was critical to their success.

CHAPTER 8
Switching Agencies

(An Unforgettable Experience)

The experience of firing BBDO and then conducting the search for a new agency for Burger King is my most vivid business memory.

It was the second and last time I successfully bet my career at Burger King. And, it was the final step in building the marketing juggernaut I had been seeking at Burger King.

It all started July 1, 1976, the day of reckoning for our relationship with BBDO. The day dawned warm and amazingly clear for a summer day in New York. So, Jeff, Les, and I walked to the agency.

To the usual morning swarm of commuters scattering northward to their offices along Madison Avenue, the three of us certainly could not have caused a curious glance. As we walked southward on the avenue the ad world had made famous, we were probably only a minor annoyance to get around. After all, who walks toward Grand Central at 9:00 in the morning?

Of the three, Les was the most nervous. It wasn't his turf. He inquired, "How long do you think this will take? We have a luncheon date, you know, with Morris Bailey and Tom McMillan (two of the major New York Burger King franchisees)."

I answered rather more confidently than I felt, "I would guess this won't be more than half an hour—unless Tom Dillon wants to make a last ditch appeal. I suspect they know why we are here. Agree, Jeff?"

Jeff said nothing, but indicated with a slight nod of his head that he agreed.

That exchange was the only conversation we had from the time we left the Essex House until we reached BBDO at 46th and Madison. The agency was in an old building with elevators that bounced you around a bit. Their executive offices were on the 11th floor.

As we emerged from the elevator, the receptionist smiled. "Good morning, Mr. Schoenleb, we have been expecting you."

"Highly unusual," I thought. "In the four years I have worked with these guys, this is the first time any receptionist ever recognized me." To put it mildly, BBDO had never been truly friendly to me.

We left the red velvet and chrome lobby as Les grumbled, "Looks like a god-damn bordello." We walked to Tom Dillon's corner office, guarded as usual by his ever-efficient secretary. "Go right in," she said.

We trooped in and immediately the three BBDO executives seated around Tom's small round conference table rose. "Welcome, welcome," greeted Tom. "I see we're all here."

We shook hands for the last time with Tom, Bob Rees, and Bruce Crawford. Both Bob and Bruce were obviously very ill at ease, but Tom had on his "another client meeting" demeanor.

Coffee was ordered. For what seemed like an eternity, we made small talk waiting for it to be poured. Finally, about ten minutes after we arrived, the amenities were over.

There was a very awkward silence. Finally, I broke it in my usual blunt way. "Well, I guess it's time to get to work." ("A horrible beginning," I thought. "You can do better than that.")

I tried again, as everyone looked up from their coffee, seemingly hanging on my every monosyllable. (I wondered if I had combed my hair.) "Tom, Bruce, Bob, we're here today to talk about the future of our relationship with BBDO. We have, as you well know, not been happy. Our adult advertising has been going downhill fast—with unbelievably poor test scores—and, more important, despite what we see as Herculean effort by Bob since he joined the account, we have no kids advertising and—"

Tom interrupted my painful monologue. "But, you do agree we're getting closer, don't you?"

"Well," I answered, "I'm not sure. Because, in truth Tom, we have really lost faith in your ability to solve our needs—not from an account group standpoint—but from a creative standpoint—what you call your bread and butter, your copy. We had a long management meeting. We reviewed where we were with you and said, in essence, we had to decide on whether we are willing to give you the time Bob tells me is needed to solve the problem. And Tom, Bruce, quite simply, we decided No."

"And so," I rushed to conclusion, "we want to terminate our relationship in accordance with our contract with you."

A short silence ensued. Tom broke it. "I see. Well I guess the jig's up. I can't say I agree with your decision. We're mighty proud of our work for Burger King. But obviously this is not a decision you reached lightly. And we, of course, must accept it. Have you chosen a successor?"

"No," Les and I replied almost in unison.

"Well, we will be prepared to help in any way we can with the transition to the new agency you select," Bruce Crawford said.

Following our preset plan if they expressed willingness to work with us, I replied, "If it's OK with you, we would like to give you ninety-days notice instead of sixty and that you remain our agency until September 30. We think we will need at least eight weeks to select your successor."

Having been offered an extra two million dollars in billings, Tom Dillon readily agreed.

And so the deed was done. It took a total of twenty minutes. We waved good-by to the receptionist, never to see BBDO again, and began our walk back to the hotel.

"Well, that went relatively smoothly," I said.

"Yeah, I am surprised they didn't raise a bigger fuss," Jeff said.

"Why? They knew that with me present there was no appeal," Les said.

"Yeah, but twenty-five million dollars went out the window. I wonder if they will ever realize how they blew this account. There's absolutely no reason for this to have ever happened," I raged.

It was quiet for the remainder of the walk back to the Essex House.

Selecting Agency Candidates

When we announced the firing of BBDO, we were ill prepared for the outpouring of advertising agency interest in Burger King. In three days we received inquiries from over one-hundred agencies around the country. It was clear that Burger King was considered a "plum" to be plucked.

I had not thought through exactly how we would conduct a search for a new agency. To rectify this, I met with Larry Krueger and Jeff Campbell. We adopted a two-part plan.

First, I would call Paul Harper, CEO of Needham, Harper, & Steers, McDonald's agency and my alma mater. I would offer the Burger King account to Needham and guarantee them the same billing income as the agency had with McDonald's. Clearly this would be the perfect move, as well as an outstanding competitive strategy, if we could pull it off.

Second, if that did not work, and we had little hope that it would, we would embark upon a four-step agency selection process.

Step One—*Identify the "specs" for the ideal agency for Burger King.* We adopted four: size, creative reputation, familiarity with kids' advertising, and media-planning and buying capabilities.

Step Two—*Identify the agencies that seemed to fit these specs.* In all, we seriously considered about twenty-five agencies.

Step Three—*Select twelve candidates for further screening.* Our plan was to then visit each candidate agency at its offices. From this introductory visit we would select several "final" candidates, the maximum being five.

Step Four—*Have each "finalist" develop adult and kids' advertising strategies for Burger King. and proposed TV ads for these strategies.* These would be presented in a "shootout." The agency's work selected would be awarded the account. (The equivalent of $200,000,000+ account today.)

I reviewed this plan with Art Rosewall and Les Paszat. Art quickly asked, "Well, if Needham turns you down—and I'm sure they will—who's going to choose between your final candidates? We need to be part of that." I assured them that they would be part of a selection committee, although, naïvely, I hadn't really expected them to want to be involved.

In the end, the final selection committee grew to eleven. In addition to Larry, Jeff, Art, Les, and myself, Rosewall insisted that Ken Horstmeyer and his two key operations VPs, Bob Bryant of Franchise Operations, and Jerry Ruenheck, of Company Store Operations be included. He also added two Pillsbury representatives, Mal McNiven, VP of Advertising, and Lou Neeb, president of Steak 'n Ale. And, at Ken's suggestion, I added a franchisee representative, Morris Bailey, the head of the New York ADI ad committee.

With a process in place, a timetable was set. The goal was to select a new agency by September 1. It was July 7. Our next two months would be totally consumed by the process of hiring the new Agency, unless Needham said, "Yes."

It was time to begin and, hope-against-hope, end it with one phone call. I called Paul Harper, the CEO of Needham. In as friendly and jovial manner as I could, I blurted out, "Paul, this is Chris Schoenleb. Long time no talk."

Paul, an ex-marine, answered rather stiffly, "Hello, Chris. It has been a long time since you were with us. What's on your mind?"

"Paul, I think you can guess. I would like to offer you the opportunity to be Burger King's only advertising agency, to handle all national and local advertising."

There was silence at the other end of the line. Paul finally replied, "Well, Chris, you know we have McDonald's as one of our major clients. We would have to resign McDonald's in order to do this."

"I am well aware of this, Paul. I understand how big a decision this could be for you. Please understand, as you consider this, that we can guarantee you equal income to your McDonald's business. I obviously need an answer as soon as possible, but I would be willing to wait several days for it."

Again there was silence at the other end of the line. Finally, Paul said "Chris, I will have to call you back. I'm not sure that we are interested but obviously we are honored that you would consider us for your entire business."

Paul called back about two days later and declined my offer. I don't remember his exact words, but essentially he expressed his loyalty to McDonald's and to the work Needham was doing for them.

With Needham eliminated, we immediately began to look at the other agency candidates. We started with three automatic selections

—Wells–Rich–Greene and Grey because of their prior contacts with me, and Leo Burnett, because they were Pillsbury's lead agency.

We quickly identified the other nine agencies to interview. Two were in Chicago, seven in New York. These were the only cities in which a major advertiser could look for a large full-service agency. (*Today, if I were looking for an agency, I would add Minneapolis and San Francisco*).

Our list of agencies included the two largest Chicago agencies after Leo Burnett and Needham, Foot–Cone–Belding (FCB), and Tatham–Laird–Kudner (TLK). (J. Walter Thompson Chicago had refused to be interviewed and had referred us to its New York headquarters.) In New York, the seven candidates, in addition to Wells–Rich–Greene and Grey, were Doyle–Dane–Bernbach, Cunningham Walsh, Ted Bates, SSC&B, Carl Ally, Esty, and J. Walter Thompson.

For the initial screening meeting, we allotted three hours for each Agency to "sell themselves" into the finals. Each was to present its credentials and allow time for discussion. In addition to learning more about their capabilities, we wanted to understand the personality of each Agency to try to determine if there seemed to be any "fit" with us.

Lifetime Lesson: The biggest criterion in an agency search, once capabilities have been satisfied, must be to find a cultural "fit." When client–agency cultures don't mesh it is inevitable that the agency will lose the client's business.

Selecting the Finalists

Having selected our preliminary candidates, we made a four-day trip, one day in Chicago and three days in New York, to meet with the twelve agencies. We spent approximately twelve hours each day on this task.

We went to Chicago first. I had hoped that we would have a Chicago agency. Having worked in a Chicago agency, I was convinced that the Midwestern work ethic and culture would be a far better fit with Burger King than New York.

Our first stop was Leo Burnett. On paper, they had everything and were our top candidate. To my great disappointment, we had a short unpleasant visit.

Burnett was openly paranoid that their client KFC would learn that we had visited. They wanted to keep our visit a total secret inside the agency. To accomplish this, the secretary who greeted us immediately whisked us up some backstairs to visit with the agency's chairman and its president in the chairman's office.

Once there, we did not get a briefing on the agency's capabilities. They simply showed us a reel of outstanding commercials, especially their Kellogg's kids' ads. They then advised us that Burnett "would seriously consider Burger King," if we would offer them the business without a competition between agencies.

Their approach astonished and discouraged us. We had wasted our time. There was no way, with our franchise community and our management group, that I could turn over the business to Leo Burnett without a competitive review.

We left Burnett with one less candidate. From there we went to Foote–Cone–Belding, Pizza Hut's agency. They were willing to openly talk to us and were willing to consider dropping Pizza Hut for Burger King. After three hours, however, we weren't impressed with anything about them, except Bruce Mason, their future CEO.

It was becoming apparent that we were not going to find our agency in Chicago. This was confirmed when we met with Tatham–Laird–Kudner, our last Chicago candidate.

The meeting took place from 7:00 P.M. to 10 P.M. with a deli supper provided for all participants. The TLK presentation was an embarrassment. The media presenter had actually memorized his presentation word for word. In the middle of it, he lost his way. We sat there for several minutes waiting for him to remember his presentation so he could finish.

After a fitful night's sleep, we headed for New York. I was beginning to worry that we might not have any viable candidates except Wells–Rich–Greene and Grey.

To complicate matters, Mary Wells had already wafted a rumor in New York that she was going to be awarded the Burger King business.

We quickly learned that this probably scared off one of our candidates. When we met with Doyle–Dane–Bernbach, the first question out of their CEO's mouth was, "We've heard that you're going to give this business to Wells–Rich–Greene. Is this true?"

We assured him this was not true, but the damage from the rumor had been done. We were treated to a rather ho-hum-glad-you-asked-to-see-our-credentials but-we-are-not-really-very-interested presentation. Not only was the agency tepid in its interest in Burger King, they failed to introduce us to Bill Bernbach, their founder and one of Madison Avenue's greatest creative icons.

We had visited four candidates and had no finalists. Our next stop was Wells–Rich–Greene. At that time, WRG was headquartered in the General Motors Building at 59th and Fifth Avenues. As we got off the elevator on about the 26th floor, Mary and her entire management team, tipped off by an employee stationed in the lobby, were standing in front of the elevator door. We walked out to applause and greetings from every member of their top management team. And, of course, I got an embrace from Mary.

Larry, Jeff, and I were absolutely wowed. For the first time, we felt like there was someone who really wanted our business. *Wanting our business and communicating this, became the key screen in this first selection process. If we didn't feel a real passion for our business from an agency, we quickly eliminated it.* We knew how hard the work would be once we hired the agency. We knew they needed this passion to have a chance to be a successful in the Burger King culture.

The three hours at Wells–Rich–Green were almost anticlimactic after our greeting. We were happy after seeing their credentials, viewing their superb creative reel, and meeting more of their people. The agency would indeed be one of our finalists.

Larry Krueger remarked as we left, "I will remember that greeting all my life."

The final candidate the first day in New York was Cunningham & Walsh. We didn't know anything about Cunningham & Walsh. But, after three hours of meeting with them, we were totally unimpressed.

Their presentation was "amateur hour." They presented to us in a small outdated auditorium with uncomfortable wooden seats. They used a public address system to talk at us, not talk with us. They seemed to have prepared their presentation an hour before we arrived. They kept fumbling over their presentation materials and came off as a totally unorganized group.

As we left Cunningham & Walsh, it was close to 10:00 P.M. Jeff Campbell turned to me and summed up all our feelings, "Well, this has been quite an experience already. I can hardly wait for tomorrow."

We headed up town to our hotel, the Pierre. This was the first and only time I ever stayed at the Pierre Hotel. I was afraid it might send the wrong message about our lifestyle to the agencies. However, it was the only place we could get rooms. You see, the Democratic Convention was in town. We were told that the Democrats wouldn't stay in the Pierre because it was Richard Nixon's favorite hotel.

On the third day, we finally found two more candidates.

We started at Ted Bates, one of the largest agencies in our search. We had chosen Bates not only for its childrens' TV work, but also because we knew of the disciplined marketing approach it had made famous over the years.

We were surprised when we walked through the entrance to the agency. There was a large waiting room but initially we saw no one in it, not even a receptionist. Then one man appeared near the door to the agency offices from the reception room. He stood about five feet four inches. He was Bob Jacoby, chairman. He had cleared the room and waited patiently for us to arrive. (I had decided to always be about ten minutes late so as not to show eagerness to any of our candidate agencies.)

Bates did not disappoint us. We saw a disciplined marketing approach, strong account team, and a good creative reel—not the inspiring reels we had seen from Leo Burnett and Wells–Rich–Greene—but good solid creative.

As we left, I looked at my two partners, Larry and Jeff, and both nodded their heads. Jeff said, "Well, I say they are a finalist unless four others are better."

From Bates we went to SSC&B for lunch and their credentials presentation. We were now beginning to relax. We added a fun new item in our rating of an agency, namely the greeting we received. Would any top WRG's or Bates'?

SSC&B was located on top of the Dag Hammerskjöld Plaza Building overlooking the United Nations. It occupied the top three floors. When we arrived, a receptionist who was one of the most beautiful women I had ever seen greeted us. "Their greeting is a ten," Jeff whispered, as we gawked at her.

We were immediately ushered into the chairman's office, a huge office that would have been equal to, or better than, the chairman of General Motors or any other major corporation's office. Complete with a monstrous oriental rug and obviously expensive antique furniture, this room was overwhelming in its opulence.

After some rather stiff introductions, we were taken to a private dining room next to the chairman's office. This spacious room also had an outside balcony overlooking the city. There, served by waiters in tuxes, we were offered cocktails and served a luncheon that must have been catered from one of the gourmet restaurants of New York. We spent ninety minutes in elegance.

I didn't know about my comrades, but I felt totally out of place. The chemistry was not going to be right with this agency.

I almost changed my mind when we went to the business part of SSC&B's presentation. We were surprised to find our old friend, Dick Mercer from BBDO presenting their creative. He was pitched as the creative group head for our business. However, the rest of the agency didn't seem to have the strength of services or the personality we desired. Also, the opulence bothered us, particularly when we thought of our franchisees coming to visit.

Indeed as we left, Jeff Campbell made a comment to SSC&B's chairman that I shall never forget. (I suspect he never has either.) "You know," Jeff said, "if you ever decide to close down your agency, you could turn this office into a five star hotel rather quickly!" To top off the opulence, SSC&B insisted on giving us a ride in a limousine to our next appointment Carl Ally—a distance of about six blocks.

After the SSC&B penthouse, the totally informal Carl Ally was almost a relief. Carl greeted us with his tie loosened, his shirttail out, and invited us to a presentation in the agency conference room. There were cardboard cups, some coffee and cookies and soft drinks offered on a metal tray that was used to carry copy around the agency.

Ally was by the far the smallest of the agencies we had selected for initial interviews. It was clear that if we hired Carl we would have major problems with network and spot television buying. Ally simply wasn't big enough to do the kind of job that we knew had to be done.

However, Carl wowed us with his passion for Burger King, and his passion for great creative. When we left, I was absolutely convinced that we had another finalist. All three of us agreed that Carl would put on a great show for our selection committee. "Who knows", I opined, "He might find another creative home run like 'Have It Your Way.' "

We went into the final day confident that we already had enough candidates—three candidates that were totally different—the full service creative powerhouse, Wells–Rich–Greene, the smaller creative dynamo, Carl Ally, and the buttoned-up marketing agency, Bates.

Our last day in New York proved as surprising as the previous two. First, we met with Grey. We were, of course, greeted by Ed Meyer who seemed to fondly remember every word I had ever said to him at P&G those many years ago. Grey quickly conveyed to us, via its presentation style and its proposal that we have an early box lunch brought into the meeting room, that it was "a working man's agency." They were also "smarter than the average bear." Grey gave a brilliant presentation of their marketing prowess. They outdid Bates in every facet of marketing strategy and planning.

We became convinced they were the smartest marketing people we had ever met. In fact, Larry Krueger thought that they ought to be a marketing consulting company, particularly after we looked at their creative reel. We were all concerned about their creative. But we had another finalist.

At this point, I was ready to go home. We had four strong candidates, and I was sure that the last two candidates were throwaways. We had chosen Esty because of their work with Nabisco, but we had not been really impressed with much else they had done. When we went there, we were totally unimpressed. It reminded us of an agency in the '30s, from the way the secretaries dressed to the formality and almost back-in-time look of the whole agency.

Last, we had added J. Walter Thompson simply because it was the largest U.S. agency, and we knew they had tremendous media buying capabilities. I was not expecting much. JWT had a stuffy somewhat old-fashioned image in the ad world.

How wrong I was! From the moment we walked into J. Walter Thompson, there was feeling of "fit." We had not encountered such enthusiasm for our business since we had left Carl Ally. When the JWT team, led by their chairman, Don Johnston, finished their credentials presentation, we had seen a good creative reel, a great media buying capability, and wonderful market research ability. Most of all we instinctively liked their people, especially the New York president, Ron Sherman, who was pitched as the man to run our account.

We left JWT and the Graybar building on an emotional high. We quickly agreed that we had five agencies for our creative "shoot-out"—Wells–Rich–Greene, Ted Bates, Carl Ally, Grey, and J. Walter

Thompson. "Now that this's done," remarked Larry, "Let's get it announced so that Chris and I can go to the Olympics." Indeed, we were going to Montreal the following week as guests of ABC as part of sponsorship of the Olympics. Jeff would stay home to keep the selection process going.

Our selections made headlines in all of the ad media press. Ours was the biggest account that had been put into play in years.

Seven Weeks of Chaos

The finalists had seven weeks to put together their proposals for the selection committee.

To keep a level playing field we provided each finalist agency a written description of the assignment to develop a presentation of a proposed marketing strategy for Burger King along with proposed advertising creative for adults and for children. We also gave them a stack of all the consumer research that had been conducted on Burger King.

In addition, we set up presentations from Dr. Saul Ben-Zev to each agency to tell what he had learned about the children's market. We had hired my old friend to give us new insights into the kid's market, and he had not disappointed us.

Last, we gave each finalist free access to talk with the franchisees or any member of Burger King management. Jeff would make sure no question was unanswered.

Then Larry and I and our wives went to the Olympics. It was there that we learned how interesting the days would be until the finalists made their presentations. As we sat in the stadium for the opening day ceremonies, we found a very familiar man sitting next to us, Ed Meyer of Grey. Larry in his barb-tongued wit chuckled, "How convenient. Isn't it unbelievable what can happen by chance."

After the Olympics, it was a chaotic time of phone calls, questions, visits from creative groups, etc. I spent almost all of my time helping make sure each agency had whatever it requested and had every question answered.

I was well aware that I had bet my job once again. If the finalist agencies failed to develop a program that the selection committee could agree was a winner, and unanimously endorse it, Burger King marketing would be in chaos. We would have great franchisee dissatisfaction, and I would lose credibility with my bosses.

With this in mind I carefully set the order of the agency presentations to the selection committee. I wanted a strong marketing agency to lead off—but an agency that probably wouldn't be the winner. Therefore I scheduled Bates to lead off. Following Bates, I wanted to have a candidate to open up the selection committee's mind to the importance of creative. This meant Carl Ally had to be second.

Then I put the other three finalists—the agencies that seemed to have the best chance of winning—in the final three slots: Grey on Wednesday, Wells–Rich–Greene on Thursday, and JWT the final day.

About three weeks before the presentations, I was so worried about the selection process that I decided to go back to New York to visit each finalist. I had to make sure that each agency understood the assignment. I also wanted to get an indication of each agency's thinking, and another feel for their cultures.

I visited each finalist for a half-day "workshop" and a social lunch or dinner. *It was a superb learning experience.* Each agency handled my visit very differently. Each visit was a microcosm of how each had decided to sell themselves.

I met Bates the first afternoon. It was obvious from the moment I came that they were clumsily playing to my ego. They fawned over my P&G background. They shared research findings that they said showed how smart I had been. Somehow they were not believable. I felt "used."

At dinner they added to my discomfort. They took me to one of the gourmet restaurants in New York and ordered a French wine that cost in the neighborhood of $500. I couldn't believe they thought this was the kind of treatment I really expected as a client.

Next I went to Carl Ally. We met all morning and I was pleasantly surprised by the work he and his creative partner, Amil Gargano, were doing.

He also totally surprised me when he took me to lunch. We went to a private club on 58th Street and ate with "the beautiful people," some of whom were sunning themselves in bikinis on the rooftop. I don't remember the name of the club but I was totally impressed with Carl's easy familiarity with the New York scene. I had grown to like Carl a lot.

From there I went to Wells–Rich–Greene. Again, Mary was charming. More important, the agency's preliminary thinking was sound and the people designated for assignment on our business were impressive. Charley Fredericks took me to a most unusual dinner. We ate in the kitchen of Christ Cella's. For some reason, I liked this kind of special treatment as opposed to the Bates approach, even though I suspect it was almost as expensive as the Bates extravaganza.

Next I went to Grey. We met all morning. We had lunch in their conference room, of course. Again a workmanlike organization sent a workmanlike message. I was not impressed with Joel Wayne, Grey's creative director. I continued to worry about whether we would get the kind of creative we needed from Grey. I was, however, totally impressed with the agency's marketing people.

Lastly, I went to JWT. Once again I was surprised and impressed. Not only was I peppered with an excellent barrage of questions, particularly on media, but when it came to discussing creative, I was surrounded at a dinner with the creative directors from their three major domestic offices. Two of them totally impressed me and became lifelong business friends—Ralph Rydholm, creative director from Chicago, and Burt Manning from New York. Both had superb agency careers. Both went on to become chairmen of major agencies.

When I left New York, I was reassured that there would be a great show for our selection committee. I didn't know who was going to win, but I was sure that Bates had the longest odds. JWT and Ally had impressed me the most.

There was one final surprise before the presentations.

Don Johnston, chairman of JWT called me. He said, "I hear you have a favorite restaurant in Miami, The Depot."

I smiled at his detective work. "Yes," I said. "It is indeed my favorite restaurant."

He said, "I understand there's even a menu dish named after you, "Crab au Schoenleb."

"Yes, there is that dish, but it's not named after me, it's named after my wife. Joanne asked them to fix crab in a certain way and they did. They liked it so much they put it on the menu."

"Can you and your wife join my wife and I next Thursday night at The Depot?"

"Sure—we'd love to."

"Good, we'll meet you there at eight o'clock."

We dutifully arrived and were surprised again. In addition to his wife, Don had brought his young son who must have been about ten or eleven years old. He said, "I know how important kids' advertising is to you so I brought along our son simply to let you know that we understand."

It was a delightful dinner; Don made it clear that JWT was "pulling out all the stops" to win.

Selecting a Winner

Finally, August 23 arrived. All the preliminary maneuvers were at an end. The week of agency presentations was at hand.

It would be quite a week. Five of Madison Avenue's "finest" pitching for the Burger King business and much more—the prestige of beating out their peers for a major client.

My task for the week was to manage the process to assure that each agency got a fair hearing and that a winner was chosen.

My goal was to gain a unanimous choice, the choice favored by Jeff, Larry, and myself. This meant I had to manage the selection committee. I had to make sure that the diverse egos on the committee were made an integral part of the process so that no one could criticize the proceedings later. This also meant, of course, that the process had to allow each committee member an equal vote—a fact that worried me because we had more nonmarketers voting than marketers.

I tried to leave nothing to chance. I even set up a "politically correct" seating chart for the meeting room. The committeee would sit at one long table with Les and Art flanking me in the "seats of power" those in the middle of the table.

Managing the selection process began the Friday before presentation week. I briefed the committee about the background of each agency. I was extremely careful not to share any of my feelings about the agencies. *The committee had to believe all the agencies were viable candidates.*

I explained how the committee would function. I introduced an agency selection criteria sheet—one for each agency—that the committee members were to use for their notes. Finally I outlined the day-to-day schedule. Even though the presentations would last no more than three hours I had scheduled only one agency presentation each day. I wanted a fresh selection committee for each presentation.

The presentations were to be made in the main ballroom of the Sonesta Beach Hotel on Key Biscayne. The committee would sit at its long table in about the center of the room with the agency having the front half of the room to use as they saw fit.

After each presentation the selection committee would have lunch with the presenting agency. There the committee could get a further feel for cultural chemistry as well as discuss any lingering questions from the morning.

To complete each day, the selection committee would meet in a separate room at the hotel to discuss that day's presentation by the candidate agency. In this meeting I hoped to gain consensus daily and thus eliminate a candidate each day. The goal: to have only two agencies to discuss on the last day.

Day One: Bates

Day One arrived. I was immediately reminded of my longheld belief about sunny days and smiled. *Every day would be sunny in Florida.*

I left the house in a very anticipatory mood. Bates was first up and I was hopeful they would make a credible showing. I knew they had done their homework from a marketing standpoint.

I picked up Larry Krueger, who lived nearby, at 7:45 A.M. We drove to the office with no meaningful dialogue. Larry rarely truly woke up before 9:00 A.M., particularly when he hadn't had coffee. We picked up Jeff at Burger King and drove to Key Biscayne. Our conversation was about trifles, mostly the exhibition Dolphin–Giant football game over the weekend.

We were obviously psychologically "up" for this. And, of course, we each made a silent prayer for Day One, "Make it good enough to keep our credibility, Ted Bates, please."

All three of us were in agreement that we did not want Bates to win. We really didn't like their people. Jeff was the most negative.

For each agency presentation, we arrived about 8:30 A.M. for coffee and rolls and "small talk" between the agency presenters and our committee. I had hoped this would get everyone acquainted before the presentations started. Naïvely I had thought it would help break the tension that was so palpable in the room before each agency's presentation began. Instead it added to the strain.

To say that everyone was uptight, including the committee, grossly understates the grip that tension held on the room each morning. When the committee finally seated themselves at the long "politically correct" table facing the agency presenters it was almost a relief to all parties.

The Bates presentation went about as expected. Bob Jacoby was very impressive in his presentation of the agency's capabilities. But, after we had had a coffee break, Bates's strategy and recommendations for Burger King were mediocre.

As expected, however, Bates's consumer research was excellent. As we soon learned, each agency would have a different take on our business. *In fact, one of the great benefits of any agency search that includes "spec" creative is that you get free marketing consulting.*

Following Bates's marketing presentation, Irv Sohn showed proposed advertising. Irv was my old friend from Needham who had written the "So Tender You Can Cut It With a Feather" copy for General Mills so many years ago. He showed us three campaigns. All three were, in my opinion, disasters, partly because the agency had done sloppy fact-finding.

The first, "Everything's a Whopper at Burger King" was a legally questionable use of the sandwich name and the wrong promise, bigness. The second, "Burger King, Fresh Food not just Fast Food" was a good promise, but not legally supportable. Burger King used frozen beef. The last campaign, "Burger King. Now you know better," had promise but had dull TV executions. Then Irv showed kids' advertising. I liked it a lot better. For the first time in four years, I saw some imaginative kids' advertising.

With that, the presentation was over. Then as we would do each day, a photographer took pictures for future publicity, and we adjourned for lunch.

At lunch, I sat with the creative folks and asked them how difficult the assignment had been. Irv replied, "Very tough. We went through over two-hundred campaign ideas. All seemed trite and awful but I was very happy with what we showed you today."

After lunch, the selection committee was convened. It was chaotic but surprisingly easy. After about an hour, all agreed that we were off to a good start. Jeff summed it up best when he said, "Good pitch, good marketing, average copy, below-average people."

We were ready for Carl Ally.

Day Two: A Creative Happening

After the usual preliminaries, Carl Ally started slowly. (He didn't seem comfortable in a coat and tie.) He began by praising the briefings he had from us on the business, "We can not plead ignorance." he concluded, "We think we know all we need to know."

He then reviewed his creative reel and made a statement about his creative philosophy. He said, "You know, TV is a straight person-to-person communication and I want to tell my story straight. That's the only way it will ever work."

After the coffee break, Carl took off his jacket and loosened his tie. He became more and more animated and passionate as the morning wore on. With his passion came great conviction. Carl presented an overall positioning which surprised us. "Ignore men," he said, "If you advertise to women and kids, you will keep the men anyway. Where can they go that suits them as well as Burger King?"

More surprising yet, he presented only one campaign for both kids and adults. The basic premise of the campaign was to use kids, all kinds of kids, to talk about Burger King. Each commercial showed an older child talking to a younger child: a fourteen-year-old talking to a ten-year-old. Each informs the younger child, "Kid, when you grow up to be my age, you'll be old enough to go to Burger King."

The executions were clever. I liked them a lot and I sensed the whole committee was impressed.

Then Carl reviewed media and his organization. It was then that we saw the real weakness of the Carl Ally agency. Carl could develop great copy but his organization was short on other talent, especially in media.

Again we broke for lunch. There I told Carl, "If you don't win, it won't be because we don't like your copy. It will be because we liked someone else's better." He gave me a worried look and promised to tell Lou Kasper where he would be from Friday on.

After lunch the selection committee was again organized chaos. But, in general we agreed to an assessment of Ally. Ally eliminated Bates. But all were concerned about Ally media capabilities and the quality of the account group.

Jeff capped off the day. As we drove back to the office, he said, "Chris, your schedule was perfect. First, we get a conventional agency that's like BBDO to pitch solid but uninspiring advertising. Next, Ally, the "maniac," comes in and breaks all the rules. No food, no restaurant, etc. and we all love it! Now it's up to the other three agencies to give us what we need. The first two have paved the way."

I hoped he was right.

Day Three: A Grey Day

There were no real surprises on Day Three. It was Grey's turn. They were the most nervous of the five agencies. Ed Meyer could barely hold a coffee cup or carry on a conversation before we started.

From the beginning, Grey's presentation was an absolute smash when it came to its marketing credentials and media capabilities. We had seen nothing like this in our two previous presentations, or from BBDO. Even more impressive to us was their thorough analysis of Burger King's marketing problem. They covered all the issues, not just advertising.

Bill Overend, a senior management account director, documented from Grey's research that the overall problem Burger King had to solve was its image as a place of large sandwiches—we were not seen as a place for families or kids. To beat McDonald's, he stated we would have to change our image, change our speed of service, and improve our dining rooms. He also suggested that our building needed upgrading and redesign.

After the coffee break, Joel Wayne presented Grey's proposed creative. The basic line he presented was "Go to Burger King where you have a picnic your way." I did not like it. My notes for that day included the following statement, "Somehow they have done everything we need but I don't like it. It is just not great copy. Ally puts them to shame."

At lunch, I sat with Joel Wayne and was thoroughly bored by his pretentious statements about creative. He and I were not on the same wavelength.

At the afternoon meeting of the selection committee, it was obvious we would have no winner that day. As I listened to the committee, I realized *Grey had made the cardinal error of any agency presentation: Their people had talked "down" to us—they had lectured us.* They communicated that they were dealing with a client they saw as less well schooled in marketing than they. Simply put, they had treated us with arrogance.

Day Four: Mary Wells

The entire committee was really up for Day Four. At last, all would meet and hear from Mary Wells, the reigning creative guru on Madison Avenue, and her creative powerhouse!

What a salesperson she was! Mary lit up the room at the pre-presentation coffee. Her smiles and her obvious confidence in her agency's abilities had every committee member predisposed to like her agency's presentation.

The meeting began with Mary showing her creative reel. It was forty-five minutes of "WOW." She followed that with a video of endorsements from some of her key clients, including one I shall always remember because I was to later work for this company for ten years, the president of Midas. Unfortunately, WRG's media and market research capabilities presented after her creative reel were not nearly as impressive.

After the coffee break, WRG began to discuss Burger King. Ken Olshan, the future president of WRG, made a brilliant presentation of the marketing situation for Burger King. It was almost as good as Grey's.

He then introduced Charlie Moss and Stan Dragoti to show the proposed creative. After a long and dramatic lead-in (Charlie Moss is a master presenter) he had us almost sold that he had the advertising campaign we were looking for. Then he showed us TV ads built around the line "Everybody Gets Their Thing at Burger King."

What a letdown! The ads were too cute and not competitive enough. But, as I sat there and watched the presentation, I became more and more enamored with working with Wells–Rich–Greene. I knew that the execution of their commercials would be superb. Clearly, WRG had the creative horsepower to do better than we had seen in the presentation, and had far better media than Ally. The agency had not hit a home run, but was clearly our best choice up to this point.

Surprisingly, the committee basically agreed with me, except for Les Paszat. Les didn't like WRG. I was sure much of his dislike was very personal. Mary Wells had made a terrible mistake at lunch. Instead of chatting with Les, she had turned her back to him and snubbed him. She spent all of her time talking to Art Rosewall. Les's ego was severely wounded. It was clear Les would need lots of convincing to support selecting WRG.

As we ended Day Four, I had a problem. I did not have a unanimous committee vote for Wells–Rich–Greene. The only creative home run we had seen was Carl Ally's.

Day Five: and the winner is . . .

The day started almost like the rest of the week. I picked up Larry and we met Jeff at the office for the ride to Key Biscayne.

There were a couple of differences, however. First, I wasn't nervous. I had concluded overnight that I would find a way to hire Wells–Rich–Greene, if J. Walter Thompson didn't top them. The longer I had thought about it, even though I knew we would have all kinds of problems with Les, I knew WRG would be able to do the job.

The second difference was that I wore a coat and tie. This would be a very special day and I wanted to dress for the occasion.

As we rode, I gave my compatriots a quick review of my overall position on what we should do. They agreed, but were not enthusiastic about WRG. Then I asked how Jeff how he thought JWT would do.

"I think they will wow us," he replied.

Larry chimed in, "I think they will win. JWT surprised us once and they can do it again. And I sure hope they do!"

While I too was rooting for JWT, I bet both Larry and Jeff that WRG would top JWT on the pitch mechanics. I was sure Mary Wells was the master of agency pitches.

How wrong I was! We arrived at 8:40 A.M. and one surprise after another began to unfold.

The first surprise was that only five people from JWT were presenting. The biggest agency came with the smallest pitch team. The five were Don Johnston, Ron Sherman, Bucky Buchanan, Joel Baumwald, and Burt Manning.

The second surprise was their creative credentials pitch. It was a home run. It began with a videotape of an eleven-year-old little girl in pigtails who introduced the presentation saying, "Don't blow it J. Walter Thompson."

Don Johnston introduced the agency by attacking its staid image, saying, "We are old but we are new because we have been through a total self-renewal process."

Bucky Buchanan followed with JWT's media credentials. He awed us with their size and network clout. Bucky's most notable quote: "One out of every thirteen prime time TV commercials on network this fall will have been placed (bought) by JWT."

Then he showed the agency's spot TV buying system. JWT had a regional buying system that had eight buying offices and, of course, Bucky promised a new ninth office in Miami if we hired JWT. He introduced each head buyer on videotape. They were all women.

Seeing all the women, Art Rosewall leaned over and said, "What a way to handle equal opportunity employment."

Ron Sherman showed how the agency would organize to handle Burger King. We couldn't read the charts but we were sure it was fine.

When we broke for coffee, the committee was all smiles. You could just feel a surge of confidence in the room. JWT had given us the feeling that they were "our kind of people."

When JWT turned to Burger King after coffee, Joe Baumwald gave us our first original look at the fast-food business for the week. JWT had done a consumer segmentation study that painted a clear path for building Burger King sales. Of course, it also set up the need for building a family business, a recurring theme throughout the week.

Then it was time for TV advertising. Burt Manning was emotionally eloquent. He had us mentally comparing his passion to Carl Ally's. He spoke for a long time without showing any ads. As he was speaking, Les Paszat leaned over and asked about his creative reputation. I assured him that Manning was one of the best.

Then Burt finally showed us his first commercial. It was for kids not adults! He was very close to Carl Alley's campaign—only this was just for kids—as he presented "You are Big Enough for Burger King."

Then he showed us a second kids' campaign! He began to sell a spokesperson, a magic Burger King. I loved it! It was clearly the best kid's campaign we had seen. I looked down the selection committee table. I could see from their eyes that most of the committee agreed.

We took a break. Larry Krueger admitted he initiated the idea because he was so excited about the copy. He said, "This is so good I was afraid I would wet my pants."

We finally saw the adult copy. When we did, Burt Manning knocked the whole idea of a long committee selection discussion out the window. He hit the creative home run we sought. He showed us five distinct campaigns. I thought three were good enough to run the next day.

As Burt's presentation was winding down, Larry passed me a note. "There is an old Biblical saying 'The first shall be last and the last shall be first." I passed this to Jeff who smiled and passed back the note to me with his comment added, "There are many called but few chosen." Bob Bryant handed me a note "We who toil in the trenches vote for JWT."

There was no doubt we had a winner. It was all over but a matter of implementing an announcement and the committee hadn't even had lunch yet.

We finally ate lunch, barely able to contain ourselves. I asked Burt Manning, "Was it hard?" He said "Yes, but we kept at it."

Finally, we went into the committee meeting. As usual, I called on Jeff first. He said with hands held high and eyes angelically looking to the ceiling, "Oh thank you God." A huge guffaw followed from all committee members. Everybody was happy. JWT had won in a landslide!

I verbally reviewed the press announcement with the committee. I wanted to wait until Monday. Ken Horstmeyer suggested that I announce it now. Everybody agreed.

I went out to the lobby to find JWT and saw Ron Sherman. He was on the house phone. I walked up and asked him if he and the others could join us in the conference room. He looked dazed and said, "Sure. Right now?" I nodded, then I couldn't contain myself for another second. I grinned, held out my hand, and said, "Congratulations! You won."

With that, Ron let a very unsophisticated hoot and a holler—something like "Oh my Gaaawd" at the top of his voice.

Burt Manning was on the phone next to Sherman and overheard our conversation. He dropped the phone, grabbed Ron in a bear hug, and literally started screaming with happiness.

In seconds a very emotional scene followed in our conference room. I have never felt such total joy and happiness, before or since, in a business situation. Don Johnston actually ran up and jumped on me. He wrapped his legs around my waist and shouted, "You've got yourself an agency."

Lesson Learned

Finding the right new advertising agency is far more difficult than it appears. It is easy to find agencies that have the capabilities a client needs. But talent and resources don't determine fit. *As a client, the key to selecting your advertising agency is to identify the agency that not only fits your culture but has a true passion for your business. This agency will put its best talent on your business and work harder for you.*

Final Comment

In later years I was involved in directing the selection of a national agency for Arby's (Chapter 10) and Midas (Chapter 15). The selection process we used at Burger King was my model for both these later agency searches.

However, I was never able to replicate the depth of the review done at Burger King. I am sure one of the big reasons for this was that I was never ever again surrounded by talent as strong as Larry Krueger and Jeff Campbell to help make the process work. The other reason was JWT's team. I never saw another agency in any pitch at any company that offered the client culture fit, the talent, the creative solution, or the dedication we saw from JWT on Key Biscayne. Result: neither of these other two selections worked out as well as at Burger King. JWT would be Burger King's agency for almost ten years. None of the other agencies I helped select lasted even five years.

Today many clients use outside consultants to help select their agency. It's a lucrative business that I have thought at times might be an occupation I should seek because of my long experience in selecting agencies both large and small.

In truth, however, I believe that the use of a third party to help put an agency and client together should not be necessary. The client understands his own culture better than any third party. If he doesn't, or if he fails to understand its critical importance, then any agency selection process he uses will fail, only to be repeated again.

CHAPTER 9
Winning the Burger Wars

(Marketing to Kids and Other Successes)

In the fifteen months that followed our hiring of J. Walter Thompson, my dream of making Burger King the fast-food marketing leader came to fruition.

After hiring JWT, I promoted Jeff Campbell to take responsibility for advertising. Jeff, like Larry Krueger, was a driven man. Extremely intelligent, with great ambition, he had learned rapidly and well. Jeff also played "good guy" and easy going, versus my "tough guy" intensity, in franchisee meetings. This was an excellent way to sell our franchisees, but it gave the wrong impression of Jeff. He was so intense that he regularly used a punching bag to vent his frustrations.

"Marketing" Public Relations

With Jeff concentrating on the advertising program, I turned my attention to the one area of marketing Burger King that was not competitive versus McDonald's—marketing public relations.

What is marketing public relations? It's corporate sponsorship of "good works." It's providing funds and manpower for unique programs designed to enrich the culture or help solve a societal need such as raising funds for medical research. A marketing PR program should make a consumer "grateful" for the sponsor and therefore more likely to be a sponsor's customer.

In truth, a marketing PR program is also a promotion designed to build name recognition and long-term consumer goodwill.

McDonald's, with its agency Golan–Harris, perfected marketing PR in the '70s and remain a master of it today. The very best marketing PR program in fast food has always been McDonald's Ronald McDonald House.

In the '70s, before starting the Ronald McDonald House program, McDonald's created a goodwill program for teens, their All-American Band. An elaborate program that selected all-star musicians from high schools around the country to play as a group at a major event like the

165

Rose Bowl, it involved McDonald's in virtually every high school in the country. It gained heaps of goodwill and publicity for the company. *It was a great marketing tool because, relative to the cost of TV advertising, it gained broad public exposure remarkably cheaply.*

As I analyzed these efforts, it was clear that Burger King had to find a way to blunt McDonald's "good guy" image. We did not need to top them, but we had to get in the "game" with programs that basically communicated that Burger King was an equally "good guy."

Understanding all this, it was still a hard sell to get the franchisee marketing committee to endorse the use of several million dollars for marketing PR programs instead of purchasing TV media time. It was an equally hard sell to Les Paszat. But, finally both agreed by late 1976.

To begin this effort, we needed PR expertise for idea generation and execution of our program. I had created a Burger King public relations department in 1975. Donna Nicol had been hired to be its director. She was relatively inexperienced but very aggressive and smart, both intellectually and politically. For her first year, however, she did no marketing PR. Instead, she handled company press releases, provided ideas to get publicity for promotions, and answered consumer letters.

Clearly, we did not have a marketing PR program. To develop one, we needed to hire a major PR agency.

Accordingly, Donna and I conducted a rather perfunctory agency search. We knew that there were only a few large PR agencies that met our specs for size and manpower. Unlike our searches for an advertising agency or a promotion agency, we made no attempt to "steal" McDonald's agency. Our budget would be less than thirty percent of what we estimated McDonald's was spending.

Within a month we hired one of the largest PR firms in America, Burson–Marsteller. Jim Dowling, who was running the Chicago office, made an impressive presentation that convinced us he understood what we needed. He became our management director, even though the account group operated out of New York. Aggressive and smart, Jim eventually became CEO of Burson.

Burson's assignment: develop a unique PR program that would appeal to families with kids. It had to be a big idea, one that would engender ongoing press and public involvement. In short, we sought a program that would match the influence we saw McDonald's getting year after year. Not an easy task.

Putting It All Together

With the addition of Burson, I finally had a complete marketing team in place. Burger King had three of the largest and best agencies in the world. And, internally, there was a strong experienced team under Jeff Campbell and Larry Krueger.

We were finally in a position to truly become the marketing force in fast food. We had the army to win the Burger Wars.

To mold this new team, and plan our 1977 program, I held a JAPS meeting in Manitowoc, Wisconsin, in late October.

It was a very successful meeting. The arrogance of BBDO was gone; finally mutual respect existed between the client and all its agencies. More important, there was an instant partnership between Rogers's organization, RMI, and JWT. They even began to work together without the third party assistance of the client.

The 1977 adult program came relatively easy. We knew we had to begin the process of changing our image from " Home of the Whopper" to "The Best Fast Food Restaurant for Families."

For adult TV advertising we no longer had "Have It Your Way." We had replaced it with JWT's new campaign designed to start the process of replacing McDonald's. The TV stated, "America Loves Burgers and We're America's Burger King." It was an interim campaign that we planned to replace within eighteen months.

For promotion we adopted two unique ideas. The first was a lucky home run. We ran a "Star Wars" glass promotion to tie in with the first *Star Wars* movie. Coke offered us the rights to show a different "Star Wars" character on each of four glasses. We had no idea, of course, what a phenomena *Star Wars* would be. Each glass sold out in three or four days. We could not get enough to supply demand.

The second promotion was an unusual follow-up to our Bicentennial poster promotion. We had learned the Olympic Committee was moving from New York to Colorado Springs and setting up an Olympic Training Center to make the United States more competitive in future Olympics. The Committee was looking for a sponsor to pay $750,000 for the Training Center's first-year expenses.

I thought, "Why not Burger King?" It would generate enormous publicity as a "good work." It could be our first marketing PR program. More than this, it was a major competitive move to overcome McDonald's ownership of the right to the word "Olympic." The symbol for the Training Centers was very similar to the Olympic symbol itself.

When queried the three agencies agreed it should be pursued. If the money could be found, they would develop ads, PR, and promotions to tie in with our sponsorship.

I then went to Pillsbury and requested that the company donate $750,000 to the Olympic Training Center in the name of Burger King so that we could become its official sponsor. (Legally, I could not use the ad fund monies for this.) The Pillsbury Foundation turned down the request.

I was very disappointed, but determined to find a way to salvage the tie-in. At the JAPS meeting we discussed the issue. Once again, Rogers Brackmann came to the rescue. He proposed that instead of donating money, we raise the money from consumers at the Burger King restaurants. He pointed out that this would create awareness of our tie-in, not only with our customers, but also with another very important constituency, our restaurant crews.

His method to do this? Sell a unique self-liquidating premium to raise money for the Olympic Training Center. Specifically, Rog recommended that we go back to Leroy Neiman and ask him to paint an "Olympic" poster. Then we would make high quality, full-sized copies of this poster and sell them at every Burger King in the country.

Under this scenario the program would not cost the company or franchisees a nickel. The total cost of the program would be about $250,000 for the painting, the printing, and shipping of the posters to the stores. If we sold one million of them at $1 a piece, we would raise the $750,000. (With 2,000 restaurants that meant each one only had to sell fifty.)

The new agency–client team liked the idea. Later, when we presented it to the marketing committee, the franchisees readily endorsed it. Result: Burger King became the first official sponsor of the Olympic Training Center.

Olympic officials and I jointly announced the sponsorship at a national press conference. This generated a spate of excellent publicity that was more than enough to justify the whole program.

We had little trouble selling one million posters, but their sale had no effect on overall restaurant sales. This lack of effect caused some franchisees to grumble that the Olympic Training Center sponsorship was a waste of money. Sadly, this attitude killed the program after the first year. The franchisees had no interest in finding ways to raise the needed funds for the following year.

To this day, I believe this was a mistake—a great marketing PR coup was lost.

Kids' Marketing Strategy

In contrast to the adult program, the 1977 kids' marketing program did not come easy. We were starting from scratch at this JAPS meeting. In fact, we basically agreed that we could not have a major new program in 1977—that the agencies needed the year to develop a complete program.

But, unlike previous meetings, we made significant progress. When we left Wisconsin, the die had been cast. We had agreed on the foundation for building a Burger King kids' program—a spokesperson.

We did this based on the consumer research Dr. Saul Ben-Zev had done for us just prior to our firing BBDO. We had thought that this report gave us the blueprint for a Burger King kids' program, and we had directed that these findings be presented to the five agency finalists.

Essentially Dr. Ben-Zev had offered two conclusions from his interviews of kids and mothers.

"First," he said, "Remember that kids are greedy. Bribe them with toys and they will want to come. *You should always have something special for kids*—and I don't mean just the crown like you do now. That's Okay, but its not news. *You need a constant stream of new items.*"

"Second," he continued, "you need a spokesperson—a real person—not an animated king. *And, I believe you should consider having this person be a magician. Kids love magic.*"

For JWT's winning creative presentation, Burt Manning had translated this research into creating a "real-person" Burger King, who did magic, as the spokesperson. We had liked the idea, but Burt and his team, headed by the now-famous author, James Patterson, had not truly fleshed out the concept into a complete marketing program.

The question at the JAPS meeting was simple, "Do we move ahead with a program built around a Magic Burger King?"

After a long discussion over the viability of replacing the old animated Burger King symbol with a real person, we unanimously agreed to adopt the new king. The task then would be to develop imaginative advertising, promotion, and PR using the Burger King in the same integrated fashion that we saw McDonald's do every day with Ronald McDonald.

This was to me the ultimate challenge. There was no marketing battle that I ever wanted to win more than this one. As the JAPS meeting ended, I summed up the task, this way, "Let's take the next six to nine months and get a Magic Burger King program put together that we know will blow Ronald McDonald right out of the water. We failed once in the kids' arena; this may be our last chance to attack the kids' market."

"Many inside Burger King and many franchisees already think we're wasting our efforts. McDonald's is too strong, they say. I don't believe that for a minute. What I do believe is that for Burger King to be the Number One fast-food hamburger chain, we have to beat the Ronald McDonald kids' program. We all believe we're the best. If we are—the proof will be in the pudding—if, next fall, we can launch a kids' program that beats McDonald's at its own game."

Corporate Battles Won

As the client–agency team came together, I also achieved two of my long-term goals within the company.

Having heard all of the agency finalists criticize our restaurant interiors, NDC finally agreed that the company needed to upgrade its restaurant dining rooms and become more competitive with McDonald's. I was given the task of developing this décor package.

After a brief review of potential firms to work on this program, I hired Bischoff–Lincoln. The firm had done excellent work for several fast-food restaurant chains, most notably Pizza Hut. What added to their appeal for me was the firm's owner, Phil Lincoln. My old friend from Needham and American Motors had formed Bischoff–Lincoln with a designer partner, Paul Bischoff.

I was pleased to hire a good friend for this task. *I have never understood those who preach not to hire friends. My experience has always been that when you know a person, communication is much easier. And, I believe a friend will always give you his firm's best work.*

Within six months, Bischoff–Lincoln was installing new décor packages in several restaurants in Miami on a test basis to determine whether the change in décor could actually increase business enough to justify the investment.

My other long-term goal was to assume management responsibility for all menu development in the company. Finally, in mid-1975, Les Paszat assigned me this responsibility and empowered me to hire a director of menu development.

At the same time we also built a state-of-the-art test kitchen. This finally gave Burger King the physical capability for an ongoing new product and product improvement program. Prior to this time, all menu development had been done in the kitchen of the Burger King restaurant nearest the headquarters' building.

The first new menu item developed was the chicken sandwich that is still on the menu today. Ironically, this sandwich was developed for economic reasons, not to fill an identified consumer demand. Basically, we were looking for a low-cost alternative to hamburger. Hamburger had risen as high as $1.00 per pound forcing our Whopper price to ninety-nine cents. We felt we needed a lower-cost sandwich to keep price value in the menu. This led us to chicken and a chicken sandwich.

John Barnes did most of the work developing the sandwich, but I had not seen him as the man to run the Menu Development department. Result: as we were introducing the new sandwich, John left the company and went to McDonald's.

We rolled out the chicken sandwich systemwide in 1976-77. It was the first chicken sandwich to be sold in a national hamburger chain, and it was a major success. It created an immediate sales increase in virtually every Burger King in the country.

A Rude Awakening

As 1977 dawned, I could not have been more pleased with my Burger King career. In five years, I had built a marketing juggernaut—a strong staff and a set of dedicated enthusiastic agencies.

Inside Burger King, I finally had all of the key elements necessary to have a cohesive marketing program for the company under my direction, advertising, promotion, public relations, menu development, store design and décor.

And I was working for a CEO who had promised me that I would be his successor.

January 1977 was, therefore, the time I least expected my future at Burger King to be forever changed. I don't remember exactly the day, but I do remember the shock. Art Rosewall called in the key executives of Burger King to a meeting. One man was missing, Les Paszat. Les had been fired, for reasons never really spelled out. Art would take control until a new president was hired. I had lost my mentor, and as events unfolded, a whole lot more.

I was not considered for the presidency. It was made clear that the new president would be hired from the outside. And he was. At the end of January in a move that shocked the restaurant world, Don Smith accepted the presidency of Burger King. Don was a big surprise because he had been named president of McDonald's about January 1st.

Don Smith became my fourth boss in five years. He came into Burger King like a whirlwind. Standing about five feet ten inches, wearing horn-rimmed glasses, he was a man who seemed to be in perpetual motion. He was what Pillsbury had sought "an operations man." He had risen through the ranks in store operations in McDonald's.

In retrospect, Pillsbury was absolutely right. An "operations man" was exactly what Burger King needed at that point in its history. The company's marketing prowess far exceeded its in-restaurant customer service and its method of food preparation. But no one was quite prepared for the personality and style of Don Smith.

For the first two months, Smith started his management takeover of the company in purchasing and operations. He had an immediate effect on the business. Suppliers who had been selling both Burger King and McDonald's quickly found that they would have to give Burger King the same price as McDonald's or lose the business.

Smith also immediately set out to revamp the company organization under a model that would emulate McDonald's. In the process, Don Smith obliterated the twenty-year culture of Burger King he had inherited.

The first thing he did was disband NDC. He wanted all franchising and real estate decisions decentralized to field operations headed by the region managers.

Smith's second step was to put great emphasis on training. He sold Pillsbury on a dream most senior Burger King executives had had for years but couldn't get funded, namely, to build Burger King University, an institution that would rival McDonald's fabled training school. Also, he immediately hired several people from McDonald's to manage the training area.

Going Backwards

Two of Don's other initial moves affected me directly and adversely. He left no doubt that I no longer had the status I had enjoyed under Les Paszat.

First, with no forewarning, he announced that the Menu Development department would no longer report to marketing. It would report directly to him, with John Barnes rehired to run it. Smith's explanation to me for this change, a move that was a devastating blow to my prestige inside the company, was one terse sentence that brooked no argument. He said, "Chris, I see menu development as strictly an operations responsibility. You have no business running it."

Second, it was widely rumored that Don had selected someone from McDonald's, or someone who had been at McDonald's in the past, to replace each member of the senior Burger King staff within a year. Don never denied this. I quickly learned through the rumor mill that my designated replacement was Art Guenther. Art had left a senior post in the McDonald's marketing department to be VP of Marketing for Sambo's. At about this time, Art was seeking a new job.

This "replacement tactic" angered me, but there was no real defense for it. It's a fact of corporate life that if a CEO wants you gone, you're gone. I was sure it wouldn't happen immediately. However to protect myself, I pursued an opportunity to join Long John Silver's as their senior VP of Marketing. After several months of courtship, I turned down the opportunity. When I did, I suggested they pursue Art Guenther. They did, and Art took the job, giving me one less worry.

Unfortunately the replacement rumor was handled differently by others in the management. It instilled a kind of fear that I had never seen before in Burger King. Some became frightened for their jobs and began responding to Don with a great desire to please. Several became "yes men" in a hurry.

Because I didn't initially see Don within the marketing area, we did not immediately get to know each other very well. Smith's lack of marketing involvement began to change in late March. He attended a franchisee marketing committee meeting in which we laid out the Magic Burger King kids' program for the first time.

As Don began to understand the proposed program, he agreed with it one-hundred percent. And, with his presidential "clout," he added an element to the program—the use of the Burger King distribution system to distribute kids' toys to our restaurants.

After that committee meeting, I was again left alone as I had been since joining Burger King. I was somewhat reassured that there was a chance, after a rocky start, that Smith and I could work together. However, in my gut I "knew" that it would be only a matter of time before Don Smith and Chris Schoenleb would clash. We were two strong personalities that had little in common.

Burger King Kids Program

The Burger King kids' program that we laid out at this marketing committee meeting in March 1977, was a complete approach for capturing kids in the marketplace. We sold it with little difficulty. Like Smith, the franchisees enthusiastically endorsed it.

The basic premise of the program was that Saul Ben-Zev was right. To attract children, we had to appeal to their greed. Therefore, the key element of the program would be to offer a new toy every two weeks to every child who purchased a sandwich at Burger King. Over the period of one year we would have to distribute twenty-six different toys throughout the entire Burger King system.

In addition the program would have an ongoing two-part kids' TV advertising campaign.

Part one was advertising that would introduce our real-person Burger King to children on network television. The campaign format was in many ways a copy of the Ronald McDonald campaign format with a different cast of characters and a new ingredient—magic.

JWT created a unique make-believe world inhabited by the "Magic Burger King" and friends. The King did magic tricks in every commercial. He also sang a jingle about himself, "I'm the wonderful, magical Burger King. I can do most anything. I love sandwiches and I love fun. Fun, fun, fun for everyone." The agency also developed several characters like the "Duke of Doubt" to interface with the King, much as the "Hamburgler" was a foil for Ronald McDonald.

Casting the right person to play the King was a major task. We needed a friendly, yet easily replicable individual. JWT solved this by developing a costume and a beard that would allow almost anyone to play the part who could portray an easy friendliness with children, and was around six feet tall and weighed under 220 pounds.

Part two of the program was advertising the continuity toy give-away promotion. The Magic Burger King was to hawk each free toy made available only at Burger King. This meant that we needed a minimum of twenty-six different toy commercials. This was an enormous workload that required a full-time client–agency team dedicated to the task. We hired Nancy Bailey as ad manager just for this program.

In addition to advertising, we needed a "Magic Burger King at-the-restaurant program." We wanted to have the Magic Burger King available for restaurant promotion visits and for grand openings just as Ronald McDonald was available for these things. To do this, we knew that we had to have at least twenty Magic Burger Kings costumed and trained to perform magic.

Like making twenty-six different toy commercials annually, this too was a tall order. Fortunately my experience at American Motors gave us the answer. At AMC I had met a very talented magician, Mark Wilson, and had kept in contact with him. Mark had done a kids' Saturday morning network TV show, *The Magic Land of Alakazam*. More than this, Mark was a "magician's magician." He was perfect for this program, and he could advise JWT on magic tricks for the TV commercials.

Mark readily accepted our proposal to put the magic we needed in the program. He worked with JWT on the TV commercials, and he set up a Magic Burger King Training Institute. He initially trained twenty Magic Burger Kings for the rollout of this program. He also outfitted each Magic Burger King with a costume and a customized "King Van" that carried the props for the magic tricks inside. (Each van was engineered to open out into a stage platform so the King could perform in restaurant parking lots.)

As the King program was being developed, RMI began the enormous effort needed to flesh out the promotion program. In many ways, this was the most difficult task in developing the program. The specifications and logistics were staggering. Twenty-six different toy premiums were needed annually. Each had to cost less than a nickel, be unique to Burger King, and be available in quantities of four million.

RMI not only had to acquire the premiums, they had to distribute them, so that every other Saturday morning, the new toy and supporting point-of-purchase materials would be in every restaurant. This in turn meant communicating with each restaurant and collecting an order for a specific premium quantity—a truly difficult task in an era before faxes and e-mail.

Entering the PR Arena

On top of advertising and promotion, we also needed a kids' marketing PR program.

Burson–Marsteller came up with an excellent idea centered around fire prevention in the home. Research had shown that fire was one of the major killers of children. Burson proposed a program to teach grade-school age children what to do to prevent fires and what to do if they became involved in a fire.

It was an elaborate program built around a cartoon character "Snuffy, the Talking Fire Engine." Snuffy was featured in a public service commercial explaining the danger of fire in the home. He was also the star of a textbook showing children how to deal with fire and a teachers' guide for the text. The textbook was, of course, offered free for use in grade schools.

In addition, we developed a program for shows in major shopping malls. This consisted of fire-prevention exhibits and a full-scale motorized Snuffy manned by a hidden driver and led around by some attendants. Each week Snuffy would go to a different shopping mall, invite children to learn more about how to deal with fire, and lecture to mothers about the importance of preventing fire in the home.

To give this program total legitimacy, we contacted the Fire Chiefs Association of America who provided us with several of their members from around the country as an advisory board. The fire chiefs were also a big help in pushing this program in their local areas.

"Pitch, Hit, And Run"

"Snuffy" was not the only marketing PR effort program we launched. We bought another program that on paper at least, had much broader appeal than Snuffy, especially to boys age eight to twelve. It seemed almost too good to be true. It gave us involvement with every Major League baseball team in America.

The program, called "Pitch, Hit, and Run," was baseball's answer to the NFL's "Punt, Pass, and Kick." Kids initially competed in each of the three baseball skills in their park district. Winners went through several elimination tournaments for the right to compete in their nearest Major League team's stadium. The winner at the Major League team's site represented that team at the national championship held at the Major League All-Star game.

Our goal was to use this program to not only to build consumer goodwill but also to get our franchisees involved with their community park districts.

Money Worries

It took us until early October 1977 to develop all of the program elements. When we did, it became obvious we had a major problem—money. When all the costs were added up, we did not have enough money from the four percent advertising fund to pay for the kids' program and maintain a strong adult marketing effort.

It was clear that the advertising fund had to be increased from four percent of sales to five percent to pay for the essential element of the program—the kids' toys. To increase the ad fund, each franchisee would have to agree—not an easy "sell" under any circumstance.

But, I had never believed in a program more strongly than I believed in this one. Therefore, I decided to go all out to sell it to the franchisees even though several had told me that they doubted that their fellow franchisees would be willing to increase their contribution.

Fortunately, we had the ideal venue to sell the kids' program and the extra one percent—a national convention.

Corporate Changes Continue

At the same time all of this was going on, a new Burger King management team was gradually taking shape. Jerry Ruenheck was now reporting directly to Don Smith on operations. Zane Leshner replaced Ray Dietrich as corporate counsel.

In addition to changes in people, Smith continued to "McDonaldize" the structure of the company. Decentralization was mandated. New Division VPs were hired—many with McDonald's background. And, Operations took over more responsibility from Marketing. The field marketing managers began to report to region managers, not marketing. Furthermore, my responsibilities for restaurant design and décor were stripped from me and returned to Operations.

Meanwhile, "to reaffirm my importance to the organization," Smith promoted me in title to executive VP. I was hardly thrilled by my new title. Nine months after he had arrived, Don Smith had effectively trimmed my job back to advertising, sales promotion, and public relations.

Don also began to meddle in the marketing department's internal organization.

One day, out of the blue, he asked me to add a new employee to the marketing department, Tom Feltenstein. Tom had been in the McDonald's marketing department as a local store marketing expert. Don wanted him to do the same for Burger King.

I protested. "I don't need him; we have our RADIUS program."

Don ignored my protests; as far as he was concerned Tom was to be hired. He offered me his rather infamous stare, smiled, and asked, "Chris, are you really telling me you don't want another "pro" on your staff?"

Cornered, I smiled back. "No," I said, "I'm not saying that at all." Case closed. Tom Feltenstein was hired.

Tom was an expert, but he never fit our culture. He was, therefore, largely ineffective. I do not remember when Tom left Burger King, nor where he went. I do know, however, that Tom parlayed his McDonald's and Burger King experience into a long-term career. He founded his own restaurant marketing consulting company and has offered many local store marketing seminars to the industry over the years.

Rocky Mountain High

The Burger King national franchisee convention was held in Colorado Springs at the Broadmoor in late October '77.

It was another of those dramatic "make or break" events in my life. I needed to sell a tough audience the new kids' marketing program—a program that I was sure was the penultimate marketing program of my career—and gain agreement from every franchisee to contribute an added one percent to the ad fund to pay for it.

I was nervous, but confident. We had a strong program. "America's Burger King" campaign was being replaced with a stronger harder-hitting advertising—a campaign featuring a strong competitive promise, "Who's Got The Best Darn Burger in the Whole Wide World? Burger King and I."

The convention itself was a happening. Franchisee attendance was very high—over ninety percent of the franchisees attended—and over-flowed the hotel into nearby accommodations. For a few days, Colorado Springs bulged at its seams with Burger King folks. Everyone wanted to meet Smith and celebrate a new beginning for the company.

The marketing presentation was the second day of the convention.

On the first day, in front of a packed house, Don and Jerry Ruenheck introduced many new operations programs. In addition, they talked about new menu items, particularly the chicken sandwich. And they pitched very hard for every franchisee to adopt the new décor packages to remodel their dining rooms. The franchisees were most enthusiastic about what they heard.

Don was so pleased with the results of this meeting that afterwards he seemed to soar with an air of superiority that he inflicted on me. Meeting him by chance outside the rehearsal area for the meeting he said rather cryptically, "I am sure you can't top today's show. I just hope you're able to sell the kids' program."

I took his "encouragement" as a dare. I looked at him and responded with fervor, "Don, we will hit a home run over the Rocky Mountains by the end of tomorrow." That conversation was probably the beginning of the end, as far as my career at Burger King was concerned. I had told Don Smith, in essence, "I can beat you."

And, indeed, the next day our marketing team did "beat" him. I presented the Burger King kids' program using Mark Wilson to introduce the Magic Burger King. At the end of the speech, I received a great round of applause So, I took a gamble and ad-libbed the Big Question, "Will you support this program with the extra one percent fund we need?" The audience yelled back a boisterous, "Yes." *Program sold.*

Then Ron Sherman and Bert Manning eloquently sold the adult advertising. By the time Burt ended our show with a 160-piece high school marching band bursting through the doors blaring out the new adult campaign music, "Best Darn Burger," he actually had many, including Art Rosewall weeping with joy.

The franchisees gave a resounding standing ovation to the presentation. We were going to have a huge marketing success in 1978.

This proved to be the pinnacle of my success and JWT's at Burger King. Today, all participants fondly remember this as their "Rocky Mountain High."

Public Successes, Private Disasters

The rest of my career at Burger King was a difficult emotional experience and remains to this day something of a blur to me.

In 1978, after the convention, the kids' program was launched and was immediately successful. Sales increased ten percent to thirty percent in most markets the first six months. More important, our consumer research showed kids' preference for McDonald's was lessening. We were starting to win the battle for kids.

The Magic Burger King shows at restaurants occurred weekly. Grand openings were held. Remodelings were done. Operational improvements in speed of service, etc. were adopted. Burger King was on the move as it had never been in its history. Over the next two years Burger King would increase its fast-food market share and its sales per restaurant and begin to ever-so-slowly close the sales-per-restaurant gap with Mc-Donald's.

Ironically, while celebrating this great continuing marketing success, my job became more and more a personal struggle to survive and prosper in the Burger King fashioned by Don Smith. My life became a whirlwind of activity in which the joy I had experienced building the Burger King marketing program was gradually squeezed out of me.

I just could not figure out how to work with Don Smith and simultaneously be a successful marketing leader. *Lifetime Lesson: It is axiomatic if you are a subordinate at any level, but particularly to a CEO, that you must adapt your managerial style to your boss's or you will fail.*

And I was failing. I became a frustrated man who was very defensive of his "turf," both internally and with the franchisees.

I respected Smith's charismatic influence on the franchisees. I also respected his ability to sell Pillsbury on long-needed capital expenditures, etc. But, I didn't think he knew "beans" about marketing or strategic thinking. Result: I was convinced that to have a successful marketing program I had to preserve the autonomy I had been given by my three previous bosses.

The problem was Smith did not agree with my assessment of his marketing capabilities nor did he seek my leadership. Instead he kept shooting out ideas in his staff meetings that he wanted pursued. Most were clearly off strategy and, worse yet, very difficult to execute. I found myself constantly arguing with Don over tactics he wanted executed—from changing an actor in a TV commercial, to selecting the kids' premium he had thought up.

In retrospect, it seems very clear that we could have made a good team, but our personalities would never let that happen. He had to be right in any clash of opinions on marketing, and I would challenge him openly when I felt he was wrong. He did not like my challenges; he seemed to prefer "yes men," something I would never be.

Still, I tried to work through the problems. And at times I felt Smith wanted me on his team. After bitterly complaining about building design and menu development being removed from my area of responsibility, Don awarded me a new area of responsibility. He appointed me to oversee Burger King Canada.

Don had hired a president for Canada, Ron White from McDonald's (naturally). I was to supervise Ron. This was, in a way, a sham because White would always report privately to Don and I would simply be in the middle. I made a concerted effort, however, to make this work because it did give me operations responsibility for a major area of expansion of the Company. And, as a result, I was at least partially responsible for growing Burger King Canada from three restaurants to over fifty in a very short period of time.

As all this transpired, my career at Burger King was being dead-ended. It was clear that my dream of being a future president had been obliterated. Don Smith would never see me as his successor. Worse yet, as I struggled with this reality, the rest of the marketing "world" I had assembled inside Burger King slowly began to fall apart.

Events started on a downward spiral at a franchisee marketing council meeting at Doral Country Club in Miami in early '78.

My relationship with the franchisees had always been tenuous. I had not wooed them enough after my initial "Have It Your Way" success. Too often I had spent time trying to prove they were wrong. Result: Several key members seemed to dislike me personally, and at almost every committee meeting they clashed openly with me.

At this meeting, a festering argument over the authority of the marketing committee versus my authority erupted once again. As I was pressing home an argument about the advertising under review, Dave Murray, a florid-faced, stocky, six-foot New England franchisee loudly interrupted me from his seat around the conference table. He said with angry disgust in his voice, "Schoenleb, when are you going to learn that you can't learn anything when you talk. You don't listen!"

I stopped talking and glared at him, then angrily blurted, "Dave, maybe it's because I shouldn't have to listen to someone who does not try to understand professional marketing—someone who thinks his opinion is more authoritative than consumer research. You are the one who doesn't listen, not me."

Then, my anger subsiding, and recognizing Smith was in the room, I quickly tried to make amends, "Sorry, let's not argue, what is it I should hear?"

This did not appease Dave. He stood up and faced me, "Chris, the role of this committee is to approve everything our ad fund dollars are spent on."

Then, pointing his finger and raising his voice, he continued "And, we are not being allowed to do that. You say our role is to give you and the agencies "input"—that you don't use us to approve anything. This is not right. We are an approval forum."

He concluded with an ominous tone, "I demand this be addressed and changed—now."

The room became very quiet. I couldn't believe that all the franchisees agreed with Dave whose ego barely fit into the room. I was confident that they knew we had the best marketing program in the industry. It was working; sales were up. Why would they want to change the basic way we operated?

Still, no one spoke. Finally I started to reply with a negative shake of my head, but Don Smith, who was sitting behind me, stood up and spoke first, "Dave, I agree with you. This committee should make the final decisions."

I couldn't believe my ears. I thought I heard Don Smith destroy my credibility with the committee and my authority to professionally run the Burger King marketing program in just one finite sentence.

I exploded with anger, "Don, I cannot be the Vice President of Marketing one more day if you empower a group of franchisees to overrule my decisions. This company deserves professional, consumer-research-based programs run by people who are full-time professionals, not part-time experts whose basic job is to run restaurants."

Dead silence enveloped the room. I had openly challenged Smith. Odds were good I was gone from Burger King.

Then Jack Jones stood up and said, "This is crazy! I don't know about you guys, but I didn't pay a franchise fee and royalties to let one of my fellow franchisees make marketing decisions. I say let Chris and the rest of the pros do it. It has worked just fine, so far."

Don Smith immediately suggested we adjourn the meeting, and finish the discussion in the morning. I left without a word and went to my hotel room. In my mind, it was Don's move. Would he back off his position on the committee's role, or was I gone?

The franchisees adjourned to the bar and discussed the same topic. Several franchisees called my room and said they would try and work out a compromise. They said that I had been stupid to challenge Don—but they would support me with him.

Ron Sherman called my room. "I'm proud of your stand, Chris. Everybody, including Smith knows you're right. You didn't, however, win any awards for tact. But, please, don't quit. It'll be Okay."

And it was Okay. Smith and I had breakfast the next morning. He claimed that he had worked the problem out with the franchisees. We would keep the Committee's role status quo.

Destroying My Team

Soon after this "victory," my marketing department world began to crumble. Don Smith called me into his office and told me that he no longer wanted Larry Krueger in any meeting he attended.

I protested. "Why? Larry is a brilliant man. He is a key member of the marketing team."

Don shrugged his shoulders and replied, "You can keep him if you want to. I am simply telling you I will not have him in another meeting with me. I don't want him in any meeting with me, ever."

Like the Tom Feltenstein incident, I was treated to a fait accompli. I was speechless. I just stared at Don as he dismissed me by answering his phone. I had no way to appeal his decision.

I considered resigning—it was obvious Don was practicing his form of "my way or the highway" management style, and I could not live with that long term. After thinking about it for a day, I chose not to leave, but did begin a job search in earnest.

In the meantime, it was obvious that Larry couldn't remain at Burger King under the circumstances Smith had created. I called him into my office, told him the news, and assured him that he could stay until he found another job. In a few months, he was gone. He became VP of Marketing for KFC.

Around the same time another ugly event occurred. I had gone on a one-week vacation. When I returned, I had a note from Don Smith, "Come and see me." When I went to see him, he said, "Jeff Campbell is now working in operations."

I was stunned. I was told that Jeff had gone to Don in my absence. Jeff told Don that he was eager to move ahead and that he wanted to know what he had to do to get to the top. Smith told him he had to have operations experience. So he asked Smith to move him into training for restaurant management. Smith agreed and made the change immediately.

It all sounded too pat, but again I was faced with a fait accompli. My two key lieutenants were now both gone after almost six years of working together. I had to rebuild my staff immediately.

To replace Jeff, I commissioned an executive search firm. It found a very personable Harvard MBA, Kyle Craig. Kyle did well, but proved to be not as strong as Jeff. He was slow to pick up all the nuances of the job but his personality almost made up for it. Everyone liked Kyle, especially because I was the confrontational leader with Smith and the franchisees.

Kyle Craig used this job as his springboard to a very successful career in restaurant management. He, like Jeff, eventually became executive VP of Marketing for Burger King in the mid '80s. Unlike Jeff he was never president of Burger King, but over the next fifteen years he was CEO of Steak n Ale and president of KFC.

I replaced Larry Krueger with his assistant, Ken Morrick. Ken was a competent researcher, but not a marketing thinker like Larry. But Ken was acceptable to Don Smith.

Final Months

As these internal events swirled about in early 1979, sales continued to grow rapidly.

Don Smith was now a hero to most. The franchisees saluted his operations-oriented leadership. I worried because I wondered whether he had any long-term innovative strategic vision. In two years, as I saw it, he had basically adopted tactics that were easy fixes and tried to emulate McDonalds, not beat them.

This could not last forever. Only the kids program seemed truly better than McDonald's. But our franchisees were already tiring of it. "Too costly" was a growing complaint. Given Don Smith's ego, it was clear that he would soon tell franchisees, as he had already told me, that we should drop the extra one percent of sales advertising contribution, do fewer premiums and go on. I was sure this would hurt a successful program—that this would weaken it enough to allow the franchisees to eventually kill it. (In this, I proved to be a prophet.)

I felt like a man trying to outrun a treadmill. I was worn out from having the double burden of rebuilding the marketing department and fighting "tooth and nail" with Smith to keep my authority over marketing.

This was not helped by events at home. One Saturday night in early January, our two teenage sons accidentally set our kitchen ablaze. By the time the fire department quenched the flames, we had no kitchen and extensive smoke damage throughout the house. For the next nine months, the home would be under substantial remodeling and repair. Besides disrupting the family, this event hurt my ability to use home as a refuge to relax and shake off the day's events.

All this resulted in my leaving town and working with the agencies, especially the gang at JWT. Ron Sherman became my confidant. He and his three key henchmen, Peter Schweitzer, Ron Burns, and Bob Norsworthy were tireless workers. No matter how inane some of my requests were as a result of Don Smith's ideas, they never complained. Sherman would always look at me and say, "Not to worry, Schoenleb, we'll save the day."

At about this time it became clear that the "Best Darn Burger" campaign had to be replaced. It had not been a home run. And, now it was not strategically right, as Smith pushed out more and more new menu items—none of them hamburgers.

In March, to buy time to develop new adult advertising, I promised Smith and the franchisees a new campaign for the October national convention. As Kyle Craig and I met with JWT to launch work on the new campaign, my first question was, "Can we bring back "Have It Your Way?"

After answering my question with a lukewarm, "Maybe," it was JWT's turn to be strategic.

We had raised a question with them in many earlier meetings, "Why is it that the only difference we can identify between our customers and McDonald's is that their customers go more often to them than Burger King customers go to Burger King?" JWT proposed that we conduct research to answer this question then develop new advertising to address the answers obtained from the research.

I loved the idea; we had not gone back to square one in our adult advertising development since "Have It Your Way." But, I was very skeptical. "What kind of research?" I asked. "Saul Ben-Zev groups?"

"No," Sherman responded. "We want to do a complete segmentation study. It will cost you $150,000 dollars."

I almost choked, "$150,000 dollars! For what? That's twice what we ever spent for any study."

Ron replied "If you want an answer that will be accurate, and research that is, in your favorite word, "actionable"—that's what it will cost, period."

"Okay", I said slowly. Then in typical clientlike fashion, I added, "It had better be good."

The Segmentation Study turned out to be very good indeed. It gave us the answer to our question. McDonald's customers came more frequently primarily because of one age group, teens and young adults aged sixteen to twenty-four. This group averaged four to seven visits weekly or more visits than our average customer did in a month. We had a road map for our next frontal assault on McDonald's. Clearly we needed to add advertising and promotion geared to this age group. JWT and RMI went to work.

The segmentation research was so impressive, I arranged for an in-depth presentation of the findings to Don Smith and my fellow management members, as well as the franchisees on the marketing committee. My purpose was twofold: (1) to lay the groundwork for selling a new ad campaign and (2) to try to re-establish research as the most important guide to marketing, as opposed to my, Don Smith's, or the franchisees' opinions.

I was successful on both counts. JWT sold a new ad campaign built around the line, "Make It Special, Make It Burger King." With an excellent catchy tune, I was sure then, and still believe today, that this campaign was the best since "Have It Your Way," and probably exceeded only once since then (by "It Simply Tastes Better").

Best of all, "Make It Special" met the critical qualification we had placed on its development, flexibility. We needed a campaign that could have special executions for different age groups, but still blend into one harmonic whole. JWT, under the direction of Frank Nicolo, finished a pool of three commercials to be shown on TV shows that reached the sixteen to twenty-four year olds, another pool of three to reach the family audience, etc.

Along with the creative, we also launched development of another Olympic tie-in promotion. In a major gamble, we had purchased the exclusive fast-food advertising rights for the 1980 Olympics. It was a $40 million purchase, almost half our projected network budget. This shut out McDonald's but it would be a hollow victory, if we did not find the right promotion to capitalize on our media buy.

All in all, with this adult program added to our continuing the kids' effort, it seemed clear that the 1980 marketing program would extend our two-year success to a third big year. We would be ready to earn another standing ovation from the franchisees at the October national convention in San Francisco.

But, I didn't get to San Francisco. While these programs were in development, I had continued my search for another job. Over the course of a year I had chatted with several fast-food chains but had not found anything good enough to tempt me to leave Burger King. This changed with one phone call from an executive recruiter in Atlanta one night in late in July.

After the usual preliminaries he came straight to the point, "Chris I represent a restaurant company looking for an executive VP and chief operating officer. It pays six figures and is a terrific overall package. They really need a man like you. Would you be interested in chatting with me and them about it?"

"Who is it?"

"Can't tell you yet. It is highly confidential."

I got a little nasty and replied "I will consider it only if you tell me who and where."

There was a pause on the other end of the phone. " Okay, But please keep it confidential. It's Arby's and it's Atlanta."

Now I paused. This sounded good. Arby's was much smaller than Burger King, but it was a national chain.

I finally replied, "I'll talk."

I went to Atlanta and had preliminary conversations with Arby's' president, Jeff McMahon. He seemed Okay, and the job had some appeal, but I was very cautious. I knew I had a very powerful and prestigious position at Burger King. I knew I would not find a bigger marketing job. However a long-term future that continued my struggles with Smith was very unattractive.

As fall began, my negotiations with Arby's continued. McMahon was offering me almost double my salary in a total remuneration package but I still had trouble facing leaving Burger King. Arby's seemed so small compared to Burger King.

Then two things happened that forever made my staying at Burger King impossible.

First, I met with Win Wallin, president of Pillsbury, and discussed my future. I asked him if there was any hope that I could become president of another division of Pillsbury. He smiled and shook his head "No."

Then I asked how he saw my future at Burger King now that Smith was CEO. Wallin was very pleasant but not very encouraging. He told me, "We see you continuing to do the job you are in right now." The thought of indefinitely continuing my life working under Don Smith was not acceptable.

Secondly, Don Smith took it upon himself to reorganize the marketing department.

He and I had been feuding over the strength of the department. He was not totally happy with Kyle Craig and had urged me to hire a stronger Number-Two guy. I had perfunctorily looked for a man but did not want to do it.

Why? Because I was sure that if I did, Don could replace me on a whim. I wanted to leave on my terms, not Don's.

Then, in early October, Don Smith hired a Number-Two man. Peter Schweitzer, the management supervisor on the Burger King business at J. Walter Thompson accepted the job.

I had talked to Peter about the job, but decided that I did not want to hire him. I was sure, in the end, that he would not fit the culture at Burger King. Before I told Peter this, Don had learned of my reluctance and had decided that he would hire Peter on his own. Worse yet, Smith didn't even tell me he had done this. Instead I learned about it in a call from Peter saying he was looking forward to coming down to work with me.

This finally "did it." I could not live with a boss who didn't even talk to me before hiring me a chief lieutenant. I decided to leave immediately, hopefully with another job.

Within seventy-two hours I cut a deal with Jeff McMahon to be Executive Vice President and Chief Operating Officer of Arby's in charge of marketing and all other aspects of operations except franchising. I would also be President of the Arby's Franchise association. Last, as part of the deal I would be given ownership of an Arby's restaurant.

I accepted the Arby's job on a Friday. The following Monday morning I walked into Don Smith's office, handed him a letter of resignation and waited for the explosion. It happened immediately. Smith became furious and asked me to leave his office.

I left and while waiting for developments phoned the agencies to advise them of my resignation. I had given a standard two-week notice and had told no one about Arby's. Still, knowing Don Smith, I was sure I'd be gone from Burger King before the day ended.

About fifteen minutes later, Zane Leshner, the chief counsel for the company, came to my office and asked me if I was willing to sign a noncompete agreement before I left the company. I said "No." Zane left and about thirty minutes later I was summoned back into Don Smith's office. He asked whether I would reconsider my decision. I again replied "No."

At this point, Don walked me back to my office and ordered a uniformed guard be placed in front of my office door. He advised me that until the noncompete agreement was signed, I would not be allowed to leave the office.

I became angry. After sarcastically asking the guard for permission to make one phone call, I phoned my neighbor, Bob Summerville, a senior partner in a major Miami law firm. I advised Bob of my situation. He told me that, if they didn't let me out of the office within an hour, he would get me out and a major lawsuit would follow.

I advised Zane of my lawyer's advice. Not surprisingly, he agreed that I could leave. I was then escorted out of the building to my car flanked by two uniformed armed guards. As I left, Dave Murray was coming in the door. He actually laughed.

What a way to end nine years with a company!

Postscript

Perhaps, the greatest irony of my career occurred sixty days after I left Burger King. The superb kids' marketing success was recognized by *Advertising Age*. The magazine named Don Smith Advertising Man of the Year for 1979.

It is traditional that the president gets the recognition rather than the people who do the work. But it was not easy to swallow. I was mentioned only once in the four-page article about my marketing program. Smith had won the award not because of his efforts, but because of the work that I had directed through J. Walter Thompson, Rogers Merchandising, and Burson–Marsteller, before he ever joined Burger King.

This award was also the end of an era. Within eight months Don Smith left Burger King to become head of the Pepsi restaurant group. (True to form, his first public act was to hire Art Guenther to be president of Pizza Hut.) Peter Schweitzer also left and returned to JWT on a different account. Peter remains there today as a senior executive of JWT Worldwide. Jeff Campbell re-emerged after his four years in Operations and became the executive VP of Marketing. He cancelled the weakened kids' program. He soon moved into the presidency by replacing Smith's initial successor, Lou Neeb. Jeff named Kyle Craig as his executive Vice President of Marketing replacement.

In less than three years, the Agency marketing juggernaut of the late '70s was obliterated. JWT had a new team; Ron Sherman was exiled from the account and left JWT to become president of Wells–Rich–Greene. RMI was fired.

All continuity of the Burger King marketing program was lost. Disaster followed in the form of the infamous "Herb" campaign.

Lessons Learned

1. *Lifetime Lesson: It is possible to usurp a direct competitor's successful marketing program, even with less marketing funds, if you can find a superior set of tactics.* Example: the Burger King kids' program

2. *Lifetime Lesson: No matter how successful a marketing program is, franchisees will tire of it and seek something new within two to three years.* Burger King's finest fast-food marketing program was killed by a combination of this ennui and a changed company management.

Final Comment

Perhaps my most profound lesson from Burger King was to experience firsthand, and observe after my departure, the devastating impact constant change in top management has on a company's long-term success.

Burger King had four CEO's in the '70s. It had at least four more in the '80s, along with six VPs of Marketing. With each changing of the boss came a changed environment. The key vice presidents under the new CEO change. In my eight years at Burger King under four different CEOs, for example, I had the longest tenure of any corporate officer before I too left.

With such top management turmoil, there is inevitably no continuity of strategy or corporate priorities. This, in turn, creates a certain paralysis of inaction by middle-management survivor—*it always seems safer to do nothing in periods of management change until one understands how to survive in a new management structure.*

As Burger King roiled in management change, McDonald's kept its team together. Fred Turner, Paul Schrage, et. al., were together through the '70s, '80s and into the '90s. They also had solid agency teams at Needham, Golan–Harris, and Burnett. They were able to have continuity at the top.

I believe this difference in management continuity is the key reason that McDonald's won the Burger Wars.

PART III
MARKETING MINEFIELDS
THREE UNIQUE CASE STIUDIES
1979–1986

CHAPTER 10
Revamping Arby's Battleplan

(A Painful Learning Experience)

For the first time in my life I joined a company while second-guessing my decision.

I kept asking myself. "Should I have left Burger King?" In many ways, I knew that I had left, not for a better job, but to escape Don Smith and the Burger King franchisees.

I kept nagging at myself, "Why Arby's?" It was a second-tier company in fast food, much as Pet was in package goods. I had not done well working for that kind of company. Perhaps my "gut" already knew the answer: Arby's would be a short, bittersweet experience.

A "Sweet" Beginning

Joining Arby's began differently. For the first time in my career I had demanded a written employment agreement, albeit a rather informal one. Jeff McMahon, the president and CEO of Arby's, provided this in a unique letter. In it, in addition to my job title and responsibilities, salary, benefits, and severance package, Jeff promised that if I performed satisfactorily, I would be named president and CEO of Arby's within eighteen months. (He told me, verbally, that he would be happy to leave the company "rat race" to tend to his private investments.)

My joining Arby's was also different in a second way. I had two bosses, not one. To understand why, a brief history must be told.

Arby's: A Unique Company History

Two brothers, Forrest and Leroy Raffel founded Arby's in '64 in Youngstown, Ohio. (Most people think the "rb" in "Arby's" stands for roast beef; it really stands for Raffel brothers.) Featuring a "natural" roast beef sandwich, the first Arby's restaurant in Boardman, Ohio, was an instant success. So was the first franchise unit in Akron, Ohio, that also opened in '64. Result: The company grew rapidly its first four years.

Disaster struck in the late '60s. The available supply of "natural" beef used for the chain's signature roast beef sandwich declined significantly.

This drove prices up and made "natural" beef too high priced to be competitive in the fast-food arena. Sales began to slide.

To stem the tide, the Raffel brothers changed the beef product. They replaced the natural beef with what many called an "artificial" product. Legally it wasn't, it could still be called beef, but it was not the beef roast that you could buy at a butcher shop. Each roast was now manufactured at a packing plant by taking chunks of beef and compressing them into an amalgam of fat and filler. This manufacturing process resulted in a very lean product that looked like beef after baking, but it did not have the texture of "natural" roast beef. Result: it did not taste like the original sandwich and Arby's lost its customer base as that company's formerly very loyal customers stayed away in droves.

With this, many franchisees added to the company's woes by stopping royalty payments. Soon thereafter Arby's filed for Chapter 11 bankruptcy. Initially, it was anticipated the Arby's chain might disappear. This did not happen, but the bankruptcy changed the inner workings of the chain forever.

Disillusioned by the Raffel brothers' financial difficulties, the franchisees banded together and formed an organization called the AFA (Arby's Franchise Association). At the same time they entered into direct negotiations with the bankruptcy court to find a way to survive on their own.

After several years of struggling while the legal wheels were grinding, the franchisees were rewarded for their perseverance. As part of the settlement that allowed the parent company to emerge from bankruptcy, a new franchise agreement calling for a much-reduced royalty (one percent) was issued to all remaining franchisees. And, the AFA was given legal ownership of the Arby's trademark. As a result, from this time forward, the franchisees controlled the Arby's system advertising.

When they gained these trademark rights, the AFA Board of Directors hired a professional marketing staff. They then set up an ad fund to pay this staff and to pay for the development of advertising materials for the franchisees and company-owned restaurants who paid into the ad fund. This staff, which included market research personnel, was not located at the Youngstown headquarters, but in Pittsburgh, home of a key AFA board member, Rick Griffith.

In the late '70s, the Raffel brothers sold the company to Royal Crown Cola (RC). RC was controlled by a gentleman named W. T. Young (the same man who sold Big Top Peanut Butter to Procter & Gamble and thus indirectly provided my first job at P&G.) RC had purchased Arby's primarily so that they could dispense their soft drinks in the Arby's restaurants. RC had not been able to break in to the almost total dominance of Coca-Cola in fast-food outlets through their normal fountain sales efforts. (This was the same rationale or driving force that led Pepsi to purchase three restaurant chains, i.e., Pizza Hut, Taco Bell, and KFC).

Following the purchase, RC moved Arby's headquarters to Atlanta near its home office. The Raffel brothers were left behind in Youngstown and a new executive team was hired.

For reasons I never learned, RC decided to hire one of the major Arby's franchisees to run the company. From the two candidates who expressed interest, Rick Griffith and Jeff McMahon, they finally selected Jeff McMahon, to be the new president and CEO. They bought his restaurants in Kentucky and the Carolinas and he went to Atlanta with his chief financial officer, Tom Klump, to set up a new Arby's "world headquarters."

Jeff McMahon

Jeff McMahon was an entrepreneur who had operated multiple restaurants as a franchisee. He lacked any previous experience as a professional manager.

Physically, Jeff was a prototypical "Southern gentleman." He stood about six feet two inches. He was prematurely gray—actually whiteheaded—in his early-mid forties. He was courtly in dress and manner. With blue eyes, a thin frame, and shock of white hair, Jeff was considered to be an uncommonly handsome man.

He also had a hot temper that bred one peculiar characteristic. Whenever Jeff became angry, his face flushed red. The angrier he became, the redder his face.

When Jeff was hired I was told he was given specific "sailing orders" from Royal Crown: "Work out a deal with the AFA Board to regain control of the marketing of the Arby's system." To accomplish this, Jeff met with the AFA Board and straightforwardly asked for their help. As a former AFA Board member he knew the Board members well. He explained what he had been assigned to do. Then he simply asked them what it would take to get to get AFA agreement to allow the company to run the AFA marketing program.

Holding all the cards, the franchisees decided to give Jeff a chance—if he would agree to certain terms and conditions. All agreed that the AFA and company needed a better working relationship.

The franchisee terms were not easy. They advised Jeff that they would not give up rights to the trademark or give up veto power over marketing decisions. However, they would agree to allowing a company executive to direct the AFA staff, if Jeff would hire an executive acceptable to them. They also agreed to name this executive President of the Arby's Franchise Association, in addition to whatever title the Company chose to give the executive.

Jeff accepted the terms, after extracting a promise from the AFA Board that he could position this deal to RC as a first step toward the company's gaining more concessions later. He then developed a list of possible candidates for the marketing executive. Two names were at the top of the list, Chris Schoenleb and Art Guenther. The Board agreed that either was acceptable to them.

Then Jeff went recruiting. It took him almost six months to finally land his man.

Thus, when I was hired, I had a dual title and two bosses. I was president of the AFA, reporting to their Board of Directors. And I was Executive Vice President of the parent company, Arby's, Inc. reporting to Jeff McMahon.

In my dual role, I was to function as the Chief Marketing Officer and as Chief Operating Officer of the company. Reporting to me in this role were not only the marketing people that were employed by the AFA and the company, but also the company store operations personnel, and the real estate and construction departments.

In effect, I was to take over the day-to-day operations of the company. Jeff was to concentrate on internal administration and gearing up the franchise sales operations, which had been relatively dormant for years as the company emerged from bankruptcy.

In practical terms, my initial tasks at Arby's were threefold:

1. Assume management of the marketing function of the AFA/company. I was to close down the AFA marketing office in Pittsburgh and move all records, files, and materials to Atlanta.
2. Take over directing the operations of the company stores, real estate and construction, and within six months close down the remaining company operations in Youngstown. (Arby's had built a large free-standing corporate facility in Youngstown. This building was to be sold.) I was to bring all operations into the new Atlanta office.
3. Develop an over-all strategy to grow the retail sales of existing restaurants and, in doing so, prepare myself to take over the reins of the company.

This was a tall order! I was starting almost from scratch in terms of people resources. When I arrived in Atlanta, I found an office full of empty desks. It was almost spooky there were so few people. I had to fill these empty desks with new hires or transfer people from Youngstown or Pittsburgh to fill them while I learned the business.

I was also starting from scratch in another way: my own credibility within the organization. *Lifetime lesson: No matter what position you take in a company, no matter what you have accomplished at other companies, you must earn "credibility" all over again when you join a new company.* This is particularly true with franchisees.

Introduction to Arby's

As I started my first day, despite deep-seated concerns about whether I should have chosen to work for Arby's, I was brimming with confidence.

I was sure that after Ernest Gallo, Burger King, and especially Don Smith, I was ready for anything.

Part of my confidence also stemmed from my belief that I could easily and immediately establish my credibility because of three major advantages inherent to my new position.

First, I anticipated a good close working relationship with Jeff McMahon. He would run interference with the parent company and help me quickly understand the franchisee culture.

Second, as acting COO, I would wield far more power inside the company to get something done than I was able to do at any previous position.

Third, I knew I had an opportunity to have a truly harmonious relationship with the franchisees. I was president of their organization. I didn't know what to expect long term from the Arby's franchisees, but I was very sure that initially I would be welcomed with open arms.

And I was. Serendipitously, my first day with the company coincided with an Arby's franchisee convention in Atlanta. I was introduced to a standing ovation.

The next day, I met the AFA Board of Directors. At first blush I liked all of them. The key members of the Board were Mike Schulson from Chicago, Russ Umphenour from Atlanta, and Rick Griffith. They were assigned to "brief" me. In their briefing, each man expressed high hopes that my new post would work out. All said that they were tired of fighting with the company.

Russ Umphenour was the most guarded in his comments. Russ, the youngest of the three, was the Arby's largest franchisee through his company, RTM. I quickly learned that he was not only on the Board of the AFA, he was also a direct competitor to the AFA marketing efforts. He had his own ad agency and sold ad materials to the Arby's system in competition with the AFA.

Mike Schulson summed up their cumulative message. "We are sure that, with your background and knowledge, you can provide the kind of vision and leadership that will enable us to bring the two systems together and build our sales."

Rick Griffith went on to explain the AFA's plans. "Our lease is up on our office space in Pittsburgh at the end of the year," he said. "Therefore, we have two months to close up shop. When your hiring was announced, we asked Darrough Diamond, who had been in charge of our marketing effort, to resign. His second-in-command also chose to quit. And our market research director—a fellow I am sure you know—Ken Morrick from Burger King—also resigned. Apparently, there was some bad blood between you?"

I nodded, remembering that Ken Morrick had left Burger King in frustration. We had not worked well together after Larry Krueger left.

Rick concluded, "In short, you will have to hire an entirely new staff to handle marketing. Perhaps that's good because at least you won't have to pay anyone to move from Pittsburgh."

I nodded again, thinking to myself, "This is worse than Burger King. I am starting with no people."

They then told me about the agency. Hopefully it would provide the continuity we all needed. The AFA employed a major New York agency, Dancer, Fitzgerald, and Sample (DFS). DFS had done all of the system's TV ads and the AFA's recommended newspaper inserts and point-of-purchase materials.

Finally Mike Schulson, a stocky, intense, tough Chicago business-man, smiled rather awkwardly and dropped the next bomb.

He said, "There is one other thing you should be aware of. In order to make the transition as smooth as possible, we have already developed and paid for the advertising and sales promotion materials for next year. The budget is essentially spent."

I nodded as impassively as I could as I absorbed this news. "This is indeed worse than Burger King," I thought. "Not only is there no staff, but there's no money to do anything!" "Of course, by the time you hire a staff and get settled in," Mike added, seeing the disbelief that I couldn't hide on my face, "we will have sold materials and begun to collect monies and you should have some funds to work with—I figure that will be April or May at the earliest."

I was surprised and somewhat relieved by this statement. Unlike the Burger King franchisees, there would be no demand for instant results. The Arby's franchisees weren't looking for an instant miracle, even though Arby's system sales were mired in a rut with no consumer traffic growth.

The briefing ended with all three men urging me to go to Pittsburgh as soon as I could to meet the outgoing staff, review the marketing materi-als, and begin to understand the marketing program.

Jeff McMahon had sat through the meeting. When it was over and the franchisees had departed, I turned to him and said, in an accusatory tone, "What a mess! Jeff, you gave me no clue that this was the situation when I joined the company. I guess all this shouldn't be a complete sur-prise. *It is generally true that in changing jobs you learn that things are at least three times worse than you have been led to believe.* But why didn't you tell me any of this? "

Jeff glared back at me; his face flushed. Then he pasted a tight smile on his face. What followed was the first indication that the personality I had seen in interviewing was not the personality I would see in working with him. He ignored my question and replied rather stiffly, "There is a lot of work to do. That's why we were so particular about the person hired for this job." And with this he cut off further discussion by bolting abruptly from the room.

I went back to the furnished apartment that I had rented until we could sell our house in Florida. I laid my weary head on my pillow and stared into space. "What a mess," I thought. "I jumped from the frying pan into the fire. I have gone from a company with a difficult culture, but great resources, to a company with a difficult culture and no resources."

Then, as many of us often do, I began to rationalize that there was another side to this. "Maybe this will work out," I thought. "I can create my own culture because there is no one to fight. I won't have to fire a lot of people, because there was no one to fire. Instead, my role is to hire and bring together a team of experts that can be my team. Then, when Jeff leaves the company in eighteen months, it will be my company."

I spent the rest of the first week reading files, organizing my office including launching a search for a new administrative assistant and answering phone calls from well wishers. I felt lost and very much alone after my ingrained routine at Burger King. My biggest task was giving phone interviews to the national and local media.

The press stories about my going to Arby's came in a rush over the first few weeks after I left Burger King. In addition to the industry press, there was a very flattering full-page article in the business section of the Atlanta evening paper about my arrival. In the article, there was speculation as to what direction I would take the company.

This publicity seemed to add to Jeff McMahon's sour attitude toward me. More than once, Jeff came to my office with a copy of an article in which I was quoted as saying things like, "We are going to make major changes in how Arby's is marketed." His face would be flushed with anger. He would say through tight lips, "I wish you would have talked to me about this before you said anything."

I was puzzled by this animosity. I thought the press was to be expected. I had earned it by my work at Burger King. I asked Jeff what harm the publicity was really causing. As I saw it, I was simply creating "good press for Arby's," as well as for myself.

This did not mollify Jeff. Of course part of the problem was that he was president of the company. It was he who had hired me but he was never even mentioned in most articles.

Marketing: The "Arby's Way"

The following week I went to Pittsburgh. There the outgoing staff and Rick Griffiths educated me about the Arby's approach to the fast-food marketplace.

The chain had survived in the '70s positioned to consumers as an alternative to hamburger chains. Arby's most successful advertising had been a campaign called "Break the Hamburger Habit" that had supported the "hamburger alternative" positioning. But, under Darrough Diamond's leadership, DFS had dropped "Break the Hamburger Habit" for another campaign, entitled "The 3 hour roast is only five minutes away"—hardly a compelling fast-food advertising line.

As I listened to the staff, the overall brand positioning and strategy they presented seemed muddled. They believed the key to marketing success was to make Arby's a "mainstream" chain, not an "alternative." Yet, they were focussed on tactics to build the visit frequency of current users, not on attracting new users.

As I learned this, I said nothing, but alarm bells immediately sounded in my cranium. *Lifetime Lesson: It never makes sense in a retail business to focus primarily on increasing user frequency versus focussing on attracting new users. New users are the lifeblood of any retail outlet.* But as important in this case, the "alternative to hamburgers" strategy made more intrinsic sense. The average customer visited Arby's once a month versus the three to four times per week customers visited fast-food hamburger restaurants. It made sense that a restaurant chain that sold one sandwich line, that is roast beef, would not attract the high frequency fast-food user. Let's face it, people, particularly teens and kids, prefer hamburgers to any other sandwich.

I resolved to address re-focussing the program to attracting new users as quickly as possible.

The staff then turned to how Arby's executed its advertising and sales promotion. What a different world! Essentially, the Arby's marketing program was a cash and carry, franchisee choice nightmare. In it, I would have less control than I had wielded at Burger King over any marketing program the system adopted.

The AFA employed Dancer, Fitzgerald, and Sample primarily to develop all ad materials needed to advertise the chain, and then sold these materials to the franchisees. The ad fund was spent for materials development and production first, not media. (Some funds were allocated periodically for national TV, usually one or two six week flights at minimum weight levels.)

The strength of the system was that the franchisees could get high quality materials for which they paid only the reproduction costs. For example, they bought tapes of TV and radio commercials to place in local markets for the minimal cost of the tapes themselves. Likewise, they purchased point-of-purchase materials, newspaper inserts, etc. for the cost of printing in large system quantities.

The weakness of the system was how these materials were actually used to market the system. It was up to each franchisee to determine how much he would spend in media in his marketing area. There was no local media planning or buying function by DFS, unless requested by a franchisee.

The AFA did try to provide some planning and coordination for the use of the materials it produced. It provided a suggested annual marketing calendar. As part of this, the AFA contracted for multimarket Sunday newspaper inserts at significant cost savings to the franchisees. It also allowed the AFA to coordinate the purchase of premiums, particularly drinking glasses. (Arby's was the pre-eminent user in the industry of this tactic.)

The problem with this plan was that it basically made Arby's a chain with little or no image advertising—the marketing plan was almost 100 percent short-term promotion focussed.

Also, this system meant that the marketing staff had to be salesmen and order takers. And, the AFA had to be able to store and ship materials efficiently. Moving from Pittsburgh we would have to find a way to do this from Atlanta. We needed a company like Rogers Merchandising.

Newspaper Inserts

The Arby's system employed a singular media tactic designed to off-set the dominant TV spending of the hamburger chains: newspaper inserts carrying multiple coupons. For most franchisees then, the key local media buy was a full-page, four-color, freestanding insert in local newspapers. Most major markets ran as many as six of these inserts a year. In these inserts would be a series of up to nine different discount coupons for half-price sandwiches, a free drink with a roast beef sandwich, etc.

Thus, the key materials sold by the AFA were themed newspaper inserts such as "Fall Value Days," "Anniversary Sale," etc. These would be preprinted except for the specific coupon offers. The Arby's franchisee could choose the themed ad he wanted, then determine his own coupon offers, and order his inserts to be black-plate printed with these offers before they were shipped to him.

Over the years, the Arby's system sales had become dependent on this use of discount coupons. *Indeed, in most markets, about forty percent of total retail sales involved a consumer redeeming a coupon.*

This in turn impacted menu pricing. Most Arby's franchisees and company restaurants inflated their sandwich prices to assure themselves a profitable gross margin on the discounted coupon sale. However, in doing this, they created a higher-priced everyday menu that reinforced many consumers' view of Arby's as high priced.

Arby's Menu

The menu itself was very limited and unique, reflecting the heritage of the company. Unlike hamburger restaurants, the typical 1980 Arby's had only one method of cooking: baking. There were no grills, broilers, or deep-fat fryers.

Thus, the menu consisted of various forms of roast beef sandwiches and other items that could be baked. To replace french fries, Arby's offered potato cakes. Instead of fried pies like Burger King and McDonald's, they offered baked fruit turnovers.

This limited menu had a major virtue that had spawned one of the keys to Arby's survival. *Unlike Burger King, an Arby's restaurant could be profitable on very low sales volume.* The operating system required very little labor. In an Arby's, one person could prepare the sandwiches and one person could wait on customers without much difficulty as opposed to a minimum staff of five or six for any fast-food hamburger restaurant.

Geography and Franchisees

Arby's was a national chain, but had almost no stores in New England or the Pacific Northwest.

The company stores formed a strong core of high volume restaurants with distribution in Kentucky and Central and Northern Ohio. The strongest franchisee organizations were in Chicago, Pittsburgh, Minneapolis, Cincinnati, Los Angeles, Long Island, Detroit, Atlanta, Dallas, and the state of Oklahoma.

It was a loose confederation to say the least. The major franchisees had built very self-reliant organizations. They operated as though they were owners of independent small chains. They paid little heed to the company's recommended operations techniques, and they did not necessarily emulate their fellow franchisees. In general, you could go from state to state and find different items on the menu, in addition to the basic roast beef menu. And you could find different building designs, different staff uniforms, etc.

The glue to keep the confederation working together came from advertising materials and product purchasing and distribution. *In both, the AFA led, the company participated.* In purchasing and distribution, the company and the AFA had formed a separate organization called ARCOP to handle the contracting for manufacturing the proprietary roast beef product. This organization, also handled contracting for distribution of this product and other proprietary or branded items including "Horsey Sauce," the paper wrapping materials for sandwiches, etc.

Getting Started

Despite the initial warm welcome, I was sure that I had very little time and no margin for error if I was to be successful at Arby's. I knew I'd be under intense scrutiny from Day One.

My initial task was therefore to build everyone's confidence that I was the right man to provide system leadership. To do this, I needed to quickly form a game plan to build system sales and then sell it to all parties.

Step One had to be fact-finding. Following my successful pattern from Burger King, I spent sixteen hours a day, six days a week in a crash course, not only in analyzing sales and consumer research, but also in trying to understand the company's operations, the franchisees, the system culture, and its people. My goal: to ferret out the marketing myths in the system.

I would do this alone; Jeff surprised me by not wanting to be part of the process. This coupled with his earlier actions confirmed that I would not have the working relationship with him I had expected.

The fact-finding had started with my Pittsburgh visit; I quickly followed this with a visit to the agency. Joe Mack, the DFS account supervisor on the Arby's business had invited me to New York for the inevitable brand review and to meet the rest of the Arby's team. There I learned about another problem. DFS was owed money and had consistently lost money on the account, "Why," I thought to myself, "does this major New York agency hang on to this business?" (The reason would soon become very apparent.)

The agency relationship, however, seemed to be off to a good start. It seemed that DFS would provide far more support than BBDO had at Burger King.

Within the first two weeks, I also learned that company restaurant sales were depressed. Every week sales were declining versus the previous year. When you coupled this with flat to declining sales in franchise outlets, and the lack of new restaurants being built (due to the lack of a good franchising program and the eighteen to twenty percent interest rates in the marketplace), the company as a whole was suffering depressed earnings.

To begin to address this, I spent a lot of time learning how the company restaurants operated. Led by Bill Ostrie, a Burger King alumnus, there were really two restaurant systems-in-one, Jeff's former stores managed by Doug Kannapel, and the Ohio stores managed by George Nadvid.

As part of this orientation, I made a trip to Youngstown. Its purpose was to understand why the company's Arby's restaurants in Youngstown averaged over $1,000,000 in sales per restaurant, versus the average system sales of less than $500,000 per restaurant. Having grown up in northeastern Ohio, I was sure it wasn't because there was a peculiar taste preference found only there.

I did not find an answer. The restaurant operations were well run, but other than that, the marketing programs were similar, the menus were similar, and the pricing similar to other areas. The only theory I could come up with was the fact that since the chain had started there, there was a loyalty to Arby's. (Later, Larry Krueger would argue a more plausible theory—that Youngstown was proof that heavy saturation TV advertising of 300 GRP's per week caused this success and that this proved the value of TV ads for the chain.)

Larry Krueger

While doing my fact-finding, I launched Step Two in building confidence in my leadership, hiring a professional staff. I started with an all-out effort to hire a new marketing staff.

First, I ran an ad in *Advertising Age*, in which I tried to capitalize on the fame I had received from the press. I invited marketers to come and join me in Atlanta to start a new era in the history of Arby's. We received hundreds of résumé's.

Second, I began to seek out people I knew in the industry, while staying away from Burger King. (Don Smith was threatening a lawsuit over my leaving with what he called "proprietary" information.)

My first phone call was parallel to my Burger King experience. As I had done eight years earlier, my first attempted hire was Larry Krueger. "Larry," I said, "How are things with KFC? Are you happy?"

"Oh," he answered cagily, "Reasonably so. Why?"

"Well, Larry, there might be a job here for you—if you would have any interest."

"Oh," he asked. "What kind of job?"

"How would you like to run a marketing department?"

There was a long pause. Finally Larry replied "I might have some interest."

"Larry, there is no one here at the moment to run marketing at Arby's. Not only would you be able to run a marketing department, you would be able to hire your own staff."

He mumbled "Mmm—Chris, what will you be doing while I do the marketing?"

"You would report to me. You would be in charge of the day-to-day work. We would work together to develop the overall strategy for the company. Come, I really need you."

Larry replied slowly. "I will have to think about it. I certainly won't say 'no' at this point."

One thing led to another and within sixty days, Larry Krueger was hired to run the marketing department at Arby's. He was employed directly by the AFA as his predecessors had been.

Larry immediately hired two associates, Tom Whitley, who had worked with him at KFC, to be director of Advertising and Sales Promotion, and Jon Ritt for marketing research. Jon had been in the Marketing Research department when I first joined Burger King.

One problem was solved. Arby's had a very professional marketing staff.

Forming a Game Plan

As I finished my fact-finding I was impressed with the potential for Arby's. The system had a solid base of distribution. It had a unique market niche with a loyal, but infrequent visiting, customer base. There seemed to be few cultural barriers to fomenting change, but there were money constraints. With flat or declining sales, the franchisees seemed ready to embrace new ideas so long as it did not require major capital investment.

On the negative side, Arby's had three key problems in the market-place, but all seemed solvable.

First, Arby's was physically "invisible" to most fast-food users. With its multiple exterior signs and building designs Arby's had no consistent physical image. *Conclusion*: We needed new signage and a building de-sign program to find a way to standardize the chain's outside appearance.

Second, Arby's was "invisible" in fast-food consumer's minds. The chain had very low top-of-mind awareness. When consumers were asked to name chains they would consider visiting, most consumers never even thought of Arby's. These same consumers did not reject the chain; most had a favorable image. *Conclusion:* We needed new advertising that would build awareness with a small media budget.

Third, Arby's menu was too narrow. Consumers viewed roast beef sandwiches as an "once in a while" choice—a change of pace in their normal sandwich eating habits. Conclusion: We needed an aggressive pro-gram to broaden the appeal of the menu.

The menu and visibility issues were really not disputed by anyone in Arby's. How these issues should be addressed was the overriding prob-lem. Up until this time, the company had not been ceded leadership in any of these areas by the franchisees. Yet, only the company had the financial resources and people to address them.

As I came to understand the depth of mistrust between the parties, I was reminded of my favorite quote from the comic strip, Walt Kelly's *Pogo*, "We have met the enemy and they is us." The task was to bring system leadership back to the parent company in all aspects of the business.

To accomplish this, I needed to make my unique two-boss position function so well it would disappear. I had to get both parties on the same page. And, to achieve my personal goals, *I had to be the man accepted as the leader who could provide system leadership.*

Leadership would not accrue to me, I reasoned, until I once again proved my marketing prowess. I had to direct the new staff to achieve major improvements in the existing marketing program. This meant find-ing better glass promotions, better coupon offers, and more effective ad-vertising.

Initially I considered spending energies on this task alone and use it as a stepping stone for winning other areas of leadership. In this scenario, I would gradually take control and put strategic changes on the back burner until I solved the AFA tactical marketing improvements.

In retrospect this go-slow approach might have been smart. I will never know. As had been my style at Burger King, I chose the "kamikaze" approach instead—at least partly because I was sure Larry Krueger did not need nor desire my working full-time on marketing.

I also wanted to be Arby's president on schedule, in fifteen months. My "gut" told me that to assure this happened, I had to "go for broke" and not wait to be given leadership. I had to seize control of all three marketplace issues simultaneously, and at the same time, dramatically improve the AFA marketing materials. I reasoned that if I succeeded in all areas, there would be no question RC and the AFA would support me for president and Jeff would be forced to honor his promise to retire.

Changing the Menu

The cornerstone to all this was to develop a successful new menu development program.

On this issue I struck political paydirt. The AFA Board members and Jeff McMahon agreed that menu innovation was indeed the way to build Arby's sales. In fact, Jeff had brought two food technologists from Youngstown and set up a test kitchen in a nearby industrial park to do just that. He had also hired Ken Breiner, a Burger King alumnus, as a special assistant to work in this area.

These men now reported to me; I put them to work. The initial assignment was to develop items that required no new equipment. We had to exploit the ovens and the big mechanical slicers for the roast beef, yet come up with new products that would have broad consumer appeal.

Initially this work did not go well. Breiner quit in frustration and joined an Erie, Pennsylvania meat packing company because the two Youngstown alumni would not work with him. The two men also had no sense of urgency. Within sixty days I decided I had to fire them as soon as possible.

I called Ken and asked him if he'd return, to head up all menu development and hire his own staff. Fortunately for Arby's, Ken had run into real problems in Erie. He jumped at the opportunity. Within a week, he was back in Atlanta and new menu development work began in earnest.

While this initial development work was beginning, we did make one immediate change in all the company stores, a change that many of the franchise stores had already incorporated. By the end of my fourth month at Arby's, we were able to announce a major expansion of the use of salad bars in the system. Jeff had liked the idea and had spearheaded getting the funds from RC.

This resulted in a spate of trade stories that usually started off with "Schoenleb makes his first move. Adds salad bars to Arby's." Jeff's name was never mentioned. His smile became even tighter and I sensed real antagonism growing between us. More and more we seemed to be competing for control of Arby's, instead of working together.

Tom Klump stopped in to see me. He was concerned about the rift between Jeff and me. He explained that his boss had a big ego and suggested that perhaps I should tone down my publicity.

I looked at Tom and I said, "Tom, I didn't generate the publicity. We simply put out a press announcement. The media, knowing me very well and not knowing Jeff at all, attributed the changes to me. What am I supposed to do, tell the press to ignore me and talk only to Jeff?"

Tom smiled, shrugged his shoulders and said, "I don't know the answer to your question. Maybe you should. But I am telling you, he is pretty upset."

As this was occurring, another bomb was dropped—this time by the agency.

Stu Upson, president of DFS, flew in to meet with me in early February. After coffee, Stu came right to the point. "Chris, we want to resign the Arby's account as outlined under terms of our contract."

Surprised and more than a little upset, I asked "Why? We have a chance to do some great work together."

He replied, "The account isn't profitable. And I am sure that with your coming to Arby's, there will be many more demands for service on this business—service that I can't afford to provide you. You deserve the kind of agency you can work with. At this point, we are not prepared to be that agency."

As I stared at Stu after this shocking statement, I couldn't help but wonder if he were a good friend of Jim Jordan. Was my reputation that bad or had something else triggered this action?

"Well," I said, "is there anything I can say that might change your mind? I don't think we've really had a chance to get acquainted, yet."

He replied, "No. As an agency, we came to the decision that it was time to end this relationship before you got into any further development of new advertising, or started any other new projects."

Stu then smiled, stood up, shook hands, and said goodbye. Our relationship was ended.

I called Larry Krueger into my office and told him what had just transpired. He said, "I'm not surprised. They haven't been paid on a timely basis for some time, and I hear rumors that they're interested in pitching for another fast-food account."

"Well," I said, "there goes any continuity on the business."

Larry grinned and replied, "Did we really need it? Now we're free to get the agency we can control. It's time to do another agency search."

"Okay" I said, "let's get at it. It's obvious though, that with our small budget, we're not going to have the same kind of dog and pony show we had at Burger King."

Larry smiled again, "You might be surprised," he said. "Arby's is a good name and I am sure that a lot of agencies would like to have it on their roster of clients."

Choosing an Agency

Larry proved to be prophetic. When we announced that DFS had resigned Arby's, we received almost as many phone calls as we had received at Burger King. We would have no lack of good candidates.

At this point, Larry and I agreed to follow the same steps we had used to select an agency at Burger King (see Chapter 8). Larry took over the prescreening process and came up with a list of agencies that he thought might be suitable candidates—all were New York based.

We went to New York to do a preliminary screening much as we had done at Burger King. This time Tom Whitley was with us instead of Jeff Campbell.

From these preliminary meetings, we selected four finalists: NW Ayer, Della-Famina & Travisano, Scali–McCabe–Sloves, and Lois–Pitts–Gershon. With the exception of Ayer, the agencies were well known for their somewhat offbeat creative products that created a lot of visibility for clients with small budgets—exactly what we sought for Arby's. Ayer was an agency much like DFS and, although we liked them very much, we weren't sure that they fitted our needs as well as the other three.

We set up a selection committee, which included Jeff McMahon and several members of the AFA Board along with Larry, Tom, and me.

We gave the finalist agencies an assignment. "Tell us how you would service the Arby's account; tell us how you would position Arby's; and show us a potential TV and print campaign to communicate this positioning."

Larry set up a presentation schedule. The first agency to present was Ayer, the agency most like DFS. Then he scheduled the agency with good creative credentials, but lacking strong account service, Della–Famina & Travisano. Of the two remaining agencies we all thought Scali–McCabe–Sloves was most likely to win the business. Larry scheduled them third with Lois–Pitts–Gershon to follow.

Unlike the elaborate Burger King review, we held the final presentations in just two days in a small hotel meeting room in Atlanta. But the "creative shootout" results were just as surprising as the Burger King experience.

Day One: NW Ayer

NW Ayer made a very impressive presentation. We were surprised at the strength of their creative and the strength of their commitment to Arby's. Then their president, Al Wolfe (a business friend I had known since Needham) dropped the other shoe. Ayer wanted a fee to handle our business that was equal to fifty percent of our total budget. We asked if this were negotiable; Wolfe was reluctant to discuss it. This was clearly unacceptable no matter how much we liked their credentials and their ideas.

Jerry Della-Famina was next. His agency made a very disjointed, disappointing presentation. At the end of the presentation he actually apologized to us. He said he had flown all night from a Mexico vacation and had never seen the presentation and that he hoped we would give him another chance.

We said "No." The agency was too clearly dependent on one man's talent, Jerry's. And, none of us had particularly liked Jerry, even though we all received autographed copies of his new book. Della-Famina & Travisano was eliminated.

This left two agencies. We were sure Scali could win the business—much as we were sure Wells–Rich–Greene would win the Burger King business. Again, we were wrong.

Day Two: Ed McCabe and George Lois

Scali–McCabe–Sloves started their pitch well. Their "credentials" impressed us greatly, especially their work on Perdue Chicken. We were also sure that there was a good fit between their culture and ours. I particularly liked Marvin Sloves, who seemed to have an excellent grasp of marketing.

But, as soon as they turned to Arby's, their new business pitch went south. We saw nothing in the presentation that really excited us. The creative they proposed was particularly disappointing. Still, we were reluctant to drop them. Larry whispered that maybe we should consider giving them and Della-Famina another chance if George Lois disappointed us too.

Then Ed McCabe slammed the door on his agency's chances with one the most inappropriate statements I have ever heard in an agency new business presentation. After he was introduced as the guru who would supervise our creative, McCabe said something like, "You know, I really don't want to write fast-food advertising. To me it's all too much the same, too much of the wrong kind of business. I don't like fast food. I don't eat fast food. I will, however, give it a good college try." To say the committee was offended by this outburst is an understatement. We already didn't like his work; now we didn't like him. But more important, we did not want any agency where the chief "creative" didn't like the business we were in.

Things were not going well. As we broke for lunch, I turned to Larry, "You know, Larry, this search is turning into a disaster. We don't have anything going for us and there's only one agency left, George Lois and his gang. And we all know that George can be a madman."

Larry smiled and said, "Yes, but he's a smart madman."

I just shook my head and made a silent prayer that my misgivings about George were groundless.

I recalled our initial screening meeting with Lois–Pitts–Gershon in New York. We were met by Bill Pitts, the partner who was the Account

Director. (Dick Gershon, the other partner, was the media expert, while George Lois was the creative guru.) Bill had shown us around their brand new offices. Finally, we reached George's office and met him. It was an experience to be remembered.

George was sitting in the midst of a very large room overlooking Fifth Avenue. You couldn't call it an office because it was too big for an office. Yet he dominated the setting. (George Lois is an imposing man. He stands at least six feet four inches with rawboned features.) He sat at a desk that was about the third of the size of a normal desk with nothing on it except a sketching pad. He looked almost larger than life. (George was first and foremost, an art director. He had started his career working for Bill Bernbach on such campaigns as the original VW print campaign named the best advertising campaign of the 20th century by *Advertising Age*.)

As we entered his office He stood up and said, "How the f—— are you?" George always used the "f" word a lot.

With that, we went into his adjoining conference room for their new business presentation. George dominated the meeting. The presentation primarily consisted of him talking about all of his "wonderful f——ing advertising." He pulled print ads out of sacks; he posted things on the board. He talked about advertising as a product that can make or break your business. George made it clear he believed it was wrong to call advertising only part of a selling strategy. He stated emphatically, "Advertising is the strategy."

He then went on to try to prove his statement. "Let me show you how we made advertising with our clients that set them apart from the pack even though they had little budgets and really didn't know what they were doing."

George spoke in such a way that his mouth always turned down on the right side and he always spoke with absolute authority. He didn't expect you to argue with him because he was "The expert." With his physical size, he was also intimidating. At times he seemed a little like the neighborhood bully.

I was fascinated by the man but leery of his personality. He would not be an easy person to deal with. Yes, he would develop highly visible advertising, but would his work be on strategy?

At any rate, following this meeting, we decided that with his obvious passion for working with us, we had to give George a finalist berth. Upon being told the good news, George had promised us we'd see advertising "so f—— good it would knock our socks off."

Now, as the selection committee assembled we would see if George could knock off some socks. If he didn't, we would still be looking for an agency.

"America's Roast Beef, Yes Sir"

When George walked into the hotel room, the first thing he did was shake each person's hand and thank them for coming. He was totally ingratiating and very down to earth—very much in the way Carl Ally had been. Everyone on the committee seemed to immediately like him.

Dick Gershon was also a pleasant surprise. Not only was he down-to-earth, he proved to be an innovative media expert. He wowed us with what he could do with media if we gave him some dollars to spend. And Dick Pitts proved to be a good strategist.

But in the end, George was the show. George presented his ad campaign with great enthusiastic energy and a sprinkling of the "f" word. All of us liked it—why, I am not quite sure to this day, but we did. Although other rationales were given, I believe, in retrospect, it was because of George's total belief in his product.

Fortunately, the campaign was also on strategy in two ways. First, it was designed to reassert leadership in the roast beef sandwich category against the competitive incursions of Hardee's, Roy Rogers, and a new Burger King sandwich.

Second, it was certainly on target to create top-of-mind Arby's name recognition. The campaign focussed upon the Arby's name. George made Arby's an acronym for "America's Roast Beef Yes Sir." And it had a memorable visual storyline. George showed Batman and Robin and look-a-likes for other famous people accepting roast beef as something they liked. It made you laugh. It made you sit up and look and say, "What was that I just saw?"

Lois–Pitts–Gershon was hired by unanimous vote of the selection committee.

Two more of my problems were solved. Not only did we have a new agency, we had a campaign to attack our lack of consumer top-of-mind visibility.

We also had in George Lois, a "creative guru" who constantly challenged us. To this day I smile at the memory of one of our meetings with George. I rejected a TV commercial storyboard he had presented, saying, "George, we can't approve that, ever; it's not on strategy."

He replied, "Chris, strategy, smatagey, if it's not good advertising who cares about the strategy?"

I replied, "I do. Advertising has got to be on strategy. You can do good advertising on strategy just as easily as off strategy, George."

But George answered pointing to the ad, "This is so f——ing good. We have got to run this."

He finally acquiesced because "I was the client," and went off to come up with something we thought was on strategy.

I grew to like George Lois very much over the time we worked together. He was a passionate, caring advertising guru. I admired his integrity. He was also very gracious personally. We had several good lunches and dinners together in which he shared his passion for sports, especially basketball.

My fondest memory of life with George were lunches at his favorite restaurant, the *Four Seasons* in New York. George always had the same reserved table by the stairs in the main room, with a bottle of his favorite Chardonnay wine chilled, awaiting his arrival for lunch. He told me he had this table privilege because he had designed the menu for the restaurant.

Vic Meinert

Lois–Pitts–Gershon was not a full-service agency like DFS. This meant we needed a sales promotion agency. I wanted to hire Rogers Brackmann, but he was still employed by Burger King.

We found a substitute for Rog—Vic Meinert. Vic was a former Coke promotion executive whom I had briefly met when I was at Burger King. Vic was like Rogers Brackmann. He was a one-man idea generator. He had his own company called PMI located in suburban Atlanta.

Vic's company was unique in many ways. He had very few employees and yet he had a large warehouse for premium fulfillment and promotion materials. His office was really an antique display area. Everything was an antique that he had purchased somewhere in Georgia.

We thought Meinert was perfect for Arby's and so did the AFA Board. Not only was he an experienced professional, he had the one thing we had to have—point-of-purchase material distribution capability. He could store materials and ship them from his large office/warehouse.

Vic was forever coming up with new and innovative promotion ideas that would have fit many chains, but not Arby's. I am sure he was very frustrated at times that the main products we needed from him were free-standing inserts for newspapers and drinking glasses for premiums.

Vic did develop two superb glass promotions during my short tenure at Arby's. The first was a "B.C." glass—a drinking glass that used the characters from the *B.C.* comic strip. The glass itself was a strange square glass with a larger bottom than top, unlike any shape I had ever seen before. It was meant to look like a primitive drinking glass. With the "B.C." characters on it, it gave us something to merchandise and advertise that was unique in the industry. It was an outstanding success wherever we used it.

The second was a classic glass for Christmas, a colorful gold rimmed decorative glass we called "Holly Berry." Arby's used this glass year after year because it was so successful.

A Grand Strategy

After eight months, the major pieces to fix Arby's were finally in place. We were ready to attack the system's lagging retail sales on all fronts.

To address the physical look of the system, we had hired Phil Lincoln's firm, Bischoff–Lincoln. His people had worked with the construction staff on a new prototype building and a new exterior sign.

The new building, quickly dubbed "Schoenleb's Folly," was designed to accommodate more kitchen equipment, particularly deep-fat fryers for french fries. It had tables and chairs and a new concept for most of Arby's—carpeting. It would open by year's end.

To attack the advertising/promotion issues we had a new highly competent marketing staff. We had a new ad agency. We had a new promotion agency that had taken over development of promotions and point-of-purchase material. Result: We had a new advertising campaign to attack top-of-mind awareness. We had the unique "B.C." glass. And we had improved point-of-purchase materials available to the system at a much more reasonable cost. Tom Whitley, working with Vic Meinert, had cut point-of-purchase material costs in half.

Last, and most important, the menu development work was beginning to bear fruit.

Based on new consumer research, we began to understand the issues. As we analyzed it, before any major changes could be made, one key issue had to be confronted. Should Arby's add to its menu the most popular and most competitive fast-food sandwich, the hamburger?

There was little doubt that hamburgers would add sales. And with hamburgers, Arby's would join the fast-food sandwich mainstream. In this scenario, Arby's might be transformed over time into a hamburger chain that also had roast beef sandwiches.

The problem with adding hamburgers was it didn't add any uniqueness to Arby's. It made Arby's much more of a "me too" concept. Worse, hamburgers would not be easy to do. They added great expense to the average Arby's franchisee in terms of equipment. It was estimated it would cost $40,000 to $50,000 to retrofit each Arby's restaurant to put in the equipment necessary to properly cook and prepare hamburgers.

Still, we had to look at this option carefully. It was exactly what a new competitor called RAX was offering with some success in their initial Midwest markets. Also, Phil Goldman, a major Arby's franchisee headquartered in Cincinnati, was selling hamburgers in his restaurants with some success.

We also had to explore the alternative scenario: other sandwiches. It had enormous appeal to me because under it, Arby's could continue to have a unique niche in the marketplace.

The question we had to answer was not what sandwiches—there were a plethora of ideas for these, for example ham, turkey, chicken, etc.—but how to position Arby's. Could we find a better positioning for Arby's than a roast beef restaurant that served other sandwiches?

As we were exploring these alternatives, I was walking down the street in New York one day and passed a delicatessen, actually my favorite

New York delicatessen, Wolfies on Sixth Avenue. The obvious thought struck me. *Why not make Arby's the first national deli*, a fast-food deli with the same kind of sandwiches a deli served but offered quicker and cheaper than a normal delicatessen? We had the equipment. We had a slicer for the meats and we even had an oven in which we could bake bread, if we wanted to.

The longer I thought about it, the more sense it made. We could create our own market, not go directly against McDonald's and the other hamburger chains. (My idea about a national deli was obviously shared by others. Witness the Subway chain, not yet a major factor in 1981.)

As I evolved my vision for Arby's, I concluded that it would be smarter to introduce the idea gradually. It was a huge change. It would frighten most people as all change does. I realized that this was particularly true in the franchisee chain culture in which I was working.

I knew that we needed to position this change first as merely a new line of sandwiches and show that deli sandwiches could have success in Arby's. If that happened, I was sure we could evolve Arby's into a full-line fast-food deli.

I went back to Atlanta and met with Ken Breiner. I asked, "Can we make deli kinds of sandwiches?"

"Sure," he smiled (Ken always smiled). "In fact, I have already been working on something I would like to show you, Jeff's already seen this and likes it."

We went to the test store and he brought out a six-inch-long submarine-style bun. He brought out salami and ham, dressed the bun, and made a delicious sub sandwich. He smiled. "See, it's easy. We don't need any major equipment—just the buns and the ingredients that can be supplied in pre-portioned packets. You tell me how many different sandwiches you need and I'll do the rest."

I asked Larry Krueger to see Kenny's work. Then I shared my national deli concept with him. Larry, in his typical taciturn way, liked the idea. He also agreed we had to go slow on exposing it to others. He concluded, "We should have at least three or four sandwiches to test the concept."

Then we began discussing another big menu issue, "price." Arby's had no low-priced sandwich. Finally I said to Kenny, "You know, as long as we are working on new products, why couldn't we have something that gives us a low-price entry into the marketplace.

Kenny asked, "What do you have in mind?"

"I'm not sure. You know Krystal does awfully well with nineteen-cent hamburgers. Maybe a Krystal-like roast beef sandwich. Larry and I both think that if we can find some way to have a sandwich under a dollar, it would really give us greater perceived price value, something we need very much."

"Ken, take this as a second project, will you? Find us a low-end sandwich, a small sandwich—some kind of sandwich that we could sell for under fifty cents and be profitable."

Ken smiled and nodded, "Sure."

Menu Innovation

By early summer we had developed a line of deli sandwiches to test. It consisted of a ham and cheese, a "sub," and two deli roast beef sandwiches—a french dip and a roast beef with lettuce and mayonnaise. All sandwiches would be on a special oblong sub-style sandwich bun.

We showed the sandwiches to Jeff McMahon who professed mild interest. But he raised concerns that something this new really needed advertising, and that we didn't have enough funds to support a new product introduction like this. I agreed with him but urged we still try it. He finally agreed to an operations test in five restaurants in Cleveland.

We then showed the new sandwich line to the AFA Board. They liked the sandwich line; several wanted to test it. I told them the company would test them first.

The Board expressed concern over a company-only test. "The company doesn't run good stores," one of the Board members, Bill Brusslin, said. "Believe me, before I put a new sandwich line like that into my restaurants, I want to have my own test experience."

I did not budge. "Look, the role of your franchiser is to develop a program to bring to franchisees. When it's already been pre-tested, the franchisees can then give their input. We take the risk. You test only after we're sure we have a potential winner. Over the years, you've not had that luxury. Starting now, we want to show you the kind of leadership you should have."

Sales of the new sandwiches in the Cleveland test restaurants did very well. Using direct mail to promote them, we gained sales increases from ten to twenty percent without much difficulty.

While this was going on, Ken came up with the answer to our second project, a low-priced sandwich. He proposed a mini-roast beef sandwich on a two-inch bun. From this, Tom Whitley, Larry, and the agencies came up with a unique packaging concept and name. They called the mini-sandwich "Hat-o'-Beef," and packaged it in a cardboard holder that was shaped like the Arby's hat. We could sell two "Hat-o'-Beef" for ninety-nine cents with a decent gross margin.

We gained agreement to test it in a few company restaurants. There was very little interest in this product on the part of the franchisees, however. They were worried it would reduce their total dollar sales if they sold this, instead of a regular roast beef sandwich.

A Growing Relationship Problem

By now, eleven months had passed. I was pleased with the progress that had been made. There was a new team in place, and we had begun the long process of changing Arby's. In less than a year, I had been able to start more menu innovation for the system than had been done in the previous five years.

Also I had built a good relationship with most of the franchisees on the AFA Board. Russ Umphenour remained a problem. He continued to actively compete with the AFA by selling free-standing inserts to the system.

The biggest problem remained my relationship with Jeff McMahon. He talked less and less to me. After I closed down Youngstown, we went two weeks with both of us in our offices next to each other and not a convivial word was spoken between us. When I would walk into his office to ask him a question, Jeff would answer without ever turning and facing me.

Finally, I went in to his office to discuss our relationship. I asked Jeff why he seemed so angry with me. He denied that there was a problem between us. He did say, however, that he felt that I had been doing too much without talking it over with him and that he did not agree with all the things that I was doing.

I pressed him for specifics. He sort of waved me off and said, "Well, that's not important. The point is you should be discussing these things with me before you do them." Ruminating on our discussion, I concluded that the problem was not me, per se, or a lack of consultation on my part. It was also Jeff. He seemed to always be surprised by my aggressiveness—my push to change Arby's—and my openness about wanting the presidency.

Also, it now seemed clear that Jeff had decided that he liked being president and he wanted to be seen as the system leader. We were indeed competing.

The frost on our relationship was noticeable to everyone in the small Arby's enclave. It got to be a standing joke that when Jeff held staff meetings, he would sit so that his back was always facing me. I would sit next to him and he would swing his chair so that he would talk to people over his shoulder to keep his back to me.

Our relationship did improve for a brief time when Jeff hired Wayne Jones from KFC to head up the franchising department. Now Jeff had someone to talk to, someone to direct on a day-to-day basis to distract him from his unhappiness with not being more involved with me.

About this time the *Atlanta Business Magazine* came and asked for an in-depth interview. Thinking that this would be good publicity for the company and for the innovations we were making, I gladly accepted. Then I told Jeff about it. He seemed uninterested, but he soon showed how deceptive that impression had been.

About sixty days later, my picture appeared on the cover of the magazine. When Jeff McMahon saw it, his face became red. He came into my office and slammed the magazine down on my desk. He asked angrily, "When are you going to stop getting publicity about what you are planning on doing and start making something really happen around here?" then charged out of my office.

When this happened, my secretary, a remarkable lady named Audrey, came into my office. She said, "That man is impossible! I don't see how you stand him. I have never been in a company where there is so much acrimony between the Number-One and Number-Two men in the company. Chris, he is out to get you. Are you sure you are going to be able to keep your job?"

Her question triggered a question already in the back of my mind. I had not wanted to consider the fact that I might lose this job. I was not happy working with Jeff McMahon, but I was hoping that he would leave in a short period of time. I could endure anything for a while.

I reassured Audrey, "Don't worry. The AFA Board is behind me and I don't think Jeff could do anything so long as I have their support." Brave words, but I realized that I could be on thin ice, especially if Jeff chose to renege on his written promise to cede me the presidency.

Reluctantly, only thirteen months after I left Burger King, I updated my resume and told friends that if they heard of good jobs that I might be available.

A Final Triumph

As in most franchise organizations, Arby's had a national convention every year. It was hosted by the AFA, not the company. Basically, it was my convention to run, just as it had been my role at Burger King.

Because this would be the first major national meeting since I had joined Arby's, I wanted this convention to be a "wow." I felt sure it would be critical to my survival to keep the support of the franchisees. We scheduled it for Palm Springs in February.

As the convention approached, almost everything was breaking favorably. Restaurant sales had been improving, the cost of advertising materials had been decreasing. New ideas had been flowing from the new marketing group to the franchisees. In addition there was a major curiosity factor. We had an agency that had never presented to the bulk of the franchisees. Most had never met me or the rest of the new marketing team.

Best of all we had some new products to introduce to the franchisees. We had the new deli line of sandwiches and the "Hat-o'-Beef." And we had new advertising to show that supported those new products—advertising that was truly a step above the quality of what Arby's had used in the past.

The convention was a smashing success. The franchisees loved the new products that we sampled at the coffee break. They liked the new advertising and the new promotions.

I was particularly pleased when a key major franchisee, George Nadler from Minneapolis, came up to us. He and his son Chuck's eyes were glowing with enthusiasm. He said, "Chris, this is the greatest thing we have ever seen since we became franchisees of Arby's. Keep up the good work."

A few years later, when I was looking for another job, the Nadlers showed me how much they were impressed by making sure that I was interviewed to become president of Arby's. (see Chapter 12).

The one clinker at the convention was George Lois. George had been given a careful script by Bill Pitts to present the new advertising. But George seemed to ignore it. He stood up and began his speech something like this: "I am happy to be here, you guys. We are going to show you the best f—— advertising you have ever seen. It is so good that I almost gave it to one of your competitors."

At this point, one of the wives in the audience was seen getting up from her chair with her hands over her daughter's ears and running from the room. The bulk of the Arby's franchisees were from the Mid-west and George's gruff, rough, coarse New York language went over like a lead balloon. We couldn't wait to get him off the stage.

After the convention, the proof of its success was quickly found. Franchisees signed up for the new programs in record numbers. And, as I recall, we were rapidly expanding the new deli sandwiches into almost the entire system by May. We were off to a great start.

A "Bitter" Ending

Then the roof caved in. Jeff McMahon called me into his office in late May. His face was beet red. As I sat down, he said, "I asked you here to request that you resign now. If you resign and you agree not to comment to the press about Arby's in any way and you agree to not discuss how you feel about this resignation with the press or the franchisees, we will honor your contract and pay your six month's severance. Otherwise, we will see you in court." I was temporarily stunned. My first thought: "How could he do this? It's so totally unfair."

As I looked at it, I had successfully accomplished all that Jeff had laid out as initial tasks. I had provided real leadership inside the company. I had hired a staff that had created an entirely new partnership between the AFA and Arby's corporate and had led development of some excellent new menu items. I had a new restaurant design and system sign, "Schoenleb's Folly," that was setting sales records.

I quickly regained my equilibrium. Jeff's methodology was crude and the timing unexpected, but not the firing itself. I had sensed that this was coming. I had come to realize that Jeff's written promise of the presidency was not going to happen. He wanted to stay; he and I couldn't live together in the same building, let alone in the same company. One of us had to go.

Somehow, Jeff had sold this same point of view to RC and the AFA Board. To a man, those who called me to say "good-by" said they were sure that Jeff had been forced to act to create a more harmonious parent company. Mike Shulson said something like, "It's just too bad you two couldn't get along."

My career at Arby's was over. Before I left his office, I agreed to Jeff's terms; there would be no advantage to fight a battle when the war was lost. I did demand and obtain assurance that Arby's and RC would follow the same terms given me relative to discussion of my resignation with the press and others.

Postscript

And so ended a strange chapter in my life. I was summarily fired while in the midst of building what I believe (to this day) would have been a major marketing success. Indeed, after I left, under Larry Krueger's direction, Arby's did rebound in sales. The deli line and the new marketing team did well. But I will never know if my idea of making Arby's a national deli chain was accurate.

After I left, many of the specific changes I had tried to institute were dropped. Jeff replaced the "Schoenleb's folly" building design with his own. "Hat-o-Beef" disappeared, etc.

Jeff McMahon stayed with Arby's until 1985. He left when RC sold the company to Victor Posner (see Chapter 12). Jeff ended his career in the '80's as president of a chain that failed, "D'Lites."

Larry Krueger stayed at Arby's until the late '80s. He is now chief marketing officer for Popeye's as he nears retirement.

Moving On

Sometimes things work out in your career better than you could ever expect. That was certainly the case with my firing at Arby's. I needed a new position quickly, especially financially. I had only six months severance pay and both of my daughters were planning to be married in the next three months.

Fortunately, because of an old boss and friend, Bob Swanson, my job hunt lasted one day.

I had kept in contact with Bob since the Needham days. He had become CEO of Del Webb, the company that developed Sun City. In early May he had called, "I know you've told me things aren't too good for you at Arby's; would you be interested in talking to someone about a restaurant chain CEO's position?"

I replied, "Sure—if it makes sense for me. What are you talking about?"

Bob answered, "I have a friend named Karl Eller. Have you ever heard of him?"

"Vaguely. Isn't he the guy that left Needham to start an outdoor advertising company?"

"Yeah, he's the guy," said Bob. "He ended up owning a company called Combined Communications which he sold to Gannett for a lot of money. After six months of working with Gannett, he resigned and went into business for himself. He now has a personal investment company he calls Red River Resources. That company bought an ice cream chain called Swensen's. Do you know Swensen's?"

"Yes, I remember Swensen's. We used to go to Swensen's all the time when we lived in Modesto. Great ice cream. Joanne really loved their hot fudge sundaes."

"Good! I agree with you, it is great ice cream. The problem is that Swensen's is losing money. Eller really needs somebody like you to fix it for him."

"Where's Swensen's headquartered?"

"Here. Karl moved it to Phoenix. Would you be interested in talking to him? I think it would be worth your while."

I was intrigued. I loved the idea of being in Phoenix so I replied "Yeah, I'll talk to him, Bob, as long as he pays my way out there."

A few days later Larry Wilson the president of Swensen's called. He explained that he was leaving his position. He said it wasn't the right kind of job for him and that he didn't really understand the restaurant business. He asked if I would come out to interview with Karl Eller and him.

So I journeyed to Phoenix where the three of us chatted for a full day. They were very open about their problems and their professed need for an expert with my background. They convinced me the problem with Swensen's was management, not the concept itself.

I came away very interested. They would give me carte blanche authority to run a chain of about 310 outlets, some company-owned, mostly franchise-owned. My task as CEO would be to engineer a turn-around, then take the company public. It seemed to be an exciting and doable challenge.

The interviews had taken place about ten days before my final meeting with Jeff. When I went home to tell my wife I had been fired, she handed me a special delivery letter. God was smiling on me. It was an offer letter to be president of Swensen's.

I immediately called Tom Chorey, my lawyer, to make sure he would develop an employment contract. Then I called Eller's office and asked if I could fly out that weekend and discuss the final terms for my joining him. He agreed.

Thus, the very day I was fired from Arby's, I flew to Phoenix to finalize a deal to become president of Swensen's. I was anxious to do this before Eller learned that I had been fired. I was sure this would reduce my leverage with Karl who had impressed me as being a very tough negotiator.

We cut a deal and I agreed to join Swensen's as its President, after my daughters' weddings.

Lessons Learned

Accomplishments alone do not assure personal success in business—even when you have the support of employees or franchisees.

Final Comment

One of my biggest mistakes at Arby's was to believe my own press clippings. The press loves to create and destroy management heroes. In the end, the press hurt me in Arby's; it gained me nothing except higher visibility in the industry that dramatized my leaving Arby's, hardly something I needed.

CHAPTER 11
Rescuing Swensen's

(Winning the Battles but Losing the War)

I was determined that Swensen's would be the final stop in my career. Now in my late forties, I wanted to stop the carousel of new companies in new cities. And Swensen's seemed to offer this opportunity. I finally had a CEO position, and, most important, I felt confident that Swensen's made sense for me even though on the surface, Swensen's appeared to be a big career gamble. It was the opposite of the big-company, big-agency successes I had achieved.

Swensen's was the smallest company, ever, in my career. Total company revenues (mostly franchise fees and royalties) were $8,300,000 the year I joined the company. I had spent ten times this amount on Burger King advertising alone. Further, Swensen's had total system retail sales of $79,000,000. It was only one-fourth the size of Arby's. Worse yet, it was a company losing money, and it had very limited financial resources.

So, why did I choose Swensen's? What made me ignore all the negtives that said I didn't "fit"?

First, it seemed to be a concept with tremendous potential. Swensen's was a unique restaurant concept. It had a great signature product—its ice cream served in cones and in soda fountain delights. It had a high-quality limited sandwich food menu. And, it had an upscale old-fashioned ice cream parlor décor that was as attractive as it was timeless.

Second, it was already the sales leader in its market niche. Swensen's had excellent consumer acceptance and name recognition.

Third, it seemed to have a culture well suited to my personality. It was large enough to have a professional staff to lead, and I'd be the boss. I had flourished at Burger King prior to Don Smith when I had been the expert and left alone to direct my area of expertise. Clearly I would have a similar situation at Swensen's.

On paper I would be reporting to my fellow members of the Board of Directors: Karl Eller and a group of Karl's friends; Steve Mihaylo, a local entrepreneur; Joe Garagiola, the famous sports announcer; Mary Galvin, the wife of the CEO of Motorola; Ike Herbert, VP of Marketing for Coca-Cola; Bill Turner, chairman of the Atlantic Argyle Corp; and Art Korf, a former McDonald's franchisee who owned a Swensen's in Scottsdale. With the exception of Korf, they knew little about running a restaurant chain.

Of course, in reality, I reported to Karl Eller who took the title of Chairman of Board but he was far more than that—he owned Swensen's. But, I was sure that Karl would let me operate with complete authority. (And he did.)

Beyond all this, Swensen's was an irresistible personal challenge—it was a strong concept that needed fixing.

Karl Eller had defined the challenge the day we shook hands and I signed a five-year employment contract. "Chris," he said, "I love Swensen's. I think it's a great concept with a great product. I really thought I could make Swensen's great, but, so far I haven't been able to. I seem to have gotten myself into a business that I really don't understand as much as I thought I did."

He continued, "The challenge you face is finding the answer to one question—is Swensen's fixable or not? You have a free hand. Do whatever you think you have to do to get the job done—just understand we don't have any money to invest in capital projects. As I see it, there is no room for any more mistakes like buying the stores we bought. The company has been bleeding my personal resources and, at some point, I won't be able to put in any more money to keep it afloat."

He concluded. "But, if you can fix this mess, I'll make sure you're well rewarded."

Swensen's History

When I came aboard, Swensen's was a retail franchised system of about 310 outlets—34 of which were company owned. Swensen's was not only in the United States, it was international. There were over forty franchised outlets in Canada, as well as franchisee stores in Mexico, Japan, Hong Kong, and Singapore.

Swensen's had been founded by Earle Swensen in 1948, when he opened a small ice cream dipping store (a retail outlet a la Baskin Robbins) on top of Russian Hill in San Francisco. He soon built a reputation of having the best ice cream in San Francisco. His business grew steadily and profitably.

Earle's success stemmed directly from his product. His ice cream was unique in several ways. First, it was very fresh. It was made in the store daily in a small machine that made only twenty gallons of ice cream at a time. Second, it had a proprietary fourteen percent butterfat formula that made a richer, creamier ice cream than competitors. It was, I believe, America's first super premium ice cream, long before Häagen Dazs would ever grace the American retail scene.

Earle Swensen was an ambitious man. After his initial success, he harbored visions of making Swensen's a national chain. But he was not wealthy—he lived off his store's receipts—and he was risk averse. Result: he basically procrastinated after one attempt to expand failed.

Then, as the story was told to me, in the mid-'60s Earle met an enterprising opportunist, Bill Meyer. Bill saw the potential of putting the Swensen's ice cream product in an upscale ice cream parlor. Bill convinced Earle to sell him the rights to franchise his Swensen's vision.

Meyer's first few franchised outlets in northern California were a success. He quickly expanded and by the early '70s, Swensen's ice cream parlors could be found throughout California.

Initially, Swensen's franchised only so-called "A" stores. These stores had an old-fashioned décor with a tin roof ceiling and limited seating in marble-tabled booths. They sold only ice cream, ice cream cones, and ice cream sundaes and sodas. The ice cream cone service and take-out service was much like today's Baskin-Robbins. But unlike Baskin-Robbins, Swensen's had waitress service. This allowed seated patrons to order and be served a litany of soda fountain treats, such as ice cream sundaes, banana splits, etc. in upscale glassware.

Most "A" stores were only marginally profitable despite evening and weekend crowds that usually overflowed the outlet's capacity. Because of this, Bill Meyer became convinced Swensen's should build bigger stores to capture this overflow business to build sales and profits. So he developed a "B" store, which was an "A" store with more seating—forty to eighty seats versus twenty to thirty in "A" stores.

The added seating in "B" stores did generate more sales, but not incremental profits. The higher rent and operating cost of the added space offset the increased revenue. This led to the inevitable conclusion that to grow profitably, a Swensen's ice cream parlor needed more than an ice-cream-only-menu. So the ever-inventive Bill Meyer added a limited menu of cold sandwiches, potato chips, etc. for the lunch period and put it into all "B" stores.

This food menu was marginally successful, but the "B" store suffered from the lack of a kitchen to prepare the food menu. It also was noncompetitive to any restaurant offering hot food. So the "B" store eventually evolved into an even larger "C" store.

The "C" store was a full service restaurant/ice cream parlor eighty to one hundred twenty-seat and a small kitchen. It was equipped to prepare a complete line of hot and cold sandwiches, including hamburgers and french fries, as well as having a take-out ice cream counter and a large soda fountain.

By the early '80s there were almost equal numbers of all three kinds of stores making the marketing of the chain's food menu a nightmare that had to be solved on a store-by-store basis, not a marketwide basis.

Bill Meyer was reportedly a penultimate salesman. But he was also an entrepreneur who never had enough capitalization. Legend has it that he was always living one step ahead of the bill collector as he slowly built Swensen's.

There was never a formal expansion plan for Swensen's. Most franchisees became sold on the concept when, by happenstance, they visited a Swensen's while on a trip to California. If they then sought a franchise, Meyer would sell it to them anywhere in the country. He also went international on an "as requested" basis.

This resulted in "outposts" of Swensen's stores in twenty-nine states outside California. There were clusters of stores in Phoenix, Kansas City, Detroit, Nashville, Austin, south Florida, and Washington, D.C. A few outlets sprouted up in Dallas, New Orleans, Chicago, Tucson, and New York City. And single "C" stores were built in places like Cleveland and Columbus, Ohio, Birmingham, Alabama, Charleston, S.C., and Chapel Hill, N.C.

Scattered distribution meant that there were insufficient ad funds to support TV advertising except in California. This in turn hurt the ability to build consumer sales. The failure to build sales resulted in many disillusioned franchisees who psychologically burned out trying to build a profitable business. Hence as many as fifteen percent of the existing Swensen's were up for sale every year.

Bill Meyer's ownership of Swensen's ended in 1980 after he met Karl Eller. Eller had always liked Swensen's. He had been a regular customer for years. In the late '70s, when the opportunity arose, Karl purchased four Swensen's "C" stores in Phoenix and became a Swensen's franchisee. Shortly thereafter, a group of nine stores in the Fort Lauderdale area came up for sale for what appeared to be a "fire sale" price. In July 1979, through his investment company, Eller acquired them.

Karl was now one of Swensen's largest franchisees. When profits did not emerge from his investment, Karl met with Bill Meyer in late 1979 to try to get help, or perhaps sell his stores to Meyer. One thing led to another and Meyer offered to sell Eller the whole company.

They struck a deal. Eller, through his company, Loel One, paid a premium price of $8,200,000 for Swensen's, then a marginally profitable company with about $5,000,000 in revenues. There is no doubt in my mind that to this day Karl Eller believes he got the wrong end of the deal.

At any rate, by the time I joined the company, Eller had owned Swensen's for eighteen months. In this period, he had moved the headquarters from San Francisco to Phoenix and had almost totally restaffed it. Aside from the Director of Franchise sales, Harry Kraatz, there were no carryover personnel from the Bill Meyer era. The new CEO, Larry Wilson, who had been working for Karl in the radio station business, was learning a whole new industry.

The net result of Eller's changes was that during this start-up period, no one really understood the business. Worse yet, the company sold no new franchises. Instead, they purchased seventeen additional Swensen's stores that had been poorly operated by failing franchisees in the midwest and Houston. By mid-1981, Swensen's had thirty-four company-owned stores in six states.

The new management did not have the expertise to make these acquired units profitable. Result: Karl spent more money not only for the restaurants but also in start-up and operating costs with no positive results. The red ink began to flow with no prospect for an early fix. This led to looking for a new CEO and my coming to Swensen's.

Building a Management Team

I tried to begin my career at Swensen's differently. I wanted to educate myself about the fundamentals of Swensen's firsthand before I took command. I was sure there were major corporate myths that had to be identified quickly, or I would fail.

My first step, then, as president of Swensen's was to ask Larry Wilson to continue to manage the company while I went to the chain's training school, "Sundae School."

At Sundae School, I was part of a new franchisee class. The professor was Mike Amos, a truly dedicated Swensen's employee. (Mike had a swimming pool shaped like an ice cream cone at his home.) In the class I learned the company's history. I learned how ice cream was made in the stores; I made ice cream sodas and sundaes. But most of all I understood how the corporate staff believed a Swensen's store should be operated.

After graduating from Sundae School, I formally became CEO of Swensen's on September 1, 1981.

My first move was to get acquainted with the staff I had inherited and I was pleasantly surprised. I found a base of talent in key staff areas that would help me move quickly. I had inherited three young but very talented managers who had worked for Eller prior to his Swensen's purchase—Quinn Williams, Carl Osterman, and Pat Doughty.

First I met with the corporate counsel, Quinn Williams. Quinn sported a baby face that belied his very aggressive, "take no prisoners" approach to business. Now in his early thirties, he had been hired by Eller directly from the University of Arizona Law School and had been part of the Eller organization for seven or eight years. He had a quick and incisive mind and proved to be one of the brightest men I have ever dealt with.

Quinn had gone through the learning curve and now understood franchising and franchising law. He would obviously be a good right arm for me in dealing with the many franchising problems that I knew had to be out there given the situation of the company.

I asked him to prepare me a detailed brief on all legal and franchising issues. He smiled, "I'm way ahead of you." (Quinn never lacked in self-confidence.) He handed me a long memo titled "Legal Briefing For Chris

Schoenleb." I chuckled, but I was impressed. One critical management base seemed well covered.

Next I met with the Vice President of Finance, Carl Osterman. Carl was a very intense, middle-aged CPA who sported a full but well-trimmed beard. After telling horror stories of his first year in which he had learned what he called "restaurant accounting" and had also coped with some "creative accounting" that he had inherited from the Bill Meyer, Carl laid out the Swensen's financial story.

It wasn't pretty. The bottom line: Swensen's was not only losing money, but it was not generating enough cash flow to pay bills. The company was, for all intents and purposes, bankrupt. Only cash infusions from Karl Eller were keeping the company afloat. Worst of all, operating losses were accelerating. They had grown greater each three-month period for over a year.

From my prior job interviews and Eller's challenge, I had understood that the company was losing money, but now for the first time I understood the total depth of the financial problem. I asked Carl for his recommendations on how to stop the bleeding.

Being a good CPA, his first comment was "Well, we have to cut overhead costs." Then he added, "But the big problem is the cash flow drain from the company-owned stores." I asked him to put together his recommendations for the overhead cost cutting. I'd attack the company store issues.

The rest of the senior staff consisted of Hank Tunney, the Operations Vice President whose responsibilities included running the company-owned stores. (Two key positions were vacant—a VP of Marketing and a VP of Franchising to sell new franchises. Harry Kraatz had quit to return to work with Bill Meyer in San Francisco on a new venture.)

My first day ended with a lengthy and painful meeting with Tunney. We discussed the operations of the company stores. They were losing money at an alarming rate. Of the thirty-four stores, less than half had a positive cash flow.

I was not impressed with Hank even though he had a lengthy restaurant operations pedigree, most notably as an employee of Art Korf in the McDonald's system. Hank's discussion with me was full of describing problems and excuses for why they existed, not solutions he was trying.

In all fairness, Hank was really not qualified for the position he held. He was not entrepreneurial; he was used to a highly structured system, not the free-flowing Swensen's environment. He seemed overwhelmed to be running an operation with very few operations manuals—a problem that was compounded because the thirty-four Company stores were in six states over four time zones.

After hearing his litany of problems, I asked Hank to give me a plan to improve our in-store labor costs. My initial analysis had shown unexplainable wild swings in these costs from store to store. I told him to get back to me within a week.

When Tunney failed to report back on schedule, I called him into my office and requested a status report. He admitted, in an offhand, why-do-you-bother-me-with-your-questions-I'm-a-busy-man attitude, that he had not done anything to address my assignment.

This infuriated me. Biting my tongue, I asked him, "Why did you ignore my request?"

He replied rather diffidently, "I didn't have time. I've been too busy. I'll get to it in the next week or two." His subliminal message was clear, "I'm the expert. I'll do things my way."

I told him to try again and sternly demanded he return with answers within forty-eight hours. When he did not return on schedule, it was clear that Hank had to be fired. Firing him would send a message to all, especially to store operations personnel, that things had to change.

I asked for his resignation the next day. Then to cover myself with a Board member, I called Art Korf to explain why.

I replaced Tunney with Pat Doughty. Doughty, a former Duke basketball player in his early thirties, had been running Eller's stores in Florida. In addition to the obvious advantage of being immediately available, he impressed me as having three other key attributes that made him the obvious choice. He was knowledgeable, smart, and he "fit" with the other two management members. Like them, he had worked for Eller prior to Swensen's. He too was a CPA.

My fact-finding continued with a review of the marketing program. Without a Marketing Vice President Swensen's relied on its advertising agency, Doyle–Dane–Bernbach–West for all its needs. DDB-West had done excellent point-of-purchase materials, radio commercials, etc., but there seemed to be no organized plan for using them.

I went to Los Angeles to meet the agency. My first impression was very favorable. But at the same time, there seemed to be a cultural "disconnect"—Swensen's and DDB–West didn't seem to "fit." We had to be the agency's smallest account by a wide margin.

It seemed obvious that the only reason they were handling the business was because of Karl Eller. They were hoping that Eller, who had earned the reputation of being a man who built big successful companies, would find a way to build Swensen's into a major advertiser.

The account executive on the business was Howard Englehart. Howard, a genial, stocky, bearded man in his mid-thirties, was a knowledgeable advertising man. He possessed a quick wit and seemed to have a real interest in the business. Even better, he understood the Swensen's system and was well liked by everyone.

A few months after meeting Howard, I talked to the agency about hiring him as Marketing VP. They gave their Okay, and Howard readily agreed to leave southern California to come to Arizona where the same salary could buy a house twice the size he had in California.

One management position remained to be filled—the VP of Franchise Sales. It wasn't long before I found Richard Pope. Richard had been working for Ramada in Phoenix as one of several executives in their franchising department. When I offered him the opportunity to run Franchising and Development for Swensen's and he met some of his fellow workers, Richard readily agreed to join us. Like them, he was young (early thirties), ambitious, and fearless.

One other important person to the company was also hired. Sonia Ford, a former English teacher with outstanding secretarial and people skills joined Swensen's as my administrative assistant. She was also the de facto office manager for our small home office staff. And she handled all customer complaints under the pseudonym of Nancy Shane.

By late spring, one of my first tasks was completed. Swensen's had a sharp young management team. Still, the key would be how we all worked together. One concern: I would have to get used to was that I was "the old man" of the group—at least fifteen years older than the average senior staff member.

Karl Eller

Working for Karl Eller was a different and sometimes difficult experience. I had admired his business accomplishments and had hoped for a good overall relationship between us, much as I had experienced with Bob Swanson.

I was disappointed. Karl was, from the first, very standoffish. Essentially, he shunned "small talk." He seemed to be a man obsessed with business and with making deals. He didn't seem to care about getting to know me personally.

I never felt we were teammates. Instead, he gave me the impression that people who worked for him were just pawns in the world of business and financial dealmaking. Most of the time, in fact, I felt that Karl and I were living on different planets. His world was populated with the "beautiful people" with whom he always seemed to be exploring possible business deals. My planet was the business of operating a company— definitely an occupation ranking below the "deal" on his planet. Hence, I could never be his business equal.

Result: We never had good personal rapport. We had, at best, a formal, strictly business relationship that never remotely became a business friendship.

Sadly, and worse yet, Karl translated his perceived superiority into rudeness in one-on-one meetings in his office. What do I mean by rudeness? It can best be illustrated by my first meeting with Karl about money. It was the first of several Swensen's financial crises.

At the end of my first month, Carl Osterman came to my office and said, "You know, Chris, we are not going to make payroll next month unless we get some money from Karl Eller." Carl was introducing me to the reality of a small privately owned company. You have to manage by cash flow and not worry too much about the P&L statement. *Cash flow is king.*

I looked at Carl and said, "Well, how do we get that money? Do we go over and ask Eller to write a check?"

"Yep, that's exactly what we do. I've already done the numbers. we have an appointment with The Man at 4:30 this afternoon."

So at the appointed hour we went to Karl Eller's office located next door to Swensen's in a separate building on the Arizona Biltmore grounds.

As might be expected of an executive who had "wheeled and dealed" for almost twenty years to build a powerhouse media company, Karl Eller had the ultimate "power" office. It was large of course—perhaps 25' × 40'. But more than this, it reeked status and intimidation.

For status: The walls were covered with pictures of Karl shaking hands with celebrities and with letters from presidents of the United States, etc., showing his high status. He had been Olympic Chairman for the State of Arizona. He had been an early supporter of the Fiesta Bowl, etc., etc., etc. There were memorabilia like footballs, trophies, and such, strewn throughout the office.

For intimidation: The office was arranged so that his oversized desk was slightly elevated and was set up to form the horizontal top of a furniture-formed T. The vertical base of the T was a long conference table that butted up to the center of Eller's desk. The conference table had uncomfortable high-backed baronial-like chairs. So, as a visitor, you sat at the stem of the T, craning your neck sideways and looking up to Karl in his "power seat" or throne.

In this office, Karl had a standard modus operandi for our meetings that can only be described as "rude." As he sat in his power seat, he accepted phone calls from almost anyone who called. It would not be unusual for Karl to answer five phone calls in forty-five minutes as we were trying to make a presentation to him. This meant there was rarely any continuity in our conversations.

At this first major meeting, Eller was cordial but, as always, impersonal. As he looked at the numbers Carl had prepared, he answered at least three phone calls. Finally he put the phone down, visibly winced, then smiled through tight lips, and said, "Well, I will get the money somehow. But there isn't much more where this comes from. I hope you guys don't have to come back for more."

Carl Osterman quickly replied, "Unless Chris pulls a miracle, I don't think this will be the last time we will have to come over here, Karl. We are going into winter and you know how sales fall in the winter. As long as we have all these company stores, we're going to continue to bleed."

Eller nodded. Then he asked about everything I was doing. He seemed interested in knowing events, but rarely commented on them pro or con. Clearly, I had my wish. He would not interfere.

Still I wanted to use him as a sounding board—every CEO needs one. I wanted him to express his opinion on my initial plans for Swensen's turnaround. I began to tell him about these plans. As I did, the phone rang. He answered, then summarily dismissed us.

If Eller had set out to intimidate me, he almost succeeded. Clearly, he did communicate that I was not as important to him as his friends or other business associates. I was a "hired hand" and, therefore, one step below him in the social pecking order.

I left the room somewhat shaken. I had not expected to be treated like a second-class citizen in a meeting that was as important to my job as the one I had just attended. Still, we had gotten the funds to continue. It was time to get to work.

Getting Started

After the money meeting with Karl Eller, I still felt the need to learn more about Swensen's before I launched what would obviously be a "do or die" turnaround effort. I started with a trip to San Francisco to meet Earle Swenson to see his original store and seek his input about the company.

Earle was a pleasant surprise. In his mid-sixties, he had flashing blue eyes and exuded the great vitality of a Norseman. He waxed eloquently an unbridled enthusiasm for his product and the company that bore his name. We seemed to instantly "connect" and maintained a good personal relationship during my tenure at Swensen's and the years that followed.

Earle had been little used by Bill Meyer. But after meeting him, I saw the opportunity to make him our corporate spokesperson, à la Colonel Sanders for KFC. I asked Earle if he would do this for expenses and he nodded yes, beaming from ear to ear to be asked to participate. Over the next few years we would develop a complete PR program to take advantage of Earle's natural charisma.

On this trip I also met with the northern California franchisees. I followed this meeting with several other trips to meet franchisees and get a firsthand feel for the Swensen's system in terms of people, quality of operations, décor etc. *Lifetime Lesson: There is no substitute in the retail franchise business for visiting actual operating retail locations. These visits always generate insights and ideas that can never be developed from sitting at a desk.*

Returning from the last of these fact-finding trips, I came to the painful conclusion. Swensen's was a flawed concept. The average Swensen's store was not generating enough profits for a good franchisee to prosper. It seemed to flourish only in high traffic tourist locations, like the French Quarter in New Orleans, or the MGM Grand in Las Vegas. *To fix the chain, we had to modify the concept. We had to find a way to reduce a franchisee's operating costs and build his sales volume or Swensen's would never truly be a success.*

I also concluded that the turnaround could not be done fast enough with internal staff. I had to bring more outside resources to the company. To do this I turned to hiring my "expert" friends in the business.

We needed retail sales promotion expertise. I called Rogers Brackmann, and his agency, RMI, became the promotion agency for Swensen's. It would be a small account for Rog, but we would have his brain working on our business.

We needed interior design expertise. Although the original Swensen's with the tin ceilings and marble tabletops had an almost timeless quality, I questioned whether an old-fashioned ice cream parlor was entirely appropriate for "C" stores. Also, the décor was very expensive. I contacted Phil Lincoln and hired his firm to study how we might "spiff up" the chain's interior and cut costs.

We needed kitchen equipment expertise. After reviewing the standard Swensen's equipment package and kitchen layout, I was convinced there were major opportunities to reduce equipment and operating costs. I called Al Bennett from Burger King. Al had retired from Burger King at a young age to make and sell "kit cars." He became enthused about returning to the restaurant business and quickly moved from his Florida home to join us.

The Turnaround Game Plan

Having mastered a preliminary understanding of the chain, I held a management planning meeting outside the office. We went to Sedona where we rented a small conference room for three days.

At this meeting, I was able to achieve three critical goals that would bring quick positive change to Swensen's

First I changed everyone's focus from "surviving" to "fixing." **Lifetime Lesson: The key first step in forging a turnaround at any company is to change management's focus from fear of failure to developing a new short-term plan that will immediately address the company's problems.**

Second, as a management team, we developed a common vision for the company's future that all believed was attainable. *This is an equally important step in any turnaround. Management has to believe its task is doable and will work.*

Last and most important, we put together a tactical game plan to turn the vision into reality. The game plan had six major elements that stemmed from one basic tenet I had insisted on—*we would turn Swensen's around primarily by growing revenues, not by cutting manpower or franchisee services.*

The plan's specifics were these six tactics:

1 *Aggressively grow the chain by selling new franchises.* Franchise fees would provide instant needed revenue. Royalties from new stores

would assure a bigger long-term earnings stream. Richard Pope was authorized two new hires to help accomplish this.

2 *Sell the company stores to new or existing franchisees*—all of them except the four stores in Phoenix and the MGM Grand. This would help stop the cash flow drain as quickly as possible Richard Pope was assigned this task to be handled personally.

3 *Focus on ways to build retail sales that did not require massive TV advertising. To me this spelled promotion and menu innovation—"news" that we could use to create more frequency of visit or build the average check.* For promotion we asked Rogers Merchandising for a good frequency-building promotion like the Arby's glass promotions. For menu development we agreed we had to invest in consumer research to provide direction for changes. We would hire Dr. Saul Ben-Zev to begin the process.

While Saul did the research, we assigned Mike Amos, and Jim Seibel, who handled R&D for ice cream, to value engineer the menu, that is, reformulate the menu specifications to lower restaurant food costs. We also commissioned them to redesign the printed in-restaurant menu.

4 *Set up national purchasing contracts for all major items used by the system.* I knew from my Arby's and Burger King experience, that we could save twenty to forty percent of our costs on glassware and on foodstuffs under such an arrangement as opposed to the every store for itself system in place. *This would allow every store to be more profitable without raising prices.*

5 *Develop a PR program to use Earle Swensen.* We wanted him to promote the company and its ice cream to take advantage of the spreading craze for premium ice cream led by the introduction of Häagen Dazs. Mary Weyenberg, a PR lieutenant in the Ray Cox organization (part of Eller's overall operation), was asked to take this task. Later she would join us as Director of PR.

6 *Gamble our precious few advertising fund dollars on Swensen's first national consumer advertising.* We scheduled four-color print ads in upscale food magazines, *Sunset, Gourmet,* and *Bon Appetite* as well as *People*, during the peak consumption summer months. We wanted to try to build on Swensen's almost cultlike following in some areas.

In addition to these six actions, we wanted to engender franchisee enthusiasm and support. So we scheduled a series of regional meetings.

Visiting Asia—The First Time

As these programs were getting underway, there was one other part of Swensen's that needed attention—Swensen's international operations in Canada and the Pacific Rim. There were around forty stores in Canada.

The Swensen's franchisee in Singapore had four stores open. In Hong Kong there were two dipping stores and in Japan there were six "C" stores.

Swensen's had no management dealing with this area on a daily basis. The franchisees were operating basically on their own. When these franchisees joined Swensen's, they had been assured that we would provide operations support. However, after Jim Seibel had set up their initial dairy supply for making mix for in-store ice cream making, they had received no ongoing operational help and no marketing help.

Perhaps as a result, the international franchisees had experienced mixed results. This was particularly true of the Asian stores. Sales were excellent in Singapore; in fact, the highest volume Swensen's in the world was there on the third floor of a vertical shopping mall. The franchisees were not doing well in Hong Kong. And in Japan, we didn't really know what results had been attained. George Tanaka, the Japanese franchisee, was not forthcoming with his operating results.

I decided to visit each of the franchisees and see their stores to understand their operations. From this tour I hoped to develop a game plan for Canada and our Asia beachhead.

One question overarched the trip—how effective could I be?

Other than Canada I was dealing with countries I had never visited. I needed time to see the countries as well as the franchisees. Because of this, I scheduled sightseeing time and used this trip not only for business, but pleasure. I took my wife and called it our vacation.

The trip began with a twenty-two hour flight to Singapore. As we deplaned into Singapore's magnificent airport, P. H. and Irene Tay, our franchisees met us. Despite our jet lag, they began our orientation with an immediate visit to the Swensen's in the airport. And as they then escorted us in their chauffeur-driven car to our hotel, we learned we were their honored guests. This meant we would be "on stage" every waking hour with dinners, shopping, sightseeing and Swensen's business.

I had started in Singapore for two reasons. First, I wanted to understand why it was our most successful operation. Second, I wanted to meet Kevin Crombie. Kevin was an enterprising young Australian who had somehow become the general manager for the Singapore franchisees.

From phone conversations I had become very impressed with Kevin. It was clear he was one-person-in-a-million for Swensen's. He understood American business. He also knew how to conduct business on the Pacific Rim and he understood how to operate a Swensen's and he understood the various franchisee personalities involved. I wanted to meet him personally, and if we meshed, to try to hire him to be the Swensen's Vice President for the Pacific Rim.

On the third day, I met Kevin for dinner at the Churchill Club, one of the few bastions of the old British occupation then remaining in Singapore. After five minutes of in-person conversation, I confirmed my phone impressions—he was bright, quick, and ambitious. More than this I immediately liked Kevin. I felt, intuitively that we could work together.

Accordingly, I didn't waste any time starting a recruiting effort. Over pre-dinner cocktails after the usual niceties about foreign travel, weather, etc., I launched a frontal assault. "Kevin, I am interested in hiring a Vice President of Development for the Far East. And you seem to be the only candidate that I have."

He seemed startled by my bluntness. He stared at me for a moment, then replied in his mixed Aussie-British accent, "Well, I don't know what to say to you. You already mentioned this to me on the phone. I admit I may have an interest, if we get to know each other better and we seem to get along. But, I'm very doubtful that you will be able to afford me."

I replied, "Why don't we drop your affordability concern for the moment? First, let's get acquainted."

We ordered dinner and spent the entire time sharing our backgrounds. Kevin was from Perth, Australia. Very ambitious, he had attended one of the U.S.'s premier business schools, Wharton. Then he had joined the Rothschild banking organization before hiring on with the wealthy investors who owned Swensen's in Singapore. And he had married Crystal, a lovely lady from Taiwan, when they were both students at Wharton.

As the evening wore on we clearly became more comfortable with one another. Finally, I turned to him and said, "Well, how do you feel about working for me? We don't have much time to determine this."

After a pause, he smiled and answered, "I am pretty comfortable, I guess."

I said, "Well then, what are your salary needs that you feel I can't meet?"

Like all good negotiators he was in no hurry to begin. He sat silently and sipped on his coffee for awhile. Then gathering himself, he began, "Well, first of all there are certain transportation needs that I have and there are several logistical problems." He outlined them. His big demand was to move to Perth, Australia, and operate as the Vice President for the Pacific Rim: Asia, Australia, New Zealand and the Philippines.

He continued, "Lastly, of course, there is the salary." He named his price.

I listened very carefully. It was obvious he had spent a lot of time putting his "package" together. He wanted the job. And fortunately his package was inexpensive considering what he could offer to us.

When he had finished, I looked at him and said nothing. I sipped on my after-dinner coffee. Two or three minutes elapsed in silence. Then I smiled, and said, "I accept."

He was totally nonplused. "You what? You accept what?"

I grinned and replied "Your terms." I extended my hand, "Welcome aboard."

He almost stuttered as he replied, "You mean you will give me everything I just asked for?"

"Yes, write it up in an employment offer letter. I will sign it and you are hired."

He smiled, shook his head, then stalled, "Well, I will have to go talk to Crystal about it."

I didn't want to lose him so I said, "Is there something you didn't tell me that you want?"

"No, no, this is everything I want."

I concluded our evening with, "Don't disappoint me, Kevin. Let's get this done before I leave."

He dropped me back at the hotel. The next morning Swensen's had a new employee, one of the finest hires I ever made for any company.

The rest of the Asian trip was a real education as I began to understand the complexities of maintaining a successful franchisor-franchisee relationship with major cultural and distance barriers.

On our way back from Asia we stopped in Vancouver, Canada. There I met our somewhat estranged Canadian franchisee, Bob Munro, and spent a most worthwhile day mending fences.

I arrived home convinced I had laid the foundation for growth in international franchising. Kevin Crombie had developed a list of priority targets to complete our franchising of the Pacific Rim. From this, we agreed to start with Indonesia, Taiwan, Thailand, Australia, and New Zealand. Each could bring in potentially sizeable income from sales of master franchising rights. And we seemed to have a solid operation in Canada that we could work with through our U.S. operations.

This alone would not turn the company around financially, but it would be an important long-term piece to building a successful public company.

The Turnaround Begins

Clearly, the biggest step toward getting well financially was selling the company stores to franchisees and selling new store franchises.

We did both.

We sold the company stores in eighteen months. Richard Pope did a magnificent job. Working closely with Quinn Williams he sold twenty-five stores (we closed three) so that by the end of '83, we had only six company stores, four in Phoenix, one in Las Vegas, and one to sell in West Palm Beach. We had indeed stopped the cash flow drain.

Perhaps, the crowning moment of Richard Pope's career at Swensen's was when he called me at home at 6:00 A.M. from a dock in Mexico. He told me he had spent a a long night on a wealthy Mexican's yacht, and that as a result he had sold the Houston company stores.

I was elated. Richard had found the perfect person for Houston. I had worried over whether we could sell the Houston stores at any price, because all were losing money. I knew we had to have a franchisee with substantial means and patience to try and change the Houston picture, and, miracle of miracles, Richard had found him.

At the same time these sales of company store were occurring, another kind of franchise sale was also occurring—franchises for new units. We opened thirty Swensen's, closed six, and ended 1982 with 340 stores spread over thirty-one states and the District of Columbia; as well as five foreign countries, with a long-sold franchise finally opening in San Paulo, Brazil.

And, with better management, increased retail sales, and lowered operating costs, we reduced the operating losses in the remaining company stores significantly. Overall we increased revenues thirty-three percent while significantly reducing the operating losses each quarter of 1982 versus '81. The company still lost $1.5 million, but this was only half of the 1981 loss. Cash flow was tight; but we no longer needed Karl Eller's wallet to survive. *In short, we had turned Swensen's around.*

As I reviewed the financial and operating plans for 1983 for the Board of Directors, I promised another four quarters of improvement over the previous year, and a slight profit for the full year. To do this, I promised an innovative marketing program to lift retail sales in existing stores and make Swensen's an even more attractive franchising vehicle.

Year II: Marketing Swensen's

As 1983 began I was happy and optimistic. All was going well. I was comfortable in my job and with my staff. I had tasted success by accomplishing the first steps toward achieving a total corporate profit turnaround. And, I had received excellent support from Eller and the Board of Directors.

As important, attitudes within the company had changed as we began to focus our efforts on building our consumer image and consumer sales instead of survival. The staff was working extremely well together. All seemed truly excited about programs that had been developed for fruition in 1983.

One little change symbolized this changed focus—we remodeled our office lobby. We wanted to communicate to one and all a first impression that "Swensen's is a winner." To do this, we acted on a suggestion my wife Joanne made and changed the mundane visitor's lobby into a partial replica of a Swensen's Ice Cream Parlor that included a small soda fountain.

And with this came a unique fringe benefit loved by all—free ice cream. All visitors and all employees could sample as much ice cream as they wanted to scoop, free, at anytime. (I found myself eating a three-scoop treat virtually every afternoon).

The year began with franchisee convention in Phoenix to lay out for them an entire year's marketing plan that was revolutionary in many ways. The plan had four major elements:

First, we made innovative changes in the basic food menu. For the first time we knew to whom we needed to target our marketing efforts—women—and what changes or additions would appeal to this target audience.

Our basis for this knowledge? The research results from my old friend, Saul Ben-Zev. It was clear from Saul's research that our best opportunity to build our food business was at lunch. And to do this, we needed to make Swensen's menu more attractive for women seeking a leisurely lunch.

Saul suggested we look at salads and unique sandwiches, that is, those made with specialty breads like pita or croissants. We chose croissants and introduced a line of cold croissant sandwiches, turkey, ham and cheese, roast beef, and an all-veggie version. They were modestly successful, but they were a start toward developing a distinctive upscale sandwich menu to add to our hamburgers.

Second, we added a new line of ice cream sundaes to appeal to another specific new target audience—chocoholics. Saul's research had shown that chocoholics were heavy users of ice cream parlors but, for them, our menu had no unique appeal. This led to the creation of three new sundaes made entirely with chocolate ingredients: chocolate ice cream (including proprietary Swensen's flavors called Sticky Chewy Chocolate and Swiss Orange Chip), hot fudge sauce, chocolate whipped cream and a chocolate covered cherry on top! We called these Chocolate Fantasy Sundaes.

Third, we announced we had developed a new ultra premium ice cream—Swensen's Supreme. Super premium ice cream was the only growing segment in the ice cream market. To build our business, we felt we had to be perceived as a competitor in this category. And we weren't.

In Saul's research, we learned that consumers had a good image of Swensen's, but felt our product was not as good as Häagen Dazs, the super premium market leader in grocery stores, now beginning to expand into the retail ice cream store business.

Based on this research we felt compelled to develop our own super premium ice cream to compete directly with Häagen Dazs. But we had a dilemma—how could we do this with minimal risk? We couldn't risk changing Earle Swensen's basic formula that accounted for the bulk of our sales.

We solved this dilemma by deciding to develop a second ice cream formula that produced a denser product with a higher butterfat content than the original. We called it Swensen's Supreme. We planned to test the appeal of this product by offering it in a limited number of flavors at twenty cents higher retail cost per scoop in a few test stores.

We couldn't make Swensen's Supreme in the store as all the regular Swensen's ice cream was made. Instead, we planned to manufacture and sell it to the stores.

We told the franchisees that we would be testing this product in '83 to see if it would give added sales. Although they agreed Swensen's Supreme was an outstanding product, they were not enthused. They were very concerned that we were sending the wrong message to consumers, that is, that regular Swensen's ice cream was not a premium ice cream. We assured them that we would learn whether this was true in initial testing before risking the success of the system.

What we did not tell the franchisees at this meeting was that if we had some initial success in selling the super premium ice cream in the Swensen's stores, we were considering selling Swensen's Supreme, packaged in pints, quarts, and half gallons in supermarkets.

Last we introduced a new store design—a prefab "A" store made as a replica of a San Francisco cable car. One of the problems with the ice cream parlor business is that it is highly seasonal. Sales in most Swensen's were more than double in the summer versus the winter. This meant that in highly seasonal locations a Swensen's could not survive even though it could do very high volume during the summer season.

We had asked ourselves if there was a way to have a small temporary Swensen's "A" store that would be inexpensive enough to allow us to place it in a highly seasonal areas like beach resorts.

Al Bennett came up with a unique answer. Working with a local specialty builder in Phoenix, Al developed 250-square-foot replica of the San Francisco cable car that could be fabricated and transported like a mobile home. Designed to serve a limited number of ice cream flavors in cones and paper cups, using ice cream made at a standard Swensen's store, this concept could make money on less than half the sales volume of an existing Swensen's. We had made two of these cable car parlors for testing.

The franchisees were excited about this concept. After some initial hassling over who could test the concept, we agreed to let Leon Todd, our Chapel Hill, N.C., franchisee test it on Wrightsville Beach outside of Wilmington, N.C. (Leon also had a full service store in Wilmington.) We put the second cable car in Phoenix and franchised it to the Weiss Bros. car wash chain. They placed it on the lot of their highest volume unit located in the heart of central Phoenix.

At the convention we also announced a number of other operational changes. Perhaps the most significant change was instigating the use of a detailed operations inspection form for our field representatives to inspect each Swensen's overall operation: its cleanliness, food service, ice cream quality, etc. I had insisted that we develop it based on my experience with such programs in fast food. It invariably improved retail sales and customer satisfaction.

The franchisees left in high spirits. They, like we, sensed that Swensen's was on the move.

Going Public

We did not announce the biggest news for Swensen's in 1983 at the convention, because we had not expected it. In November 1983, Swensen's became a public company with its stock traded on NASDAQ.

I was genuinely surprised when Karl Eller called me into his office in late April and informed me that he wanted to take the company public. He quickly gained Board approval to hire a regional brokerage house in Los Angeles, Bateman Eichler, Hill Richards, to begin the process.

This proved to be a major distraction. I spent hundreds of hours in the going-public process which added to an already long workweek.

My first role was to answer all strategic questions, explain corporate plans, etc. to the underwriters. Fred Krimm, Bateman Eichler's partner in charge of this process, did much of his company's preliminary due diligence. Fred's first question was, "Will Swensen's be profitable in 1983?"

I replied, "I think so. If things continue the way they are, yes. It depends upon how many new franchises we sell, how many stores open, and when we finish selling the company stores. The best I can promise is that we will have eight straight quarters of improved operating results. And I'm sure that we can continue the quarterly successes in 1984 and be profitable."

Fred didn't like my answer. This meant Swensen's could not go public promising it would be a profitable company in 1983. Then, obviously quickly strategizing that Swensen's stock would have to be sold on future potential, he asked, "What do you think the odds are that Swensen's could be successful in the supermarket ice cream business with your new super premium product?"

I replied, "I don't know. You and I both know it will take significant time, money, and manpower to put together such a program. But, clearly it's a major opportunity, and if we get funds from a public stock sale, we will pursue it."

Fred Krimm liked that answer.

And so began the difficult process of going public. It took six months of hard work to put together the paperwork for the SEC, the stock prospectus, etc.

The next step was a "road show." After an initial meeting in Phoenix starring Karl Eller, Fred set up meetings with stockbrokers in Los Angeles, San Francisco, Dallas, Chicago, New York, and, of all places, Fresno, California, to sell the initial public offering shares. At these meetings, Pat Doughty and I were to sell the shares by selling the programs we had developed to assure growth and profitability.

The meetings went well. Two of the star attractions of the road show that helped make the sale were pictures of the new cable car store for Wrightsville Beach and providing sample tastings of Swensen's Supreme.

Finally, in early November, it was accomplished. Thirty-three percent of Karl Eller's shares in the company were sold to the public at $5.00/ share. Result: we had over $4,000,000 in the bank and one new board member, Fred Krimm.

I was rewarded with a handsome raise, and a major stock option. Karl Eller had kept his promise. If we succeeded in 1984 and beyond, I would be a wealthy man.

Year III: Building a New Swensen's

We ended 1983 with a loss of over $285,000. Primary reason: we opened ten stores less in the fourth quarter than we had planned.

Still, despite our fourth quarter woes, I began my third year with great optimism. The Swensen's system was growing in size and strength. We had opened thirty-seven new stores, twenty-one in the United States, four in Canada, and twelve outside North America, including five in Indonesia and two in New Zealand. We also had closed twenty units (ten in Canada) as we began weeding out the nonpaying franchisees. Swensen's was now in thirty-three states and eleven foreign countries with a total of 357 stores.

We had come a long way; but we still weren't profitable; 1984 would be crucial. I knew it would not be easy despite my assurances to the underwriters and Board of Directors.

To help make sure we succeeded, I held another out-of-the-office management planning meeting immediately after our public offering—this time in Tucson. We all needed to catch our collective breath and make sure we understood the plans to reach the profit goal for 1984. We also needed time to rebuild management camaraderie. We had made several key people changes in 1983.

When Carl Osterman left, we had replaced him with Larry Field. Larry had been the Swensen's auditor for Price Waterhouse and was a logical candidate for the position. However Larry was young and we knew we needed to go public with a more experienced person as CFO. Result: We restructured the company promoting Pat Doughty to senior VP of Finance and Development. Richard Pope and Larry Field would report to him.

In order to keep Quinn happy and recognize his efforts, we named him senior VP of Legal and Administration. Purchasing now reported to him.

This left an opening for a new senior VP of Operations. After several months search, we hired Bob Puccio for this position. He had over twenty years of operations experience but he quickly showed he was not up to the task. This hurt results in 1984, and cost me credibility with the franchisees.

The immediate result of all this, however, was to free me up to focus on three areas—building sales in the existing stores, the supermarket ice cream project, and international franchising efforts.

At the Tucson meeting, in addition to some serious planning sessions, we had some fun playing golf together and relaxing over several good meals. I wanted to offer this as a minor, but meaningful, reward for two long years of toil.

But, I also had a serious business purpose—namely to ensure I got the best thinking of these executives and engender their personal commitment to the business plans of the company. *Lifetime lesson: To obtain the best work from your management team, you must first build personal rapport with them and foster rapport among them. This can never be done if executives know each other only in an office setting.*

We formulated an aggressive, somewhat risky game plan for 1984. It consisted of the same basic elements as 1983 with four major additions.

First, we would honor our going-public pledge to develop a program to test market Swensen's Supreme ice cream in supermarkets.

Second, we would finally get the entire revamped food menu rolled out to the system. We had developed a line of large "gourmet" salads, a Cobb salad, Chef's salad, etc. These were served in spectacular fashion in large special glassware. Added to the croissant sandwiches, we now had a "signature" luncheon menu especially targeted to women. And these items, along with our ice cream specialties, would be featured in our new award-winning menu. (The menu's design had been awarded first prize for the casual restaurant concept category in the National Restaurant Association's (NRA) annual design contest.)

Third, we would add a new specialty parlor ice cream item, waffle cones. As a trade-up product, versus regular cones, it would add sales volume and profits to a key area of the menu.

Last, we would step up our efforts to sell territorial franchise agreements overseas. We had already franchised Kuwait, Taiwan, and Guam. And we had unsolicited nibbles of interest from Venezuela, Western Europe, Israel, China, and South Africa.

Now the plan called for seeking franchisees for Australia, Thailand, Korea, the Philippines, and Malaysia to complete our expansion in the Pacific Rim. We budgeted $700,000 income from this activity for 1984. Without this income Swensen's would not be profitable.

We again started the year with a franchisee convention—this time at the original MGM Grand (now Bally's) in Las Vegas. We held it there to get maximum attendance. (Vegas always attracts top convention attendance in every franchise organization).

Also, we wanted to showcase our newly remodeled "B" store inside the hotel. The remodel design had been a stunning success, both physically and financially. (Sales were up over twenty percent since the remodeling had been completed.) Result: We launched a program at this meeting to encourage franchisees to refurbish the interiors of their restaurants.

The convention was a huge success. Attendance and optimism were both at an all-time high. Earle Swensen summed up the consensus that emerged from the meeting when he spoke at the franchisee award banquet the last evening. He boomed out to the assembled audience, "I never thought I'd see the day when my name would be on a public company. But then I never thought I'd see the day when there would be so many successful, optimistic businessmen and women in one room talking about how to increase their sales of my ice cream."

He concluded, "Thank you Karl Eller; thank you Chris. I'm sure this is just the beginning of our bright new future."

Supermarket Ice Cream

We spent six months and $500,000 of the public-offering money to develop a program to sell Swensen's Supreme ice cream to supermarkets.

As the only Swensen's executive who possessed a packaged-goods marketing background, I took the role of brand manager for this project to expediently complete the development work. Furthermore, as CEO, I could ensure speedy decisionmaking.

My objective for this program was to "do it right"—not cut corners in any area, including ad support. This was a highly competitive business. It would be a war for space in the supermarket freezer case. We literally had the funds to try this just once.

The first step was to hire a package design firm to develop a unique package design for the supermarkets. Our goal was to find a design that communicated high quality, and would "stand out" in the supermarket ice cream freezer section to achieve maximum consumer visibility.

We hired Soyster and Orenthal (S&O), a major package design firm in San Francisco, for the task. S&O created what I believed was an outstanding package for Swensen's Supreme. They proposed a brown and embossed gold package. It had a look unlike anything in the supermarket. More than this, it seemed to shout "highest quality" in its overall consumer impression.

While doing this design work, we attacked a key second step—contracting with an ice cream manufacturer to produce and distribute the supermarket product. With some reservations, we cut a deal with Foremost Dairies, the firm that was already making the Swensen's Supreme for the Swensen's stores. They had plenty of excess capacity to accommodate us in their Los Angeles plant. However, this was an old plant, and we had some concerns about whether we would be able to consistently get the high quality product we had formulated.

Third, we launched the most important step of developing a marketing program. For this, we needed a new advertising agency. (DDB–West had resigned). We needed a highly skilled packaged goods agency, regardless of size, to develop a strategic positioning and the advertising and media plan that resulted from it.

Once again I called upon a good business friend—this time Jerry Fortis, to provide the service needed. I had known Jerry and had worked closely with his wife, Dixie, at Needham. They were talented creative directors with extensive packaged-goods credits. They prided themselves on being good strategic thinkers as well as creators of advertising.

In the late '70's, the Fortis's had founded their own advertising agency, Fortis–Fortis–Westerfield, in Chicago, and had built a twenty-five million dollar agency by the time I contacted them. I was sure they were the right people to assign the task of developing a strategic positioning and advertising for Swensen's entry into the supermarket ice cream business.

They did not disappoint. In addition to a solid introductory plan that included a full-page four-color newspaper insert, they wrote and produced a memorable TV commercial—one of the best ever TV spots for ice cream. Using the old song, "You Made Me Love You," it featured an "ice-cream-o-holic" who could not resist eating the new Swensen's product. It thoroughly captured and captivated the viewer while selling the quality and taste of the ice cream.

Our final step in the supermarket ice cream project was to select a test market. We chose the state of Arizona for two obvious reasons. First, it was a strong area for Swensen's. We already had good name recognition. *If the product did not sell well in Arizona we had no hope of successfully selling it in markets in which we had low name recognition.*

Second, it was an area we could easily supervise. But more than this, we owned retail Swensen's parlors in Arizona. Therefore we could accurately measure the effect the supermarket product launch had on the parlor business—a key issue to our franchisees.

Finally, everything was in place. I reviewed the ambitious launch plan with the Board of Directors. We were seeking a ten percent share of market in a highly competitive, seasonal, low-margin business. The plan was front loaded to spend eighty percent of every profit dollar we estimated would be generated in year one in advertising and sales promotion in the first ninety days of its launch. Result: We would lose money in 1984 on this product, putting further strain on generating a corporate profit.

The Board approved the plan, with the understanding we still projected a profitable year.

In June, we launched Swensen's Supreme with great fanfare. It quickly gained distribution in all major chains, except Safeway. By August, we had gained great initial success. We had slightly exceeded our initial wholesale sales goal. More important, based on trade feedback, Swensen's had gained a thirteen percent market share of the supermarket ice cream sales in Phoenix. Also, sales in our parlors seemed to have been positively influenced by the program.

So far, so good. But the real test was just beginning. The issue: Could we maintain sales and distribution for the next nine months with far less ad support? We had to know this before we could consider expanding the product.

Eller's Surprise: A Nightmare Begins

As all this was happening, Karl Eller made a major decision about his investment in Swensen's.

In early August he called me into his office and introduced me to a Terrence Greve and a Willard McNitt. These gentlemen, through a holding company, owned controlling interest in Foremost Dairies. Without explaining why, Karl asked me to update them on the Swensen's. It was a short, cordial, but somewhat stiff meeting. I was soon dismissed, and as I left I couldn't help wondering what Eller was up to.

I soon found out. A few days later, Karl dropped a bombshell. He advised me that he had sold forty-two percent of Swensen's to Foremost Dairies in exchange for ownership of two Foremost ice cream manufacturing plants, one in Fort Worth, Texas, and one in Los Angeles.

I was stunned. To this day, I don't know why Karl did this. On the surface it looked like he was seeking a graceful way out of Swensen's as soon as possible. He denied this. Perhaps he did it for the reason he gave me, that is, to strengthen the company. I do know this move effectively changed the future of Swensen's forever.

The immediate impact of the sale was a major change in the composition of the Swensen's Board of Directors which, in turn, changed management control. Here's how I explained the change to our shareholders, employees and franchisees in a letter dated August 17, 1984:

> This agreement gives Foremost approximately forty-three percent of the company's total shares outstanding. Swensen's Chairman of the Board, Karl Eller, who, prior to the agreement, controlled sixty-seven percent of the company's stock through his interest in Loel One Inc., will now control approximately 38 percent of the company's stock.
>
> Foremost and Loel One have agreed to vote their shares in such a way as to cause four persons named by each to be elected to Swensen's nine member board, with the ninth member your company's president. Additionally, Foremost and Loel One have agreed that any action by the Board of Directors would require a two-thirds majority vote.

Thus, three years after becoming CEO, I effectively had a new reporting relationship. No longer could I advise Eller of my plans and be assured of Board support. I would need Foremost's agreement to all plans as well.

As this announcement was sent out, the first major glitches in the three-year turnaround plan emerged. Supermarket sales had slowed. It looked like we would lose more money than expected. Worse yet, two significant franchising problems had arisen within days of the Foremost deal.

Problem Number One: Kevin Crombie had not delivered two territorial franchising deals in our 1984 plan that could have added up to $700,000 to earnings.

Problem Number Two: Our former company-owned stores in Florida (the old Eller stores) were a huge threat to our earnings. The franchisee purchaser was in financial trouble; if sales did not improve we would have a large uncollectable receivable to write off.

Both problems were unanticipated and would, therefore, be an unpleasant surprise to our new Board. Our fourth quarter would be a disaster unless we found some answers quickly.

With more than a little concern that I was making a tactical mistake, I decided not to cancel a long-planned trip to the Orient. This meant I would have to forego any immediate efforts to woo the new Board members. It also meant I would have to leave the Florida problem for others to address. I assigned Doughty and Williams to finding an answer to Florida.

Then I warned Karl Eller of the possible problems. He was not pleased and stated that I had "better not let it (a bad fourth quarter) happen."

Visiting Asia: A Second Time

I'd planned a second trip to Asia in September for almost a year. It was to be an arduous forty-one day trip to twelve cities in eight countries, a trip that would take over 25,000 air miles to complete. As on the first trip, my wife accompanied me.

Kevin Crombie had done a remarkable job of building Swensen's in the Pacific Rim in the thirty months since he had joined the company. Through his efforts, the company had more than doubled its distribution. We had opened eighteen stores in two years and now had twenty-eight parlors open. We had new franchised stores in Indonesia, New Zealand, Malaysia, and Taiwan, as well as additional stores in Singapore, Hong Kong, and Japan.

In building Swensen's Pacific Rim presence, Kevin had attracted a very different franchisee than we had in the United States. Unlike our financially struggling U.S. franchisees, all the Pacific Rim franchises were part of large profitable firms or were owned by very well-heeled entrepreneurs. In either case, Swensen's was a small part of their overall businesses.

However, like the United States, most were struggling to make their Swensen's profitable. And Kevin felt that all critically needed "a presidential visit" from me to reaffirm to them the wisdom of their involvement with Swensen's and to be reassured of the company's continued commitment to the region.

Beyond this, Kevin also sought help in franchising. He had not been able to close deals in Thailand or Australia—deals in the works for almost a year without closure. He hoped my presence would give the negotiations a final push to closure. We had to find a way to do this by year-end.

From the beginning to the end, this trip was a whirlwind of meetings, business dinners, and social visits with our franchisees. All were most gracious hosts as each pushed his agenda of Swensen's issues and concerns. For the first time, I gained a full appreciation of the difficulties Kevin dealt with daily.

In addition to furthering my understanding of our Pacific Rim franchises, the trip seemed fruitful in reassuring and encouraging our existing franchisees. Two of them, the Kwok's in Hong Kong and General Foods in New Zealand, used my visit to generate publicity. I gave a speech to the Hong Kong Rotary on "Restaurant Trends in America," and had press interviews afterward. In New Zealand, in addition to press interviews, I was a featured guest answering consumer questions about ice cream and Swensen's on an hour-long call-in radio show.

At first, the other purpose of my trip, namely to sell franchising deals in Thailand and Australia also looked promising. Kevin had scheduled follow-up meetings with well-qualified interested candidates in both countries.

In Thailand we conducted protracted negotiations with a Thai millionaire family, the Assaro's. Finally, at a dinner the family head (the senior Mr. Assaro) hosted for us in his compound, we struck a deal. He would commit to buy the franchising rights to the country and build five stores in two years. We would collect only $100,000 upfront, but we had a sale. The formal papers would be drawn up.

In Australia the franchising effort was less productive. We spent eight days meeting with prospective franchisees in Perth, Sydney, and Brisbane. Kevin had planned to sell franchising rights on the east coast to one dairy company and on the west coast to another. Despite seeming great interest, and several lengthy negotiations with these companies, neither deal came close to fruition. At best, we could hope for a deal in six months.

Then the proverbial roof caved in. While we were in Sydney, Mr. Assaro notified us that he had made a mistake and killed our deal for Thailand.

As I returned home, exhausted from six weeks of travel, I felt the long-term results would be positive. But I worried that I had spent too much time to return without a major income producing franchising deal.

I worried my trip would be perceived, especially by the new Board members, as a poor use of my management time—that it would seem as though I had "fiddled while Rome burned."

Final Months

Indeed, I returned to Phoenix and found myself in a seriously crippled presidency. Swensen's three-year financial success story was in shambles.

Sales of the supermarket brand continued to drop. We would sustain a bigger loss than we had projected to the Board in our most pessimistic model. Further, the franchisees were threatening to sue us and withhold royalties if we tried to expand the supermarket product.

But, by far the biggest problem was Florida. The new owners of Eller's former stores were not paying royalties or paying down the note they had signed to finance the stores' purchase.

As Quinn explained it, we had two options—both bad. We could get a court order to take them over and operate them, or we could let them drift into bankruptcy and perhaps lose the stores forever. Either way, we were faced with a major earnings hit. We either wrote off the profits of our sale in 1983, plus assuming operating losses to keep the stores open, or we wrote off the value of the assets.

I chose the less expensive short-term alternative of taking over the stores.

With this action, and the loss of the planned-for Pacific Rim territorial deals, we were faced with a quarter in which for the first time in three years we would not beat the previous year. Swensen's would not be a profitable company for the entire year.

I advised Eller of the bad news. He had obviously been forewarned and was not surprised. He seemed somewhat detached but generally supportive. Then, as our brief meeting ended, I understood his lack of emotion. He said, "Look, Chris, these things happen. Go see Alan Meyer and see if you and he can work together to straighten this mess out."

His message seemed clear: "I won't support you unless you sell Foremost." I was bitter at this message. On my planet, I had saved the company and made Eller a lot of money. But, obviously, on Karl Eller's planet that was yesterday. I was in danger of being an expendable pawn.

As advised, I hurried up to San Francisco to talk to Alan Meyer. As president of Foremost, he had been designated by the other three Foremost board members as my contact.

It was a difficult meeting. From the beginning we had very poor personal chemistry. I wonder to this day if Meyer had decided he wouldn't like me before we ever met. He had telegraphed his approach to me when he told me he would "squeeze me into his busy schedule," but would not be available for lunch or dinner. In other words, our first meeting would be "strictly business."

When we met in his office in a San Francisco skyscraper, I was confronted by a younger man—early forties I guessed. He was about six feet one inch tall, slim, well-dressed, with sharp, cruel eyes and short-cropped hair. He didn't smile nor immediately look up when I entered the room. Clearly he was going to try to intimidate me.

I had expected this and set out to disarm him. Putting on my P&G business manner, I spent little time in the usual formal chitchat that executives use when first meeting a fellow executive. In a very formal businesslike manner I presented a memo that described our Florida problems and our revised earnings forecast.

He seemed shocked at my news, even though I was sure he wasn't hearing new information. Then he warmed to his task. In what seemed to be a carefully rehearsed diatribe, he scolded me over a lack of good communications. Then he demanded, in a very boss-to-subordinate manner, that I involve him in all major future Swensen's operating decisions. He made it clear that he wanted me to operate as though Swensen's were a Foremost subsidiary.

Somehow I was not surprised by Alan Meyer's grab for power. It confirmed my worst suspicions. And, for once in my life I chose to be conciliatory. I asked him," "Well, given your desire to be more involved, Alan, how would you prefer we worked together on next year's plan?"

He stared at me for a moment. I think he had girded himself for an argument and was surprised with my quiet response. He rose from his chair, and began pacing, "Chris, I'm glad you asked. Let me outline for you right now what we have in mind in terms of the overall approach to the business. Then I would like to review the actual plan you come up with before the Board meeting."

He went on, "We believe in the conservative approach. We expect you to focus on maximizing profits. We want to see a plan that will guarantee a profit in 1985 without increased sales or new stores. We believe you must cut back on manpower. We don't think we should be investing in new products. We do think we should expand the supermarket ice cream test; but on a pay-as-you-go-basis—no more fancy investment spending plans. Swensen's is not P&G."

He stopped for a moment, stared intently at me then asked, "Any questions or problems?"

I did not answer his question. I was not about to let him see how upset I was, as he thoroughly trashed my commitment to growth and the promises I had made as we had gone public. Instead, I smiled, stood up, shook his hand and said, "I've got to run. Thanks for your time and your candor. I understand what you want."

He issued a parting shot as I strode out the door, "Chris, just remember, it will be very hard for us to support you unless you follow the approach I just outlined for you."

As I walked away, I thought, "Nice guy; I think I would've liked Attila the Hun better." I was also sick at heart. Clearly I not only had a new reporting relationship, I had a Board group that wanted to dictate how I should manage the company. I was being told what to do. If I followed them, I would be CEO in name only. If I ignored them we'd have a deadlocked Board.

As important to me personally, I had made public promises to employees, franchisees, and the underwriters of the public offering, to pursue a growth strategy. This commitment could not be kept if I followed Meyer's edict. If this happened I would lose a lot of faith and trust that I had fostered over three years.

I did not like my choices. I had no foxfole to hide in. I discussed my dilemma with Eller. He surprised me by assuring me he would back me, if I proposed to the Board a profit plan I felt was right for Swensen's.

That was all the encouragement I needed. I advised Meyer by phone that I would tone down my aggressive plans, but continue them. There was silence at the other end of the line.

With a sense of foreboding I put together a proposed plan for 1985. It showed the company adding people and overhead costs but making a profit from our core parlor business, primarily because of the sale of franchising rights in Australia, reselling the Florida stores, and increased royalties. We now had 387 stores open, up 30 over the previous year.

The plan also showed that we would continue to lose money in the supermarket business but that we wanted to continue the test program. I included more TV advertising in the plan. To pay for all this we showed we would make a sizable profit from the ice cream manufacturing business.

It was not the plan Alan Meyer had asked for. It continued the aggressive growth plans I had championed when we had gone public. I saw no other choice *because I did not believe I could be an effective CEO if I changed game plans and lost my credibility with the franchisees or stockholders.*

I went to see Meyer again. I tried to sell him on my plan. I argued that my plan would potentially generate as much profit as the plan he sought. He shook his head, but agreed to review it with his Board faction. I left with little hope, knowing this kind of man would see my plan as insubordination.

In mid-December I presented the plan to the Board and explained that we had publicly obligated the Company to aggressive expansion and asked for their support.

I didn't receive it.

Following my presentation the Board took a break. After the break Karl asked me not to return to the meeting. The Board then met in private and left without even saying good-by. It was clear that I had lost.

After a miserable Christmas week in which I had no communication with any Board member, I met with Eller for breakfast on December 31. I was too upset to remember many details of our conversation. I do know that it was agreed I had to leave. I told Karl I would resign but only if I could collect the fifteen months' severance in my employment agreement. He agreed and the deed was done.

I went back to the office. I wept as told my staff my fate; then left. It was the hardest single day of my career.

Postscript

Like my fate, the story of Swensen's after 1984 does not have a happy ending.

Pat Doughty replaced me as CEO. Within sixty days, Eller undid the Foremost deal. He returned the ice cream plants to Foremost and regained his shares in Swensen's.

Karl was now CEO of Circle K convenience stores, and it was clearly in his best interest to rid himself of Swensen's. Within eighteen months he sold all his shares and the company to a Long Island firm, Steve's Ice Cream.

The stock was delisted. Swensen's ceased to exist as an independent company. Over the years since 1987, Swensen's outlets have closed and the chain has gradually disappeared.

Earle Swensen died in 1996 with only a few Swensen's still in existence.

Lessons Learned

1. *The president has to be the chief marketing officer of any restaurant company.* In effect, he is the all-powerful brand manager I had dreamed of being when I held the title at Procter & Gamble.
2. *The biggest difference in managing a privately owned versus a publicly owned company is in financial reporting.* A public-owned company has to focus on predictable quarterly earnings; a privately owned company should always focus on maximizing cash flow.
3. *A CEO's job performance cannot guarantee his job security.* Such "hired hands" are truly pawns of an owner's egos and his dealmaking. Karl Eller apparently sacrificed my career at Swensen's for what he saw as the "greater corporate good." Owners and Boards of Directors for companies, big or small, take similar actions routinely in American business. Corporate buyouts and corporate restructurings spawn them. In all these actions, I believe that rarely would an individual employee, no matter what title he or she held, be their concern.

Final Comments

I left Swensen's with a "template" for a successful management take-over of a franchise chain restaurant company. In many ways, it is as ruthless as the course of action Eller used with me.

The "template" had five guiding principles *that I believe will still work today*:

1. *Quickly evaluate your staff.* Replace those who do not "fit" with your personality or do not have the professional skills you seek.
2. *Make an early Herculean effort to assure yourself of franchisee support.*
3. *Spend several months learning the facts before making any changes.* Spare no effort to identify all the corporate myths as you gain understanding of why certain stores or franchisees succeed and others don't.
4. *Put together a game plan to build sales of existing stores.* This will prove your management skill to everyone quicker than anything else. *Key to doing this in any restaurant chain are three programs: new menu items, new advertising, and remodeled restaurant interiors.*
5. If at all possible, hire any new outside suppliers and new management personnel needed from the pool of friends and former employees whose loyalties and skills are well known to you.

CHAPTER 12
Waving the White Flag at Bojangle's
(Trying to Save a Restaurant Chain)

After my abrupt departure from Swensen's I was depressed. For several weeks I did nothing about finding another job, other than to call friends to seek their help in finding another position. (Over the years I found they helped me the most in relocating.)

Toward the end of January, I finally got my act together. I awarded myself a temporary job—finding a president's position in another restaurant chain. This would mean leaving Phoenix and going through a third inter-city move in six years, but there seemed to be no other choice.

Finding another job can be a full-time occupation, as many of my executive compatriots can attest.

My job-search methodology was rather mundane, but it worked. I would get up each morning and spend from 8:00 A.M. to 12:00 A.M. job seeking. I would scan ads in *The Wall Street Journal*, *Advertising Age*, and *Restaurant News* and answer ads that seemed appropriate for me. I also made a list of people to "network" with and faithfully called one or more of them each day. I also sent my resume to every executive search firm for which I could get an address.

Friendly search firm executives told me that I could expect to be out of work six months to a year. But, within thirty days, I had two leads.

The first came from a search firm that contacted me about the presidency of Arby's. Jeff McMahon was gone. Arby's had been bought by Victor Posner. I was intrigued with an opportunity to return to Arby's, after being banished just four years prior. Quoting Professor Henry Higgins, I thought, "How delicious! How delightful!"

The second opportunity was to become president of Bojangles', a chicken and biscuit chain headquartered in Charlotte, North Carolina. The chain had been purchased by Horn & Hardart (H&H), whose CEO was Barry Florescue, a man I had known peripherally over the years. Barry had been a successful Burger King franchisee with great ambitions. He had taken control of H&H in '77 and had resuscitated it by finishing the conversion of their famed Automats into Burger King's and Arby's. With this success under his belt, he had led H&H to purchase Bojangles' in

1982 from its founder, Jack Fulk. Jack had stayed on as Bojangles' CEO but had resigned at the end of 1984.

I pursued both of these opportunities with vigor. (I was not enjoying my forced retirement.)

I traveled to New York to H&H headquarters to visit with John Gerlach, the president, to sell him on my suitability for the Bojangles' position. I called the Arby's franchisees and solicited their help in gaining the Arby's position. (It was then that I learned that I had been sought out by Arby's because of George Nadler, one of the key Arby's franchisees who owned all the Arby's in Minneapolis.) I also called Larry Krueger to get as much information as I could about Arby's, post-Jeff McMahon.

By late March it was clear that both companies were very interested in me when they both invited me to on-site personal interviews.

Victor Posner

Arby's was first. I flew to Miami to meet with Victor Posner, the now infamous entrepreneur who collected companies like some of us collect baseball cards.

This interview was like none I had ever had in my career.

When I landed in Miami, Rene Mottrum, an attractive, middle-aged, bleached blonde met me. She introduced herself as executive VP of Victor Posner's companies and told me that she would be my hostess for the day.

It was early afternoon. Our first stop was Victor's headquarters' building, an old hotel on Miami Beach. I was told that most of his 200+ companies were run administratively from this building. In addition, because this had been an old apartment/hotel, he maintained several luxurious suites for guests within the building.

I was assigned one of the rooms, then given a tour by the chief financial officer. After a brief look at the executive offices he took me through the accounting department.

I was amazed. I had never seen anything quite like it. I saw dozens of desks. At each desk there was a clerk slowly going through large baskets filled with paper. I was told that these were the accounts payable clerks for all of Posner's 200+ companies, including Arby's. Larry Krueger had told me that Posner had a policy of dragging payments on bills for as long as he could. By passing these bills in these baskets, he was apparently very successful in doing this.

After this tour, Rene announced that it was time for my interview with Victor Posner. We were to go to his home on Fisher Island. The home turned out to be the old Playboy mansion. As befitted a mogul of his background, Victor's house was guarded. It was several minutes before we were finally admitted.

Upon entering, we went down a short flight of stairs and traversed a long corridor. Finally we entered a large room with a floor-to-ceiling window overlooking the Inter-coastal Waterway. In the room, there was a huge semicircular couch facing the window. Probably thirty feet in total length, the couch did a lazy semicircle around the room. In front of the couch's center section was a large coffee table with a bank of three telephones.

Rene directed me to sit down at the end of the couch and left the room.

Posner soon appeared. He was a burly man, probably in his early sixties, dressed in a white bathrobe and a pair of beach shoes. A man he introduced as his lawyer accompanied him. The lawyer was dressed in coat and tie and looked very professional but somewhat ominous.

As he visually sized me up, Posner sat down in front of the bank of the phones and immediately answered a phone call. He uttered a few gruff sentences, barked an order, and hung up. It seemed obvious that Victor Posner was a bully showing off. Finally he turned toward me and began the interview.

Surveying this scene, I became convinced that I would never want to work for Victor Posner. Although I had seen him in operation for only a few minutes and "felt" the kind of organization he was running for only a few hours, I was totally turned off.

From then on, the interview became fun. I was sitting on the couch about fifteen feet away from Posner. When he asked me questions, I decided I would start sliding down the couch getting ever closer to him as I answered them. By the time I got within eight feet of him, he seemed to become very nervous. He said, " Stop! What do you think you're doing?"

I replied, "Well sir, I am just trying to get close enough to hear you clearly."

As I recall, he spoke in a somewhat guttural New York accent, which was indeed sometimes difficult to understand, but not to hear, because he spoke very loudly. He gave out a visceral grunting sign as he absorbed my obviously false answer. He looked at me with a bit of puzzlement, gave a sort of half-smile and said, somewhat accusingly, "You aren't afraid of me, are you?"

I smiled. "No," I said. "Why should I be? You're looking for someone who knows how to run a restaurant chain. I know how to do that. Further, I know Arby's. I hired many of the current staff. I know all the key franchisees. I truly understand the company."

The phone rang, Victor answered it, then looked up, and waved his dismissal. The interview was over. Rene reappeared and guided me out of the mansion. I left convinced that I didn't want to work for the Victor Posner organization.

As we left, Rene invited me to dinner. We went to a private club. There, seemingly to Rene's surprise, Posner joined us. We spent several hours getting better acquainted. The more I got to know Victor Posner the less I wanted to work for him.

As we left, Rene was very pleased. "Victor doesn't usually join us for dinner unless he is very interested in the candidate," she said. "I am sure you will get a job offer if you are interested."

The next morning I equivocated on my resolve to not work for Posner. I met more people within the Posner organization. All were people with whom I was comfortable, and most seemed to be very competent. At the end of the day, I told Rene that I was interested in a job offer. I rationalized to myself, "A bird in the hand is worth more than two in the bush—who knows, maybe if I stay away from Miami and negotiate enough freedom to operate, I could make the Arby's job work."

Bojangles'

The following week I went for interviews to Bojangles' headquarters in Charlotte, N.C. There I was met by Barry Florescue.

These too were out-of-the-ordinary interviews. The day started with my meeting several of the key officers of the company who would report to me, including the three men who formed an office of the presidency in the absence of a CEO, Howard Singer, Chuck Trego, and Andy Stubl.

Following these interviews I had a long lunch and discussion with Barry. From this it seemed obvious that I was going to get a job offer at the end of the day.

First, though, I had one more interview hurdle, Cameron McCray, president of the Bojangles' Franchisee Association. "Cam" was a native North Carolinian—a man I would describe as a classic "good ole boy." He was young and very street smart. We seemed to get along well.

Later that night over a congenial dinner, Barry offered the job—CEO of Bojangles' reporting to him as CEO of the parent company, Horn & Hardart. I asked for the offer in writing and promised I would answer him within a week.

And so, by early April, I had a job offer in writing to be president and CEO of Bojangles' and another offering me president and CEO of Arby's. Both had similar total compensation packages that exceeded my Swensen's remuneration.

Even though there was an obvious appeal to return to Arby's in triumph after my ignominious exit four years earlier, choosing between these offers was not difficult. Bojangles' seemed far more attractive. It was an exciting growth vehicle. Indeed Bojangles' had been widely honored as one of the fastest growing, most successful new chain restaurant concepts in America in 1983 and 1984.

Also the concept was built on a solid foundation, its unique menu. It had two proprietary signature products, Cajun-spiced fried chicken, and made-from-scratch-in-restaurant Southern buttermilk biscuits. These biscuits tasted better than any biscuit I had ever eaten—even all those I had sampled when we were trying to match Southern biscuits with Bisquick.

And, Bojangles' was a market leader. Bojangles' restaurants that had been established for a year or more in the Carolinas were averaging sales of almost one million dollars per outlet. They were the highest sales volume chicken fast-food restaurants in America.

Last, I liked the ownership better. Although I was not totally comfortable with Barry Florescue, he seemed preferable to Victor Posner. (Later I would wonder if this assessment had been correct.)

Result: I accepted the Bojangles' job with an employment contract that called for many fringe benefits like stock options etc. and a one-year salary-plus-benefits termination clause.

A Unique Culture

I arrived in Charlotte, North Carolina, in mid-April, 1995 to become president and CEO of Bojangles'. In doing so, I stepped into the shoes of Jack Fulk, the founder of Bojangles', and inherited his office, part of a sprawling set of offices located in a closed retail strip center.

It was from the beginning an almost surreal experience. To understand why, you need to know the history of Bojangles', and the personalities of Jack Fulk and Barry Florescue.

Jack Fulk was not a corporate man, nor a cultured man. Jack was a self-made, profane, shrewd Carolinian businessman who preferred to conduct business through old friends and cultivated lifelong friendships with key suppliers.

Jack had been a Hardee's franchisee who had participated in the launch of the fast-food biscuit breakfast menu at Hardee's. In the mid-'70s he sold his Hardee's franchise to begin building his own restaurant concept with a long time friend, Richard Thomas.

Essentially they developed Bojangles' to be a hybrid or dual menu concept.

For breakfast there was a biscuit sandwich menu. It was, because of the quality of the biscuit, an improved version of the original Hardee's biscuit breakfast: sausage biscuit, ham biscuit, and bacon and egg biscuit sandwiches, grits and red-eye gravy, etc.

For the rest of the day there was a spicy chicken menu. The chicken was sold a la KFC. The spicy chicken was similar to Popeye's as were the side dishes of dirty rice, spicy pinto beans, and German cole slaw. There were no sandwiches and no french fries on the menu.

What set Bojangles' apart from its competitors was the quality of its food. It was extraordinary for fast-food, primarily because much of it was prepared fresh and/or from scratch in the restaurant.

Jack Fulk had personally worked with suppliers to develop the key proprietary elements of the Bojangles' menu—the Cajun spice for the chicken and the emulsifier for the biscuits. The formulas for these were some of the best-kept secrets since the Coca-Cola formula. Only the president of Bojangles', and the supplier who made the key secret ingredient, had access to them.

Jack and Richard named their new restaurant concept, Bojangles', after the fabled African-American dancer. When I asked Jack why he chose this name, he never offered a specific reason. He said they just liked it.

A Bojangles' restaurant was very visible. Its predominate exterior color was a garish orange. In addition there were theatre marquee-type lights under the outside overhang surrounding the dining room and encircling the sign. The sign was a black script-written logo on a yellow background.

The first Bojangles' restaurant was primarily a drive-thru facility. It opened in a lower-income area of south central Charlotte. Its success became legendary in Charlotte. This restaurant grossed well over $1,000,000 in retail sales in its first year. This was unheard-of volume for a fast-food chicken restaurant. Soon, a second much larger full-service restaurant, a prototype for future expansion, was opened. Located in a more upscale location, its volume exceeded the original restaurant.

The key was breakfast. Bojangles' did about forty percent of its sales by 10:00 A.M. Bojangles' breakfast business was so successful and executed so well in this new prototype, that it was widely rumored McDonald's had sent its key operations people down to study the operation. McDonald's was particularly interested in how this Bojangles' processed three orders per minute through the drive-thru for breakfast.

In the late '70s and early '80s Jack and Richard expanded Bojangles' rapidly by building company-owned restaurants in Charlotte and by franchising outside Charlotte in North and South Carolina. Almost all of the franchisees were local, well-connected, wealthy Carolinian businessmen.

By early 1982, there were fifty-two Bojangles', all in the Carolinas. Average sales per restaurant were about $900,000 or more than double KFC, the fast-food chicken chain market leader. Then, as the history was related to me, Horn & Hardart approached Fulk and Thomas about buying the chain.

After prolonged negotiations, a deal was struck. To this day I do not understand how this deal could have happened. Perhaps the final purchase offer—$12,000,000 in cash—was just too much money for Fulk and Thomas to turn down for what Thomas was quoted as saying was originally a $10,000 investment.

It certainly was not a deal with any corporate culture match. Jack and Richard were part of a "good ole boy" network of bible-belt Carolinian businessmen. They were the absolute antithesis of the new owners of their company—Horn & Hardart, a Jewish-led New York holding company.

When the deal was finalized, Thomas left. Fulk stayed on as CEO of Bojangles'. He was promised a free hand to run the company with one imprimatur—H&H wanted rapid growth.

And H&H got its wish. In the years 1982–84, about 250 new Bojangles' were opened. Throughout this period, Jack Fulk continued to be the heart and soul of the company. Standing about six feet two inches, with intense deep-set eyes, thick black eyebrows, and a shock of gray hair, he cut a wide "macho" swath wherever he went. He was virtually a living legend among all the Bojangles' employees. To some he was an all-knowing genius. To most, he was a sometime tyrant who instilled great fear.

Still, the entire staff was intensely loyal to Fulk. They were also essentially people who did Jack's bidding. Many were not highly educated, nor were they professionals with years of experience in the various key disciplines of a chain restaurant franchisor: operations, real estate, finance, marketing, purchasing, training, franchise law, etc. But, they believed in Bojangles', took great personal pride in its success, and worked long hours to make sure the company succeeded.

Because of this, only Jack could foment change, not Horn & Hardart. Only Jack's requests and instructions were heeded. Horn & Hardart had to go through Jack for any information. And, as it was told to me, Jack paid little heed to most questions or requests for "reasons why" restaurant operating results did not meet H&H guidelines, particularly food costs.

This attitude enraged Barry and his New York management. A bitter culture clash ensued. H&H was accounting oriented and used to operating restaurants with tight cost controls. The Jack Fulk crew was top-line sales oriented and considered cost controls a necessary evil.

At first, however, the infusion of H&H capital to expand Bojangles' somewhat masked this conflict. Bojangles' restaurants were franchised in Virginia and Florida. And franchise development agreements were sold for Dallas, Washington, D.C., and Chicago. Florescue himself bought a development agreement for New Jersey and another for West Palm Beach, Florida.

Fulk expanded into all four key cities in Tennessee: Memphis, Nashville, Chattanooga, and Knoxville with company-owned restaurants. Barry Florescue converted some of his personal Arby's in south Florida and some of H&H's Arby's in New York City to Bojangles'.

However, none of these expansion stores did the sales volumes of the Carolina stores. I was told that in Tennessee Fulk poured in manpower to build the top line while, at the same time Florescue demanded reduced labor costs. Fulk largely ignored him.

Frustrated, seeing his acquisition beginning to founder, and sure he knew how to run the chain better than its founder, Barry Florescue continually demanded performance, his way. Fulk continued to ignore him. Both were proud egocentric, win-at-all-costs men.

Barry had more power, and he used it. He gradually replaced key members of Fulk's staff by ordering that his people be hired. He replaced the chief financial officer with Chuck Trego. He brought in Howard Singer, a real pro at site selection and development of restaurants as Vice President of Development. (Singer had been at Burger King and Kentucky Fried Chicken in similar capacities.) Finally, Barry brought in his own Operations man, Andy Stubl. On paper, all reported to Fulk but they talked directly with Barry almost daily.

Fulk had little patience with his "masters" from New York. Over time, he too became frustrated. It was apparent to him that they were going to run things their way regardless of what he told them. After over a year of the bitter feud, he resigned.

Result: When I joined Bojangles' there was a decided lack of morale within the company. And it had a very split personality in terms of its culture—those that paid no attention to the H&H people and those that were sure they needed to work with the H&H people to keep their jobs.

In short, internally, chaos reigned.

Getting Started

It was clear from Day One that I had to modify my takeover template outlined at the end of Chapter 11. My first priority had to be to reunite and motivate the internal staff—a task I had totally underestimated when I had interviewed. For this, I had only myself to blame. I had been too enamored with the concept and the sales growth numbers to see the cultural problem.

This was, without doubt, the most difficult corporate cultural/people problem I ever encountered. (In some ways I complicated the problem. I was a "Yankee" in charge of a "good ole boy" Carolinian culture restaurant chain. And, I was a born-again Evangelical Christian reporting to an aggressive Jewish Chairman of the Board.)

This task was also made even more difficult by timing. As I arrived, so did three other major new hires, Eric Newman who was to be the lawyer, Jack Keilt who was to be in charge of franchising, and Art Benes who had been hired to run purchasing.

As I made my assessment of the new hires and existing personnel, Bojangles' people problems quickly became clear. The management that built the company was largely gone. The newly hired executives were expert in their field, but were not knowledgeable in the ways Bojangles' had been built. Worse yet, only one, Eric Newman, was a Carolinian. All others were cultural outsiders. Result: When they began to assert their authority, most had major relationship problems almost immediately with the franchisees and internal employees.

In some ways the people/culture problem was the "good news." Despite the obvious culture clash, the new team was talented. All I would need to do to finish out the management team was hire a Vice President of Menu Development and replace a weak Vice President of Marketing, Will Claybourn.

The "bad news" was Bojangles' "success."

Before accepting the presidency, I had seen all of the sales numbers and the growth plans for Bojangles'. There were retail sales problems in the newer expansion markets, but the data showed that Bojangles' was growing in sales and profits every quarter. Furthermore, Barry and John Gerlach had assured me that Bojangles' had excellent financial fundamentals for continuing this success.

Now several weeks into fact-finding and searching out corporate myths, I was personally shaken when *I found the biggest corporate myth of my career—Bojangles' "success."*

Bojangles' success was not as it appeared. Bojangles' had opened so many new stores on such a small base—250 stores in less than three years on a base of fifty-two stores—that a possible concept-crushing problem had been partially masked.

The problem: Bojangles' restaurants outside its North and South Carolina core area had sales volumes approximately fifty percent or lower than those in the heartland. This was not a "start-up" problem as I had been led to believe. Sales in noncore area restaurants open more than a year were not growing and showed no signs of improving. These stores were unprofitable either as a company-owned or a franchisee restaurant.

To put it another way, half the chain was sick and the other half was healthy. But the sick half was the targeted growth area! Worse, the healthy half, the Carolinas, also had a major company-owned restaurant problem—sales were flat and profits declining. In short, Bojangles' was reporting record sales and growth on the outside, but it was rotting on the inside.

This basic problem had been significantly abetted by a corporate acquisition made six months before my arrival. John Gerlach had championed the purchase of a chicken and biscuit chain called "Biskit's" in north Florida for $14,000,000. There were forty-one Biskit's restaurants between Orlando, Jacksonville, and Tampa-St. Petersburg. Added to the restaurants that Bojangles' owned and operated in South Florida and five existing franchised stores in Tampa, this purchase made Bojangles' a major force in the fast-food business in Florida.

Unfortunately, Gerlach had bought Biskit's for its distribution, not its sales success. Although the chain had a menu similar to Bojangles'—the major differences were in the quality of the biscuits and that Biskit's sold only nonspicy Southern fried chicken—Biskit's average sales volume was under $400,000 per restaurant, less than half Bojangles' average.

John, with Barry's backing, had assumed that if he remodeled and renamed them Bojangles' and introduced the Bojangles' menu, he could drive the volume of the restaurants to $800,000 per year.

This didn't happen. In six months Biskit's restaurant consumer sales barely grew. In short, the Biskit's acquisition was a staggering mistake. The restaurants in Orlando and Jacksonville were suffering a P&L loss of about $400,000 a month. Worse yet, the franchisee in Tampa, to whom Gerlach had immediately franchised seventeen of these restaurants, was suffering similar losses and not paying royalties or debt payments.

This purchase had been made in November of '84. H&H had chosen to capitalize all operating losses as start-up costs for six months. Therefore, none of these operating losses had appeared on the books when I had seen a profitable Bojangles' earnings report. Nor had I been verbally advised of this accounting maneuver in any of my interviews.

Not surprisingly, then, I was stunned when Chuck Trego and Muni Saltoun, the H&H CFO, advised me that these operating losses would hit the books from May forward. Result: Thirty days after joining Bojangles', I found myself in a world turned upside down. I was CEO of a company that was losing money not making money.

I smelled a rat. Clearly, I was in a position to be the fall guy for others' bad decisions. I confronted Barry Florescue and John Gerlach with my suspicions and demanded some answers.

"First," I asked, "Why didn't you tell me about the Biskit's accounting maneuver before I was hired?"

They denied they were trying to hide anything. Barry indignantly replied, "You saw the books; they're public records. You're an experienced restaurant CEO. If you missed the Biskit's accounting it was your own fault. It was disclosed in the footnotes of the annual report."

Barry went on in a more soothing tone, "Besides, what are you worried about? I'm sure that you'll fix the Biskit's problems. All Bojangles' needs is good marketing—and that, my friend, is your specialty."

I heard Barry's unspoken answer too, "We didn't volunteer our dirty laundry—it might have scared you off." And this immediately raised my apprehension that there were other problems hidden in the deals Barry had made with which I would eventually be confronted.

I instinctively shuddered. I realized I was alone in a real mess. Barry was a proud, ruthless man. He would never take the fall for Bojangles' poor performance. He'd get rid of Gerlach first. Then if the problem wasn't fixed it was clear I would be next.

Perhaps even more disheartening was my analysis of the cause of Bojangles' problems versus theirs. They saw marketing as the problem. I saw marketing as a needed fix, but not the answer to Bojangles' problems. I *knew the key fix needed was better store operations.*

I told them so, "Gentlemen, I will fix the marketing; but Bojangles' needs more help elsewhere. Its company store operations "suck." The chain has expanded too fast to allow adequate store-level training. We can't build sales when the restaurant operations are so poor that some stores run out of chicken or biscuits at peak sales hours. And I am told that this happens all too often."

Barry did not want to hear this. His face glowered and he responded in an angry raised voice, "Bulls—t!! A few operating glitches should not be your focus! Andy Stubl can fix those. You fix marketing, and you get Keilt to sell some franchises. Do that and everything will be fine."

Barry then went on to say, in a very calm rambling dialogue, that he was convinced that good advertising and promotion would bring the non core restaurant volumes up to the same levels as in the Carolina's, thus assuring the future success of Bojangles'. He ended by saying that I had the reputation of being a "marketing genius," and he was sure that I could fashion a solution.

While wanting to share their enthusiasm for my talent, I was deeply disturbed that they did not share my perception of the depth of the operations problems. They viewed it as an excuse, not as the critical problem it was.

Why were store operations so critical?

First, virtually fifty percent of the Bojangles' restaurants were company owned. These restaurants provided the bulk of sales and profits, not franchising fees or royalties as had been the case at all my previous restaurant chains. This changed the internal dynamics of how to manage for profits. *The first focus had to be on fixing company-owned outlets. The success of the franchisees was secondary.*

Second, the strength of Bojangles' was its food. Research showed that consumers chose Bojangles' because they literally loved the quality and taste of the menu. For people who sought the kind of food found in this market niche, Bojangles' food quality towered over its competitors.

This resulted in our repeat customers being the most loyal customers ever found in the restaurant industry. Eight percent of our customers accounted for eighty percent of our volume. Indeed, it was not unusual for a Bojangles' customer to buy breakfast every morning, seven days a week, at the same restaurant!

But, the key problem for the chain was also its food. The food that made Bojangles' famous was difficult to prepare. Much of it was made from scratch daily instead of being pre-prepared and ready-to-cook as was the norm in other fast-food restaurants. The biscuits, for example, were made from "scratch," requiring a skilled biscuit maker to be present in the restaurant at all times. Biscuits that were more than twenty minutes old lost their flavor and within an hour became like rocks. In short, Bojangles' was a fast-food restaurant in terms of service, but more of a full-service restaurant in its backroom preparation of the food.

This, in turn, put a premium on well-run in-restaurant operations to assure proper food prep and proper food rotation. To achieve this we had to have well-trained, experienced restaurant managers—and Bojangles' did not have enough of them.

This critical need had grown progressively into a bigger and bigger problem because of rapid expansion and Barry Florescue. When Fulk announced his departure, many of his key operations people left the company. Many were worn out by the job's difficulty, but most were driven out by Barry Florescue's demand that they reduce their food waste and other costs to improve profitability, a demand that they knew they couldn't execute without harming food quality.

Result: As the quality of the in-store management became poorer the quality of the food became poorer. Indeed, as I joined the company the quality of operations even in the heartland company stores was deteriorating rapidly. This, in turn, caused sales to plateau and begin to turn down throughout the Bojangles' company store system.

Barry Florescue

As I truly began to understand the problems I had inherited, I began to believe that perhaps the biggest problem of all was the Horn & Hardart CEO, Barry Florescue. In his mid-forties, Barry was an accountant by trade, who had grossly inflated ideas about his business abilities. He saw himself as a dealmaker a la Karl Eller. He also saw himself as a restaurant operations and marketing expert.

Over time, he was successful at none of these things. Barry Florescue was, instead, a strong-willed, egocentric bully who, I came to believe, stretched the bounds of business ethics to the legal limits. Barry was used to getting his way, any way he could. He was a man who built his wealth by buying four percent of the Horn and Hardart stock in 1977 and parlaying this into control of the company through a bitter proxy fight masterminded by his close friend and brilliant lawyer, Donald Schupak.

Barry was also a man who hated to lose. He preferred to litigate rather than accepting a settlement of any issue on less than his terms. More than any man I ever knew in business, Barry seemed to believe the end justified the means. He had bet his business reputation and Horn and Hardart's future on making Bojangles' a major national success. He could not, therefore, stay away from meddling in the day-to-day operations of the company.

A Terrible Realization

As I completed my first thirty days at Bojangles', I finally understood the immensity of the problems to be addressed and the conditions under which I would be operating. I felt like I had a thousand-pound gorilla on my back—a gorilla that for the first time in my career, I was not sure I could successfully handle. Everywhere I turned there were problems that needed solutions and I had neither the resources nor the manpower to address all of them.

More than this I had a boss who was already making my life miserable—more miserable than Don Smith ever had. Florescue would use monthly review meetings with the management team to harangue us for not instantly solving problems created over several years. At these meetings he took the role of an omnipotent, omniscient bully. It was almost as though he believed that all he had to do was demand success and he would achieve it.

I summed up the situation to my wife in one sentence, "I have taken a near impossible job and have a near impossible boss."

Still I plowed forward. In retrospect I wonder why I accepted my fate and tried to make the job work. It was another "kamikaze" career decision—one that my gut instinct warned was foolish.

Building a Foundation for Success

To have any chance of success, it was clear that I had to address multiple priorities simultaneously and make no major mistakes.

In addition to addressing company morale and building a post-Jack Fulk culture, I had to evaluate the management, reconcile the franchisees and suppliers to my leadership, and improve company store operations. Most of all, I needed to craft a business plan to determine exactly what to do with Bojangles'—especially how to market it. Amazingly, there was no plan.

I became a man in perpetual motion. I toured of all the company-owned restaurants, including three days of looking at the former Biskit's restaurants to understand the problems firsthand. On this tour I wanted to show the restaurant managers that I cared about them and their problems. They had to be convinced that I was not another "bastard from New York."

Almost simultaneously, I addressed marketing. I met with the advertising agency hired by Florescue, Scali, McCabe, and Sloves (Scali). To my pleasant surprise, they welcomed me with open arms. The Arby's experience was never mentioned, but Sam Scali, not Ed McCabe, was in charge of the creative work. I never saw Ed.

Scali had been first frustrated by the Fulk–Florescue donnybrook, then by lack of direction from Will Claybourn who Barry had emasculated by allowing him no decision-making capability. They were anxious to make their mark and saw my arrival as a golden opportunity to do so.

I learned all this in a brand review in their New York office. We quickly agreed to start over and treat Bojangles' as a new account. I wanted a well-thought-out consumer positioning and, of course, brilliant TV advertising. I left New York believing this could happen. Messrs. Sloves and Scali had done outstanding work for other clients and they seemed motivated to do this for Bojangles'.

Along with new advertising, it was apparent that new menu items offered an almost sure road to sales success. Why? The answer lay in two key facts.

First, Bojangles' did only twenty percent of its business from 10 A.M. to 4 P.M.—yet, this part accounted for up to sixty-seven of the fast-food restaurant industry sales. Lunch was a huge opportunity! And it would give us real news to advertise.

Second, the franchisees wanted two menu additions. They wanted a sweet roll for the breakfast business, and french fries to add to the chicken menu.

To launch work on new menu items, Bojangles' had to have two new key resources, a test kitchen and someone to manage it. Fortunately, neither was a problem.

As part of the H&H makeover of Bojangles', the company was moved thirty days after my arrival into a "Taj Mahal" new headquarters—two stories in a new office building for offices and, on the ground floor, a state-of-the-art test kitchen. It was the best test kitchen I had ever seen.

I had started a search for a Vice President of Menu Development and a Director of Consumer Research as soon as I joined Bojangles'. Here too I was fortunate. Within sixty days, I was able to hire two highly competent former employees from Arby's: the always-smiling Ken Breiner for the menu development post and Jon Ritt for research.

I also added familiar marketing personnel—this time from Swensen's. Howard Englehart was hired to replace Will Claybourn. Howard had been "downsized" at Swensen's and was delighted to find employment. In addition, Mary Weyenberg joined us in a new post, PR Manager. Like Howard she had been fired by Pat Doughty and needed a job. She would report to Howard, but she would work directly for me on speeches, meeting planning, etc.

Mary turned out to be invaluable in another role. She became the person who built bridges between the "Fulk people" and the "H&H people." Naturally gregarious, she would meet everyone in her role as editor of an internal employee newsletter and learn their concerns/frustrations. I called her "chief morale officer" as she convinced me to hold employee functions like a bowling tournament, a softball game, and a Christmas party.

As all this was occurring, I still needed fast answers in a number of crucial areas that I had no time to review personally, nor staff that I could trust to address them. To get these answers, following my takeover template, I added three outside resources I had used at Swensen's. All knew their specialties and me. Each would report to me directly until I could sort out the management team.

I hired Rogers Merchandising to investigate our promotion needs and recommend a plan. Phil Lincoln's design firm was hired to recommend store design improvements that would also reduce costs. And I brought Al Bennett on board, as a one-man consultant, to do a thorough review of the store equipment. I was sure he'd find improvements that would more than justify his fee.

Finally, to top off the first sixty days, I attended a franchisee convention in Charlotte. It had been planned to try to calm their concerns over what they saw happening between Fulk and Florescue. But now it would be used to introduce me.

This meeting was a "make or break" occasion. I knew enough of the Carolina businessman's mentality and franchisee cultures, in general, that if I didn't make a good first impression, I would never get the chance for a second.

The meeting went surprisingly well. I was introduced as the meeting's first speaker; then spent an almost nonstop thirty-six hours talking one-on-one with the franchisees.

I was surprised at their sophistication and pleased they seemed open to my leadership. Later it became clear that they would have welcomed anyone they saw as strong enough to, as they often repeated, "Keep Barry Florescue from ruining Bojangles'."

Then came the meeting's close. Facing the audience of about 150 people, I shredded my written script in front of them, then walked to the front edge of the stage and gave an emotional speech. I talked about why I believed in Bojangles' and how I would address all their concerns starting with the menu. Finally I asked for their support. I stated that the chain's greatest need was to have the franchisees and the franchisor reunited and working together.

They seemed receptive. I received a standing ovation. After the convention I had dinner with Barry Florescue and John Gerlach. They were very pleased with my progress. For a few days, I became more optimistic about fixing Bojangles'.

Fortress Bojangles'

I needed a game plan to address all our major problems. To develop this, I used one of my favorite tactics, a management meeting outside the office. I took a cadre of Bojangle's management to Asheville, North Carolina, for a three-day meeting. The meeting was set up on dates that I knew Barry couldn't attend. I had two purposes for the meeting, and he would not be helpful for either.

We had to become better acquainted as a management team and build esprit de corps among us. Many of us barely knew each other. And, we needed to share a common vision of our problems and participate in formulating a game plan.

We had a good meeting. The group became better acquainted with each other and seemed to become more comfortable with one another. In general, this was as talented a group of executives as I had ever dealt with, anywhere. Jack Keilt and his newest hire, Bill Thelen, were particularly impressive. They were inventive strategic thinkers and good salesmen. If anyone could sell a franchise they could. Only Andy Stubl was a question mark. He was not strong enough to run all the company store operations without help. Andy was a "doer," not a problem solver.

We struggled over developing a game plan, however. We all knew that we had no chance of overcoming the immediate operations problems and the Biskit's problems. This meant we had no hope of meeting the profit plan goals set by H&H six months earlier, or even the lower forecast H&H had made a few months earlier. It was clear 1985 would be unprofitable, regardless of any effort we could make.

We were in a deep hole that would, over the next six months, inevitably grow deeper without a miraculous turnaround. Growth had stopped; no new restaurants were being built. Few if any new franchises could be sold when the operating results outside of the Carolinas were revealed.

As important, sales in existing company-owned restaurants were declining; and the 158 stores in total would be unprofitable. Tennessee and the Biskit's markets were very unprofitable and offset the still excellent profits from the Charlotte area restaurants.

Finally, virtually all the key outside-of-Carolina, franchised markets were in sales and profit trouble, including Dallas, Houston, Tampa, Washington, D.C., and Barry's stores in south Florida. Only the franchisee restaurants in the Carolinas were thriving.

By the end of the second day of discussion, the only way out of the mess was apparent. We dubbed the resulting plan, Fortress Bojangles." This was a four-part strategy built on a "survival" premise, namely that we had to protect our strong base of success in the Carolinas and focus on fixing the internal problems of the chain, before we grew it. This meant we would:

1 *Make training and people retention the focus of operations' programs for the remainder of the year, not food and labor costs.* The key issue to address to raise company profits was improving restaurant operations. Only trained personnel could solve this need.
2 *Halt all expansion outside the Carolinas until we found the answer to why Bojangles' consumer sales in this area were not equaling or even coming close to sales in the Carolinas.* Furthermore, in this outside area—we dubbed it the "noncore" area—we would not "rescue" franchises that failed; we would allow them to disappear. This meant the chain would shrink, perhaps by fifty or more restaurants.
3 *Franchise all the company restaurants in this non core area, except in south Florida.* We would use these Florida restaurants as our test area to address the noncore sales problem.
4 *Aggressively advertise and promote the business inside "Fortress Bojangles',* that is, North and South Carolina. We would defend our market leadership position at all costs.

Selling this to Barry Florescue would be very difficult. He was on record with stock analysts that expansion would be slowed, but would continue. He still publicly proclaimed that the only real problem was marketing and that Chris Schoenleb would fix that in short order.

Four Programs for Survival

Beyond this, we formulated a 1986 strategic plan that had four key programs to be developed for implementation in January. We felt these programs, coupled with operations' improvements that would be in place by then, would create an improved Bojangles' restaurant concept—a concept for expansion in the non core area after it proved itself.

The most critical of these was a new menu to broaden the appeal of Bojangles'. It had to be the weapon to build consumer sales because I was sure it was the only tactic that would work for every Bojangles' restaurant. Outside the core area it was clear from the data available that the existing menu had limited appeal. Inside the core area new menu items could provide "news" to advertise and promote, instead of a discount on buckets of chicken or biscuit sandwiches.

I also knew from my experience at Burger King, Arby's, and Swensen's that *new menu items would help address our internal cultural problems.* The excitement they created always improved company morale and gave added impetus to in-store training.

The issue, then, was what items were our best bets, and how fast we could get them ready for market. We had no in-depth consumer research to direct this effort, nor time for it. Instead I had to rely on input from franchisees, the internal staff, my "gut instinct," and Ken Breiner.

To keep my political powder dry, I also had to involve Barry Florescue and his ideas. I knew he'd love the idea of new menu items. They would give him fodder for the stock analysts and the H&H Board.

To get started, I met with Ken Breiner. I told him the importance of his assignment and gave him carte blanche to go all out to develop products in four areas:

1. *Lunch.* I was convinced this was our greatest opportunity to add sales in our core area. Bojangles' was a fast-food restaurant chain without a sandwich on a bun, everyone's fast-food staple. I asked Ken to develop a chicken sandwich and find an easily cooked second meat sandwich, but not hamburgers.
2. *New side dishes, starting with french fries.* I was sure this was a no-brainer profit improvement opportunity. Every fast-food chicken chain in America had french fries except Bojangle's.
3. *Nonspicy chicken.* We needed to test having a second chicken line, a la KFC. By far the largest part of the fried chicken market was basic salt and pepper spiced fried chicken (I called it southern fried chicken).
4. *A breakfast sweet roll.* The franchisees were convinced it could be a big seller.

Ken smiled. "I love it! Don't worry Chris you'll have all of it in six months or less."

I smiled back. I loved his "can do" attitude. " Ken, I'll promise the sweet roll and french fries by the end of the year. Do those first, then go for fixing lunch."

He shook his head. "No, I'll do it all—and I'll simplify the in-store chicken prep that Barry keeps asking about. I promise! You gave me that beautiful test kitchen. Watch it pay off."

The second key program was an aggressive advertising and sales promotion program. We followed the model plan we used at Burger King to have programs that addressed all three methods of building sales—attracting new customers and gaining increased sales from existing customers through more frequent visits or from a higher sale per customer.

To build the customer base, we directed Scali to develop a plan and advertising creative to exploit the new menu items in television, radio, and newspaper. At the same time we asked Rogers to develop plans to increase average check, particularly at breakfast, and traffic-building promotions.

The third program was a new building design, already in the works through Phil Lincoln's and Al Bennett's work. This design simplified the kitchen layout, spiffed up the dining rooms with carpet and a different seating décor, and cut construction costs significantly. I approved building this new prototype for a new company restaurant in Charlotte that would open in January.

The fourth program was a special company-owned restaurant operations program designed to address the quality of store operations and the morale of the employees. It too would be ready for launch on January 1.

Six Months of Bad News

I returned from Ashville convinced we had a workable program. As the staff scattered to execute their part of the plan, I had a big assignment. I had to sell Barry Florescue.

As I contemplated how to do this, *I realized* I was not really the CEO of Bojangles'. I had no freedom to operate, as I had enjoyed at Swensen's. Worse yet, I had no contact with the Horn & Hardart Board. They would hear only from Barry and Muni Saltoun. It was clear that I could easily be made a scapegoat for Barry's mistakes.

At any rate, I went to New York for a private meeting with Barry to sell Fortress Bojangles'. To have any meaningful discussion with Barry you had to talk one-on-one. When Barry had a group meeting, he was "on stage." He had to show that he was boss. He had to win any discussion. Alone, he could be reasonable.

Before seeing Barry I met with Muni. He had a bushel of bad news. He advised me that we would be taking over the franchisee's stores in Dallas.

Since this violated the very first key tenet of our Fortress Bojangles' plan. I told Muni that as CEO of Bojangles' I would not do it.

Muni shrugged his shoulders and said, "I don't blame you for not wanting to do this, but we have no choice. Therefore you have no choice. Barry will explain."

Muni went on, "There's worse news, Chris. You will have to take over all the Tampa-St. Pete stores. Those folks are going out of business, and as part of our Biskit's deal with the banks, we are obligated to keep them operating."

I was horrified. "Muni, this is absolutely nuts! If we take over the twenty-two stores in Tampa and five in Dallas, we'll be buried financially and stretched over the breaking point from an operations manpower standpoint. I have nobody I can send to either place without hurting our existing Carolina's business!"

Muni shrugged again. "Look, Chris, I can't do a thing about this."

I soon learned why. Barry appeared. He was friendly, almost congenial. As we shook hands, he said, "Chris, great to see you. Come on in (to his office). We have lots to talk about."

I responded with gallows humor, "Please, no more news!"

The day was spent learning about the deals that had been made to sell the Dallas expansion and acquire Biskit's, and why we had to take over these losers.

Dallas was particularly galling. Associates of the famous junk bond salesman, Michael Milken, owned it. Barry had used Milken's services for much of Horn & Hardart's borrowing. Barry told me he had to take back Dallas "to stay in Milken's good graces."

When I finally tried to broach Fortress Bojangles', Barry would not discuss it. He told me such strategic decisions were not mine to make, but his. "Your job is to work with the existing system and fix it with good marketing. You're our doer, not our strategist."

In retrospect, this was a second time I should have resigned. I couldn't execute my plan to try to save the company; it would be Barry's plan. But, I didn't quit. Instead I laid out the four programs for '86. Barry loved them, especially the new menu items and the advertising/promotion plan development.

I went back to Charlotte hoping for the best, but feeling that thousand pound gorilla growing even heavier.

I can't overstate the devastating impact that the Dallas news and the Biskit's news had on my staff. To keep them from total despair, I convinced most that we would have to begin Fortress Bojangles' as a corporate guerilla warfare tactic—that we'd follow the philosophy as much as we could without making it a formal strategy.

As the year wore on, the overall corporate earnings worsened about as we expected, but they were far worse than Barry claimed he had expected. He began to harass all of us with daily phone calls offering advice and warnings to make more progress or else.

This constant pressure, coupled with simply dreadful management review meetings with him each month led to further internal and manpower problems. It became clear we were not making progress in operations and Howard Englehart was ineffective with Barry. I concluded we had to find two key new lieutenants, a senior VP of Operations and a senior VP of Marketing. Surprisingly, Barry agreed.

We were making progress, however, on other fronts. Ken was making magic happen in the test kitchen. He did exactly what he said he would do and more. He would have seventeen new items ready to introduce.

In advertising, we approved a new well-strategized and well-executed ad campaign. It was not a once-in-a-lifetime campaign, however, and I worried that it was not strong enough to create traffic on its own. (My worries were, unfortunately, justified.)

Last, we were able to close Dallas and several other major company restaurant profit losers. We also refranchised ten restaurants. Fortress Bojangles' had started despite Barry Florescue.

Unfortunately, none of these actions made a dent in the year's results. We did not see any positive results from the advertising. And, just as we felt some progress was being made in restructuring the company-owned restaurants, Barry dropped another set of failing franchise restaurants on us to operate—his. Somehow, he got the H&H Board to acquire the twelve restaurants he had as a franchisee. All were losing money.

I shed no tears as 1985 ended. I found myself nominally in charge of a chain financially wrecked by overzealous expansion and a parent company that insisted on taking over and operating restaurants performing so poorly that they had negative cash flow.

The 1985 Horn & Hardart annual report spelled out the disaster. It reported a $27,000,000+ drop in an operating income from $14,321,000 in 1984 to a loss of $13,225,000. Over $23,000,000 of this drop was blamed on Bojangles'. Here's how it was explained in the annual report in which as I had expected only Gerlach's deal was scapegoated (Predictably, too, John resigned):

> The Bojangle's loss, before nonrecurring charges, resulted from a 10% decline in average unit sales volume, losses stemming from the operations of Biskit's Inc. restaurants acquired in 1984 and continued lower sales volume experienced in new markets. In addition, due to a slowing of franchise growth, the sale of franchise development contracts and franchise fees were $1.7 million lower in 1985 than 1984.
>
> The number of company operated restaurants increased to 167 at year end 1985 from 143 in 1984. Included in this increase are 44 units repurchased from franchisees including 17 units which were franchised at the time of the Biskit's acquisition.

The company also opened 11 new restaurants, refranchised 10 and closed 21 restaurants.

The misery continued as we entered 1986. We were forced to take over yet another set of franchisee stores that H&H did not want to fail. This time it was Washington, D.C.

Still, my hope was that Bojangles' had reached bottom—that we could start showing real improvement as our 1986 program was launched with as much positive PR spin as we could muster. We had excellent programs. The question was were they strong enough to truly reverse the existing trends. The key would be whether the new menu would build traffic and whether this traffic would be well served in company-owned restaurants, or whether our operations woes would continue.

It was clear, too, that this program had to work to protect my career. I needed positive trends to use with potential new employers. (Not surprisingly, I had resolved that to leave Bojangles' at my first opportunity.)

Launching the "New Bojangles' "

We started the year with a meeting to introduce the restaurant managers to the four programs that we had developed and motivate them to believe in the new management.

We spent two days introducing and hyping the "New Bojangles'," a company we stated had a great future for those that embraced the planned changes and made them work.

The first program we introduced was the new menu. We showed seventeen new menu items that would be gradually introduced system-wide over twelve months. Some, most notably the salads, would be in-market tested first. The seventeen items are listed below by mealtime occasion:

Breakfast—We added elements of a traditional breakfast: A scrambled eggs and bacon (or sausage) platter, and a Cinnamon Twist sweet roll (made from leftover biscuit dough) We also added "Egg Boats," a unique scrambled egg dish.

Lunch/Dinner—We put in elements of a mainstream fast-food sandwich menu but made it as unique and as appealing as possible. We showed a line of five sandwiches. a spicy chicken sandwich a country-fried steak sandwich and, of course, a nonspicy grilled chicken breast sandwich, fixed three ways, deluxe (lettuce and tomato) chicken 'n bacon, and with lettuce and mayonnaise only. With these sandwiches, we added a unique potato side dish, seasoned french-fries.

Then to seek some uniqueness for women we displayed four entrée salads: chef, chicken, garden, and taco-chicken.

Finally, we showed a second chicken. We called it southern-style (it was essentially the Biskit's product) to be served as a choice instead of spicy. We completed the new menu by adding mashed potatoes and country-fried steak platters.

Marketing Program

We laid out a twelve-month marketing calendar that had part of the new menu introduced each quarter, starting with the sandwiches, fries, and the Cinnamon Twist.

We previewed the new TV, radio, and print ads to support the introductions. And, on top of this, we launched a Bojangles' version of the Burger King RADIUS program and a schedule of ongoing promotions to build visit frequency and encourage add-on sales to build the average check.

This was the most extensive marketing program I had put together since the Burger King kids' program. In effect it was an all-out assault to broaden the customer base of the chain by adding new menu items that were outside Jack Fulk's original Cajun concept. It would forever change Bojangles' from a niche marketer to a more mainstream fast-food concept.

To be called a success it had to increase sales a minimum of ten percent in the heartland and at least twenty-five percent in the non-core areas.

New Building Design

As part of the meeting, we took all attendees to see a new prototype restaurant we would open with as much positive PR as we could the following week.

The new design had a revamped kitchen, a new less garish exterior and interior. It was significantly less costly, and had more efficient service capability. It was a big hit with the restaurant managers.

Operation P.R.I.D.E.

Our fourth program, the one we developed to help fix Company-owned restaurant operations was dubbed Operation P.R.I.D.E. This was the most all-encompassing program of its kind I have ever seen.

Here's how I introduced it in videos to every employee, in a speech to all store managers and in the "Operation P.R.I.D.E. Employee Newsletter":

> "What is Operation P.R.I.D.E.? The single most important event in Bojangles' history. It's our opportunity to be the best fast food chain in America . . . our means to give to you—our restaurant management and crew—the tools you need to achieve excellence in customer service.

P.R.I.D.E. is an acronym–each letter stands for a word:

P = People
R = Resources
I = Initiative
D = Determination
E = Excellence

And these five words summarize the philosophy that Bojangles' Operation P.R.I.D.E. is built upon:

> Bojangles' *People* are its greatest *Resource*. It will be through their *Initiative* and *Determination* that we will achieve *Excellence* in customer service.

> Operation Pride is not a program—it's a philosophy—a philosophy that is found in only those companies that achieve excellence within the fast food industry. But in order for it to be a philosophy it cannot only apply to the operations group. It has to apply to every single department and every single employee in the Bojangles' system. It means that every single one of us has got to embrace it, endorse it and believe in it.

In Operation P.R.I.D.E. we put a plethora of special programs. Eight programs, for example, focussed on rewarding and recognizing excellence in restaurant customer service. These ranged from a mystery shopping program in which the shopper paid instant rewards to an employee giving proper service, to employee-of-the-month recognition plaques, to special bonuses for restaurant managers whose restaurants scored above ninety-five percent on operations inspections, etc.

Hope Fades

As I reviewed all the elements of the plan, my template for success was in place. Similar programs, less elaborate and complete, had worked at Burger King and Arby's. Indeed, all of us "outsiders" were confident that in any other chain, the new menu items and new advertising coupled with this all-inclusive dynamic operations incentive program would build sales.

The question on all our minds, however, was whether the Bojangles' veterans would decide to adopt the program or continue to resist change, as they had for over the year since Jack Fulk had left. And, there was the "unthinkable concern": Would the program be strong enough stop the downward earnings spiral?

The next three months after this all-out program launch were a blur of disappointment and frustration.

The bottom line was that despite some initial success we failed to reverse the company's fortunes. Bojangle's continued to spew forth earnings' losses. And with this lack of success we started to lose key employees and some of the management team. Howard Singer left, as did our computer whiz, Dave Bush.

Along with this I made hiring blunders. I hired a new VP of Marketing, Jim Maruna, then I fired him in sixty days. It was the worst hiring mistake I ever made. I also hired a new VP of Operations from Godfather's Pizza, Joe Gillette. He too failed to perform.

On top of this, Barry Florescue became more and more antagonistic. He seemed to have convinced himself that I was the cause of Bojangles' problems. He had a horrible temper and would explode with highly personal venomous attacks on me whenever any new piece of bad news struck. It seemed obvious Barry was pushing me to quit to vindicate his position.

It was clear by April, my one-year hiring anniversary, that my days were numbered at Bojangles'. I knew that the only hope for Bojangles' was Fortress Bojangles', and no one at H&H wanted to listen to this strategy.

Final Months

I was miserable, but decided to wait for the axe to fall. I believed conventional wisdom that quitting without another job always makes finding a new job more difficult.

In retrospect, it's clear that I accepted the inevitability of my demise. I spent the summer fending off Barry's incessant phone calls and trying to "care take" of the business. I also made several valedictory speeches to the AMA and MUFSO in the hopes of sparking someone's interest in hiring me.

It was impossible, however, to ever get inured to the actions of Barry Florescue. As the summer months wore on, he seemed more and more angry and upset. This in turn led some truly bizarre behavior, not always at my expense. One such incident became an instant legend at Bojangles'.

As a symbolic cost-cutting measure Barry had demanded that we reduce our Watts lines for long-distance phone calls from six to three. At the same time, he edicted that no phone, not even mine could override the Watts line. All long-distance calls had to use the Watts lines.

On one mid-summer visit after Barry had spent the day looking for new cost savings, he realized he had forgotten to make a major stock market trade. It was 3:50 P.M., when he ran into my office, summarily ordered me out and grabbed my phone to place his trade. He had ten minutes before the market closed.

He tried to place his call but it would not go through. The three Watts lines were in use. I was outside my office door when he discovered he was not going to be able to complete his call. From the noise in my office, he seemed to go berserk. First he bellowed several obscenities. Then when his final phone call try failed, I heard a loud stomping, as though he was jumping up and down on something. Finally the door opened, he rushed out and left the building.

I walked into my office to find a mess. On the floor was a totally destroyed telephone. He had apparently jumped up and down on it and smashed it.

My tenure at Bojangles' ended in early fall—the exact date of my last meeting with Barry Florescue is lost in the mists of my mind. The meeting itself was equally unmemorable. He flew in on his private jet with his lawyer and summarily fired me. I was escorted from the building as Barry announced my "resignation" and that a Carlos Garcia was replacing me.

Postscript

Even after leaving, my problems with Barry continued. He was an angry vengeful man. He declared financial war on me, and true to his overall modus operandi, sought litigation, not accommodation. He apparently wanted me to suffer a financial hurt and personal integrity questions.

He reportedly launched an internal investigation of my expense accounts to find some indiscretion so he could threaten me with a fraud lawsuit. Then he slowed the processing of my exercise of a stock option and threatened through his lieutenants not to honor it. Finally, he refused to recognize my written employment agreement for one year's salary as severance pay. He would pay nothing.

I called my lawyer, Tom Chorey, and a legal battle was begun. I expected to win because I possessed signed original documents that entitled me to the stock option proceeds and the severance pay. I also had signed copies of all my approved expense reports. There were no fraudulent charges, and I knew this would prevent Barry from possibly changing any report to aid his investigation.

I didn't totally win the legal battle. In the end, to avoid mounting legal costs and drawn out litigation, I agreed to six month's severance. In return, H&H honored the stock option and agreed to stop their threats of a fraud lawsuit. But, Barry had gotten his "pound of flesh" by choosing to litigate rather than honor a written promise. His deeper pockets financially made him a successful bully.

Nine months later, I indirectly received the first and only major public explanation that Bojangles' failure was not my doing, but Barry's mistakes.

In a June 15, 1987 article in *Forbes* magazine, Florescue's career was thoroughly trashed. In the article titled, "Why Didn't They Pay Him to Stay Home?" the series of financial maneuverings he had made were exposed as the huge mistakes that caused Bojangles' earnings demise in 1985-86.

Here's in part what was written:

> Last year the Bojangle's chain lost $47.6 million in sales of $90 million. Bojangles' parent, Las Vegas-based Horn & Hardart Co., lost $28.4 million on $405 million in revenues.
>
> Horn & Hardart. Once famous for its Automat restaurants, long a must for visitors and New Yorkers alike. How did the company go astray?
>
> Look no further than Barry Florescue, 44, who had been Horn & Hardart's chairman and chief executive officer since 1977.
>
> During Florescue's ten-year reign, Horn & Hardart's only significant success has been in one area Florescue knew little about and did not mess with: the Hanover House mail-order catalog division.

Barry was finally dismissed from H&H sometime after this article was published. Shortly thereafter, Bojangles' was sold to venture capitalists. Since then, Bojangles' has survived another ownership change but has continued to thrive in the Carolina's. The Fortress Bojangles' strategy was proven correct. Of the old management, only Eric Newman remains.

One final personal note: Whenever I visit the Carolinas I am a still a loyal Bojangles' customer. The biscuits and chicken are still the best, as are the seasoned french fries, the Cinnamon Twist, and the luncheon sandwich menu that we introduced.

Lessons Learned

1. The ambitions and greed of one man, if he has the reins of power, can destroy a thriving company and the careers of many men, even in this era of strong boards of Directors.
2. ***Lifetime Lesson: Expansion of a successful restaurant chain concept must be done slowly enough to assure that a company's infrastructure can manage it and that regional differences in consumer's tastes are learned.*** I could not overcome the original mistake that of rapidly introducing Bojangles' outside its heartland without testing. The owners assumed that Bojangle's would have the same concept strength everywhere.

Final Comment

This was my final job in the restaurant industry. The Bojangles' experience convinced me that my ambition to be a restaurant chain CEO had led me down a road of no return. I did not want to be used and abused again. Someone else could be CEO of the next restaurant chain seeking "better marketing, etc." It was time to bury ambition and seek a safe haven.

As is chronicled in Chapter 13, this led me back to Chicago and the advertising/marketing world, but not to a "safe haven." By the late '80s, corporate "downsizing" would begin. There were no companies that offered the safety of long-term employment, particularly if one was a high-level marketing executive.

PART IV
FINAL BATTLES
1987–1997

CHAPTER 13
Drinking My Own Kool-Aid
(The Perils of Advertising Agency Ownership

Relatively secure financially from earning two CEO salaries for most of my time at Bojangles', I took a month's vacation before considering seeking another job.

During this month the phone didn't ring. For the first time in my career, executive search firms, knowing that I was "on the street," did not seek me out. I began to wonder whether my public failure at Bojangles' had poisoned my career permanently.

In mid-November, I finally sat down to review career options. *Lifetime Lesson: Before seeking a job, you must realistically assess how executive search firms, corporate and agency human resource directors, and your peers will perceive you. Without this, you could waste much of your effort seeking a position you simply will not be given an opportunity to be interviewed for, no matter how much you believe in your ability to handle it.*

In this case, there seemed to be three options: (1) another presidency of a restaurant chain, probably as a CEO for a turnaround chain (This was an option I did not want, but clearly it was a possibility.) (2) a corporate marketing position, or (3) ownership of my own business —every P&G brand manager's ultimate dream. My preference was to return to corporate marketing, preferably outside the restaurant industry. But this was, at best, a long shot, so I decided to pursue all three options.

As I began the job search, I was hopeful that I could replicate my experience after leaving Swensen's and easily find several good opportunities.

My hopes were quickly dashed. From the start, based on phone calls to friends and friendly executive search firm recruiters, the early lack of phone calls was not a fluke. Perhaps because of my age (fifty-two), or, perhaps, because of the Bojangles' fiasco, I seemed to have very little marketability.

No restaurant chain seeking a new president, for example, was interested in Chris Schoenleb. That door seemed to be permanently barred. Likewise, as I had feared, no company seemed interested in hiring me in a marketing position. I had been a CEO and was, therefore, in the minds of search firms and corporate executives, overqualified to be a chief marketing officer.

And last, after spending almost sixteen years in the restaurant industry no one outside that industry, even advertising agencies, showed any interest in hiring me.

After ninety days only one opportunity had developed–part ownership of a small Chicago advertising agency.

Fortis–Fortis

The agency opportunity was with Fortis–Fortis, the agency we had hired for Swensen's. Jerry and Dixie Fortis were seeking a new partner.

I had learned this during my last months at Bojangles' when the Fortis's came to visit us in Charlotte. Jerry was a fine golfer, and I had vainly hoped that his skills would enable us to do well in a member/guest tournament. During the course of this three-day weekend, Jerry, Dixie, and I talked searchingly about the possibility of my joining them. Their former partner, Bob Westerfield, had left and they professed to be overwhelmed with managing their agency without him.

This partnership was not a new idea. I had first been intrigued by the possibility of going into business with Jerry and Dixie in 1979. They had contacted me about joining them when they were starting their agency. These two had compiled an impressive set of creative credentials. Dixie, for example, had been named Ad Woman of the Year in Chicago in the mid-'70s. They had left key agency positions with McCann–Erickson, one of America's largest and most successful advertising agencies, to begin their agency. (Jerry had been the Managing Director of the Chicago office.)

The three of us had seemed to fit. I was a seasoned marketer and account manager; they were talented hard-working creative people. Also, we seemed to share a common set of values. But at that time, with two kids in college, I was afraid of the financial risks involved.

Now, as the phone remained silent, the risks seemed more attractive. Furthermore, I was becoming convinced that the agency business offered me the only way back into the mainstream of advertising/marketing—my career path of choice.

Returning To Chicago

In late January 1987, I flew to Chicago for in-depth discussions with the Fortis's about joining them.They seemed very open, sharing their financial books, their hopes, and their dreams.

Initially, my biggest concern was the agency's small size and the type of clients it had. I knew Fortis–Fortis's business didn't fit my talents or interests. The agency needed to have one or more national advertisers to really fit my expertise.

But it didn't. Fortis–Fortis was billing only about $15 million dollars with all clients headquartered in Chicago. The agency's biggest client was the Oldsmobile Dealers Association of Chicago. There were four other major clients: Ram Golf; Hinckley & Schmidt, the bottled water company; Pepe's, a Mexican restaurant chain; and the Colonial Bank group in Chicago. Only Ram and Hinckley & Schmidt advertised outside the Chicago market.

I soon learned that there was a second and potentially bigger concern—profitability.

Fortis–Fortis was an agency on the brink of financial problems. Basically the agency had too much overhead, but the overhead (people) really couldn't be cut because everyone was needed to enable Fortis–Fortis to be a full-service agency (account, creative, media, TV commercial and print production services in-house) and thus make it a viable competitor for most new business.

The agency was breaking even financially, but only because Jerry and Dixie were paying themselves about one-fifth what they could have earned as creative group heads at a major agency. The problem was that they had not replaced their biggest client, the Mexican restaurant chain Chi Chi's that they had lost about two years prior to this. Chi Chi's had billed from $7 to $12 million and had been their only major national account.

Clearly the agency needed new business to be secure financially, but neither Jerry nor Dixie had the time to mount a full-fledged new business effort. They saw a third partner who could also run account groups as the answer to this need.

It all seemed ready made for me. I saw Fortis–Fortis as an opportunity that I was confident could be built into a sizeable agency, quickly. So, despite the obvious risks involved, and despite my wife and other close friends telling me I would never be comfortable in such a small business, I became more and more enamoured with returning to the Chicago ad agency business and putting my name on the door.

Eventually all of this led to discussion of the key issue for any partnership, the "price of admission" or the deal for the prospective partner.

The Fortis's seemed anxious to make it as attractive as possible. They were willing to sell a one-third partnership in the agency for a very modest price, $30,000, or one-third of the book value of the agency. And, they were willing to pay me a salary equal to their combined salaries. (This was about half my income at Bojangles'.)

This proposed deal seemed fair and added to my interest. As important, there were still no other potential jobs on the horizon. In mid-February, I advised Jerry and Dixie that I was ready to become their partner.

Surprisingly, and perhaps in retrospect, wisely, the Fortis's were reticent to finalize the partnership. Instead, they proposed that I try out the new job before I invested. They wouldn't pay me, but they would pay my expenses.

I agreed to this arrangement and moved to Chicago in late February to begin a second career in the advertising agency business.

The first few weeks went well. I quickly became immersed in the financial administration of the agency. My job was to be the agency president and COO. As president, I was in charge of all accounting and internal administration. All account personnel reported to me, while Jerry had the creative personnel reporting to him. And of course, I was to be in charge of developing new business—the agency's biggest need.

Initially, I took over management of the Hinckley & Schmidt Bottled Water, Colonial Bank, and Pepe's Restaurant accounts. However, because I was a temporary employee, I did no work on new business.

It was not an easy adjustment to go back to advertising agency life, especially working with small clients as a temporary employee. I worked long hours four days a week, and commuted to Charlotte every weekend. (I had rented a one-bedroom apartment in downtown Chicago and made no plans to move to Chicago).

Still, I liked being out of the day-to-day pressures of my previous jobs, and there were still no other job prospects on the horizon. I decided to push for a finalization of the partnership.

Fortis–Fortis–Schoenleb

After two months, Jerry, Dixie, agreed to formally put together our partnership. Partnership documents were drawn up and, after the usual legal wrangling between their lawyer and mine, we finally signed the papers. In late April 1987, the name of the agency was changed to Fortis–Fortis–Schoenleb (FFS).

I was truly excited. I was sure that, with my notoriety in the restaurant industry and with the business friends I had throughout the marketing world, my joining Jerry and Dixie would be big news in the advertising world, and this would help us to immediately gain significant new business.

I was wrong. The world little noticed or cared about the press release we issued announcing Fortis–Fortis–Schoenleb. It was buried in a one-line sentence in the *Chicago Tribune* and on a back page of *Advertising Age*.

Despite this, I was optimistic that we could quickly build Fortis–Fortis–Schoenleb into a $30 to $40 million dollar ad agency, and make the agency very profitable for we three partners.

My optimism was short lived. It was soon very clear why Fortis–Fortis had not succeeded in attracting new business. Potential national account clients, the clients that Jerry, Dixie, and I would have been most comfortable working for, saw our agency as too small. Despite our personal backgrounds, they did not even invite us to present our credentials to them.

Conversely, the clients that did seek out Fortis–Fortis–Schoenleb were the kind we were least interested in handling. They were owners of small entrepreneurial companies that had $100,000 to $1 million advertising budgets and were not willing to spend significant funds for television commercials or print ads to do the kind of creative work that the three of us were most comfortable producing.

To counteract this problem, I tried to sell companies with major national advertising budgets to give us special assignments to show them that we could produce great work at a reasonable price. Jerry and Dixie had been successful in doing this in prior years. It was, in fact, how they had originally landed the Chi Chi's account. I contacted as many business friends as I thought would be receptive to such a presentation, but struck out every time. Although most were cordial, they expressed no interest in giving us such assignments.

Then in late May, Dick Good, a business friend and a former P&G brand manager who headed his own marketing consulting firm, asked us if we would be interested in working with his client, Bill Knapp, a regional restaurant chain headquartered in Battle Creek, Michigan. It was small, but had potential. We, of course, said "yes" and landed our first new client.

A Failed Merger and Its "Fallout"

About this time, I also received a fateful phone call from Ron Sherman, my old JWT friend from Burger King days. "Schoenleb," he said, "What are you doing in a tiny Chicago agency? I don't care if your name is on the door. Don't you feel like a duck out of water? How can you possibly be happy in a $20 million dollar advertising agency? You used to spend that much money for breakfast!"

I laughed. It was good to hear from a dear friend. "Ron, I'm just happy to be out of the restaurant industry and out of the messes I've been in the last few years. It's probably true that I don't really belong in this kind of agency but I hope it can become a bigger agency. At least, that's what I'm trying to do."

He responded, "Chris, trust me—it'll never work. Do me and yourself a favor, come and talk to us. As you know, Ross–Roy out of Detroit owns our agency. Ross–Roy is run by Glenn Fortinberry, my old buddy from J. Walter Thompson. Glenn wants to talk to you." (Glenn had been part of the new business team when we first visited JWT in New York.)

I was confused and asked, "Why call him? What's up?"

"Well, Ross–Roy is looking into opening a Chicago office and Glenn has always liked you. Perhaps we could put together a deal where your agency became part of Ross–Roy. Then I would be running the New York office and you would be running the Chicago office and we could have some great times together just like we had back in the BK days."

This sounded like manna from heaven. "Ron, that sounds like a great idea. Would you set it up?"

He replied, "I'll get back to you."

I advised the Fortis's of my phone conversation, and reminded my partners of our precarious financial situation. "We need to pursue this. Maybe this can jump-start our growth. I know these guys, you'll love 'em!"

Jerry was not enthusiastic about the idea of becoming part of Ross–Roy; but he agreed that I should pursue initial discussions. As I recall, he said something like "Well, Chris, this is not something we ever want to do again—you know, be part of a bigger agency. That's why Dixie and I left McCann–Erickson in the first place."

Still, I went to Detroit and met with Glenn Fortinberry. It was a good meeting. Glenn had done a remarkable job of turning Ross–Roy into a full-service agency from what had been, basically, a promotion agency working with one client, Chrysler. He now also had a major full-service client, K Mart, and had been on an agency acquisition spree that had included purchasing a New York agency that he had hired Ron Sherman to manage.

As a result of our meeting, Glenn agreed to visit Chicago to meet with Jerry, Dixie, and me. He also expressed interest in hiring me to work for Ross–Roy in Chicago if he didn't make a deal involving the Fortis's.

Several weeks later Glenn came to Chicago. From the first, even though Glenn was one of the most congenial, easy-going, likeable people I have ever known, Jerry and Dixie bristled. It was obvious my partners wanted no part of Ross–Roy. It was also clear from this meeting that we would never be able to make a deal to become part of any bigger agency.

My hopes for my new career sank. In my mind, my partners' surprising mindset doomed Fortis–Fortis–Schoenleb to being a small insignificant player in the Chicago agency scene unless we had a major stroke of luck.

After the meeting, I confessed my frustrations to Fortinberry, "I am sorry, Glenn. I had no idea my partners were so adamant against any kind of association with another major agency. I wouldn't have invited you over had I understood their true feelings."

He replied, "That's Okay, Chris. I don't think it would've worked out anyway. We need a bigger presence in Chicago than Fortis–Fortis–Schoenleb could have given us. I'm really more interested in getting your services than your agency's. Would you be interested in helping us with a new business presentation we are about to make?"

I thought a minute. I had been partner in my own ad agency for less than three months and was being asked to work for another agency in a new business presentation. It was something I should not have been interested in.

But I was. I was now sure that Fortis–Fortis–Schoenleb was doomed to mediocrity and that I'd never realize my goal of returning to big-time advertising through FFS.

After a long and painful hesitation I replied to Glenn, "What do you have in mind?"

"Well," he said, "Ron Sherman is putting together a team to pitch the Arby's account out of our New York office. I know you know a lot about Arby's and you could be a big help to us. We would be willing to pay you a consulting fee for your time. And I am sure that you could do this in such a way that it would not interfere with your work at your own agency. If we win the business, however, we would like to talk to you about running it for us, perhaps by setting up a new Ross–Roy Chicago office."

The lure was too much. I agreed to Glenn's proposal. I would be helping Ron Sherman pitch the Arby's business to my long-time associate, Larry Krueger.

I told my partners nothing of this conversation. I continued our new business efforts for the agency, pursuing regional restaurant chains and any other mid-sized account that announced an agency search. However, on the next two weekends I met with Ron in New York to work on the pitch for Arby's. We spent several delightful evenings reminiscing over the good times at Burger King. (Sadly, these would be our final times together. Ron died two years later from cancer.)

In addition to the fun, I learned about the art of being a good agency pitchman from a master agency account manager. Sherman, the best ad agency account manager I have ever known, was very concerned about my agency personality. He spent hours coaching me to take on what he called a "more acceptable agency personality." "Schoenleb," he said, "You are too much like a client. You scare potential clients. You need to soften up and let people see that you are open to their ideas instead of always trying to sell them your ideas."

Listening to Ron, I wondered more than ever why I had been eager to jump back into the advertising agency world.

The day came to pitch the Arby's business. Larry Krueger marched in with his entourage. We gave a three-hour credentials presentation. I was shown as the man to run the business. All seemed to go well, but within a week we learned that we had not made the finals for the Arby's business.

So much for friendships being able to gain access to major pieces of business!

Final Months

Meanwhile, things were getting worse for Fortis–Fortis–Schoenleb. We were losing money with no immediate prospects for improvement.

The Oldsmobile account had cut back its billings due to lower car sales. Colonial Bank had decided not to run the radio and TV campaign we had pitched. The Bill Knapp account proved to be a lot of work for very little billing.

The only bright spot was Hinckley & Schmidt Bottled Water. We were able to convince them to do a high-profile TV campaign. For this, we produced what I still consider to be one of the classic bottled water commercials of all time.

As all this occurred, my relations with the Fortis's became more strained. Jerry and Dixie, both very heavy cigarette smokers, were obviously discussing many agency matters without me behind closed doors and a cloud of smoke. It seemed clear that a showdown of sorts was coming.

To try to repair our relationship, which had never been good after the Fortinberry visit, and try to help the agency financially, I offered to take no salary for a month or two, if they would do likewise. Jerry declined to discuss the matter.

About this time, a senior partner of an executive search firm called. His question: "Would I be interested in interviewing for the presidency of a major franchising company?"

Surprised that I would hear such a question after nine months of a silent telephone, I hesitated, then asked, "What company are you talking about?"

"Well, we're not really supposed to tell you, but it's Midas, the muffler company."

"Midas," I said, "I've obviously heard of the company, but I know nothing about it. Where's it located? How big is it?"

I sensed a smile at the other end of the phone. "Well, Midas is headquartered here in Chicago. It has over 1,700 stores nationwide and an ad budget of over sixty million dollars. Midas is looking for a president of its U.S. operations who would be the probable successor to the current CEO."

"Sounds interesting. I'd definitely like to learn more about the job. But first, let me ask you a question. Why me? I don't know much about mufflers even though I was in the car business at one time."

The reply was typical "headhunter speak." "You have the two major pieces of background we have in the specs for this job, marketing and franchising."

An interview was soon set up. I spent an afternoon talking with the CEO and president of Midas, Ron Moore, and the senior VP of Human Resources, Brian Burhoe. I came away intrigued. Midas was a "quiet giant" in its own industry that seemed to enjoy its relative anonymity. It was, and remains today, the largest specialty auto repair chain in the world.

Further, Midas was not a turnaround situation. It was a very profitable franchising company with growing sales. Equally important, I sensed in both Brian and Ron two men who shared the same set of values about people and management that I did. I was very comfortable with both of them.

A few days later, Burhoe asked me to take the next step in the Midas interviewing process—a half-day psychiatrist's interview to determine my psychological suitability for the position.

By early August, I had met the psychiatrist and apparently "passed." Burhoe asked me to come back for a final "make or break" interview with an executive of Midas' parent company, IC Industries. So at 7:30 A.M. one morning, IC executive VP, Bruce Chelburg interviewed me in a unique and somewhat intimidating fashion. He stood behind his stand-up working desk during the entire interview.

The interview went badly. I was not sharp at such an early hour. Worse yet, Chelburg and I had no personal chemistry. He seemed annoyed that I was there, and he seemed much too concerned about the many jobs that I had held.

Result: I was not surprised to learn several weeks later that I was a losing candidate for the U.S. presidency of Midas.

Meanwhile, the business at Fortis–Fortis–Schoenleb continued to worsen. And, unknown to me, my partners had come to a decision. They would dump me. They dissolved our partnership in a letter that I found on my desk. In it they used many angry words and phrases and blamed me for virtually all the agency's problems.

I was stunned by the letter's content. I was equally upset that my friends couldn't or wouldn't discuss the matter directly with me. The bottom line, however, was clear. The five months with my name on the door of a Chicago agency were over. The partnership was not working. And as owners of two-thirds of the agency they had the right to throw me out with no buyback of my investment. The agency had lost all book value since I had joined it.

I ignored their threats of a lawsuit, packed up my personal belongings and left with no dialogue, other than a brief verbal rebuttal to all their self-serving accusations.

Postscript

The Fortis's did not seek a replacement for me. The agency continued in business for several years even though they lost virtually all their accounts except Ram. Finally, in the early '90s it closed. Jerry became VP of Marketing for Ram; Dixie became a freelance creative writer.

Ross–Roy never opened a Chicago office.

Lessons Learned

1. Your talent and experience must fit the job opportunity. Owning your own business will not change this ultimate fact of business life.

2. When negotiating with a future employer, or partner, you must focus on listening to what is truly said, not on those things you want to hear.

Final Comment

This whole experience was very bitter Kool-Aid. Perhaps the biggest lesson from it was an understanding of the difficulty and frustrations of owning a small advertising agency.

CHAPTER 14
The Midas Way
(Business Lessons in a Unique Culture)

For the first time since 1956 I was without a job or a paycheck and at age 53, I was a man with very few job opportunities.

As I considered career options only one came immediately to mind. I would become a consultant. (Isn't that what all marketing and advertising executives do when out of work?) I decided I would be better off staying in Chicago to do this. Accordingly, I ordered business cards for "Schoenleb and Associates Consulting" and prayed that I would get lucky and find a client quickly.

At the same time I followed a career **Lifetime Lesson: If at all possible, never burn your bridges with a possible employer or former employer.**

I called Brian Burhoe at Midas and asked for his permission to meet with Dr. Paul Bomrad, the psychiatrist who had interviewed me as part of the Midas interview process. It was a good excuse to re-establish contact with Burhoe and I thought it would be prudent to know as much about myself as possible. Perhaps I had been fooling myself about my own abilities all these years.

Brian readily agreed; then casually asked me, "How're things going?" When I told him my situation, he said he might have something to talk to me about in a few days.

Encouraged, I met with Dr. Bomrad. He gave me the best pep talk I had heard in years. He told me that in his tests I had emerged as a competent, well-rounded executive, and an excellent leader of men. He was convinced that I would have no trouble finding a management position in a major company. He even volunteered to contact some investor friends to let them know of my availability.

The next day I called Burhoe and thanked him for allowing me to meet with Dr. Bomrad. Brian acknowledged my thanks, then asked, in an almost offhand manner, "I'd like to explore a job possibility with you. What's a good time to talk?"

With hope rising in my pores, I replied, as casually as he had asked the question. "Most anytime. What do you want to talk about?"

He responded, "Let's have lunch Friday."

A Fateful Lunch

Several days later we met at the Plaza Club, a private dining club on top of Chicago's Prudential building.

Brian Burhoe was (and still is) a soft-spoken, heavy-set, bearded executive about six feet tall with soft, inquisitive eyes. In his mid-forties, he conveyed a genuine caring attitude about people. I had instantly liked and trusted him when we first met. (I later learned my reaction was par for the course. Brian invariably gained the trust and confidence of everyone with whom he dealt.)

About halfway through lunch, after discussing the niceties of family and Chicago, Brian leaned forward, smiled, and put the reason for our lunch in play with a bombshell opening question. "Tell me, Chris, would you ever consider taking a position below the presidency of a company?"

I stared at him for a moment, then offered the "yes" answer he probably expected to hear. (He had obviously chatted with Dr. Bomrad before this lunch.)

I spoke passionately about my desire to return to the strength of my talents and the happiest moments of my career, namely, to be a Marketing VP again. I pitched Brian very hard to hire me to replace the Midas Marketing VP.

Brian smiled. "You are aggressive," he said. "But, Chris, I'm not here to discuss a marketing job. The Marketing VP position is filled."

Then he paused, as if considering whether to go on with what had obviously prompted lunch. Finally, he said, "We do, however, have an opening that I believe you could handle very well. In fact, there's no doubt that you're overqualified for it."

Pausing to observe my noncommittal response, he went on, "It's for the position of Vice President of Franchise Operations for the eastern half of the country. The current VP for the east is being moved back to his old position as VP of Real Estate. The VP of Real Estate recently resigned to become president of Sparks Automotive."

He continued, slowly emphasizing every word, "This job's strictly operations, not marketing, and, it doesn't report to the CEO. It's three levels down. It reports to the Executive Vice President of Marketing and Operations, Russ Richards. Russ reports to Bill McCarthy, the new president of U.S. Operations, who reports to Ron Moore, the CEO."

Burhoe then concluded his foray by returning to his first question and restating it. "Do you think you could take a position that's this far down the corporate pecking order? I would think that it'd be very hard for a man like you."

I thought for a moment; then replied, "Well, I think I could. I'm sure it'd be tough for awhile, but if the job were attractive enough, I'd be interested in considering it. Tell me more."

In providing this response, I followed another *Lifetime Lesson: In any job interview, you should always sell yourself to the prospective employer and earn a job offer. Then, and only then, should you decide whether you really want the job.*

Brian went on and described the job. Essentially, it was a position responsible for all new franchise sales and royalty income from Midas shops in the eastern half of the United States. Four region managers and their staffs—about forty men and women—reported to this position.

When Burhoe finished the job description, I stared at the table and said nothing. This was not a job I would have sought—it wasn't marketing. But my survival instinct reminded me forcibly that it was a top management job, a job in a major corporation outside the restaurant industry, and it sounded like a job I could do.

I looked at Brian's inquisitive eyes, took a deep breath, and replied, "Brian, you know I need a job, and, clearly, this is a job I could do. Obviously I'd prefer a marketing job, but I'm interested."

He stared at me one more time, then dropped a last bomb, "There's one more thing, Chris. This job cannot pay you the kind of money you've been making. You would have to be willing to take it for far less salary than you earned as president of Bojangles'."

I nodded (I had expected this), and answered, "I'm not surprised; how much less?"

"Well," he replied, "why don't we stop our conversation at this point? Since you're willing to consider this position, I need to discuss the matter further with Ron Moore, Russ Richards, and Bill McCarthy. If they all agree that you're a good candidate, then I'll have you come in and meet with them. At that time, if it still makes sense to do so, we can talk about the particulars of salary, and so forth."

Hired!

Within a week I met with McCarthy, talked briefly with Ron Moore, and had a short discussion with Russ Richards. It all seemed rather perfunctory. A job was offered, and after some negotiations relative to moving my wife and our permanent home to Chicago, I was hired.

As I accepted the offer, I anticipated that this would be an entirely new job experience for me. For the first time ever, I planned to concentrate on earning a paycheck, not on building a career. I vowed to keep my head down, make no "waves," and focus on earning money for retirement.

The night before I joined Midas, I had dinner with my old friend, Rogers Brackmann. I described my new position this way, "You know, Rog, I think Midas is just what the doctor ordered for me at this juncture in my life. I've got a good position in a company that doesn't seem to have the kind of pressures or problems that I have dealt with in the restaurant industry the last sixteen years."

Rog nodded, but then replied, "You know, Chris, Midas was a client of ours for several years. I think you're going to be surprised at how much work there'll be. Midas may be a market leader, but their marketing program is really back in the Dark Ages.''

He continued, ''If you get involved in marketing—and I can't imagine you not sticking your nose in it, regardless of what you say—you're going to be a one-eyed man in the land of the blind. You're going to see so many things to do that could improve the way Midas marketing is run that it will blow your mind.''

Then he added a warning, ''Chris, when this happens, don't try do your usual thing and fix everything at once. Go slow. Take your time. These folks don't like a lot of quick changes.''

As always, Rog proved prescient.

Learning the Midas Way

One of my favorite books is Robert Heinlein's *A Stranger in a Strange Land.* That title was a perfect description of how I felt the day I joined Midas. As Brian Burhoe led me to my new office the first morning, the reality of not having to take over and run a company finally sank in. For the first time in over fifteen years I would not be expected to create major changes the first six months on the job. I was no longer The Boss, and I was suddenly not totally sure I could adjust to this lower station in a company.

Beyond this, I knew I had entered a very unique company culture that I would have to find a way to become part of, or fail. Although Brian Burhoe and Ron Moore had somewhat prepped me about the Midas's culture and history, I was still amazed at what I found.

To help you understand my amazement, let me share four unique elements in the Midas culture—each very different from any other company I had ever worked for as an employee, or as an agency executive.

Franchisee Relationship

The most profound element of the Midas culture was the company's relationship with its franchisees (or ''dealers'' as they were called within Midas). There was a sense of family and partnership in the relationship that I had never seen before. Indeed, the major dealers were friends with one another and saw themselves as personal friends of the top management. They also believed they were an integral part of managing the company.

Midas was their company. They were proud of its success and took much of the credit for it. And, most important, they actively exercised power within Midas through their own organization, the National Midas Dealers Association (NMDA). The NMDA had, in fact, de facto control of most key decisions on operations and marketing.

To understand how this happened, you need a brief history lesson that begins at Midas's founding in the '50's.

In the '50s, car sales were booming, making the muffler replacement business larger each year. The average muffler on a new car became worn out in about eighteen months. So, if you owned a car for five years, you could expect to replace your muffler at least three times.

Nate Sherman founded Midas in 1956 to capitalize on this booming market. As he conceived it, Midas was to be a chain whose sole function was replacing mufflers and tailpipes. It would be the first national specialty vehicle repair shop chain in America. (Until Midas, auto repair generalists, the auto dealers, independent auto repair shops or gasoline stations did all muffler replacements.)

Such a chain concept had advantages for everybody. For Nate it provided a retail outlet for his products. He owned and operated IPC (International Parts Company) a manufacturing company that made mufflers and tailpipes. For the consumer, such a specialty outlet offered muffler replacement that would be quicker and cheaper than existing repair shops.

Because Sherman saw himself as a manufacturer not a retailer, he chose to not own retail muffler repair shops. From the first he franchised his specialty muffler shop idea. He sold the first franchise to Hugh Landrum in Macon, Georgia.

Sherman named the chain MIDAS, not in honor of the fabled king, but as an acronym for *M*idas *I*ndependent *D*ealer *A*ssociation.

The chain was an almost instant success. Midas revolutionized the muffler replacement business. It became to muffler replacement what McDonald's was to the sale of hamburgers—a better mousetrap.

Why? Because Nate added a magic marketing ingredient. He founded Midas with the concept that when the Midas dealer sold a muffler to a customer, the dealer would replace that muffler free, should it fail to work properly, for as long as the customer owned the car—in effect, a lifetime guarantee on the muffler.

The Midas guarantee was one of the greatest marketing moves in the history of retail marketing. It was, I believe, the first lifetime guarantee offered for any consumer product that would routinely wear out.

Midas grew very rapidly. Almost 100 shops were opened throughout the country in its first year. Dealers who were later dubbed the "founding fathers" of Midas owned many of these shops. All of them built multiple outlets and profitable businesses in the '50s and '60s.

In many ways, these dealers reminded me of the major franchisees at Arby's. Each operated their own fiefdom in a major city and were united to the other Midas fiefdoms by the brand name, the mufflers Nate sold, and by the guarantee. Each had his own in-shop procedures for running a Midas shop that were quite different. Of course, each felt he had the best methods for running a Midas shop.

However, unlike Arby's where a corporate leadership void existed, all dealers acknowledged Nate's leadership of Midas. His word was law much as in any other franchisee-franchisor relationship.

In the early '70s this initial culture of Midas suddenly changed. Nate Sherman relinquished the day-to-day management of the company to his son, Gordon, and began phasing himself out of the business. Soon, however, Nate became disenchanted with the way Gordon was running the business. A huge fight ensued between father and son for control of the company.

When the dust cleared, Nate had regained control of Midas. He then sold it in 1972 to IC Industries, a growing conglomerate funded by its original holding, the Illinois Central Railroad.

Even before the purchase of Midas by IC Industries, the dealers, already concerned about the power struggle within the Sherman family, formed their own association, dubbed the National Midas Dealers Association (NMDA). They quickly used it to protect themselves from their giant, well-heeled new franchisor.

From the beginning, the NMDA was a unique franchisee organization. It was a lot like a labor union in its dealings with the Company. Funded by monthly dues from its members, the NMDA held its own conventions and hired its own staff headed by a retired labor lawyer named Myron Gordon.

Myron, a shrewd, slightly built, street fighter, was empowered to negotiate with the management of Midas on anything from the franchise agreement wording, to approval of a new Midas shop location, to changes in the product line, etc. Through its leaders the NMDA presented a united front for these negotiations and insisted that the company work with them or else. The "or else" was the dealer's option to not purchase many of their auto parts other than mufflers from Midas.

As a result, the dealers inserted themselves in any management decision of Midas that effected the day-to-day shop operations or profits—especially advertising. Starting in the mid-'70s, any major program that corporate managers wanted to institute for the Midas system had to have NMDA support or it would fail.

The NMDA had influence on all major Midas corporate policies that directly influenced their business but one—Midas wholesale product pricing. The dealers accepted the company's assurance that the products the dealers were required to buy from Midas would be competitively priced.

Midas Corporate Culture

The second unique feature of the Midas culture was the company's management philosophy and practices. It had two delineating facets.

First was management's risk-averse mindset in the late '80s and early '90s. The internal Midas culture fostered maintaining the status quo. Both Russ Richards and Ron Moore focussed everyone inside Midas on optimizing the existing system, not altering it.

The second unique facet of the corporate Midas culture was its internal workforce. In some ways, like the dealers, it too was a family. Midas was an organization that prided itself on the continuity and longevity of its employees. When I joined Midas, anyone who had worked for the company less than ten years was considered a newcomer. Indeed, of the officers of the company, only two, Terry Reynolds, Vice President of Manufacturing and Distribution, and Bill McCarthy, the new President of U.S. Operations had been with the company less than ten years.

People knew each other and for the most part, liked and trusted each other. Many departments were led by managers who had come up through the ranks, and like Ron Moore, they were proud of the company and its growth.

This longevity of employment gave the same strength to Midas that I had found in only one other company, Procter and Gamble—a relatively smooth running, loyal infrastructure.

Unlike P&G, however, this longevity also contributed to a major weakness at Midas, a dearth of promotable aggressive middle-management talent. Midas did not routinely seek nor attract the kind of top talent found at P&G. The company hired competent hard-working people, but like Bojangles', most of these people were longer on a good work ethic and loyalty to Midas than senior management potential.

For the marketing department this was a special problem. Midas had tried to train long-term employees from other disciplines for marketing positions. Many of these men and women were eager to learn but did not have the capability needed for the job, especially to deal with the dealers.

When you couple this kind of workforce with the dealers' influence on corporate policy and programs and add Ron Moore's personality, few decisions of any consequence were permitted to personnel below senior management. Midas was managed almost totally "from the top."

Planning Process

All this leads to the third unique major cultural element within Midas—its unique joint marketing planning process.

For advertising and in-store operations, the company brought any new program to the dealers for their input and involvement, before trying to launch it in the systems. The NMDA had a standing committee of a dozen dealers that would meet three to four times a year to listen to proposed programs, review ad materials, etc. Normally, a dealer committee would ask for changes to whatever was presented. Result: Virtually nothing was agreed to in just one meeting. Thus almost no marketing or operations program could be planned or executed in the Midas system in less than a year.

As a chain in the retail business, this lack of nimbleness was a huge weakness.

This planning process also put a huge emphasis on an annual Midas sales convention (always held at an attractive resort or Las Vegas) to "sell-in" an annual plan by showing new ads and new programs. Literally all substantive plans for the retail Midas shops were developed for presentation at these meetings.

Faith in TV Advertising

The last key of the Midas cultural element was an almost cultlike belief in the power of TV advertising to build retail sales.

This belief stemmed from fifteen years of experience that a well-run Midas shop's sales increased substantially when TV ads ran. Indeed, for most of those years a marketing plan was really just a media schedule.

This facet of the culture was a direct result of hiring a national advertising agency, Wells-Rich-Green (WRG) around 1970. In the '70s and early '80s, WRG developed a series of brilliant and funny TV ads that helped grow Midas sales exponentially. These commercials were, in my opinion, some of the best work Wells-Rich-Green ever produced for any client.

Midas Evolves: More Cultural History

In its entrepreneurial culture of the '50s, '60s, '70s, and '80s, Midas changed only when events forced the issue. Result: In the first thirty-five years of its history, Midas made only one major successful change. It added brake repair in the late '70s.

Because this fact is so important let me elaborate and tell you a little more history.

In the '70s, the competitive environment in which Midas operated changed significantly. Other chains sprung up to compete directly with Midas. All were "clones" of Midas in terms of services offered and in offering lifetime guarantees on mufflers. Most even used the same colors, yellow and black, for their signs and buildings.

Two of the clones, "Tuffy" and "Car-X" were founded by Midas franchisees who had pulled down their Midas signs and formed the new chain with their former Midas shops. The other two major "clone" chains that appeared were "Speedy" and "Meineke."

All began to nibble at Midas' heels primarily in the Northeast and Midwest. Although no clone was a major competitor nationally, each one's growth resulted in making the competitive climate sharply different by city.

The second and biggest change in the '70s came from a new federal law specifying that a catalytic converter must be installed on all new vehicles' exhaust systems. The catalytic converter required that a vehicle use unleaded gas instead of leaded gas. The combination of the catalytic converter and unleaded gas significantly reduced the corrosion on mufflers. Mufflers that used to wear out every eighteen months would last almost three years. In effect, the muffler replacement business was cut in half by this technological development.

This technological change was not immediately felt at the retail level. The growth of the car population, and the fact that people were holding on to their cars longer during the high inflation times of the late '70's, hid this reality until the mid-'80's.

Nevertheless, the handwriting was on the wall. Sales would fall unless Midas adopted a second major repair service. Following the lead of several of the founding fathers who had been offering brake repairs for several years, the company adopted brake repair as this service.

Midas introduced brake repair service nationally in 1979, and it was an almost immediate success. Why? Because the company again pioneered use of a lifetime guarantee—this time on the brake shoes and pads that it sold.

The '80s were halcyon days for Midas. While the muffler business remained healthy, the brake business grew rapidly. In fact, by the late '80s Midas repaired more brakes than any other chain.

On top of this, the Midas TV advertising was truly in a class by itself in the auto repair industry. The term "Midasize" was coined. The chain dominated TV spending in its category with inventive, funny commercials.

While all this was happening, however, Midas lost two of its greatest strengths.

First, its united dealer body began to unravel. In the areas where salt was used to thaw snow on the roads in the winter, the so-called northern rust belt, the muffler replacement business remained a Midas shop's dominant business. However, in the so-called sunbelt, California, the south, particularly Texas and Florida, the muffler replacement business became secondary to the brake repair business. As this happened, the dealers in the south and west demanded more advertising for brakes; the dealers in the northeast and midwest resisted.

Each year the dispute became more heated. Result: Midas changed how the chain's advertising dollars were spent. Midas went from being primarily a nationally advertised chain to being primarily a locally advertised chain. By the mid-'80s, about seventy percent of the advertising dollars were spent locally.

Result: another key strength was lost. Midas's biggest advertising advantage over its regional competitors—its ability to use national media—was largely erased.

Getting Started

When I joined the Midas franchisee–franchisor family I was virtually ignored by my fellow employees and my staff.

One reason was because everyone who reported to me was in the field. The four Region Managers were headquartered in Atlanta, New

Brunswick, New Jersey, Taunton, Massachusetts, and Cleveland. (Each Region Manager had about ten staff members—district managers, technical trainers, and a field sales promotion manager (FSPM). The FSPM, universally called a "Fizzboom", was the number-two man in each office.)

On this first day all I could do was call each Region Manager and introduce myself. All seemed friendly over the phone and, at the same time, understandably reserved.

I had replaced Gordon Kaiser who returned to his area of expertise as VP of Real Estate. Gordon was a genial, highly intelligent man. Gordon's modus operandi was, in general, to avoid decisionmaking. He had positioned himself to be primarily a communicator, relaying Russ Richard's decisions to the regions and relaying their responses to Russ. He had been a "hands-off manager." This meant that the Region Managers ran their regions autonomously.

Gordon's system had worked reasonably well, but I knew immediately that it was a system with which I could never be comfortable. If I were to be held responsible for results, I wanted to take a more active hand in directing the staff that reported to me.

Near the end of this first day Ron Moore "dropped in" and started my real "indoctrination" to Midas. Moore grimaced a quick, "Hello." Then he contemptuously dropped a page from the *Chicago Tribune* on my desk. I looked at the page. It was the daily column written by George Lazarus, the well-known ad columnist for the *Tribune*. The column had a blurb reporting my going to work for Midas.

Moore said, in a sarcastic, accusatory tone, "Chris, we have hired a lot of folks around here but we have never had anyone's coming to the company announced for us by George Lazarus. You must be something special."

I had been told in interviews that I would have to take a very low profile with the media. Both Russ and Brian had advised me to keep my name out of print that this was a real "No-No" with Ron Moore. Thus, this mention in the Lazarus column and had obviously gotten me off on the wrong foot with the CEO.

I replied as noncommittally as I could, "Ron, I have no idea who gave him this information or why he'd find it important enough to put it in his column. But I assure you I had nothing to do with it."

Standing at least six feet two inches and leaning accusingly over my desk at me, Moore stared at me in disbelief.

I stared back in the harsh silence, then put my foot in my mouth, "However, you know, over the years I did do a lot of things that made me well known in the marketing arena."

At this explanation Ron uttered a loud "harrumph" and in a very sarcastic tone said, "Yeah, I know, you've told me, you're a marketing genius. Well, we will see how well you work in this environment, Mr. Genius." With that welcoming blast, he abruptly left the office.

Finally, as the day was ending, Brian Burhoe came to my office and asked, "Well, how did it go?" I told him it had gone well except for the Lazarus column incident, but that I was surprised that I hadn't been able to talk to my new boss, Russ Richards.

Brian looked at me and slowly shook his head, "You mean you didn't go and talk to Russ?"

I replied, "No, should I have? I thought he would invite me to talk to him."

Brian smiled, "Chris, you are no longer running a company. If you're going to work well with Russ Richards, you're going to have to make all the moves. He is expecting you to come to him, not him come to you."

The next day I met with Russ Richards and began my working relationship with a unique and talented individual. Although he possessed no college diploma, Russ was very smart with a quick wit and an encyclopedic memory. He was respected by all and seemingly adored by some who worked for him. Most important, the key dealers respected and trusted Russ. Russ Richards was the critical link in maintaining the close family-like Midas franchisee–franchiser relationship that had grown over the years.

In our initial meeting, Russ was brusque. He essentially laid out his modus operandi in one sentence, "Chris, come to me when you have questions or need a decision." Then he added, "You're a veteran. I don't expect to have to spoonfeed you. I assume you'll find out what's happening in your regions, go to M.I.T. (Midas Institute of Technology) to learn how a Midas shop is run and after that you'll spend time getting to know the dealers. After that maybe I'll have some specific things I need done. And, Chris, always remember, I don't like surprises."

In short, I was on my own. Russ was not going to overtly pave the way for me with the Region Managers or the franchisees.

Wells–Rich–Greene's "Welcome"

To top off the first week, I met with Larry Singer, the Managing Director of the Wells–Rich–Greene Chicago office.

Singer had called to suggest that we get acquainted. I accepted a breakfast date and went expecting to make a friend. I had assumed that Singer had talked to Ken Olshan who was then president of WRG and/or Mary herself. Both knew me well. I assumed Larry would know the. that I always liked Wells–Rich–Greene, although I had never hired the agency.

We met in the cavernous coffee shop near the fountain of the Hyatt Regency-Chicago. Breakfast was pleasant at first. Singer was gracious in a very businesslike manner. It was obvious from the start that he was very bright and used to being "in charge." A well-dressed, heavyset, chain smoker, he somehow seemed out of place in the Midwest. He was too urbane, too businesslike to fit the Chicago agency scene. He reminded me of ad agency executives I had met in New York.

After exchanging pleasantries and talking briefly about our mutual acquaintances in Wells–Rich–Greene, Larry came to the real reason we were having breakfast. Surprisingly blunt and to the point, he leaned across the table and, in a somewhat intimidating manner, said, "Chris, I don't know what you are doing at Midas, but let me tell you I don't think you are going to succeed there."

I was stunned. This was the last thing I expected to hear from the agency executive in charge of the Midas account. Still, I hoped that he was trying to be a friend in a backdoor sort of way. So I asked, "What do you mean?"

He replied, "Well, first of all, the dealers really run the company. You're not going to be able to tell them how to market their businesses, as I understand you've done in other places. Secondly, they are in charge of the advertising program. I work closely with them and I don't expect them to welcome your participation."

I grew wary. "Larry, I'm not in the marketing department and may never be."

He smiled rather grimly and replied, "I don't believe that. I am sure that Midas didn't hire you to replace Gordon Kaiser. I'm sure that one of these days you and I will be working together. That's why I wanted you to know how things are."

Still somewhat puzzled, I stared at him across the table for a minute and then said, "Larry, I guess I don't quite get your message. What exactly are you trying to tell me?"

He sighed, then replied, "Just this, Chris, you're not right for Midas. You're not going to be able to do the things here you've done in other companies. You're not going to ever be happy here."

I sat back, amazed. I couldn't believe what I had just heard. Here was the account manager for my company's agency "welcoming" a new corporate officer by warning him he wouldn't succeed. He had offered no statements like "I'll help you." Rather, he had proffered words and tonality that clearly communicated, "Chris, I don't want to work with you. I'm not going to help you."

As I absorbed this, I concluded Larry was trying to intimidate me. I wondered if he feared that if I got the marketing job it would be bad for him and WRG. Whatever the case, I had an enemy.

And I had heard enough. I stood up, looked at Larry, smiled and said, "Thanks for breakfast. I'll keep your thoughts in mind," and left him sitting there. That began seven years of a very difficult relationship, and it finished a very difficult opening week.

When I added this meeting's results to Moore's welcome and Russ Richard's approach to me, I saw very clearly the difficulty I faced to become an accepted member of the Midas culture. I may have been over-qualified for my job, but I was the new boy on the block in a deeply ingrained corporate culture.

I had expected to struggle but had not expected to find a management and ad agency that added to the difficulty. It was clear that I would be tested, and through this, I would have to gain corporate culture acceptance or fail.

It also seemed clear that the only road I had to gain acceptance and power in Midas was through the dealers. If I could sell myself to them, I was sure I could earn Moore's and Richard's continued support.

Ironically, because the key dealers did not want the company's operational help, the only easy way open to me was to get involved with the dealers was in the advertising and promotion planning done in each ADI. My "operations" job was then, from the first, largely focussed on retail selling tactics and local media plans.

New York

As hoped, the opportunity to begin selling myself to the dealers came quickly.

At the end of my third week, Ron Moore called me into his office. He peered over his reading glasses from behind his massive desk and, in his most intimidating manner, said, "Schoenleb, we all know you're a marketing genius. We also know that you have been president of several companies. It's time you earned your keep at Midas."

As was usual then, I was somewhat taken aback by Moore's verbal abuse. I choked off a natural urge to answer his sarcasm with my own and replied as pleasantly as I could, "I always like to earn my keep. What do you have in mind?"

He glowered at me. "Well, if you're as good as you say you are, you can solve a problem we have with the New York dealers."

For the first time I wondered why Russ Richards wasn't in the room. After all, I reported through him to Moore. But, brushing this thought aside, I asked, "What about the New York dealers?"

"They're out of control. They're blaming WRG and us for their losing sales to Meineke. They're insisting that we make special New York-only TV commercials. Worse yet, I just finished talking to Harold Forkus about this and he's convinced that Simpson (the Region Manager who reported to me) is not strong enough to deal with the New York market."

"What do you want me to do, Ron?"

"Just this. I want you to attend every future New York ad committee and ADI meeting until further notice. I want you to prop up Simpson and represent the company. I want you to make sure that the right things get done in this market." He paused, then pushed forward one last zinger, "If you're as good as you say you are, you'll solve this problem."

I left Ron's office not knowing quite what to make of his attitude toward me, but clearly I had an assignment. (In later years I learned Moore had believed that his tough attitude toward me was necessary because he feared I wouldn't be a team player. Over the years he became more comfortable with me and our relationship became much more open and friendly.)

I attended my first New York City Midas dealer meeting the following week.

ADI meetings in Midas were like those at Burger King. They were held to discuss marketing plans for the market and to agree on media plans and promotions to be run in the market. They were attended by all the franchisees. Each had one vote.

Normally, these meetings were run by the agency at a hotel ballroom two to three times a year. In the case of the major markets, however, there was usually a smaller ad committee composed of the major dealers in the market that met more often. Usually this committee met with the agency and the corporate regional personnel at least once every other month.

In the New York ADI, there were fifty-six dealers. The ad committee was composed of eight franchisees selected by the dealers themselves. This committee was empowered by the dealers to represent them to make all advertising decisions for the market.

My New York assignment began with an advertising committee meeting held in Wells–Rich–Greene's Manhattan offices. The agency was represented by its New York account executive and its senior field manager, Stan Flaum. In addition to me, Midas was represented by the FSPM, Jay Gray, and Robert Simpson.

The committee was composed of three dealers from New Jersey, two from Long Island, two from the city itself, and one from Connecticut. Three men, Howie Lichterman, Larry Goetz, and Harold Forkus dominated it.

Howie, one of the founding fathers, had over twenty-five Midas shops in New Jersey and was the market's largest dealer. Goetz, about twenty-five years younger than Lichterman and Forkus, owned all of the shops in lower Connecticut. He was a highly volatile but very intelligent dealer. He was well known to be the most outspoken dealer in the Midas System except for the legendary Harold Forkus, another founding father.

Forkus had been the second president of the NMDA. He owned about ten shops on Long Island and was the original New York franchisee. He professed little use for anyone who disagreed with him and he had the ability to shout louder and longer than almost anyone in a meeting.

As was their habit, the dealers came late for the meeting—almost an hour late. Forkus arrived last and made an almost royal entrance, complaining boisterously as he entered that the meeting should never have been held at the agency because it was too hard to get to Manhattan.

The meeting finally began. It lasted six hours and was, in my eyes, a disaster for the company.

Lichterman sat next to me and chain-smoked cigarettes the entire meeting. He argued with almost every presenter in a very emphatic but low-key manner. As he did this, he seemingly carefully made sure that his cigarette smoke wafted in my face.

Larry Goetz sat across from me. Whenever the agency made any significant point, he would shout that it was wrong. He would then rant that no one listened to the dealers and that he was not going to put up with such nonsense any longer. In each case, he pointed his finger at me as if to say, "What are you going to do about it?" Forkus remained relatively quiet except to loudly affirm his agreement with Goetz.

Finally, WRG showed their proposed New York media plan for the next two months and asked, "What do you want to do?" The dealers argued with each other; then gutted the proposed plan and adopted a media plan they felt was better. The agency did not argue with the result.

WRG then showed creative—the TV spots available to run. The dealers didn't like them and demanded that New York-only creative be made. The agency agreed to look into it.

In short, the dealers bullied WRG by asserting that their media expertise and advertising copy expertise was better than a professional agency's. And to my horror, the client, Robert Simpson, said nary a word. He did not challenge the dealers nor did he support the agency. As a rookie Region Manager from a more genteel area, the South, he seemed stunned by the dealers' seeming animosity towards him and their overt lack of respect for WRG.

I now understood the New York situation and the dealers. My first reaction was that they seemed to be much like the New York Burger King franchisees. They were tough, but probably good businessmen who sought company–agency leadership they could respect. To lead them, I knew that I had to seize control by directly challenging these dealers' marketing expertise. And, I had to challenge them immediately, or risk being a cinder in their eyes.

So, at the end of the meeting, I stood up and said, "Gentlemen, this meeting has been a disaster. I promise you that there'll never be another meeting like this one. The issues you've raised will be addressed at next month's meeting. I not only assure you that we will address the issues you've raised, I promise you that all of them will be addressed in a manner that'll make good marketing sense, even if some of the answers don't please you."

Larry Goetz looked at me a little startled and glared, "So what makes you in charge?"

I stared back at him and replied as firmly and emphatically as I was able, "Because, I am and you know it."

With that, the meeting was over. Howie Lichterman then turned to me and said, "I think I'm going to like you. Why don't you come out with me to my house for dinner and meet my wife?"

I had passed my first test. Better yet, over the next four months I was successful in helping build a consensus among the committee to adopt more aggressive advertising and promotion plans to attack Meineke and seek to regain Midas's pre-eminence in the market.

Making Progress

Soon after this trip to New York I went to St. Petersburg to meet the Orns family. The Orns owned virtually all the Midas shops in Tampa-St. Pete and were the most powerful dealers in the southeast. Without their support, it was very difficult to get any program launched in the south, particularly in Florida, one of Midas highest retail volume states.

This meeting was easier than New York. The Orns were most cordial. Lonnie Orns and his brother-in-law, Dave Kitenplon, were running the day-to-day operations, and I spent the morning getting acquainted with them as they took me around to their shops.

Jerry Orns, Lonnie's father and another of the founding fathers, was still very involved in the Tampa franchise. He joined us for lunch. I have never met a more intense, no-nonsense businessman than Jerry Orns. He quickly provided my next test. We had not even made it to the restaurant entrance before Jerry turned to me and said, "What do you think of Wells–Rich–Greene? I understand you've got a lot of marketing background. I'd be interested in what you think."

I thought for a moment. I could duck the question. But it wasn't in me to do so—nor did I sense that this would be smart with a man like Jerry Orns. I answered him as bluntly as I had been asked. "Jerry, I think that Wells–Rich–Greene is a fine creative agency. However, based upon what I've seen so far, their media planning and buying leaves a lot to be desired."

Jerry smiled broadly, clapped me heartily on the back as we walked into the dark restaurant from the bright sunlight and said, "You know, I think we're going to get along. You're a straight shooter. My only worry is that you won't be employed this time next year. Guys that talk like you don't last very long." He laughed.

While there, I learned the Orns' and Dave Kitenplon were avid golfers. Because I had learned over the years in dealing with franchisees that a competitive golf game can usually improve communications, I came with golf clubs whenever I visited them.

About this time, the NMDA held their annual convention. As was their custom, the NMDA invited the top company officers to the final day of the meeting for an afternoon of golf and an evening banquet.

When I got there, I didn't know anyone except for a few New York dealers and the Orns. I went to the banquet expecting a cold shoulder. I was surprised. Larry Goetz, my steely-eyed opponent at the first New York ADI meeting, saw me and said, "Chris, join us. Lonnie Orns and I are saving you a seat at our table."

Things were looking up. Clearly I had passed my first tests with these key franchisees. They were welcoming me as "a breath of fresh air."

Remaking Field Operations

For the first four months I focussed on understanding the culture, gaining key dealers' support and trying to modify my abrasive, take-charge personality to work for Russ Richards and Ron Moore.

Probably because of the dealers, I began to make progress with Richards more quickly than I had expected. He gave me surprisingly wide freedom to operate. He told me, "Schoenleb, I can see that you're a pro. I'll give you lots of rope. Just don't surprise me or I'll let the dealers hang you."

I decided to make my first foray into changing things within Midas. I picked an area I was nominally in charge of—the regions and how the Region Managers ran their day-to-day business. Up to this point they had been allowed to operate as they had under Gordon Kaiser. I wanted to begin installing the kind of disciplined systems I'd used in fast food including a uniform set of priorities for all regions to follow, standardized reports, and, most important, a new approval system that required the Region Managers to review all dealer relationship issues with me before any action was taken.

I met with the four Region Managers in January in Atlanta to lay out these changes. As our two-day meeting evolved, their discomfort grew. One of them, Rob Tertzakian from New England, finally challenged me, "Chris, if I'm understanding you right, you're telling us that from now on you will approve what we do in our regions. We are not free to manage as we see fit."

I replied, "Rob, I'm telling you that you have a boss who wants to make sure you learn how to do your job to the best of your abilities and that you follow corporate dictates. I am a hands-on manager with a lot of experience. I can be of help to you if you will work with me."

I imposed the changes that I sought, but I did not make a sale. Result: I had a constant internal struggle. Only one of the four Region Managers, Reed Vought, stayed on the job. Within eighteen months, two resigned and Robert Simpson transferred to another corporate position.

Final Dealer Test

After about seven months, Russ Richards announced, "I am going to see the Katz's. I want you to come with me."

The Katz's were then, and are now, Midas's largest dealer. The two brothers, Art and Cal Katz, built their first Midas shop in the '50s in Akron, Ohio, then went on to build or buy 112 Midas shops throughout Ohio, western Pennsylvania, upstate New York, and Jacksonville, Fla.

The Katz's were a feared power within the company. Owning so many shops made them the largest dealer purchaser of Midas products. And they were demanding customers.

Of the two, Art was the most feared. He was a gruff no-nonsense businessman with a raspy intimidating voice. He did all the Katz's purchasing. He was well known for phoning executives or clerks and yelling at them if he was displeased with a corporate situation or action.

Cal, the younger brother, was more congenial than Art, but still a hard-driving businessman who managed their shop operations. A third Katz, Cal's son Randy, handled the Katz's advertising and real estate functions. His no-nonsense style, more like his uncle's than his father's, also caused consternation with most everyone who met with him.

The Katz's were obviously important, but I had stayed away from them. They were Russ Richards's "private account." They talked to Russ whenever they wanted some action taken by the company. Corporate scuttlebutt had it that anyone who got between them and Russ would get mowed down.

When we met, however, the Katz's surprised me. Unlike their reputation, they were friendly and most cordial. The meeting went well and as it was ending, Russ asked me to follow up on several issues with the Katz's in about a month. He was, in effect, turning them over to me. It was his biggest vote of confidence in me so far in my tenure at Midas.

So, as requested, I went back a month later without Russ to meet with the Katz's. Knowing that the best time to meet with them was on Saturday, I went to Toledo for a morning meeting. We met for bagels and coffee at 7:00 A.M. in the Katz's rather unorthodox office, a one-square-block building, and I met several of their non-Midas friends who stopped in regularly to chat.

By the end of the morning, we had made some progress on a number of issues relating to marketing and training, and it was clear that the Katz's were willing to work with me. This was underscored when Cal asked if I played golf. When he heard "Yes," he invited me to bring my clubs for our next meeting. This started my friendship with the Katz clan that continues today.

Wells–Rich–Greene

Because one of my key tasks as the VP of the East was to make sure that effective marketing plans were in place in all eastern markets, I worked closely with Wells–Rich–Greene, and soon learned the ponderous and awkward account management structure WRG had developed to handle Midas.

WRG had a field office and an account executive for every Midas region. All the AEs had less than three years agency experience, and were given no decision making authority. Like Midas, WRG was managed from the top. All AEs reported to Stan Flaum who was headquartered in New York. But Larry Singer managed the account from Chicago with several AEs and a media planning group and required Flaum to clear all decisions through him. Result: Any routine decision could take days.

On top of this, WRG's creative group for Midas was in New York. The media buyers were in New York, but the media planners were in Chicago.

It was the most dysfunctional agency organization I had ever worked with. Built on the premise that Larry Singer's presence in Chicago was more important than daily face-to-face interaction between all key personnel on the account, it crippled the agency's ability to work with the dealers effectively in local markets. And it led to all kinds of local media planning and buying snafus.

In viewing this, I was reminded again of an old adage about the agency business, **Lifetime Lesson: An agency will, in general, perform only as well as the client demands.** Simply put, the WRG organization and the problems it caused with the dealers existed only because the top management of Midas allowed it.

Why did Midas management ignore the WRG field problems? Almost solely because of the agency's TV creative product.

I had learned this almost as soon as I joined Midas. WRG's TV creative for the previous year had not been effective. The dealers were demanding an agency change to fix this and address their complaints about local TV buying. Then, at the annual sales meeting, Mary Wells personally introduced a new campaign, "Nobody beats Midas, Nobody." The dealers loved it, and the demands for action were quieted. Result: The company demanded no changes from WRG to address what I knew were legitimate dealer complaints.

The local market agency issues really bothered me, and I couldn't let the issue disappear. I was sure, based on the data I'd seen, that WRG was wasting millions with poor spot TV buying in local markets, and that this, in turn, was hurting retail sales. The local spot TV prices they were paying seemed sky high. (I had a real sense of history repeating itself. WRG's media inadequacies were a mirror image of the problems I had seen with BBDO at Burger King.)

Despite my initial resolve to make no waves at Midas, I pushed hard on this issue but I gained no support from Richards or Moore. This made me a maverick within Midas, but I saw no alternative if I was to keep the support of the dealers.

I went to Russ Richards regularly and pushed for the power to fix the problem. My usual plea went something like this, "Russ, when are you going to let me take over marketing? WRG is getting away with murder out in the field. Good TV commercials aren't enough to demand from our agency. We need and deserve better media buying. I know I can get if you give me a chance."

Russ would usually smile and say something vague like, "All good things come in time, Chris."

Marketing VP Again

In July of 1989, Russ Richards apprised me that "my time had come." I was appointed Vice President of Marketing, replacing Ralph Linder who was taking early retirement. I was also, in effect, promoted. Bill McCarthy had resigned and was not replaced. Russ now assumed the role as the Number Two man in the company, and I became his right arm for marketing.

The marketing job was similar in scope to Burger King's. It had the traditional responsibilities of public relations, advertising, sales promotion, and market research. Also, like Burger King, I inherited a too-small, woefully inexperienced staff to handle these responsibilities. None had any agency experience, and only one had worked in another corporate marketing department.

However, unlike Burger King, I had no ability to make immediate personnel changes. At Midas, unlike the fast-food companies, there were well-established personnel policies that prevented any manager from hiring or firing without a detailed process of performance reviews that would take six months at a minimum.

Clearly, I had a major on-the-job training task, and I needed to find immediate help from any available resource.

Knowing this, and knowing that the best marketing talent in Midas was the retiring VP of Marketing, Ralph Linder, I asked him to stay as VP of Advertising. Ralph had solid experience outside Midas and was a well-versed marketing talent. He had been ineffective at times at Midas largely because he had the wrong personality. He was not a confrontational person in a position that needed a someone willing to constantly battle WRG and the dealers for the marketing leadership of the system. Fortunately, Ralph was willing to work for me. He stayed three years and was an invaluable ally.

The other key marketing employee was Jerry Brown, the Director of Market Research. Jerry was the one of the longest-term employees in the history of Midas. He had started with Midas at age nineteen and had learned market research on the job. He had already been with the company for thirty-five years.

Initially, Jerry was a big question mark for me. I wondered how a man who had neither a formal education, nor had ever worked for a market research professional, could possibly be the person to direct a market research department. But, this proved to be a non issue. Jerry's intelligence coupled with his willingness to learn made him a real asset. Together we developed a solid department and program that I believe became the best in the automotive after-market industry.

Beyond these two men, I knew I would have to rely on the company's agencies. I understood WRG, but I did not know the other three specialty agencies used by Midas. Each, like WRG, had a long-term relationship with the company and was entrenched in the culture.

I spent my first weeks meeting each of them and was pleasantly surprised.

The largest of the three was TMP Worldwide (TMPW). Through TMPW, Midas was the second largest yellow pages advertiser in the United States, spending about $16,000,000 annually on over 6000 different yellow page ads. Midas dominated the medium in most markets versus its competitors in terms of ad size and number of books used.

This was an extremely important advertising program. It's hard to overstate its impact on the Midas system's retail sales. Experience, confirmed by consumer research, had shown that as much as fifty percent of all business in a Midas shop was a direct result of a consumer seeing the yellow page ad!

Midas had hired TMPW in the early '70s. The agency was managed from the beginning by a one-of-a-kind executive, Lance Johnson. When I visited the agency for the first time, TMPW welcomed me with open arms. Johnson met me for breakfast and, in direct contrast to my WRG experience, opened his conversation with, "How can we help you?"

After a brand review, I was convinced Midas was in good hands. TMPW seemed to be a rock of strength. Their thirty-seven person staff that worked only on Midas had experience and depth. Beyond this, Lance Johnson became a close confidant and friend on whom I relied for Midas history and insights about key dealers.

For promotions, Midas used a small firm, Lunardi and Associates, run by Rich Lunardi and his wife, Karen. Rich was a talented art director and an aggressive promoter. He made a perfect team with Karen, who was a direct mail expert. Over the ten years Lunardi and Associates had worked for Midas, it had become an almost in-house art department. It had also developed a complete direct mail program for the Midas system. Like TMPW, the Lunardi's were receptive to my coming, and we quickly formed an excellent working relationship.

The third major outside resource was Midas's PR agency, Golan–Harris—the same agency that had built the great public relations programs for McDonald's. To say the least, the prospect of working with this agency excited me. I was sure that Midas could use marketing PR.

Midas was a very small account for Golan–Harris, but because Midas had been a client since the early '70s, the agency honored this longstanding relationship by providing excellent service. Al Golan handled management of Midas personally. And the AE, Jim Kokoris, was one of the most talented PR professionals I ever met.

Because my predecessors had not understood the principles of marketing PR as it had been used in fast food, Golan–Harris's talents were, in my eyes, being underused. Their work was confined to routine press releases about new store openings, and new franchisees.

When I met Al Golan, I asked for an agency review and for the agency to generally discuss the role of PR. At that meeting I was welcomed like an old friend as I expressed the fervent hope that we could use their McDonald's expertise on Midas. At subsequent meetings and long lunches, as we struggled with how we might bring marketing PR programs to Midas, Al Golan and I became good business friends. (We also enjoyed sharing "old war stories" about the "Burger Wars.")

Taking Control

The one major obstacle to achieving control and leadership of all the outside agencies was Larry Singer. I had to change his modus operandi so that WRG took its primary direction from me and the Midas marketing department, not the dealers. We had to work together to deal with the ad committee, or I would fail.

In our initial meeting in my new role, I directly asked Singer to do this. He didn't respond, nor did he change his handling of the account. Clearly, I had a problem that had to be solved, or my statements to Russ Richards on how I would fix marketing would be seen as hollow bravado.

Not long thereafter, WRG presented a proposed twelve-month network media buy and stated it would be bought in the next day or two. In other words, the agency had adopted the pose that this was a courtesy presentation for informational purposes, not one for client approval.

It was the opening I was looking for. I deliberately didn't approve the proposed buy and advised Singer that WRG was to make no purchases until I had time to review the plan in detail.

Singer grumbled, "You are getting in the way of progress. We have to make these buys now or we cannot maintain the rates we negotiated."

Not believing him. I replied, "If that happens, you should've been smart enough to send this plan over sooner. As your client I'm going to take whatever time is necessary to review plans to spend our annual network budget before any buy is made."

Then Larry became angry. He burst forth, "Wait a minute. Who's the expert here? Who's making the decisions here? I'm telling you that you can't hold us up. We know the best way to do it."

I responded, "I'm not sure who the expert is, Larry, but I am the clients, and I will tell you if we are going to make this buy. Until you are ready to accept that, this meeting is over."

The point was made. From that point forward, Midas corporate became Larry Singer's primary client not the dealers. Further, Singer shrewdly reorganized to help address his obvious personal relationship problem with me. He hired a former JWT account supervisor, Bill McCann, to run the account on a day-to-day basis, minimizing his personal contact with me.

Bill McCann proved to be an excellent account manager, but the spot media buying problems remained a major problem. Because of this, I called Ken Olshan and raised my concerns over the field problems and Singer's management of the account.

Within twenty-four hours, Ron Moore called me on the carpet. Angrily, he said, "Chris, you are to never call Ken Olshan again. He's my responsibility. If you have problems with Singer, solve them yourself in Chicago."

Clearly, I had no management support to change WRG's practices. This stifled and frustrated me, but I went back into my foxhole and resolved not to let losing this battle cause me to lose the war. I bided my time, but never stopped pushing for media-buying improvement. It took three years, but this was a war I eventually won (See Chapter 15.)

Midas: a Sinking Ship?

When I took over marketing I was surprised to find that there was no formal marketing document describing the overall Midas marketing strategy.

The only strategic document I found was a five-year plan that Midas submitted annually to its IC Industries parent, now renamed the Whitman Corporation. While the five year plan discussed the strategic issues of the business in broad sweeping generalities, it was, in general, an exercise in number crunching. *Like so many of these corporate documents in America, it was a financially oriented exercise, not an actionable marketing document.* It was useless as a basis for an annual advertising, promotion, or public relations plan.

I now understood how right Rog Brackmann had been. I was truly a one-eyed man in the valley of the blind. I found blank stares and shrugged shoulders in the marketing department and WRG when pursuing a marketing strategy document. Only Ralph Lindner understood the need for a strategic plan, but he felt it was useless to write one because the dealers were only interested in tactics and in his mind, they "called all the shots."

Professionally, I could not accept this. *Lifetime Lesson: (First learned at P&G) The first priority for developing any marketing plan is identifying the strategic issues to be addressed. Only when these are understood can you develop an effective plan.*

Failing to find such a document, I had no choice but to personally review all the available data and develop a strategic document. One more time I was seeking the facts and the corporate myths.

First I did a ten-year sales analysis. Then I discussed the five-year plan with Russ and the financial planners. Finally, I searched the files for meaningful consumer research. There was little available. The best information was a five-year-old segmentation study.

Still, I pieced together a startling set of findings. Midas had four critical problems, and not one was being addressed. Absorbing how serious these problems appeared to be and the lack of action being taken to address them, I questioned whether Midas would survive ten years. I concluded the company's success was similar to Bojangles'—a house of cards about to fall.

Here's what I found;

Critical problem #1: Fewer mufflers were being replaced every year, and this trend would soon accelerate. Chrysler Corporation had just announced use of a stainless steel muffler. A stainless steel muffler would eliminate any muffler replacement for the first seven to eight years of a car's life and, perhaps forever outside the rust belt. If the history of other declining markets was any guide, I knew that this market shrinkage would intensify competition with the other muffler specialists for the remaining business. We could face an all-out price war that would destroy the dealers' and company's profitability.

Critical problem #2: Midas brake business had stopped growing. After ten years of solid, double-digit growth, Midas brake retail sales were almost flat versus the previous year. No one knew why. No basic research had been done about the consumer's perception of brake repair done by Midas. Typically, the dealers were sure it was an advertising problem.

Critical problem #3: Midas had failed in its late '80s effort to add a third major repair service—the front-end business, that is, wheel alignment, wheel balancing, etc. After a fast start, the business had not grown; in many markets it had begun to die. Dealers had purchased $25,000 to $50,000 worth of equipment that was now lying largely idle in their stores.

Critical problem #4: The Midas system's retail shop image was shoddy. Many shops were over twenty years old and needed a facelift. This contributed to the fact that many younger consumers saw Midas as old and out of date.

In short, all three of Midas's core businesses were in trouble and the chain needed remodeling.

Alarmed, I discussed the situation with Russ. He stated his firm belief that I was overly worried—that we had a lot of time to consider making changes, and that he did not want to alarm the dealers. Let me be perfectly clear, here. None of the four problems I identified were unknown to Midas management, the agency, or the dealers. I was not plowing new ground. My degree of alarm and the need for urgent change was however very new. Most of the Midas culture except for a few dealers saw the problems as a long way off—problems for successors or the next generation to address someday.

I thought we needed to address each problem head-on immediately. But, the only action Russ approved was to pursue the brake sales slowdown. Result: We immediately launched two major consumer research studies on the brake business.

The first was an in-depth study to identify the demographic profile of our brake customer and to learn consumer perceptions of Midas versus major competitors.

When this study was completed, we presented the findings to the NMDA and Midas top management. The findings created a great furor. Essentially, this research said that Midas was in trouble in its brake business because the sales-building tactics being employed were attracting consumers, but not retaining them.

The dealers had been building their brake business primarily through price advertising. They were routinely offering brake package specials for $69.00. However, when consumers would come to purchase this special, most were advised that they needed additional repairs not included in the package price. Result: many consumers ended up spending $200 to $400 for their brake repairs.

The package price advertising was not illegal because there was a disclaimer in every ad that stated the price covered only replacement of the pads and shoes and, that if other work had to be done, it would cost more. Many consumers felt, however, that they had been misled. Result: Even though customers were generally satisfied with the quality of the work, they were not likely to return to Midas.

I proffered the conclusion that the brake package price ads should cease. The dealers did not agree. Management was unwilling to overrule the dealers. Price advertising continued.

A Wake-up Call

The second research study was a basic ATU (attitude usage and awareness) study. Unlike any previous study done by Midas, this was not a national study per se. It was a study conducted in the top twenty-five Midas retail sales markets in the country. Our objective was to determine market share and consumer attitudes toward Midas for its three major services, mufflers, brakes, and front-end repair in each major market.

The results from the ATU study were surprising. But, unlike the brake study, these findings were accepted by most and provided the basis for a long-needed Midas system wake-up call. Basically, the research provided two key findings that shook the culture to its core, particularly the key dealers.

1. *Midas was not perceived by consumers as superior to its clone competitors, or other competitors.* This directly challenged the Midas system's biggest corporate myth—its belief that consumers perceived Midas as better than any competitor. Worse yet, this lack of superior image meant that Midas was seen as "high priced" versus all competitors except the auto dealers, and therefore very vulnerable to loss of market share.
2. *The WRG Midas brake advertising had been largely ineffective.* Despite years of outspending competitors in brake TV ads, Midas had very low in "top-of-mind" awareness as a place to repair brakes, and Midas's market share of brake repair service was very low in all markets. ***Lifetime Lesson. In any business you must first build " top-of-mind" customer awareness before you can expect to increase sales.***

We presented these findings orally to every major ADI to try to sell this research. Why? Because I was sure, based on my Burger King experience, that if presented right, this research could begin to change the Midas culture's basis for marketing and advertising decisions to consumer research, rather than the negotiated consensus of agency, corporate and dealer opinions.

This approach paid off almost immediately. Key dealers understood the importance of consumer research and expressed support for its use in marketing planning.

Developing a New Marketing Program

Perhaps the biggest reason for acceptance of the ATU research was that it provided direction for a new strategy that most of the culture accepted as valid without consumer research.

The key finding was that the reason consumers chose one place for auto repair over another was trust. *If consumers trust a repair shop, they are more likely to take their car to be repaired there even if they have to pay more money.*

All this resulted in gaining agreement with Moore, Richards, and the dealers that we had to find programs that would address customer trust. To most within Midas this meant new advertising, but I saw it as the opportunity to build an integrated marketing effort using TV advertising, marketing PR, and an in-shop program to equip shop employees with new methods of customer handling that would pay-off any promises made in the advertising.

Fortunately, we already had a major "piece of the puzzle" in place. Midas had initiated its version of the latest management "rage," TQM (Total Quality Management) the previous year. As part of this, a new in-shop operations system had been developed to upgrade in-shop customer-handling practices and improve customer satisfaction—thus improving customer trust. Dubbed TCS (for Total Customer Service) this program had been rolled out just prior to the research findings and was given added impetus by them.

Project Safe Baby

The need to build trust brought a focus to our efforts to develop a marketing PR program—the second element sorely needed for the new marketing program.

Four criteria were set for this program, criteria that I believe should be used for any company's marketing PR effort:

1. It had to address and help solve a genuine societal need.
2. It had to be associated with Midas's business segment, autos, and trucks.
3. It had to be unique to Midas, not someone else's program, like the Marine's "Toys for Tots" that Midas had been part of for years.

4. It had to be an affordable program that would involve every Midas retail location.

This was a tall order, and after several months Golan–Harris admitted they had found nothing that totally fit the criteria.

Then Ron Moore came to the rescue. "I know no one will listen to my idea, let alone do anything about it—especially a marketing genius, but there is a program in England that one of our competitors ran. It exactly fits your criteria. They gave away child car seats and installed them free at every shop. It generated a ton of favorable publicity for them. I'll send you a copy of a newspaper story on the program."

I immediately told Golan–Harris of this idea and gave them the newspaper article. I asked them to explore whether a similar program made sense for Midas. I did this in spite of Moore's sarcastic challenge that had initially angered me. ***Lifetime Lesson: Never fall prey to the "not-invented-here syndrome" that so many agencies and corporate executives suffer from.***

This was the birth of a superb and nationally honored marketing PR program we eventually called "Project Safe Baby."

The essence of the program was to sell Century child car seats at every Midas shop at wholesale cost. With this seat purchase we also gave an instructional video on how to properly install the car seat and another Midas guarantee. We promised to reward anyone returning the car seat after it had been used with a coupon for Midas repair services worth the cost of the seat (about $43.00). We also developed a TV commercial and TV public service spot (a PSA).

It took eighteen months to work out the details of Project Safe Baby in test market and an industry crisis (described later) to sell management and the dealers on doing it nationally.

The program lasted five years and by any measure it was highly successful. Midas became known in consumer advocate circles and in state and federal government agencies as a leading advocate of child safety in cars. Almost 250,000 Century car seats were sold. Many purchasers were first-time visitors to Midas and became future customers. Several of these purchasers later wrote that the seat had saved their child's life.

Not surprising, Project Safe Baby won all major PR awards during its second and third year of existence. But perhaps the finest accolade came from Al Golan himself. He stated that this program was one of the two best he'd ever done (The other? Ronald McDonald House).

Changing the Rules

We still lacked our biggest weapon, a new TV campaign to replace "Nobody Beats Midas, Nobody".

The strategy was clear. We needed a campaign that would sell "trust" in a manner in tune with the '90s, not a campaign from the '70s or '80s like "Trust the Midas Touch" (an early '80s campaign). Ralph Lindner and I insisted that the ads not use the word "trust." We argued that when someone says "trust me" that the first thing most of us think is "I can't trust that guy."

As this work began, I also hatched another major quarrel with WRG. I proposed that any advertising campaign we developed be pre-tested with consumers before airing it.

Larry Singer did not agree. He pointed out that Midas had never used standard creative research techniques to measure a TV commercial's effectiveness, yet Midas had run great advertising over the years.

I rejected this argument and insisted on research. I wanted to avoid the "I like it" versus "I don't like it," arguments in the NMDA marketing committee and within Midas as the sole basis for selecting new campaigns.

Surprisingly the dealers supported this idea. Mike Glad, a key dealer and chairman of the marketing committee for many years, endorsed the idea of research for decisionmaking as did Glad's successor as chairman, Larry Goetz.

A major hurdle to building a consumer-driven program had been achieved. For the first time choosing a new Midas advertising would be partially based on creative research.

This was particularly important, because all the TV advertising Midas had run over the years had been directed at men. It was advertising that had either a good guffaw or a hard edge/hard sell to it. It was the kind of advertising easiest to sell to dealers or a male management team.

This kind of advertising had not necessarily been wrong. Until the '90's auto repair had been basically a male-dominated purchase. But, by the '90's more than fifty percent of the people who brought vehicles to a Midas shop were women, and forty percent of all women no longer relied on a man's opinion on where to take a car for repair. Conclusion: Midas needed advertising that would have universal appeal, not just appeal to men.

The Sears Fiasco

As all this work was in progress, disaster struck the auto repair industry.

The California Bureau of Auto Repair (BAR) had run an undercover operation in which they took a previously inspected car to several Sears' outlets in northern California and found that Sears tried to sell them repairs and parts that were not needed. This became national news and reinforced in the consumer's mind that they could not trust chain auto repair facilities.

This greatly impacted Midas's business. Brake sales fell like a rock. For the first time in history, total annual retail sales for the Midas system declined from the prior year.

The Midas family was frightened. Changes began to occur. In this crisis, the NMDA and the company agreed that all advertising offering brake repairs for a package price had to cease. There would be no more $69.00 brake job advertising.

Indeed, for the first time in my marketing tenure, changes were demanded. The dealers and Moore turned to the agency and the marketing department and demanded a program to stop the sales decline.

The stage was set. A once-in-a-lifetime opportunity to show the power of an integrated marketing effort was thrust on me. Fortunately, we did not need new research; the Sears fiasco totally reinforced the need to build trust. We simply needed to complete our trust strategy and tactics development.

This would not be easy. We needed to have the program ready in six months to be launched at the '93 national sales convention. The key ingredient still missing was a new TV campaign.

I prayed for WRG's creative magic to appear one more time.

The "Midas Way"

The agency brought in a new creative team headed by Jonathan Cranin—a creative talent it borrowed from its P&G business—to get fresh thinking.

Jonathan developed and showed three different campaigns to the marketing committee in early fall. The dealers didn't like any of them. They complained that they were being shown "feel good" advertising, not the hard-hitting advertising Midas needed. Most wanted to keep "Nobody beats Midas, Nobody" instead of running any of the campaigns presented. However, they did agree to consumer test these campaigns to see if consumers reacted differently.

The test results were very definitive. All three tested well, but the research said one campaign was a potential home run. The campaign employed a new theme line, "The Midas Way, The Way It Should Be." It was based on consumer testimonials from letters sent to Midas.

What made the campaign stand out was its use of a visual technique that had never been used before. Visually, the commercials opened with the sound of a typewriter putting words on the screen, "Dear Midas" and then, with words from the actual letter scrolling across the bottom, pictures unfolded at the top dramatizing them. The real letter writer would narrate his or her own letter and be seen at the end of the commercial. Further, the real Midas employees who had fixed the letter-writer's car would be shown replicating their service.

The strength of the campaign was its believability. The Midas Way campaign wasn't dismissed as "just advertising" because the letter writing was a visually interesting way to introduce the testimonial to consumers. And the letter writers were genuine, not actors. It attracted and kept viewers watching.

Selling this campaign was a tough job despite the exciting test results. There was a general unease in the culture with this more indirect selling approach. All were concerned that the advertising might be too soft sell. But in the end, all agreed to take a chance on the campaign.

For the sales convention, the agency developed six commercials. When the dealers saw the commercials, they didn't know quite what to make of them. Their wives loved them but they weren't sure this was an answer to what they viewed as a life-and-death situation for their business.

Following this mixed review, we launched the "Midas Way" campaign in March 1993 and reintroduced the TCS program. Project Safe Baby was launched in April. Sales immediately went up. In fact, for the next twenty-four months sales increased month after month versus the previous year.

We had turned the business solidly around.

Now What?

The campaign launch and the immediate few months afterward were the high point of my marketing career at Midas. The "Midas Way" campaign would last for three years and win a gold Effie from the American Marketing Association for being the most effective ad campaign in its category in 1994.

However, the critical issues facing the company had not been solved. No effort to remodel the stores had been begun. No effort to build suspension sales had worked. And muffler sales continued to spiral downward.

The sales turnaround had occurred because of increased brake sales. But much of the sales increase was not from increased customer counts, but, rather, was attained from charging more for brake repair and not offering package price discounts.

In truth, the "Midas Way" program had only bought Midas time to address these issues, and it gave credibility to the use of consumer research to solve them. It solved nothing.

The difficult times were about to begin.

Lessons Learned

1. Applying marketing principles that built sales in a fast-food franchised restaurant chain can work in a specialty retail automobile repair chain. I believe they would be equally successful in building sales in any retail franchised chain in any business category.
2. Accepting a lesser job after being CEO is possible, but not easy. Your previous jobs make you a marked man.

Final Comment

In many ways Midas is a classic marketing case study.

Midas literally invented, then dominated, an industry category that started to rapidly shrink and will perhaps disappear altogether in the twenty-first Century. It is a company that succeeded for almost thirty-five years primarily by using entrepreneurial instinct, not classical marketing techniques.

Unfortunately, as time passed, it also became a company that cherished the status quo. If ever there was a company that embraced the management philosophy "If it ain't broken don't fix it," it was Midas from 1987 to 1993.

While at Midas, I was never sure why this status quo mentality existed. In retrospect, I believe it was the caused by a combination of five factors:

1. *The company's success in the marketplace.* Holding a dominant market share, with sales and profits increasing annually, it was easy to continue to ignore potential future problems.
2. *The company's manufacturer–wholesaler mindset.* Unlike all other franchised chains in which I had worked, Midas's greatest source of revenues/profits was not from royalties or company-owned retail outlets, but from wholesale product sales to the dealers.
3. *The parent company's influence.* IC Industries seemed to view Midas as a "cash cow" that could help fund other parts of the conglomerate. They may have limited capital investment in the '80s.
4. *The difficulty of selling change to a body of franchisees that was growing old.* Most of the major dealers were in their sixties and prosperous. They shared IC's aversion to capital investment. Many were more interested in maximizing profits than investing in change.
5. *The personality of CEO Ron Moore.* Moore was a twenty-five-year employee of Midas. A dedicated, hard-working executive, he'd worked his way up to the presidency in 1982 from his initial position as a warehouse manager. He presided over the company's steady success in the '80s. Moore was very proud of this success and clearly communicated to all that his goal was to optimize the existing business model, not change it. In doing this, he took as one of his key jobs the protection of the Midas concept from radical modifications.

    Also, Moore was also far more tactical than strategic. Perhaps as a result, he tended to micro-manage. He directed much of his staff's energies to managing the status quo.

By happenstance it became my role to try to sell Midas (dealers and company management) to address the rapidly changing marketplace. Ironically, I didn't succeed at first partly because the "Midas Way" advertising and other trust programs—traditional solutions for Midas—were too successful. They masked the danger of the bigger issues and slowed any real impetus for change for two years. This in turn led to years of frustration and organizational chaos described in Chapter 15.

Only when sales and profits waned in '96 did the Midas culture finally accept the need for change. *Lifetime Lesson: There is no more difficult task in business than trying to sell change when the company's sales and profits results mask the problems you are trying to address.*

CHAPTER 15
Corporate Chaos and Surrender

(Final Lessons—déjà vu Burger King)

Major change had started to infiltrate Midas even before the Sears fiasco.

It had begun when the founding fathers ceded control of the NMDA to the next generation of dealers led by Elie Revollier, Steve Altheimer and Lonnie Orns, all sons of major dealers. This new generation saw their ascendancy to power as a mandate for change, and they wasted little time in seeking it.

First they pushed Myron Gordon into retirement. Then they began to demand changes in the one area of Midas policy that the founding fathers had left solely to the company's discretion, wholesale product pricing. Convinced that the company was charging noncompetitive prices for mufflers and brake pads and shoes, items the franchise agreement required they purchase from Midas, the new leadership angered Ron Moore by demanding "changes or else" in the product prices offered through the Midas wholesale distribution system.

The sales crisis fomented by Sears slowed the new leadership's demands, but as retail sales recovered, the NMDA began to push again at the very core of Midas' profitability, its wholesale product pricing to the Midas dealers.

A New Agency Structure

The new NMDA leadership also began attacking Wells–Rich–Greene. Mike Glad, chairman of the marketing committee, came to company management with a familiar problem—how poorly WRG's media department bought local TV and radio.

This time Mike had more than a complaint, he had proof. Mike had been given a presentation from Horizon Media, a media-buying company, that showed that Horizon could buy thirty percent more spot TV in his markets than WRG had bought for the same budget. (Mike owned shops in Fresno and San Francisco.) He demanded that Midas hire Horizon, or any media-buying company the company chose, for spot-TV-buying in northern California for a yearlong test.

After years of trying to fix the WRG media-buying issues, I was totally receptive to this idea but I didn't have the authortiy to do this. I needed Ron Moore's approval.

Things, therefore, really looked up when I learned that Ron Moore was also receptive, but for a non media reason. In his search to optimize sales of the existing Midas concept, he had come to believe that Midas needed stronger local marketing. Moore was convinced that Midas needed local promotions and localized PR efforts, and he was willing to test use of smaller regional agencies for this kind of effort.

WRG, seeing its Midas income threatened, asked for a meeting with the NMDA leadership and Midas management to address the issue. At this meeting, Ken Olshan acknowledged some local-buying problems, then surprised us by offering to use a media-buying company owned by WRG for Midas local markets instead of using the buyers inside WRG.

This was a classic error. Olshan in effect confirmed that WRG knew their spot TV media purchasing was poor. Moore and the NMDA agreed to test using a media buying service and/or a local agency for local markets.

At long last, I was given carte blanche to test replacing WRG's buying of local media.

From the beginning this test was not just to determine whether these regional agencies and/or media-buying services could buy media better than WRG. There was little doubt that this was true. The real test was to learn if Midas could integrate its national agency with regional agencies/media buying services to create a more effective marketing capability.

I was convinced we could. McDonald's and other fast-food chains used such a system, as did the automobile industry. In effect, it was a system in which national advertising sells the image of the company; the regional agency promotes off this image using local offers and promotional incentives to build the business.

The first task was to hire a media-buying company. After carefully researching the firms available, I interviewed three—two in New York, one in Chicago. From this, after a presentation to Midas management, a winner was selected—Horizon Media, the New York firm owned and managed by Bill Koenigsberg. Bill had been the individual who originally presented to Mike Glad. I assigned Horizon to buy Northern California and, at Larry Goetz's request, the New York City ADI.

After hiring Horizon, the next task was to develop a test of the use of regional agencies. To do this, we wanted to test an urban market and a regional area with several small markets. Accordingly, we chose to hire an agency for the Philadelphia ADI and one for the southeast United States, headquartered in Atlanta.

We had only sixty days to find these agencies but I was determined to do it as professionally as possible. As selection criteria, we set up two search screens: (1) The agency had to have billings of more than $20 million and (2) the agency had to have had fast-food or other franchise advertising experience, working under a national agency umbrella.

Utilizing the agency *Red Book* for selecting candidates, then setting up appointments for credentials presentations from each agency, I formed a selection committee consisting of Mark Jones, VP of Operations, Bob Sand, the field marketing manager, Ralph Linder, and myself. The plan was to visit the selected city to interview each candidate agency. From this interview the committee would select an agency without further ado.

Oh the stories I could tell about these and the later regional agency searches. Each agency that we met with was an education in people and how regional agencies survive.

Our first search for an agency in Philadelphia was almost prototypical of the experience.

We found that most of the agencies in Philadelphia that passed our screening criteria were branches of New York agencies. We didn't want to employ these agencies because we did not want to create any possibility in WRG's mind that we wanted to replace them as a national agency. At the same time, it looked like we had no choice. None of the other agencies we interviewed in Philadelphia even remotely convinced us that they were right for our culture and our needs.

We left Philadelphia discouraged. We hired no one. Our best candidate was McCann–Erickson, a branch office of the New York headquartered agency, but it was clearly not a true regional agency.

We scoured the *Red Book* again and identified a new candidate—an agency we had rejected for initial screening because it had less than $20 million dollars in billing. The agency was LevLane, named after the co-founders Bruce Lev and David Lane. Its president, David Lane was a veteran account man who had worked on the McDonald's business at another agency before founding his own. Bruce Lev was a young creative hotshot who bubbled with enthusiasm as well as talent.

We went back to Philadelphia to meet with LevLane and with McCann again. It was no contest! We were so impressed with LevLane that we immediately hired them.

In retrospect, LevLane proved to be the best regional agency hire we would make. They proved to be one of the most responsive, intelligent agencies I have ever dealt with at any level.

Atlanta was a further education in local regional agencies. However, in this case, we were able to select a winner rather easily—Austin Kelly. The owner, Austin Kelly himself, had built an excellent $60 million agency in a town that has always been a deathbed for advertising agencies. At the time, Austin Kelly was Pizza Hut's regional agency, and we were convinced that the infrastructure they had for Pizza Hut could be used for the Midas system throughout the Southeast.

The regional agency/media buying service test was launched.

Midas Reorganizes

By 1993, organizational change was not confined to the NMDA. Midas reorganized.

Apparently convinced that to get more focus on local marketing, the company had to have better localized decisionmaking, Ron Moore hired A.T. Kearney to develop a plan to reorganize the company. Its goal: to decentralize the control that Moore and Russ Richards had used to manage Midas.

Kearney worked with the management for over six months and finally came up with a plan that was deployed in April 1993, the month after "the Midas Way" campaign was launched.

The plan split the company into into four divisions, each managed by a Divisional VP. Reporting to the Division VPs were region managers, a marketing manager, a development manager, and technical trainers. The Division VPs reported directly to John Warzecha, who was promoted to Sr. VP of Operations. Warzecha reported directly to Moore. Thus, as a result of these changes, Russ Richards' job responsibilities were cut in half, his power immensely diminished.

As part of this reorganization, Kearney also recommended beefing up the corporate marketing department. At last I could add sorely needed staff by hiring professionals as directors of PR, Field Marketing, and Advertising (Ralph Linder had finally retired).

This reorganization, added to the NMDA leadership changes, began a five-year implosion of the old Midas culture.

The initial fallout was a year of internal chaos as the management struggled to implement a new culture. New managerial personnel were hired from the outside, and others were promoted from the existing manpower. Used to the heavily centralized decision making culture in the past, all struggled to learn how much authority they really had.

Beyond this, there was a threefold change in the Midas company-dealer relationship that shattered the old "family" relationship forever, and doomed WRG.

1. The former close personal relationships many of the key dealers had developed with Midas management were damaged. The divisional VPs were now to be the dealers' key decision maker—not "good ole" Russ or Ron. Because of this, the entire dealer–company relationship became a renegotiation to determine if the NMDA still held sway over the corporate policies that affected them. This, in turn, gave added impetus to a growing distrust between the dealers and company.
2. The power of the NMDA committees was diminished. No longer was all policy nationally implemented. Regional differences were permitted and encouraged.
3. The control of individual ADI marketing plans was ceded to the Divisional Marketing Manager. A new position, this individual was to work

with the agency to develop media plans, promotions, local Safe Baby programs etc. for each ADI in his or her division.

Citing the obvious success of the regional agency/media-buying service test, the divisional marketing managers were convinced that only if all markets had a regional agency or buying service, could they have the local "arms and legs" to plan/execute the local plans mandated by the reorganization.

Thus in June 1993, WRG lost all local market responsibility for 1994. This represented a $40,000,000 loss of billings and made Wells–Rich–Greene our national agency only, with $20,000,000 billings for creative and network media.

We spent the remainder of the year hiring an agency network of twelve more regional agencies. When the dust cleared, Midas had agencies in Boston, Philadelphia, Atlanta, Tampa, Pittsburgh, Detroit, Chicago, Minneapolis, Kansas City, Dallas, Denver, Phoenix, Seattle, and Honolulu. Horizon remained as our only media-buying service and handled California and the New York ADI.

Building on Success

Entering 1994 I was truly optimistic. Retail sales were growing monthly at a greater rate than any period since the mid-'80s. Midas would finally exceed one billion dollars in retail sales. And the Midas marketing program was given much of the credit for this success.

More important, I had built the beginnings of a marketing juggernaut. First, I had added professional staff to the marketing department including a twenty-three-year pro in PR, Bob Troyer from Firestone, and Rich Brayer, a fifteen-year advertising and promotion professional, as Director of Field Marketing. We had also added a young University of Illinois Ph.D. candidate in Consumer Research, Bob Thompson. Thompson gave Jerry Brown the in-house expertise in research techniques and analysis that he had sought for years.

Second, I had added a new national agency to develop advertising to Hispanics. By 1994, over ten percent of our potential customers were Mexican, Cuban, Puerto Rican or other Spanish speaking immigrants. After a mini search in which we interviewed agencies in Florida and California, we settled on one of the biggest and best Hispanic agencies—Leo Burnett in Chicago. As P&G's lead Hispanic agency, they had a proven track record that gave us a tremendous new resource.

Third, I finally had a professional local marketing capability. We had experienced agency pros (from our fifteen regional agencies) in major markets and four Divisional Marketing Directors—two hired from outside Midas with ten-plus years of experience. In all, we now had 120 people, as opposed to only twenty agency–company staff when I had assumed the marketing helm in 1989.

Beyond all this, consumer research was now being employed routinely inside Midas. We were doing many small studies for promotion development, yellow page ad copy, etc. For many of these studies, we used my old friend, Saul Ben-Zev. He still had the ability to hear consumer truths and provide actionable solutions to consumer issues.

Also as part of this newfound reliance on consumer research, I gained agreement to conduct two major consumer research studies—another national ATU study, and a market segmentation study. My goal was to use these studies to blast the culture out of its complacency and finally address the immediate problems caused by stainless steel mufflers and the shoddy retail image.

My almost euphoric state lasted less than six months. Destruction started almost immediately, when another internal organizational bombshell struck. It was announced Russ Richards would retire in three months.

The entire Midas culture was shaken. Everyone waited for the next shoe to drop. We didn't have to wait long. Three months after Russ left, Dick Krant was hired as General Manager, Midas United States.

Dick Krant

Krant was introduced to the Midas culture with great fanfare. Moore announced that Dick was his replacement long term —perhaps two to three years. In this role, Krant was given management responsibility for the U.S. company and would report to Moore, who remained CEO.

Krant, a man in his early forties, came to Midas with a glittering resume. After graduating from Dartmouth he had begun his career in sales with Pepsi. From there he had joined Tenneco where he had rapidly ascended the management ladder in jobs at three Tenneco subsidiaries, Speedy/Car-X, one of the Midas clones, Monroe, and Case.

Of critical importance, in retrospect, all of Dick's jobs had been in companies that were relatively more sophisticated than Midas in terms of internal systems, particularly in computerization of information. Most had been filled with aggressive personnel, not unlike P&G.

Initially, Dick Krant seemed to be exactly the leader Midas needed to address the chain's long-term strategic issues. He was, from the first, a very proactive manager for change. He was not afraid to challenge the status quo. And, he was a man in a hurry to prove himself to his many audiences—Moore, Whitman, the franchisees, his staff, and his fellow senior officers. He gave the impression that he had come into the company with a mandate to create change.

From the first, however, Dick had problems coping with the culture and in developing good working relationships with the veteran staff who reported to him, starting with me. Even though I could have been one of Krant's strongest allies for changing Midas, it didn't take long for us to lock horns.

It started at our first get-acquainted session. He called me into his office and opened our acquaintanceship without a smile and an accusatory tone of voice. After a very perfunctory "Hi," he asked, "Chris, why don't we have a written marketing strategy? I would think that a man with your background would always have such a document."

Irked by his immediate attack on my professionalism, I swallowed hard and tried to be friendly: "Welcome to Midas, Dick. I'm glad you asked about a planning document. None has ever been required until now. But I've done a shorthand version of one for my annual presentation to the dealer marketing committee. I brought you a copy of my last presentation—I gave it last month—and a copy of our current marketing plan. Also, here are copies of several key pieces of consumer research you need to read. And, by the way, when you're ready, I'll have the agency present our advertising campaign and its rationale."

He didn't smile, nor even acknowledge the stack of papers I handed him. Instead he switched to another topic. "Look, Chris, I expect marketing to be run here like it was run at Pepsi. My old boss was from P&G and he taught me how to develop and implement marketing."

With this, Krant went to a small chalkboard on the wall of his office and began to lecture me on the fundamentals of marketing. (One of Krant's biggest idiosyncrasies was his use of a chalkboard to communicate. He invariably illustrated his key points with shorthand graphics—almost like computer icons.)

I couldn't believe it. After almost forty years in professional marketing, my new boss, a man with half of my experience, was lecturing me on the fundamentals of developing a marketing strategy and tactics like P&G—a company I'd worked for, and he hadn't. I was most uncomfortable, and angry. Krant was giving me a first-class professional insult.

When Krant finished his illustrated lecture, I couldn't help myself. I grabbed the chalk, went to the board, and proceeded to correct my teacher. "Dick, apparently you didn't learn it all. Here are two areas of marketing you failed to mention as critical to success—packaging and the competitive environment. And ironically, these are two of the biggest areas we need to address at Midas, as you will quickly see if you read the research I gave you." He seemed a bit surprised at my reaction; then curtly dismissed me without further ado.

So much for a good start.

Krant had apparently approached each of his direct reports similarly. Both Terry Reynolds (senior VP Manufacturing and Distribution) and John Warzecha (senior VP of Franchise Operations) told me that he had lectured them on how to do their jobs.

Still, we all hoped for the best, as Krant made his first major move barely thirty days after he was hired. He employed a management consultant to lead his senior staff in a strategic planning exercise from which a new long-term strategic plan would be formulated.

Initially this planning exercise was a breath of fresh air. Virtually all of us were in agreement that we had to update Midas and were eager to do so. Krant was reinforcing with us that he was the man who could make it happen.

However, ninety days later, when it was finished, the planning exercise appeared to have been largely a subterfuge. After many vigorous discussions, it seemed that only Dick's ideas were adopted. He had obviously come to Midas with his own agenda.

Worse yet, by the time the planning session ended I was faced with a real dilemma. For the first time in my career as the officer responsible for consumer marketing, I was saddled with an overall strategy that I was convinced was wrong.

Krant had not agreed with my deep-rooted belief that the biggest problem Midas faced was its image as a muffler specialist. He saw this image as an opportunity not a problem. He insisted that the company's long-term goal had to be to dominate the muffler repair business and gain sales by doubling Midas's market share over five years.

I had vehemently argued against Krant's conclusion. It was my view that Midas had to change its identity in the eyes of the consumer. We had to stop being called Midas Muffler.

Krant had not totally rejected this, but his direction was that our job was build a broader business on Midas roots as a superior purveyor of muffler repair, not seek a whole new identity.

I had never been more frustrated in my marketing career. I was so sure he was wrong, I committed political suicide, by stating my view one more time on the last day of our strategy workshop. "Dick, I just can't buy your strategy. You set a goal to double Midas retail sales in five years. You show that virtually all this sales growth will be in brakes and suspension or front-end repair. Yet, you say we must also focus on exhaust and work within our existing image as a muffler specialist.

I can't say it more strongly—hear me please—this will not work!"

Dick replied irritably, "Are you saying you won't develop a marketing plan on this strategy?"

"No. What I'm saying is that no matter what programs are developed under this strategy, we cannot make a sow's ear into a silk purse. They will fail long term. We must address the problem Midas has —namely that we are still seen as a tired old muffler shop that does other services; not a chain that is an expert in all three services."

I went on, "Read the consumer research. It's clear. We are known as Midas Muffler. Unless and/or until we can be known as Midas, the brake experts, or some other name, we will never be able to convince consumers we aren't a muffler shop that does brakes, and this will seriously hinder our ability to get the brake sales we need. It's very clear that this is our problem right now."

This was not a battle I could win that day. I knew that Krant would react like most corporate chieftains when challenged in front of others, he would insist on his way—just as I had done as CEO many times in my own career. But I wanted my concerns on the record.

And I didn't win. Dick just angrily stared me at for a few moments, then told me that my argument had already been considered and rejected. He then closed the meeting by handing out a detailed description of thirteen major assignments to change Midas.

As originally conceived by Krant, two kinds of projects were assigned. First, virtually every major internal operating system in manufacturing, distribution, and management information would be computerized and streamlined to provide lower operating costs. Secondly, a series of programs were to be designed to improve retail sales, including, at long last, a new building design to provide a basis to remodel all existing shops.

These projects, if completed, would truly transform Midas. And ironically, it was the new Midas I believed in, but it was to be marketed under our current name and positioning and that, in my mind, doomed gaining any marketing leverage from the changes.

The projects were complex and required dedicated teams of employees to complete them. It quickly became apparent that most would take far more time to accomplish than Krant was ready to accept. He had totally underestimated or refused to accept the difficulty of engendering change in the entrenched Midas culture. Virtually all the key changes he sought were delayed far beyond a timetable he thought reasonable.

Because of this, Krant became frustrated and in the process made the life of his staff very difficult. At almost every staff meeting he was critical of virtually all aspects of Midas, including its people. He expressed total incredulity that Midas could be the market leader with its many internal shortcomings, particularly in computerization of information systems. Over and over he would harp on the fact that he was used to weekly sales, not monthly sales a month late. And he would continually complain that Midas had an impossible marketing system—that we should be able to change marketing plans in a week; not the three months minimum time we faced in our decentralized franchised system, etc.

All of this lowered morale and put Krant's direct reports in a defensive, reactionary mode. Instead of worrying about problem solving within their area of responsibility, they focussed on reacting to Dick's constant barrage of questions and/or suggestions.

In doing this, Krant was not only a disruptive intimidating bully, he also directly undermined the new decentralized franchise operations organization. He wanted to make all key decisions in every area and over two years he gradually returned Midas to a top-down management mode.

The dealers' initial reaction to Dick was muted, but friendly. The new NMDA leadership professed great frustration with Moore as being an "out of touch" CEO. They wanted a new leader with whom they could build a relationship.

However, they had difficulties in accepting Krant. Dick's aggressive push for change had not, in their view, included enough dealer input. They felt left out of their traditional role in the Midas decision making loop. And when they tried to insert themselves they were relatively unsuccessful.

Corporate Guerilla Warfare

My personal problem remained. How could I direct Midas marketing under a strategy I didn't believe in?

I was in a position with no convenient foxhole to duck into. If I developed a marketing program on Krant's strategy, I was sure it would fail and my job would be in jeopardy. On the other hand, if I didn't develop programs under Krant's strategy, I would be insubordinate and surely lose my job.

Fortunately, Krant initially stayed away from marketing. He did not push for quick action or try to micro-manage me, as he was doing in several other areas of the company. Still I had to move forward and lead development of new marketing programs. As I did this, my personal objective became to convince Krant of the validity of the strategy I believed in.

To do this, I adopted a personal strategy that I had employed on occasion throughout my career (See Chapter 12 on Fortress Bojangles')—corporate guerilla warfare.

In corporate guerilla warfare, you always mask your disagreement with a corporate mandate while trying to sell or resell your idea that has been rejected, or would be rejected if proposed. In this mode, your tactic must be to find one or more ways to give the individuals who block approval of the idea, reasons to reconsider their position without "losing face."

Following this tactic, I tried to proactively bring Krant into marketing meetings to begin to build rapport with him. My rationale for this was to not only change his mind, but also to gain this very intelligent man's input and agreement.

In doing this, I was following a **Lifetime Lesson: Never be afraid to get those who oppose you involved in your area of responsibility, before they demand access. It's far easier to deal with people who are invited into your tent, than to try to keep them outside.**

Perhaps the best guerilla warfare tactic is to create the illusion that the idea you need to sell is not yours, but theirs. I knew that's what had to happen with Krant. And it did. Over the following three months Dick changed his mind on the long-term market positioning he sought for Midas. By February 1995, at the annual Midas sales convention, he decreed that Midas should seek to shed itself of its muffler specialist image and reposition itself in the marketplace as a repair chain that did multiple services.

Dick, in fact, now began pushing for Midas to broaden its services to include maintenance: selling oil changes, batteries, wiper blades, etc. At the sales meeting he showed his diagram of his new vision of Midas. It would compete for all routine maintenance services done by auto dealers as well as offer its three basic repair services.

Two Critical Assignments

This overall new strategy led to launching two key marketing assignments. Both have had a profound effect on Midas to this day.

First we held a meeting with the top management of Wills-Rich-Greene and gave a twofold assignment that I explained this way:

> "Please give us a new name that will help reposition Midas away from being a muffler specialist in the marketplace. We need a name to replace "muffler." Up till now we have just said Midas in our ads. To this, the consumer always adds "muffler." We have to bury "muffler" and become a much broader-based auto repair chain in consumers' eyes. Within the next several years Midas shops will be doing add air conditioning repair, maintenance services, batteries, tires, and who knows what else. In addition, we'll remodel the exterior and interior of the Midas retail shop.
>
> We think to successfully build our business as this new entity, Midas needs need a new moniker. We need to do what Xerox has done. They have morphed to "The Document Company" from "The Copier Company." *The problem is simple, but oh so profound, "What do we call ourselves?"*
>
> *We also must have new TV ad campaign to tell consumers this new name and positioning. The "Midas Way" is losing steam in the marketplace. It's not adding sales today, and it won't put new customers in Midas shops tomorrow for new services."*

The second assignment was to launch a new building design image project. For this, we hired Babcock & Schmidt, a corporate design firm. Bill Babcock was an old business friend. After his hiring, he and I met privately. His first question confirmed that we had the right firm. He asked, "Chris, to do what everyone wants done, Midas needs more than a new building design. In my professional opinion you also have to redesign the Midas logo. May we add this to the assignment?"

I almost shouted with excitement, "Yes. Krant wants to do this, but be aware that Ron Moore will probably not ever approve such a change. He does not believe it necessary—but let's give it a shot."

The seeds for a new Midas were finally growing.

WRG's Final Days

Spring 1995 marked the beginning of the end for Well–Rich–Greene's long tenure as Midas's national ad agency.

Larry Singer went all out to try to lead his new creative team (Jonathan Cranin had left the agency) to develop the new campaign we had requested, but with little success. The biggest reason for this failure was that none of the proposed new campaigns addressed our first question: "What do we call ourselves?" WRG simply would not or could not address this.

I have never been sure why WRG failed to deliver anything remotely resembling an answer to our twofold assignment. But sadly, as spring became summer, we rejected all the work presented, most before it could be shown to the dealers.

This lack of progress reinforced the NMDA's pressure on us to fire WRG. Led by Larry Goetz, they were sure it was time to get "a fresh perspective on our business." They placed weekly calls asking me to take action. But, as with BBDO at Burger King, I resisted. I knew that it would cost us a year's time to get any new agency fully integrated into our system.

Finally, after a very difficult creative meeting I came to the decision that every client makes before he fires his agency, namely that WRG could not solve our assignment. I went to Krant and told him we needed to consider firing WRG. He agreed and gave Larry Singer an ultimatum, "We need significant progress in the next thirty days or we will seriously consider hiring a new agency."

Thirty days later, on July 6, 1995, Wells–Rich–Greene made its final creative presentation to Midas. Like all previous meetings, WRG still ignored the question, "What do we call ourselves?" Instead they paraded five different creative campaigns all basically designed to sell trust humorously. They were funny, but not on strategy. WRG simply didn't get it.

After the presentation, Moore, Krant and I all agreed, albeit reluctantly, that we needed a new agency. And so, after twenty-six years, Wells-Rich-Greene was fired.

Selecting A New Agency

Shades of Burger King. As I looked at the Midas situation, I was struck by how remarkably similar WRG's demise compared to BBDO's twenty years earlier.

We had the difficult task of replacing an agency that had generated an immensely successful ad campaign, but was fired within three years of its launch. And this task was thrust on us for a similar reason. Agency management had failed to produce advertising for an assignment given by the client in an atmosphere made tense by overwhelming negative pressure from the franchisees. Furthermore, in both cases, the franchisees had become hostile because of the agency's failure to provide competent field service and local media buying.

The similarity with Burger King didn't end there. Midas was a household name, and as such, was like Burger King, a coveted client name for any advertising agency.

Seeing all this, I tried to duplicate as much as possible the search procedure we had used at Burger King as described in Chapter 8.

I set up a three-person screening committee from the marketing department to develop a preliminary list of candidates that fit our criteria and select the ones that would be visited by the committee for preliminary screening. From this screening visit the committee would select five finalists.

Then, as at Burger King, the agency finalists would have two months to prepare a strategic presentation with for-instance creative to a large selection committee. At Midas this committee would include the three screening committee members, five corporate executives (Moore, Krant, Warzecha, Jones, and Ray Snipes, a former divisional VP now in charge of Product Management), and two franchisees (Larry Goetz and Lonnie Orns). Each would have one equal vote.

The screening committee consisted of Rich Brayer, director of Field Marketing, me, and a newcomer, Zeynep Gunduz, who had been hired as Director of National Advertising and Promotion just in time to attend the final WRG presentation.

Zeynep was my last hire at Midas, and the person I had selected as a possible successor when I retired. She was hired after a long search. A talented and charming mid-thirties DDB–Needham account superviser, Zeynep impressed Burhoe, Moore, and Krant so much that they gave me authority to hire her at a starting salary $30,000 higher than previously had been permitted for the position.

The initial part of the agency search went well. Our search criteria were virtually identical to the Burger King search. We sought a large full-service agency that had the creative capability to develop outstanding strategically relevant TV. And, we hoped to find the agency in Chicago.

We identified thirteen agencies to visit initially, but only five were in New York. What a difference twenty years had made in the major agency landscape. The stranglehold on talent held by Madison Avenue twenty years ago had disappeared.

In mid-July 1995, we visited Grey, Bates, Grace & Rothchild, Deutsch, and McCann–Erickson (Jonathan Cranin's new home) in New York. We followed this with meetings in Chicago with Leo Burnett, Tatham–Euro–RSG, DDB–Needham, Foote–Cone–Belding and J. Walter Thompson. We then headed West to see three powerhouse strategic and creative agencies, Fallon McElligott in Minneapolis, and Hal Riney and Goodby–Silverstein in San Francisco.

From this point forward, the parallels with Burger King disappeared. First, we liked six finalists, but, in the end, had only three. We lost two of our favorites, McCann and Burnett—the two I was sure had the best chance of winning—because of John Smale, chairman of General Motors. Smale ruled that Midas was a client conflict for McCann, Buick's agency, and Burnett, Oldsmobile's agency. They would have to resign these huge accounts to serve us. (Interestingly, Ford allowed JWT, its agency, to compete and did not see Midas as a conflict.)

Then another of our favorites, Goodby, chose to withdraw from the selection process after their initial visit to our corporate headquarters.

This left us with a final threesome of Fallon, Needham, and J. Walter Thompson, Chicago.

A Selection Process Gone Awry

After this initial fallout, the agency selection process never fully recovered. Unlike the Burger King experience, this selection process seemed over before the committee ever met. As the three candidates tried to woo us with their prowess over the two months up to the selection committee presentations, only one seemed to fit—DDB–Needham.

As we gathered in early October, it was clear in our preliminary committee meeting that Needham, through a deft set of maneuvers led by their new business manager, Jan Zweirin, had convinced Moore, the dealers, and most of the other committee members they were the best choice.

As at Burger King, the three finalists put on a good show for the selection committee. We gained the benefit of three proposals for a new long-term strategy. All were well thought-out; all had merit. All reinforced our belief that Midas had to reshape its consumer image or fail longterm.

But, as I had experienced before, the show was also full of surprises. And this time, unlike Burger King, these surprises created a very divided selection committee and a painful final selection process.

J. Walter Thompson presented first and gave an unexpectedly impressive presentation.

Led by its Chicago president, Steve Davis, JWT stated categorically that its consumer research showed that Midas suffered from "muffler vision"—most consumers did not know Midas shops did repairs other than mufflers. The agency was convinced that Midas had to change its identity with consumers to reach its sales goals.

JWT proposed that Midas change its descriptor from "Midas Muffler" to "Midas Auto Systems Experts." They presented an impressive rationale for this name; then showed a unique new point-of-purchase graphics idea that would help communicate the new descriptor. It incorporated computer-like icons for each repair service offered.

More than this, JWT proposed that Midas adopt a "killer line" that could be used in ads and at the shop level. The line was "What can we do for you today?"

Last the agency played a proposed radio campaign that used "Click and Clack," the auto mechanics who gave repair advice every Saturday morning on National Public Radio (NPR), and suggested that they could be our spokespeople to sell this new name and positioning.

When their pitch ended, JWT's stock had risen with all of us. Still, in general, we were not sold on the agency, primarily because it seemed to lack the creative and account talent of the other finalists.

Fallon followed in the afternoon. The pitch team wowed us with their strategic thinking and daring creative but proved to be very weak in media and people perceptiveness. The committee came away from the pitch very concerned that Fallon would not be easy to work with. Pat Fallon had made it clear to us that he would resign a business if he disagreed with a client on creative strategy. Creative judgment would be "their way or the highway," hardly the Midas way.

Thus, as we entered the Hyatt ballroom the following morning for the final agency presentation, the selection committee was prepared to anoint DDB–Needham. However, Needham, led by Keith Reinhart, their CEO and legendary creative guru, proved to be a devastating disappointment. The agency's strategic thinking was not as crisp as Fallon's and JWT's. Worse yet, they showed a creative product that was mediocre.

The selection committee was to convene after Needham's presentation but it was clearly in disarray. Their favorite agency had given the poorest presentation.

Knowing this, I quickly gained agreement to delay the committee meeting for three hours to have time to develop a concise review of each agency's presentation and develop the best case for hiring each candidate. We would use this as a basis for the committee's deliberations. Zeynep would present the case for Needham, Brayer for Fallon and I would do JWT.

When the committee met, we made the three presentations. Discussion then began and a preliminary secret ballot was taken. From this, the committee eliminated Fallon, but remained divided into three camps:

1. Start over—we have no suitable winner.
2. Hire DDB–Needham—the agency with the best cultural fit and best talent. We surely can get their work redone and make it acceptable to all.
3. Hire JWT—the agency that gave the best presentation and an exciting creative idea, Click and Clack.

Finally, after a long discussion, I was able to eliminate option #1, with an impassioned speech that argued that the committee had no assurance of achieving better results by starting over. I concluded with a plea, "Please replace WRG now. Either of the two remaining agency finalists is far superior to WRG."

Another secret ballot was taken. The vote was a tie. At this point, Ron Moore asked each committee member to argue openly for his choice. Moore stated he favored Needham but could live with JWT. Similar comments were echoed by others, until Larry Goetz made an impassioned plea for JWT. He argued that "Click and Clack" could be a real winner.

When the next ballot was cast, JWT, which had my vote from the beginning, was an eight to two winner. Once again the parallels with my Burger King days emerged; J. Walter Thompson was hired.

Six Months of Bad News

When I had switched agencies in the past at Burger King and Arby's, a new advertising campaign had been the basis for our choice. This gave breathing room to inculcate the new agency to the company culture and allowed the agency time to hire needed account people, etc. This period, commonly labeled the honeymoon period, usually lasts at least six months.

JWT had no honeymoon. They struggled for survival almost from Day One. Three major problems contributed to this:

1. *Midas Management.* From Day One, JWT had three clients, Dick Krant, Chris Schoenleb, and the Midas dealers, especially Larry Goetz. Each operated independently of the other and, therefore, gave conflicting requests.

   I needed to be THE client to be effective in my role as marketing VP, but JWT never insisted upon it; nor could I totally solve the problem internally. Neither Goetz, nor Krant saw any reason to work through me, but expected me to accommodate them and sort out any conflicts they caused with the agency. **Lifetime Lesson: No agency can be effective if it does not have clear direction from its client.**

2. *JWT account management.* The initial account group was even weaker than we had initially perceived. This led to numerous communication problems best illustrated by how they handled my request for a proposal to build a Midas Internet website.

   Convinced that Midas had to have a presence on the Internet, I requested Burnett, TMPW, and JWT to make formal credentials pitches for what I viewed to be a new media assignment. TMPW and Burnett went all out to secure the assignment. JWT gave a second-rate pitch, then complained that they had misunderstood the assignment when we awarded the account to TMPW.

   Following this, Steve Davis changed personnel, but the initial damage was never totally assuaged.

3. *JWT creative.* The initial lack of a new ad campaign was compounded by a fiasco over the idea that had swayed many of us to select JWT, the use of the NPR personalities, Click and Clack, to introduce the

new Midas positioning. This had been a skeletal idea for a campaign, executed only in radio in the new business pitch. We wanted Click and Clack for TV as well. After showing us some promising initial TV storyboards, JWT advised us that Click and Clack were no longer interested in working for Midas. Upset, I asked for a face-to-face meeting with Click and Clack and their agent in their hometown, Boston.

The meeting was held. There I learned Click and Clack's agent had advised JWT of their noninterest in advertising Midas almost immediately after doing the radio tapes. And even when I offered them a $1,000,000+ talent fee, Click and Clack refused to reconsider their decision. We had hired JWT for an idea that was DOA.

The net result of these three problems was that less than thirty days into our new relationship, JWT had to start over to develop new creative with multiple client direction and a weak account group.

Worse yet, sales were declining; the "Midas Way" campaign seemed to have spent its effectiveness.

We were in a real crisis mode. We did not have the luxury of time to assure proper testing of new concepts. It was November and new creative was needed for an already announced new campaign launch in March. We had already committed media funds for a major heavy-up of TV weight primarily in the NCAA Final Four basketball tourney.

Analogies

The advertising goal was clear. We needed to persuade consumers that Midas was no longer the brand they all knew and trusted as "Midas Muffler." We had to convince consumers that Midas had changed over the years and had become as expert in other specialty services as it had always been in muffler repair.

JWT had sixty days to develop and do preliminary testing of this new campaign. These days were some of the most stressful in my career. We held meetings virtually day and night. The holidays were a blur in which we had a special dealer creative subcommittee join us in directing and reviewing JWT's work.

From this emerged an ad campaign that tested "fair" in the limited testing that could be done in the time allotted. From a practical standpoint, it was a gamble, but we had run out of time for more work if we were to launch in March. And all involved felt that the campaign had promise and could work.

The campaign was called "Analogies." It conveyed a simple message. Cars had changed. They had complex systems, not just parts to repair. And as this change had occurred, Midas had changed to be experts in repair of more than just muffler systems. Midas had used their competence in muffler repair to become technical experts in brake and suspension systems repair. Midas was now an "Auto Systems Expert."

An actor, delivered this message as the Midas spokesman. He dramatized the need for system repairs through the use of analogies. For brakes, for example, he was shown trying to play a piano that had a one key that was out of tune. He pointed out that just as a piano needs all its parts working properly to play a tune, a car's braking systems need to have all parts in perfect repair. And that to repair a car's braking system you needed an expert to check out the entire system—Midas.

To emphasize change, and to add pizazz to delivering this message, I reluctantly endorsed JWT's fervent recommendation that the commercials be filmed away from a Midas shop in an old warehouse. In this I broke *my own cardinal rule of retail advertising—Always show the building or place of business in TV advertising of a retail chain.*

As the TV campaign went into production, we put the finishing touches on a whole new look for the Midas advertising program, including a new approach to media. We added network radio as an adjunct to TV.

Also, we hired JWT to replace Lunardi for point-of-purchase materials thus giving the agency total charge of Midas' consumer communications. In doing this, we added one more element of change and lost valuable experience—a move that would haunt us later.

Beyond this, we put together a thirty-five-minute video to communicate the entire new program to the dealers and corporate employees prior to its March launch. The video featured Moore, Krant, Steve Davis of JWT, and me explaining the importance of the new descriptor, "Auto Systems Experts," and showed the new point-of-purchase materials as well as storyboards of the new TV commercials in production.

As this video was mailed to each dealer, I worried about the TV campaign. So much rode on its effectiveness. It would make or break this initial effort to convince the Midas customer that Midas was more than a muffler specialist.

To reassure myself, I went to the production shoot in California to see the set and view rough film footage. It was about midway through the two-week shooting schedule.

When I saw the set, and the rough film, I was appalled. I saw disaster. The commercials did not remotely resemble the storyboards. The set was artsy, not down to earth. In the rough film, the scenes in the commercial were dark, almost spooky. And finally, the film had too many short scenes (cuts) which made the message hard to follow. My conclusion: The analogy message was butchered.

I halted production long enough to meet informally on the set with the director and the JWT creative team. I said in a very agitated loud voice, "This is not what we approved. It won't work! You have to brighten it up, and slow it down."

They didn't agree. They argued that they had just tried to make the commercials more visually interesting—that when I saw the final edits they would be spectacular.

I did not believe them, but I did not stop the shoot. In retrospect, I should have listened to my gut and paid the short-term price of an aborted shoot.

When we saw the commercials in finished form, I was sick at heart. I was sure that they wouldn't work and that the whole repositioning would be slowed, perhaps aborted. I wanted to keep them off the air, but I was overruled by timing—we had promised the dealers new creative—and Krant and Moore, who thought the ads had a chance of working.

The commercials aired on schedule in early March. Within sixty days, the creative research we now had time to do right, the dealers, and retail sales confirmed my darkest fears. This advertising campaign was a bomb. It did not communicate to consumers, nor motivate them to visit Midas. We needed a new campaign as quickly as possible.

While the advertising campaign was developed and launched, another key project, the new Midas building and exterior sign, also ran into serious trouble. Bill Babcock and his staff had systematically developed a proposed new corporate image. Meeting monthly with John Warzecha and me over the summer months, they had created an exciting new interior and exterior Midas shop design. Their proposed design gave a striking new look that featured a red-and-gray exterior and a high-tech red-and-white interior.

The design not only modernized the Midas shop and made its interiors far more consumer friendly, it buried the familiar yellow and black colors that Babcock stated were immediately identified by consumers as "muffler shop" colors.

Babcock also proposed a new corporate logo that minimally modified the well-recognized forty-year-old Midas sign. He wanted to modernize the old English letters of the black Midas logo and add a red exterior edge that looked like a new moon on the familiar yellow oval background.

Babcock presented the new image and logo with great fanfare to Krant, Moore, and other senior Midas officers the week after JWT was hired. To my enormous disappointment, they did not approve the new design. Although all agreed the new design was attractive, most were clearly uncomfortable with adopting it. In their eyes it was too radical a change.

Anticipating this, Babcock proposed that Midas remodel one existing company-owned shop to the new design. This would help everyone visualize the retail viability of the design, give us a way to research consumer reaction to the change, and provide a vehicle for obtaining dealer comment.

With some reluctance, Babcock's proposal was approved. And about 100 days later, the remodel of a company-owned shop in northwest Chicago was completed. Ironically, it was the same day we approved the Analogies campaign.

I loved the new building image design. So did consumers. Consumer research showed that the new logo and new exterior design was readily seen as a newer, more modern Midas. Customers oohed and aahed over the clean bright new interior, and over the months, sales jumped in excess of fifty percent in the remodeled facility.

But the new design was not adopted. The dealers and company store operations personnel did not like the exterior red or the primarily white interior. They liked the look of the interior, but were sure it would be too hard to keep clean.

And the new logo was buried. Ignoring the consumer research, Moore flatly refused to consider changing the logo. It was, for him, a change that did not need to be done.

In short, the new design was derailed, but not discarded. The research and sales results were too good to ignore. After a series of heated meetings, the project was salvaged by agreeing to have Babcock develop a new exterior design and a modified, less-white interior, as well as drop the new logo.This delayed the start of any possible remodel of the system for at least a year and was a serious setback to building a new image for Midas.

Personal Problem

There was one other major negative factor in this time period, my personal health.

In the midst of firing Wells–Rich–Greene and launching of the new image project, I began to experience a mysterious loss of strength in my wrists as well as numbness and paralysis in my hands. Alarmed and fearing I had Parkinson's Disease like my father, I went to a neurologist. After a series of tests, he offered no finite diagnosis, but opined that I might have Lou Gehrig's disease, Amelo-Lateral-Sclerosis (ALS). He suggested a second opinion. The second neurologist was "almost sure" I had ALS.

If true, this was a death sentence. I was told I would die from ALS in two to three years.

I told no one of my plight, not even my family, and tried to ignore this diagnosis as I went through the Fall. But I became steadily worse. By Thanksgiving, my wife, suspicious of the worst, insisted I keep an appointment at the Mayo Clinic in Phoenix. There in mid-December, the neurologist confirmed to both of us that I had ALS. He gave me eighteen months to three years to live.

After a long difficult week of soul searching and prayer with my family, I decided to return to work and not reveal the diagnosis as definitive. I needed to work for my sanity; it would keep me from dwelling on my future if I had ALS. I also had some hope the doctors were wrong.

So, during the critical repositioning campaign development and building image project, I lived with a personal death sentence. As 1996 progressed, I became steadily more crippled.

I am not sure, in retrospect, how this disease influenced my decision-making. I do know it greatly shortened my temper and reduced my stamina. For the first time in forty years, I worked a nine-to-five workday and traveled as little as possible.

This in turn led me to turn over more and more responsibility to Zeynep Gunduz. And I began to seriously consider retiring before I lost all my physical capabilities.

Six Miserable Months

Midway through 1996, Midas marketing was in disarray. We had expended our budget on an advertising campaign that had failed to communicate change and had not built sales. Worse yet, we had made no real progress on launching a new Midas. The new look Midas building was still in development, and a new logo was not going to be a reality.

Predictably, the dealers turned to price promotion to try to revitalize sales. Month after month, virtually all major markets developed special commercials through their agencies and offered brake repairs at a discount—usually twenty-five percent off brake shoes and pads.

This did flatten the sales decline but, in the process, it created another Dick Krant-generated problem. Krant became focussed on finding new promotion ideas to salvage a very optimistic sales projection for 1996. He demanded that the corporate marketing staff take over promotion development. He wanted new ideas, with supporting point-of-purchase materials and advertising, sent out to the markets to control what was to be run in the following months.

In doing this, Krant deprived Midas of the inventiveness of its dealers and the regional agencies—a basic strength of the regional marketing system we had employed in prior years to generate effective new promotions.

Overwhelmed by the combination of my declining health, the struggle to save the new building design and leading JWT in its effort to find a new ad campaign, I did not oppose Krant's program. I also failed to make sure expenses were closely monitored for this unbudgeted work. I knew we had budget problems; we were spending funds to placate Krant, but did not know how badly overspent we had become until it was too late.

In the end, Krant's promotion tactics did not work. Sales were flat as we began planning for 1997—a plan we would present in early November at the Midas Sales Convention.

More than this, Dick Krant's personal plans were in a shambles. The "New Midas" Krant had promised was not materializing. And his goal of building sales from one billion to two billion in five years was exposed as an impractical dream. This in turn had caused a major decline in corporate profits. Midas would miss its profit forecast to its parent company by over $5,000,000.

Last Hurrah

I soon learned the importance of personal health—an issue I'd never faced before. As we began preparations for the sales convention I was operating on about fifty percent of my previous years' capacity.

I had received an optimistic mid-year medical report from another neurologist. He stated flatly that I did not have ALS. He opined, however that I would become crippled over time, but never die from my mysterious ailment. Clearly, my health was deteriorating to the point I had to consider early retirement.

I postponed any thought of retiring, however, until after the November convention. I did not want the disastrous year we had experienced to be my career swan song. I wanted another chance to sell changing Midas to "Auto Systems Experts" from "Muffler Specialist." If I had to leave, I wanted to go out a winner.

I pushed my staff, the agencies, and myself for a marketing program that would build retail sales and support the New Midas. I would sell it at the convention with all the oratorical skills I possessed.

To begin the planning process, I held two meetings to engender systemwide support. Needing to rejuvenate their enthusiasm as well as tap into their ideas, I met with the presidents of our most effective regional agencies at a two-day conference in Chicago. Led by Tom Moroch (president of our Texas agency), David Lane, and Bill Koenigsberg, I heard an earful of good ideas.

Then, I met with the dealers. They were still supportive; they gave me a definite, but nonverbal, vote of confidence, even as they lashed out at JWT for its poor creative and national media plan.

From all this, it became clear that the plan needed three key elements to have any chance of working.

First, we needed a way to return optimism to the dealers so that they would aggressively support the New Midas. To do this we had to have a new, thoroughly tested ad campaign that was not only strategically correct and worked with consumers, but had TV commercials that would excite the dealers. *There is no greater truth about marketing in franchised companies than the fact that success starts with the franchisees liking the advertising.*

Second, we needed a method to jump start retail sales to assure an instant reversal of the stagnant sales trend. This was translated by all to mean Midas needed an exciting new promotion—ideally a national offer that could be featured on network TV to lead off the year.

Third, we had to be able to announce that we were ready to move forward with the New Midas. This meant the new building design had to be ready with a program to begin encouraging dealers to remodel their shops. Interestingly, the regional agency presidents pushed harder for this than any other fix. They were convinced that Midas would not survive without upgraded facilities.

The sales convention was held in Orlando and was the best attended conference in a decade. We had assured that when we announced that Colin Powell would be our featured guest speaker.

I arrived exhausted. In addition to putting together all elements of the marketing program and writing and rehearsing speeches to sell it, I was concerned about all details of the convention itself as part of my overall responsibilities in leading the marketing department.

Midas conventions were always a combination of speeches and entertainment. But, this was to be a special meeting. It would celebrate Midas's fortieth Anniversary, and because of this, it was a convention of the entire company. European, Canadian, and Australian dealer and company personnel were attending. Worldwide attendance was a first, and it placed added stress on everyone.

Beyond this, the marketing plan remained a huge concern. It had still not been finalized when I reached Orlando.

The ad campaign was done and showed promise. Because it was humorous and returned to selling "trust" we were sure we had better consumer advertising and that the dealers would like it. And we had completed the new image shop design that had been approved by all. A full-sized model interior would be displayed at the trade show exhibit that was always part of a Midas convention.

But the lynchpin of the plan, the national promotion to kick off the year was not finalized. We had developed the idea, but we had not yet gained the final agreement of the NMDA.

I had personally conceived and overseen development of the idea. It would be the biggest promotion ever attempted by Midas—a nationally advertised $40 consumer rebate on any brake repair. I was convinced that this would be the strongest promotion the company had ever run and that even its huge cost would pay out because of increased customers.

However, because each dealer would be required to help fund part of the $40 rebate offer, I had to gain the NMDA leadership's endorsement of the idea to assure dealer support of the promotion in each Midas shop. And as the Orlando meeting convened I did not yet have this support.

The day before the entire marketing plan was to be presented to the convention, I met with the NMDA board. After a few anxious moments, they agreed to support the promotion. One last time I had lived up to Ron Moore's favorite description of me, i.e. "kamikaze pilot."

This hurdle breached, I presented the 1997 marketing plan, the new building design and a host of other marketing initiatives that I was sure would further our fledgling efforts to reposition Midas in the marketplace.

The dealers gave the plans an enthusiastic reception. I was optimistic that we finally had the New Midas underway.

Final Months

The actual results of this marketing program were mixed. The rebate promotion was a huge success. It garnered the biggest monthly brake retail sales increase in the history of the company. But the TV advertising was not effective and adoption of the new building design and "Auto Systems Experts" was slower than hoped for. (But it did start.)

It was indeed my final program. Three months after the convention, I was forced to step down from being the Midas Marketing VP. Ill health and Dick Krant combined to make this happen.

Dick was under heavy pressure to produce a good sales year. He wanted to control marketing. His excuse to demand my leaving was that I was responsible for an overexpenditure of over $3,000,000 in the ad budget largely caused by the added promotion work he had demanded. We both knew this was a convenient excuse, but with my nerve disease I was more than ready to step down to a less stressful position, if a deal could be made.

After some initial angst on everyone's part, a deal was made. Krant created a new position for me, Vice President Marketing Planning. By March 1997, I was no longer in charge of Midas marketing.

In my new role I did some special assignments, but I was largely a figurehead. It was an ideal job. I could work at my own pace, as my health continued spiraling downward. I had hoped to hang on for another year, but I couldn't do it. I formally retired eight months later, October 31, 1997.

A luncheon, hosted by Ron Moore, and a fun-filled roast given by the Marketing Department were held to celebrate my retirement.

My forty-one year marketing career had ended.

Postscript

By the time these retirement luncheons were held, it was clear that the internal Midas culture in which I had toiled for ten years was imploding. Dick Krant had resigned in June 1997. Along with this news, it was announced that Midas was being spun off by its parent company, Whitman, to be a publicly owned company (MDS) on the New York Stock Exchange.

Shortly thereafter, Midas lost the two men who had nurtured the internal Midas culture for almost twenty years. Ron Moore announced his retirement effective with the spin-off. Brian Burhoe also retired to care for his seriously ill wife.

Thus, when the spin-off occurred in January 1998, Midas had a new CEO from Pep Boys, Wendel Province, and a shell-shocked internal culture.

For example, after Krant left, all remaining stability in marketing vanished. David Lush was hired as my replacement as VP of Marketing. Under Lush's leadership, Project Safe Baby was discontinued and the regional agency network ignored. Lush fired JWT and hired Foote–Cone–Belding Chicago. Nine months later, Lush was fired. Foote–Cone was also fired in less than a year. After years of stability, a third Marketing VP and third agency were hired in less than three years.

Since Wendel Province has become CEO, he has radically changed Midas. He has retired, replaced and/or restructured virtually of the old management team. He has sold off Europe and Australia. He has adopted the new image program, including the new logo, and a modified descriptor. Midas is now calling itself, "Auto Repair Specialists."

The New Midas introduced in the 1996 convention is finally largely in place. However, it will take five to ten years to determine if Midas will succeed with its new image. I'm betting it will. In fact, I'm back in the fray! After several years of retirement, my health has improved. (The ALS diagnosis was wrong, as were other medical predictions that I would be a total cripple.) Result: The Midas dealers have hired me to be their executive director. I'm now part of their world, dealing with the Midas management on their behalf, as their new Myron Gordon.

But, the story of this new job and how it feels to change sides after thirty years as a corporate executive dealing with franchisees is for my next book.

Final Lessons Learned

In looking back, from P&G to Midas, two lessons stand out.

1. *Very little of the work in which I invested so much intellectual and emotional energy has endured.* There is no vast legacy of work, just grist for several historically interesting marketing case studies, and one enduring advertising slogan that truly identified a major company for all time, "Have It Your Way." Perhaps the New Midas will be another.

   In retrospect this is not surprising. Marketing is primarily devoted to problem solving today's issues. It addresses the strategies needed to build sales and brand equity today. As the marketplace changes, strategies must change, programs, ad campaigns, and PR programs must be replaced.

2. *Marketing myths and corporate cultures continue to exist today.* And I believe that the **Lifetime Lessons** in this book are wisdom and truth that still apply to the corporate marketing world—the New Economy or Old. I believe that all can be useful to anyone battling corporate marketing myths

Final Comment

In my Foxhole Tales, you met many people—some much more talented than others. Talent is important, but I hope I have convinced you that talent does not guarantee marketing battlefield success. It's the entry ticket. I have shown you that a person's talent must first fit the culture in which he or she works.

Equally as important, every marketer still must confront and destroy marketing myths. To do this in the corporate world, the real success determinant is attitude. **All the successful people I worked with, and for,**

shared a passion for truth. They went the extra mile in terms of time and effort to understand their company's marketplace and consumers they had to sell. You can't win marketing battles in any corporate culture without this passion. But with it, in a culture suited to your personality, you will find the ammunition to succeed.